The Giant Encyclopedia
of
Theme Activities

the GIANT

encyclopedia of theme activities for children 2 to 5

*Over 600 Favorite Activities
Created by Teachers
for Teachers*

Illustrated by
Rebecca Butcher Schoenfliess

gryphon house
Mt. Rainier, Maryland

© Copyright 1993, Gryphon House, Inc.

Published by Gryphon House, Inc.
3706 Otis Street, Mt. Rainier, MD 20712

Cover Design and Illustration: Beverly Hightshoe

Library of Congress Cataloging-in-Publication Data

   The Giant encyclopedia of theme activities for children 2 to 5 : over 600 favorite activities created by teachers and for teachers / illustrated by Rebecca Butcher Schoenfliess.
     p. cm.
   Includes index.
   ISBN 0-87659-166-7 : $29.95
   1. Education, Preschool—Activity programs.
LB1140.35.C74G53
372.13'078—dc20

93-22373
CIP

Alphabet

3+ Alphabet Friends 13
4+ Letter Treasure Box 14
4+ Alphabet Soup 14
4+ Coconut Tree Fun 15
4+ Letters Go 'Round 16
5+ Fun With Magnetic Letters 16
5+ Ice Fishing 17

Animals

2+ Noah's Ark 18
3+ It's an Animal 19
3+ Footprints 19
3+ Worm Watch 20
3+ The Best Ears 20
3+ Be an Animal 21
3+ Animal Parade 21
3+ Animal Pictograph 22
4+ Finding the Animal's Home 23
4+ Myrtle the Turtle 24
4+ On the Trail of Forest Animals . . . 26
4+ Lace-A-Bear 26
4+ Black Bears and Baubbles 27
4+ Habitats and Eating Habits 28
4+ Ocean Animals 29
4+ Ocean Reef Diorama 29
5+ What's Inside? 30
5+ Classification of Amphibians 31

Art

2+ Worm Painting 32
2+ Shiny Constructions 32
2+ Helpful Paint Hint 33
2+ Toothbrush Painting 33
2+ Stained Glass 34
3+ Ice Dancing 34
3+ Tissue Fireworks 35
3+ Texture Bears 36
3+ Paper Quilt 37
3+ Let's Make an Impression 38
3+ Corn Shuck Painting 38
3+ Tissue Paper Water Transfer Collage . . . 39
4+ Epsom Salts Painting 39
4+ Tissue Square Leaves 40
4+ Stained Glass Windows 42

Birds

3+ Snow Owl 43
3+ Peaceful Doves 44
3+ Black Owl 45
3+ Bird Words 46
3+ Making Bird Feeders With Paper Rolls . . 46
3+ Bird Mobile 47
4+ What's in a Bird Nest? 48
4+ Our Fine Feathered Friends 49
4+ Robin 50
4+ Penguin 51
5+ Dangling Birds 52
5+ Wild Ducks 53

The Body

2+ My Body 54
3+ Balloon Person 54
3+ Beanbag Body Toss 55
3+ Body Bingo 56
3+ Healthy Teeth 57
4+ Shadow Tracing 57
4+ Growing and Changing 58
4+ Body Tracings 59
4+ Who Am I? 59
5+ Organ Tunics 60

Circus

2+ Six Clowns 62
2+ Elephant Headbands 64
3+ Create a Shape Circus 64
3+ Under the Big Top 65
4+ Clown Costumes 67
4+ Big Top Show 68

Clothing

2+ Shoe Monster 69
2+ Toddler Shoe Search 69
3+ That's Hats! 70
3+ Mitten Match 70
3+ Shoe Pair 71
4+ A Hat Is Not Just a Hat! 72

Colors

2+ Flower Garden 73
2+ Stone Search 73
2+ What Color Is My Apple? 74
2+ Mixing Colors Inside Plastic Bags 75
3+ The Color Box 75
3+ Rainbow Simon Says 76
3+ Doodly Doo Colors 76
3+ Human Dominoes 78
3+ Crayon Color Match 78
3+ Color Bingo 79
3+ Color Game 79
3+ The Color Red 80
3+ Color Wheel 81
3+ What Do You Get? 82
3+ Shady Dealings 82

CONTENTS

CONTENTS

3+ Color Telescopes 83
3+ Clothespin Sticker Match 84
3+ Red Rover, Red Rover Let the Colored
    Leaves Come Over 84
3+ Go Batty 85
3+ Eraser Sorting 86

Our Community

2+ A Visit to the Pet Shop 87
3+ Getting to Know You 88
3+ Making My House 88
3+ Democratic Free Time 89
4+ Where Does All Our Mail Come From? . . 90
4+ Mail Carrier 91
4+ The Letter Carrier 91
4+ Library Fun 92
4+ Block City 93
4+ Collections/Antique Shop 93
4+ Flower Shop 94
4+ Pounding Stump 95
4+ Cast Your Vote 95
4+ Block Play: Building a Town 96
5+ Our Own Newspaper 97

Cooking

2+ Brown Bear Bread 98
2+ Rice Cake Creatures 99
3+ What's Cooking? 100
3+ Pizza Day 102
3+ Sweet and Sour Fruit Flavors 102
3+ Cooking With Literature 103
3+ Cinnamon Roll-Ups 104
3+ Applesauce 105
3+ Cherry Pie 106
3+ Olden Days—Making Butter 107

Crafts

2+ Playdough Design 108
2+ Create a Creature 108
2+ Country Clay Hearts 109
3+ Sometimes I'm Afraid 110
3+ Camera 111
3+ Puzzle Pin 112
3+ Balloon Tissue Paper Painting 113
3+ Pearl Necklace 113
3+ Dying Wool 114
4+ Class Quilt 115
4+ Unique Hats 116
4+ Make an Alligator Purse 117
4+ Papier-Maché Masks 118
4+ Paper Bead Necklaces 118
5+ Picture Frame Weaving 119

Dinosaurs

3+ Dinosaur Eggs 120
3+ Dinosaur Footprints 120
3+ Dinosaur Dance 121
3+ Dinosaur Toes and Toenails 122
3+ Dinosaur Collage 122
3+ Dinosaur Hatch 123
4+ Dinosaur Dig 124
4+ Dinosaur Dip 125
4+ Dinosaur Bookmaking 126
4+ Dinosaur Hunt 126
4+ Nameosaurus 127
4+ Big Foot Dinosaur 128
5+ Fossil Hunt 129

The Environment

3+ Bucky the Recycle Beaver 130
3+ Our Trash 131
3+ Oil Slick 131
3+ The Balance of Nature 132
3+ Litter: An Eyesore 133
4+ Recycling 133
4+ Ocean Mural 134
4+ Recycled Paper Bowls 135
4+ Composting 136
4+ Great Clean-Up 136
5+ Green Tree 137

Fall

2+ Leaf Coloring 138
2+ Leaf Crunch 138
2+ Apple Picking 139
3+ Leaves Are Falling Down 140
3+ Autumn Leaves 141
3+ Leaf Bookmark 141
3+ Apple Tasting Party 142
3+ Going Nuts 142
3+ Nut Sorting 143
4+ Leaf Prints 144
4+ Nature Collage 144
4+ Flower Bulb Sorting 145
5+ Fall Poem 146

Families

2+ Just Mom and Me 147
3+ Family Banner 148
3+ Taking Care of Babies 149
3+ Where We Live 149
3+ Say "I Love You" With Coupons . . . 150
4+ Potato Print Family 151
4+ My Clothespin Doll 152

Farms

2+ Paint the Barn 154
2+ Stick-the-Spot-on-the-Holstein 155
2+ Farm Animals 155
3+ Old MacDonald's Mural 157
3+ Farms 158
3+ Same and Different 158
3+ Cow Milking 159
4+ Goat Mask 160
4+ Duck, Duck, Goose! 162

Food

3+ Fruit Picker 163
3+ Stone Soup Day 164
3+ Food or Not Food 165
3+ Bananas 165
3+ Grapes 166
3+ Lunch Basket 166
3+ Paper Pizza 168
4+ Before and After Foods 168
4+ Corn 170
4+ Nutritional Menus 171
4+ Let's Make Lunch Week 171
4+ Good Foods to Eat 172
4+ Shopping Lists 173
5+ Set the Table for a Balanced Meal 173
5+ What Part Do We Eat? 174
5+ Food Storage Center 175
5+ Food Fun Game 175
5+ Answer Robot 178

Games

2+ Beanbag Toss 179
2+ Fishing Game 180
2+ Memory 180
2+ Milk Jug Drop 181
2+ Lock and Latch Board 182
3+ Stop and Go Game 182
3+ Tick-Tock 183
3+ Let's Go Fishing 184
3+ Spoon Partners 184
3+ Rainbow Toss 185
3+ Up and Down 186
3+ Guess What I Am? 187
3+ File Folder Games 187
4+ The Describing Game 188
4+ Cookie, Cookie, Who Has the Cookie? . 189
4+ Coupon Game 190
5+ Tic Tac Bears 192

Gardening

3+ Red Wagon Flower Garden 193

3+ Building the Yellow Brick Road 193
3+ Planting a Garden 194
3+ Planting Bulbs 194
3+ Garden Collage 195
3+ Growing Radishes 196
4+ Zucchini Squash Plants 197
4+ Seed Wheel 198
4+ Planting Graph 199

Group Projects

3+ Changeable Art 200
3+ Murals 200
3+ Tube Art 201
4+ Friendship, the Perfect Blendship 202
4+ Togetherness Flag 203
4+ Hamster Maze 203
4+ Castle Creations 204
4+ Spelunk! 205

Health and Safety

3+ Brushing the Alligator's Teeth 206
3+ Mr. Yuk 206
3+ Syringe Painting 207
3+ Medical Collage 208
3+ Operation Cast 209
3+ Fire Safety 209
4+ Finger Cast Puppets 210
4+ What Makes Our Bones Strong 210
4+ Sneeze Experiment 211
4+ Safety 212
4+ Phone Home 213

Holidays

3+ Wrapping Presents 214
2+ Birthday Celebrations 214
3+ Birthdays! Birthdays! 215
3+ Halloween: Spider's Web Game 216
3+ Halloween: Melt the Witch 216
3+ A Charlie Brown Halloween 217
3+ Halloween: Pumpkin Mosaic 218
4+ Halloween: Sewing a Spider's Web . . . 219
4+ Halloween: Pumpkin Windsock 220
2+ Thanksgiving: Tom Turkey's Feathers . 221
3+ Thanksgiving: Trick That Turkey 221
4+ Thanksgiving: Handy Turkey 222
3+ Hanukkah: Menorah Game 223
3+ Hanukkah: Menorah Match-Ups 223
4+ Hanukkah: Menorah 224
2+ Christmas: Holiday Wreath 225
2+ Christmas Presents 226
2+ Christmas: Recycled Paper Ornaments . 226
2+ Christmas: Santa, Santa, Walk Around . 227

CONTENTS

3+ Christmas: Handy Holiday Wreath . . . 228
3+ Christmas: Rudolph the Red-Nosed
    Reindeer 229
3+ Christmas: Santa Pocket 230
3+ Christmas: Nutcrackers 231
3+ Egg Carton Christmas Tree 231
3+ "Christmas Joy" Photo Gifts 232
3+ Christmas: Glittering Pine Cones 233
4+ Christmas: Egg Carton Tree 233
4+ See-Through Christmas Tree 235
5+ Bulletin Board Christmas Tree 235
4+ Kwanzaa: Light the Kwanzaa Candles . . 236
4+ Martin Luther King, Jr. Day: Friendship
    Circle 237
5+ Martin Luther King, Jr. Day: I Have a
    Dream 238
4+ Chinese New Year Celebration 239
5+ Chinese New Year's Day 240
2+ Valentine, Valentine, Red and Blue . . . 241
2+ Valentine's Day: Heart Scepter 241
3+ Valentine Magnets 242
3+ Valentine's Day: Musical Hearts Game . 242
3+ Valentine Game 243
4+ An Owl Valentine 244
4+ Valentine's Day: Ladybug's Family . . . 245
4+ Valentine's Day: Heart Game 246
4+ St. Patrick's Day: St. Patrick's Day
    Treasure Hunt 246
2+ Easter: Let's Match Our Eggs 247
3+ Easter Egg Match 248
3+ Easter: Scrambled Eggs 248
3+ Mother's Day Bath Salts 249
3+ Grow a Plant for Mother's Day 249
4+ Mother's Day Coupon Holder 250
4+ Mother's Day: Mouse and Cheese
    Bookmark 252
4+ Mother's Day: A Butterfly Gift 253

Insects

2+ Butterflies 254
3+ Catch and Look Box 254
3+ The Very Hungry Caterpillar
    Becomes a Butterfly 255
3+ Fingerprint Ants 256
3+ 3-D Spider Web 256
3+ Crayon Shaving Butterfly 257
3+ Busy Bees 258
4+ Dancing Spider 259
4+ The Caterpillar 260
4+ Butterfly Kite 260
4+ 3-D Spiders 262
4+ Bumble Bee 263

4+ Symmetrical Insects 264
4+ Lady Bug 264
4+ A Caterpillar Becomes a Butterfly 265

Language

2+ The Three Little Pigs 266
2+ Goldilocks and the Three Bears 266
3+ A Kangaroo? 267
3+ Teddy Bear Picnic 267
3+ Magic Mirrors 268
3+ Play and Language 269
3+ Old West Role Play 269
4+ Special Friends 271
4+ Let's Make a Telephone 271
4+ Western Wear/Equipment 272
4+ A Kangaroo Without a Pocket? 273
4+ Rhythm Language 273
4+ Cookie Cookbook 274
4+ Flannel Board Story Box 274
4+ A Silly Cookie Story 275
4+ What's in the Box 276
4+ Using Descriptive Words 276
4+ Poetry Dramatization 277
4+ I Am a Monster 278

Money

3+ Money Bag 279
3+ Musical Money 279
4+ Coins 280
4+ Piggy Bank 281
4+ Let's Go Shopping 282
5+ Money Pots 284

Movement

2+ Turkey Trot Races 285
2+ Can You Climb Like a Monkey? 286
2+ Ball Kicking 286
3+ Making Imaginary Applesauce 287
3+ Leaf Dance 288
3+ Goldilock's Walk 289
3+ How Can We Get From Here to There? . 289
3+ Bubble Fun 290
3+ Monkey See, Monkey Do 291
3+ Velcro Obstacle Course Lines 291
3+ Balancing Beanbags 292
3+ Shadows 292
3+ Blanket Dancing 293
4+ Color the Movement 294
4+ Kangaroo Broad Jump 294
4+ Kangaroo Tag 295
4+ Preschool Olympics 296
5+ Fun With Opposites 297

Music

2+   Exploring Sound Through Music 298
2+   Dance Along Songs 298
2+   Dancing in Paint 299
3+   High in the Sky, Low to the Ground . . . 300
3+   Beanbag Rhythm 301
3+   Tone Color 301
3+   The Old Woman Who Swallowed a Fly . 302
3+   Dancing Angels/Pounding Hooves . . . 304
4+   Songwriting for Rhythm Instruments . . 304
4+   Beethoven Brush Art 305
4+   What Does the Music Sound Like? . . . 305
4+   Making Horns 306
5+   Color Match Musical Notes 307

Native Americans

3+   Totem Pole 308
3+   Indian Sand Painting 309
3+   Pocahontas 309
4+   Canoes 310
4+   Native American Tepee 311
4+   Weaving 312
4+   Kick Ball\Native American Style 312
4+   Triangular Tepee 313
4+   Making Indian Necklaces 314

Nature

2+   Setting Up a Home for Worms 315
2+   Worms 315
2+   Snipping Grass 316
2+   Lily Pads 316
3+   Worm Watch 317
3+   Nutty Mobile 318
3+   Snails 319
3+   Shell Snail 319
3+   Worm Farm 320
3+   Dirt Day 320
3+   Tree Bark Rubbings 321
3+   Nature Wreaths 322
3+   A Tree Is Nice 322
3+   Build a Pond 323
3+   Over in the Meadow 323
4+   Snail Race 324
4+   Sunshine and Moonlight 325
4+   Pollination of Flowers 326
4+   I Spy Soil 326
4+   Borrowing Bags and Sharing Trays . . . 327
4+   Tree Houses 328

Numbers

3+   Monkey Line 329
3+   Number Lotto 329
3+   Number Puzzle Cards 330
3+   Number Hunt 331
3+   Matching Bears 332
3+   Count the Cars 332
3+   Fingerplay: Five Little Candy Canes . . 333
3+   Let's Count 334
4+   Buzz Buzz 334
4+   Numbers 336
4+   Pots of Gold 336
4+   Road Blocks, a Counting Game 337
4+   Number Puzzles 338
4+   Planes Up High 338
4+   Teaching Numbers Using Playdough . . 339
4+   Monkey Face Finger Puppets 339
4+   The Number Train 340
5+   Doggie, Doggie, Count Your Bones . . . 340
5+   Wonderful Web 341

Nursery Rhymes

3+   Baa Baa Sheep 342
3+   Peter's Pumpkin 344
3+   Humpty Dumpty 344
3+   A Story in Sheep's Clothing 346
3+   Wee Willie Winkie 347
3+   The Eensy Weensy Spider 347
3+   Humpty's Broken 348
3+   Musical Puppet Play 348
3+   Jack and Jill 349
3+   Hickory Dickory Dock Clock 349
4+   Milkweed Pod Cradles 350
4+   Nursery Rhyme Play 351

Outer Space

3+   Rocket Ships 354
3+   Constellations 354
3+   Adventures in Space 355
3+   Fluorescent Constellations 356
3+   The Twilight Zone 356
4+   Space Station 357
4+   Star Box 358

Pets

2+   Kitten, Kitten 359
3+   Kritter Kare 360
3+   Classroom Pet Store 360
3+   Frog Egg Fun 361
4+   Frogs 362
4+   Pet Show and Tell 363
4+   Let's Vote on a Name for Our
     Classroom Pet 364
5+   Graphing a Frog's Life Cycle 364

C O N T E N T S

Plants

3+ Writing and Singing a New Seed Song . 366
3+ Jack's Beans 366
3+ The Function of Plant's Roots 367
3+ Sunflower 368
4+ Hand Print Tulips 369
4+ Sensational Sprouts 369
4+ Water Lily 370
4+ Effect of Water on Seeds 372

Science

2+ Melt Down 373
3+ Underwater Exploration 373
3+ Monthly Guessing Jar 374
3+ Magnet Painting 374
3+ Hand Magnet Scavenger Hunt 375
3+ Guessing Tools and Machines 376
3+ Ice Castles 376
4+ An Inclined Plane 377
4+ Ramp Races 378
4+ Water Table Science 378
4+ Waterfall Science 379
4+ Let's Make Predictions 380
4+ Straw, Sticks and Bricks 381
4+ Carbon Paper Transfer 382
4+ Things That Float 382
4+ Magnet Testing 383
5+ Magnet, Yes or No? 384
5+ Transparencies 384
5+ What's That Green Stuff? 385

Seasons

2+ Art Appreciation 386
3+ Yummy Chicken Soup 386
3+ Matching Seasonal Items 387
3+ Four Seasonal Trees 388
3+ Monthly Calendar 388
4+ The Months of the Year Go Round . . . 390
4+ Four Seasons Game 390
4+ Days of the Week 391
5+ Seasons in the North and South 392
5+ Big Book of Months 393

Self-Esteem

3+ I Dress Up—I'm Still Me! 394
3+ We Are Changing/We Are Growing . . . 395
3+ A Very Special Person 396
3+ My Special Hand Print 396
3+ Feeling Sentences Game 397
3+ Tape Recorder Talk 398
3+ Search and Identify 399
3+ "Me" Balloon 400
4+ I Know You! I Know You! 400
4+ Color Yourself 401
4+ Faces of the World 402

Senses

2+ Feet Painting 403
3+ Stewed Pears 403
3+ Food Roulette 404
3+ Texture Finger Painting 405
3+ Sensory Bear 405
3+ Feely Boxes 406
3+ Simon Says in Sign (Language) 407
3+ Family Signs 408
3+ Sign and Do 409
3+ Mr. Senses 410
3+ Smell Bags 410
3+ Feel Box 411
3+ Scent Matching 412
3+ Texture Corner/Divider 412
3+ I Can Do 413
3+ Roll Over 414
3+ Scent-Sational 412
3+ Veggie Shuffle 415
3+ Touch 'n Such 416
4+ Mud Finger Paint 417
4+ Foot Feelings 417
4+ Sign Language 418
4+ The Sense of Sight 419
5+ ABC Braille 420

Shapes

2+ Shapes Spectacular 420
2+ Round and Round 421
2+ Shape Awareness 422
3+ Magnetic Shape Pick-Up 423
3+ Passing the Shape 423
3+ Triangle Angel 424
3+ Take-Home Flannel Board Kit 426
3+ Shape Pets 428
3+ Triangle Size Seriation 428
4+ Sing a Song of Shapes 429
4+ There Was a Little Mouse 430

Sound

3+ House Sounds 432
3+ Hello Game 433
3+ Sound Lotto 433
3+ Now Hear This! 434
3+ Wood Xylophone 435

Spring

3+ Spring Mud Painting 436

3+ Lilacs 437
3+ Meet the Spring 437
3+ Spring Cleaning 438
3+ Flower Colors Match Up 439
4+ Spring Is Here! 440

Starting School

2+ Pick an Apple—To Learn Your Name . . 441
2+ Teddy Bear Picnic 441
3+ Photo/Name Match-Up Game 442
3+ The Name Game 442
3+ Class Quilt 443
3+ Unpack Your Bag 444
3+ My Name 444
4+ Circle Time Interviews 445
4+ Our Big Class Family 446
4+ Name License Plates 447
4+ Kangaroo Buddies 448
4+ Learning Addresses 450

Summer

3+ Watermelon 451
3+ Pack Your Bags 451
3+ Let's Go Camping 452
3+ Making a Classroom Campfire . . . 453
3+ Under the Sea 453
3+ Beach Wreaths 454
3+ Beach Party 455
3+ Sea Collage 455
3+ Seaside Collage 456
4+ Camping Week 457
4+ A Day at the Beach 458
4+ Beach Scene 459
4+ Luau Play 459

Transportation

2+ How Do I Get There? 462
2+ Tire Prints 462
3+ Constructing a Car 463
3+ Airplane' 464
3+ Tugboats 465
3+ Carpet Boating 466
3+ Mayflower Boat 466
3+ Vehicle Collage 467
3+ Egg Carton Choo-Choo 467
3+ Paper Plate Car 468
3+ Road, Sky or Water 468
3+ Car Painting 469
4+ Building Bridges 469
5+ Transportation Tally 470
5+ Mass Production 471

Weather

2+ Mr. Weatherbear 472
3+ Weather Game 472
3+ Puddle Game 474
3+ Cloudy Visions 474
3+ When It Rains, Where Does It Go? . . . 475
4+ Rainbow Mobile 476
4+ "I Think the Weather Is..." 477

Wind and Air

3+ Wind Sock 478
3+ Wind-O-Meter 478
3+ Making Windsocks 479
3+ Full of Hot Air 480
3+ Cotton Ball Race 480
3+ Blowing Game 481
3+ Bubbles 481
3+ What Can We Move by Blowing? 482
4+ A Windy Day! 483
4+ Let's Be the Wind 484
4+ To Move or Not to Move 484
4+ Air, Rain, Sunshine 485

Winter

2+ Soft-Snowman 486
2+ Fun With Ice 486
3+ Winter Fun 487
3+ Snowflakes 488
3+ Igloo Art 488
3+ Belly Bingo 489
3+ Building Snowpeople 490
3+ Making a Picture Book Sequel 491
3+ Building a Snowman 491
4+ Snow Fun 492
4+ Snowman! 493
4+ California Snowman 493

Zoo

2+ Stick Snakes 494
3+ The Lion's Whiskers 494
3+ Alligator 495
3+ Making Authentic Snakes 496
3+ Zoo Animals 496
3+ Olie Octopus 497
4+ Snakes! 500
4+ Lion: King of the Animals 501
4+ Tiger Bag Puppet 502
4+ Paper Zoo 503
4+ Panda Puppet 504
4+ Zoo Classifications 506

CONTENTS

How to Use This Book

Wouldn't it be great if you could call upon the creative resources of teachers from all over the country to help you plan the day, the week, or even the month? Now you can! In response to a nation-wide contest, teachers sent us their best ideas and activities that they use with children in their classrooms. The activities in this book are ones that teachers use every day, and they work!

We took 625 of the very best activities and divided them into 48 chapters. Each chapter is an encyclopedic unit. In any one unit you will find activities from different curriculum areas—art, dramatic play, cooking, science, music, and so on. An integrated approach to each topic is, therefore, possible. Each activity is arranged in a ready-to-use format. We are proud to bring you the excellent work of so many teachers.

The format for each activity is as follows:

Age

The age appropriateness for each activity is a suggestion. Each teacher is the best judge of the appropriateness of an activity, based on her or his prior knowledge of the children and the children's responses to the activity.

Introduction

The learning objective and/or additional information about the activity is presented in a short introduction.

Materials needed

A list of readily available materials is included.

What to do

The directions are presented in a step-by-step format. Patterns and illustrated directions are included where needed.

More to do

In this section, additional ideas for extending the activity are provided.

Related books

Many activities list titles and authors of popular children's books that can be used to support the activity.

Related songs

Some teachers included suggestions of original songs or well-known songs to integrate the activity into another area of the curriculum.

The book has two indexes. One is a skills index. It lists the pages of the activities that support the development of basic skills such as problem-solving, following directions, eye-hand coordination, matching, letter recognition, counting, estimating, language development, and so on. The second index contains words and phrases that are used throughout the book.

To pull this massive work together, we drew upon the expertise of two editors, Caroline Barnes and Carol Reynolds Petrash, who were ably assisted at a critical juncture by Justin Rood. We trust that you will benefit from the years of experience reflected in this book.

Alphabet Friends

3+

The children become alphabet detectives and learn to recognize letters as they search for objects displaying alphabet letter tags. This simple game can be played with endless variations just by changing the alphabet objects you choose.

Materials needed

One or two items for each letter of the alphabet. (For example: a toy alligator for A, a small ball for B, a large mixing spoon for S, or a zipper for Z.) Mark each item with an alphabet letter tag using masking tape and a marker, and place the items in various inconspicuous places around the room.
Large alphabet cards or pieces of posterboard or oak tag, each showing one letter of the alphabet (capital letters only).

What to do

1.   Gather the children on the rug or in your circle area and teach them the following rhyme: "We are walking on quiet feet. Alphabet friends are what we seek." Tell them that there are alphabet friends all around the room. They will know them by their alphabet letter tags (show an example.) Each child is to find one alphabet friend and return to the circle.
2.   Let the children search while reciting the rhyme. Give assistance when needed.
3.   When all children have returned to the circle, hold up one alphabet card and ask all children whose objects have matching alphabet tags to stand up and bring their items to you. Name the letter and object and display them together.
4.   Continue the game until you have gone through all the letters and collected all the objects.
5.   Following this, display the items in an alphabet center.
Note: You do not have to go through the whole alphabet each day. You can choose to work only on certain letters each day until you have gone through them all. Just be sure to have enough objects so that each child can find one.

More to do

Once the children have learned to recognize and name the letters, you can just ask for the objects to be brought forward by naming a letter without showing the letter card. Of course, always help if a child is unsure.

—Carol G. Taylor, Pineville, LA

Letter Treasure Box   4+

This activity will help children learn the letters of the alphabet and associate them with a variety of objects whose names begin with the same sound.

Materials needed

Box with a lid
Decorations for the box
Variety of objects beginning with the letter being taught

What to do

1. Decorate the box and lid. This will be the treasure box.
2. When teaching a new letter put the letter on the outside of the treasure box.
3. Place various items that begin with the letter around the room. Conduct a treasure hunt for those items. The hunt could take place inside or outside the classroom.
4. Encourage children to bring small things from home to add to the letter box.
5. Change the letter on the treasure box whenever you introduce a new letter and conduct more treasure hunts.
6. Allow the children to look at items in the box during free time.

More to do

At the end of a letter study, make a big poster of the letter. Then call children one at a time to get a treasure from the treasure box. Attach the treasures to the poster or draw pictures of them on the poster. For older children, print the word under the item or picture. Leave the poster up in the room during other letter studies.

Related songs

"Alphabet Sounds" by Barbara Milne on *Sounds Like Fun*
The Muppet Alphabet Album

—Cindy Bosse, Crystal Springs, MS

Alphabet Soup   4+

Children learn to recognize and properly sequence the letters of their first name.

Materials needed

Construction paper
Markers
Glue
Envelopes
Scissors

What to do

1. Using capital letters, print the name of each child on the outside of an envelope.
2. Cut small circles out of the construction paper.
3. Print one letter of the child's name inside each circle.
4. Place the circles with the letters for each child's name inside the envelopes with their names on them.

5. Cut the remaining construction paper into the shape of spoons or bowls.
6. Gather children by asking a few to come and play Alphabet Soup.
7. Begin by helping each child recognize their name on the envelope when it is given to them.
8. When everyone has their envelope, have the children open them. Encourage them to say the letters they recognize. Who has similar letters in their name?
9. When the children are ready to move onto the next step give them each the cutout of a spoon or bowl and encourage them to paste on the letters of their name in the correct order. Children who are having difficulty can be encouraged to look at their name printed on the envelope.
10. After the children have finished putting the letters in order, again encourage each child to read aloud the letters in their name.
11. Gather another group of children to participate in the activity.

More to do

The children could make alphabet soup for snack one day.

Related books

Alphabet Soup by Kate Banks
Growing Vegetable Soup by Lois Ehlert

—*Melissa Browning, West Allis, WI*

Coconut Tree Fun

4+

The children learn to recite the alphabet.

Materials needed

Chicka Chicka Boom Boom by Bill Martin Jr.
Cassette tape to accompany book
Flannel board
Flannel coconut tree and letters
Butcher paper
Paint
Alphabet letters cut from paper

What to do

1. Make a coconut tree and alphabet letters from felt.
2. Cut alphabet letters from construction paper.
3. Read the book to the class.
4. Listen to the tape together and encourage children to join in.
5. Allow children to reconstruct the story on the flannel board.
6. Let children paint a giant coconut tree on butcher paper and display on bulletin board along with the construction paper letters.

More to do

Make a class alphabet book using pictures the children draw for each letter.

—*Laura Chadd, Haviland, KS*

Letters Go 'Round 4+

The children will learn to recognize letters while playing this game.

Materials needed

Flashcards, each with a letter on one side and a picture representing that letter on the other
Blank index cards (preferably large ones)
Colored markers

What to do

1. Count the children.
2. Put the flashcards on the floor in a semi-circular pattern, one card per child.
3. Have the children sit on the floor by the cards.
4. Ask each child to pick up the flashcard that's in front of him and look at the letter. Give them about one minute to do this.
5. Ask the children to turn the cards over and look at the pictures.
6. Hold up an index card with a hand written letter on it and say "Would the person that's holding this same letter please come to the middle of the circle."
7. After the child is standing in the circle, have him show the children the letter that he is holding and identify that letter (if the child identifies the letter incorrectly, just ask the other children to help that child identify the letter).
8. After the child identifies the letter, have him turn the flashcard over and identify the picture.
9. Ask the child a question about his picture.
10. Follow this procedure until each child gets a turn to identify his letter and tell about his picture. After this, the children should sing the Alphabet Song.

More to do

Play games using letters. Example: have the children sit in a circle. Announce, "all of the children whose names begin with the letter 'A' stand up, turn around and touch your friend." Another extension could be to have the children play only with toys that have letter labels on the containers. If the room is not set up this way, the teacher could label the toys for a day.

—Denise Hodge, Brooklyn, NY

Fun With Magnetic Letters 5+

Here children enjoy a unique book about alphabet letters and will practice identifying letters on a magnetic board.

Materials needed

Lowercase magnetic letters a to z
Chicka Chicka Boom Boom by Bill Martin
Magnetic chalkboard (or board that can be drawn on)
Chalk (or dry erase markers)

What to do

1. Draw a coconut tree on the board and arrange all letters at the bottom.
2. Read the book, *Chicka Chicka Boom Boom*. Ask questions such as, "What did the letters do? What happened to them? Why did they fall out of the tree?"
3. Read the story again, this time acting it out with the letters on the magnetic board.

4. Read the story a third time and have the children come up, one by one, and move the letters up and down the tree.

5. Put out the letters and board for children to play with during free time.

More to do

Make a tape recording of the story. Put out upper case and lower case letters. Have children match the upper case letter with the correct lower case one. Have a chart showing the upper and lower case pairs nearby so that they can check their matching.

—Nicole Geiger, Elicott City, MD

Ice Fishing

5+

Here's a fun way for your oldest children to practice recognition of letter sounds.

Materials needed

Paper
Bucket
Aluminum foil (or any shiny silver paper)
Magnet
Paper clips
Stick
String
Pictures or items whose names begin with the letters you are working on
Alphabet chart

What to do

1. Make a fishing pole out of the stick and string, and attach the magnet to the end of the string.
2. Cut fish shapes out of paper and attach one of the pictures to each fish with a paper clip.
3. Put the fish in the bucket and cover the top of the bucket with the foil.
4. Tell the children that you are going to go ice fishing.
5. Cut out a circle in the center of the "ice" (aluminum foil).
6. Let each child use the fishing pole to catch a fish.
7. Have them identify the sound that the picture on the fish begins with.
8. Have them find that letter on the alphabet chart.

More to do

Begin a unit on Eskimos. Talk about magnets. For younger children, draw alphabet letters on the fish and have them match or identify the letters rather than the sounds.

Related books

Dr. Seuss's ABC by Dr. Seuss
Animalia by Graeme Base

—Suzanne Sanders, Cherry Hill, NC

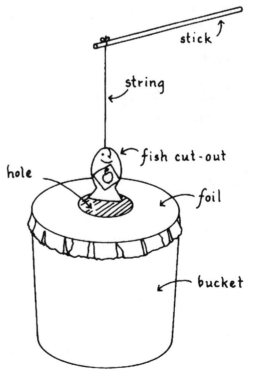

Noah's Ark

2+

This activity enhances fine motor skills, encourages cooperative interaction, expands experiences in mixed-media activities and increases knowledge of animals.

Materials needed

Large piece of butcher paper for mural collage
Magazines with animal pictures
Scissors
White glue
Craft sticks
Brown paint
Construction paper in different shades of blue
Paintbrushes

What to do

1. Draw outline of Noah's Ark on large piece of butcher paper. Set up materials around table to maximize interaction.
2. Place paper with ark outlined on the floor or across a table.
3. Children glue the craft sticks down to fill in body of ship. Let this part dry.
4. Have the children paint all the craft sticks brown. Let the paint dry.
5. Children can cut or rip blue paper into small pieces and glue all around the ark for the water and sky. (Other materials can be used such as cotton balls, tissue paper or felt.)
6. Ask the children to look through the magazines and cut out pictures of animals.
7. The children glue animal pictures all around top of ark. Fish can go in the water, birds in the sky, etc. Let dry.
8. Hang up for all to see.

More to do

Bake cookies in animal shapes. Do a language experience activity with question, "What would you take with you if you went for a trip on Noah's Ark?"

Related books

Two by Two—The Untold Story by Kathryn Hewitt
Noah Built an Ark One Day by Colin and Jacqui Hawkins
Noah's Ark by Peter Spier

—Pam Laptook, Dallas, TX

It's an Animal

Children will sort a variety of objects or pictures into categories: animals or not animals.

Materials needed

Plastic replicas or photographs of animals
Other objects or pictures of objects

What to do

1. Put the objects or pictures into a container or basket or spread them on a work surface.
2. Present the objects or pictures to the children.
3. Have the children sort the objects or pictures according to whether or not "It's an animal!"

More to do

Focus the children's attention on specific features of the objects or pictures in order to verbalize specific characteristics of animals. Encourage the children to think of their own examples of "animals" or "not animals." For a more advanced activity, sort them into groups according to different kinds of animals.

—Barb Lindsay, Clear Lake, IA

Footprints

The children will learn to identify the footprints of various animals.

Materials needed

Construction paper—white and black
Glue
Glitter—clear or silver
Animal stickers (optional)
Whose Footprints? by Masayuki Yabuchi

What to do

1. Cut out animal footprints from black construction paper using the book, *Whose Footprints?* by Masyuki Yabuchi, as a guide.
2. Read *Whose Footprints?* to the class.
3. Set out the glue and glitter, and give each child a sheet of white construction paper. Show the children how to add glue and glitter to make "snow."
4. Have each child select one animal's footprints and glue to their paper over the snow.
5. Write the animal's name under the footprints on each piece of paper. If animal stickers are available, have the child place the appropriate sticker next to the animal's name.

More to do

Older children with cutting skills can cut out their own animal footprints. Make human footprints by having the children step in paint and then onto paper, or by tracing the children's feet and having them paint or color inside the outlines.

—Maxine Della Fave, Raleigh, NC

Worm Watch

3+

In this activity, the children will compare different kinds of worms and how they look, feel, smell and act.

Materials needed

Soil
At least two different kinds of earthworms
Shallow pans

What to do

1. Fill the pans with soil and add a few earthworms.
2. Have the children sit in small groups with the worm pans.
3. Discuss with the children what the worms look like—their color, shape, texture and size.
4. Allow the children to gently handle the worms. Encourage them to comment on how the worms feel.
5. Record the children's comments.

More to do

Give the children crayons or markers to draw worms. Record their comments about their drawings. Give the children pieces of cooked spaghetti and paint. Let them dip the spaghetti in the paint and move the spaghetti on the paper as if it were a worm.

—*Constance Austin, Dallas, TX*

The Best Ears

3+

The children will observe and evaluate different animal ears as they learn about the sense of hearing.

Materials needed

Animal ears cut from construction paper, or ear patterns to be used by the children
Headbands cut from construction paper

What to do

1. If you do not use pre-cut ears, have the children trace and cut patterns for donkey, cow, horse, pig, sheep and dog ears.
2. Using any book that has pictures of animals, point out the animal's ears, paying special attention to the direction in which they point.
3. Look for advantages and disadvantages. Which kind of ears would be better in a wind storm, donkey ears or pig ears? Which do you think hears better?
4. Have each child choose which kind of ears they would like to have if they could exchange ears with an animal. Discuss each child's choice.
5. Fit each child for a head band and either attach the pre-cut ears or let the children trace, cut, and mount their own ears.

More to do

Have the children search through magazines for pictures of ears and make a collage.

Related books

Old MacDonald Had a Farm by Colin Hawkins

—*Elaine H. Root, Garland, TX*

Be an Animal

The students will role play animal movements and sounds either spontaneously or in imitation of others.

What to do

1. Think of specific animals to role play such as a bird, cow, dog, cat, etc.
2. "Warm-up" the group by standing and doing stretching exercises.
3. Choose a small group of children and quietly suggest an animal for them to role play. The other children try to identify the animal that has been chosen.
4. Each child gets a chance to role play an animal. The children may decide within their small group which animal they will role play.

More to do

Discuss with the children what it might feel like to be an animal. Ask the children about their personal experiences with animals.

—Barb Lindsay, Clear Lake, IA

Animal Parade

The children will learn to walk or move like a particular animal and can choose a characteristic of that animal to make and wear.

Materials needed

Construction paper
Music (optional)
Masking tape
So Can I by Margery Facklam

What to do

1. Read the story *So Can I* to the children. Ask them what kind of animal they would like to be if they weren't human.
2. Help the children make a body part of the chosen animal to wear. (For example, an elephant's nose can be attached with a piece of tape or tied around the head with string. Rabbit's ears can be attached to a paper headband.)
3. Attach the animal part to the child with tape or string.
4. Have the children parade around the room moving their particular animal to music. They can also make their animal sound.

More to do

Discuss different animals and where they live. Talk about differences in pets, wild animals and farm animals. Have a classroom pet such as a fish, hamster or rabbit.

—Renee Kapusniak, Webster, NY

Animal Pictograph

3+

In this activity the children will learn to produce pictographs.

Materials needed

Resealable plastic bags
Animal crackers
Markers
Oaktag or posterboard
Glue (glue stick or paste works best for this project)
Ruler

What to do

1.   Prepare one plastic bag for each child in your class. Fill each bag with five or six different animal crackers.
2.   Prepare a graph outline listing each animal.
3.   Give each child a bag of animal crackers and explain they will be used for the lesson and they will be able to eat them in a few minutes.
4.   Have each child remove crackers from the bag and identify the animal shapes. Talk briefly about the animals. How are they alike and different? Where would you find these animals, etc.
5.   Ask each child to select their favorite animal from the cookies in front of them and set it aside.
6.   Allow children to nibble the rest of the cookies. Explain that each child will glue their favorite animal to the graph next to the animal names. Be sure that the graph is flat on a desktop for gluing.
7.   Tell the children they have created a pictograph. Have children study their newly created pictograph. Discuss the longest line, shortest line, etc. Count how many cookies are in each line. Discuss what this pictograph shows them.
8.   Give your graph a title and post it where the children can see it.

More to do

Use the graph as a springboard into Animal Week. Feature a different animal each day and discuss each animal in depth. For example: bear habits, types, habitat, etc. Create other pictographs using the children's favorite colors, shapes, breakfast cereals or even pasta shapes.

Related songs

"Animal Fair"
"The Bear Went Over the Mountain"
"Three Blind Mice"

—*Karen Megay-Nespoli, Massapequa Park, NY*

Finding the Animals' Home

After participating in this activity, children will understand that different animals need to live in different habitats (a principle basic to understanding environmental concerns).

Materials needed

Crayons/markers
Scissors
Glue
2"-3" pictures of polar bear, shark, monkey, giraffe, duck, mountain sheep, beaver, owl
11" x 14" paper divided into 8 sections

What to do

1. Divide the 11" x 14" paper into 8 sections and design a different habitat for each section. You may use photocopies of photographs or simple sketches. The habitats to include are an ice flow, undersea coral reef, jungle trees and vines, grassland with acacia trees, a marsh with water and reeds, a rocky crag, a river bordered by trees and a large old tree with a nesting hole in it.
2. Prepare a set of papers for each child in your class.
3. At circle time, discuss how different animals like to live in places and how each type of animal needs special things from where they live. Explain that an animal's habitat provides it with food, shelter and the right type of environment for life. Easy examples are panda bears who need bamboo plants, sea otters who need kelp beds and koala bears who need eucalyptus. Some creatures can eat a wide variety of foods and survive in a wide variety of climates and so are found all over the place such as coyotes and people!
4. Pass out pictures of the animals and the habitats. Let the children color the animals while you talk about them.
5. Let them color the habitats while you talk about them.
6. Have the children cut out the animals.
7. Ask the children to paste the animals into the correct habitat. Work on the project as a group, so that everyone places the animals correctly. Note: This activity can be divided up into several sessions, depending on the age of the children.

More to do

Talk about animals that live in your area, what the main habitats are, and the niches that they fill. Go on a nature hike to a pond, grassland, forest, marsh, seashore, etc. and keep a list of all the animals you find (birds, bugs, all living things).

Related song

Sing to the tune of "The Farmer in the Dell"

Oh the polar bear needs the ice, etc.
Oh the monkey needs the trees,
Oh the shark needs the sea,
Oh the goat needs the rocks,
Oh the beaver needs the pond,
Oh the duck needs the marsh,
Oh the giraffe needs the leaves,
Oh the owl needs a home,
Oh the people need them all.

—Dixie Havlak & Family, Olympia, WA

Myrtle the Turtle

4+

In this activity the children will create a turtle while learning about its basic anatomy.

Materials needed

Turtle pattern
Green or brown construction paper
Scissors
Construction paper—any color
Glue
Newspaper
Stapler
Marker

What to do

1. Using the turtle body pattern, cut turtle body parts out of green or brown construction paper. Be sure to draw in the diagonal lines and dots on the turtles back, or "carapace."
2. Cut out hexagonal "scoots" using any color of construction paper.
3. Have children glue the scoots onto the turtle's carapace and tummy, or "plastron."
4. When the glue has dried, cut (or have the children cut) along the diagonal lines on the carapace pattern, being sure to stop at the dots.
5. Overlap the paper on either side of the diagonal. Cut about one inch and staple. The finished turtle's back should resemble a bowl.
6. Fill the back with crumpled newspaper, align the tummy with the back and staple all the way around the turtle's body.
7. Glue the head together and glue the neck flaps onto the turtle's body. Scoots can be glued on to cover up the neck flaps.
8. Glue on or draw in eyes.

More to do

Make a bulletin board display of a pond adding some of your turtles and other wildlife and plants including fish, insects, aquatic plants, snakes and frogs.

—Leslie Kuehn Meyer, Vermillion, SD

Turtle Body Pattern

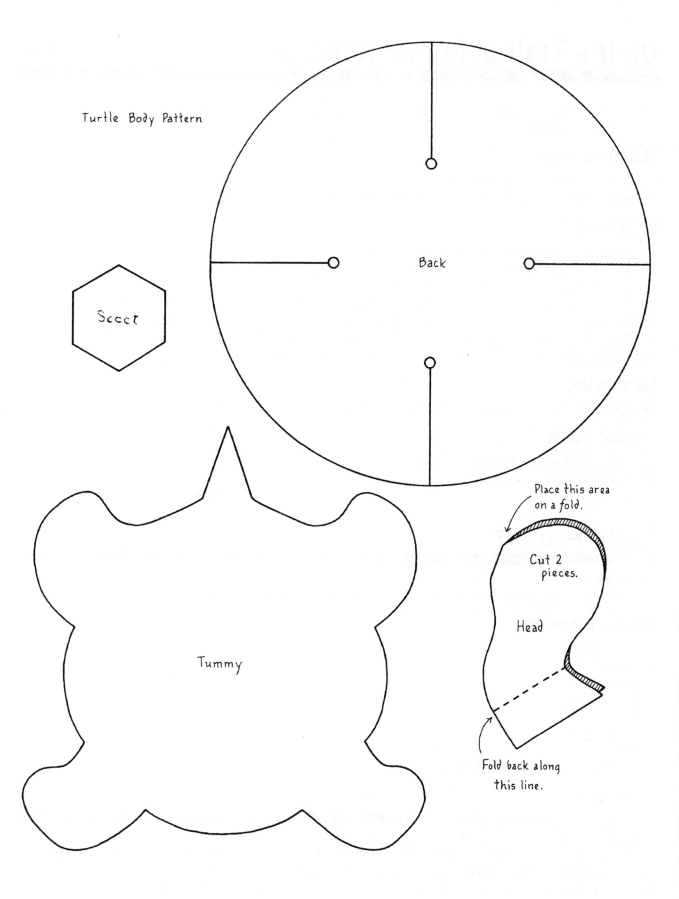

Back

Scoot

Tummy

Place this area on a fold.

Cut 2 pieces.

Head

Fold back along this line.

On the Trail of Forest Animals

4+

The children will improve their memorization skills and learn about some common wild animals, including their tracks and habitats.

Materials needed

Books by Jim Arnosky (see below)
Plastercast of the paw print of a raccoon or another animal

What to do

1. Make or obtain a plaster cast of an animal paw print.
2. Read aloud the book *Raccoons and Ripe Corn* sharing the illustrations. The second time it is read aloud, have the children point out the small, nature details found on each page.
3. Show the children pictures of the prints of a dog, a bird, and a raccoon. Show the plaster cast of the animal paw print to the children. Tell them simply how the cast was made. Let them touch the paw print.
4. Read aloud *Deer at the Brook*, sharing illustrations. Re-read aloud, having the children point out special details in the illustrations. Share with the children the experience of seeing a live deer.

More to do

Make a game of matching animal prints (dog, duck, child, etc.). Plaster casts of the children's hands could be made.

Related books

Raccoons and Ripe Corn by Jim Arnosky
Deer at the Brook by Jim Arnosky

—*Christina Chilcote, New Freedom, PA*

Lace-A-Bear

4+

This activity will improve the children's eye-hand coordination and fine motor skills.

Materials needed

Bear pattern
Brown felt
Scissors
Hole punch
Yarn
Plastic needles
Stuffing
Movable eyes, flat buttons and glue (optional)

What to do

1. Trace and cut out two felt bears for each child. Punch holes 1/2 inch or so apart around the outside edges of the bears (do two at a time so the holes correspond).
2. Give each child a plastic needle with yarn and two felt bears. Demonstrate carefully how to lace the two bear sides together, leaving an opening at one end so the bear can be stuffed.
3. When all the bears are laced, help the children stuff their bears and lace up the last few holes.
4. If desired, have children glue on eyes, button noses, and yarn mouths.

More to do

Talk about hibernation and make a home for the bears to hibernate in. Have children tell adventure stories about their bears.

Related books

Sleepy Bear by Lydia Dabcovich
Corduroy by Don Freeman
A Pocket for Corduroy by Don Freeman

—*Christina Casey, Malvern, PA*

Black Bears and Baubles 4+

The children will use fine motor skills to roll, cut and decorate dough.

Materials needed

Bear-shaped cookie cutters
Ingredients for air-hardening dough (salt, water and cornstarch)
Saucepan
Hot plate
Mixing bowl and spoon
Measuring cups
Black tempera paint
Gold ribbon, small beads, pompons, and moveable eyes

What to do

1. Prepare the dough according to the following recipe:

    Mix 2 cups salt and 2/3 cup water in a saucepan. Cook at medium heat for 4-5 minutes.
    Remove from heat.
    In a separate bowl mix 1 cup cornstarch and 1/2 cup water.
    Stir into cooked mixture until smooth.
    Cook again over medium heat until mixture is thick, stirring constantly.
    Take off heat and allow to cool.
    Cut into pieces. This dough dries at room temperature.
    Keep excess in an airtight container in a cool place, preferably a refrigerator.

2. Cut the gold necklace ribbons and mix the paint ahead of time.
3. Have the children roll out the dough and cut out bear shapes using the cookie cutters. With a pencil, poke holes in the ears of each bear so that the necklace ribbon may be added later.
4. Set the dough bears aside to harden.
5. Have the children paint their bear shapes black. Let the painted bears dry for 1-2 hours.
6. Give the children moveable eyes and pompons for noses these to the bears' faces.
7. Help the children lace the ribbon through the ear holes to form a necklace. Now the children may string beads onto their necklaces for added decoration.

More to do

Sing "Teddy" to the tune of "Bingo Was His Name":

There was a little tiny bear
And Teddy was his name-O.
T—E—D—D—Y,
T—E—D—D—Y,
T—E—D—D—Y,
And Teddy was his name-O!

—*Lisa Lang, Parkerburg, WV*

Habitats and Eating Habits

4+

In this activity, the children will explore the different habitats and eating habits of a variety of animals.

Materials needed

Green construction paper
Scissors
Pictures or models of meats
Toy worms (plastic fishing lures with the hooks removed look realistic)
Animal pictures

What to do

1. Cut the green paper into leaves and strips to resemble blades of grass. (You will need quite a few so cut a lot.) If the children in your classroom are skilled in using scissors they can help do this.
2. Take a look at the animal pictures. As you show each picture to the children, talk about the various animals. Where do they live? What do they eat? How is where they live and what they eat different from where the children live and eat?
3. Divide the room into several "Feeding Stations" and place "food" in the different areas. Use grass (green strips of paper), leaves (cut from green paper), meat (from your kitchen area or use magazine pictures), and worms (toy ones).
4. Tell the children that you need animals to fill up the feeding stations. Since no real animals are available, we will pretend to be animals.
5. Start with the grassy meadow. Ask what kind of animals eat grass. Cows? Horses? Sheep? Goats? Have the children name several animals and then ask for volunteers to go to the area and "graze." (Caution them not to actually eat the paper, etc.)
6. Continue until all of the feeding stations are filled with appropriate animals. Then let all of the animals graze for a while as you walk from area to area.
7. As you walk, ask the children to tell you what kind of animals they are pretending to be and what kind of food they are eating. Talk about the places that the animals live and compare them to the houses or apartments in which the children live.

More to do

Plan a field trip to a local farm or zoo. As you tour the grounds and view the various animals talk about the places they live and the foods they eat. It would be nice to plan your trip so the children can see the animals being fed.

Related books

The Mixed-Up Chameleon by Eric Carle
One Two Three: An Animal Counting Book by Marc Brown

Related songs

"Animal Walks"
"Save the Animals, Save the World"
"Zany Zoo" by Hap Palmer
"Walter the Waltzing Worm" by Hap Palmer

—*Virginia Jean Herrod, Columbia, SC*

Ocean Animals

The children develop hand-eye coordination through tracing and cutting and learn about oceans and the animals living in them. They also develop an awareness of quantity by graphing.

Materials needed

Construction paper
Stencils
Crayons
Clear or blue-colored plastic wrap
Shoe boxes
Tape manila folders
Glue
Baby Beluga by Raffi

What to do

1. Collect as many shoe boxes as you can. Ask your students to help.
2. It would be helpful to have stencils of ocean animals for the children to trace. Use a manilla folder to cut out ocean animal shapes.
3. Read the book aloud to the children. Talk about the animals that live in the ocean. What will happen to them if the water is polluted?
4. Pick out all of the animals shown in the text. Name them and draw them. Let the children pick out their favorite and draw it. Graph the results of their choices.
5. Make your own ocean complete with fish. Directions:

   Have each child color the inside bottom of a shoe box blue.
   Have children trace or draw and color different ocean animals.
   Glue some of the shapes onto the bottom of the box and suspend others so that they float freely in the box.
   Assist the children in covering the top of the box with the plastic wrap—secure with tape.
   At last, an ocean full of fish!

More to do

Sing the song "Baby Beluga."

—*Lori Erickson, Harris, MN*

Ocean Reef Diorama

The children learn about ocean reefs and create a scenic representation of one with water life figures and plant-like details. This is a good alternative to an actual classroom aquarium setup.

Materials needed

Large cardboard box
Thin cardboard
Blue construction paper
Manila paper
Crayons or markers
String or yarn

Scissors
Stapler
Tape
Newspaper
Sand
Rocks

What to do

1. Line the interior of the large cardboard box with light blue paper.
2. Have the children trace out the shape of a fish or other ocean animal on manila paper.
3. Back this shape with another sheet of manila paper and cut through both sheets when cutting out the animal.
4. Staple the two sides of the ocean animal together, leaving a 5" length open for later stuffing.
5. Let the children design and color the sides of their fish or animal.
6. Stuff their figures with crumpled up newspaper and staple closed.
7. Draw, color and cut underwater plants from thin cardboard.
8. Hang the water animal figures from string inside the large box.
9. Prop or tape the cardboard plants on the ocean floor of the large box.
10. Scatter sand and rocks around the ocean floor of the large box.

More to do

Set up a small aquarium with live fish and plants. Discuss possible reasons for the various colors, shapes and sizes of the animals.

Related books

The Aquarium Book by George Ancona
Grover's Adventure Under the Sea by Tom Cooke

—Linda Barrett, Chicago, IL

What's Inside

The children will learn to distinguish animals that are born alive from those that hatch from eggs.

Materials needed

Egg shapes cut from white or colored paper—approximately 5" tall
Crayons or markers
Scissors
Paper fasteners
Pictures of animals which hatch from eggs and those that do not

What to do

1. Cut egg shapes from white or colored paper, two for each child. For older children, provide line drawings of egg shapes, and allow them to cut their own.
2. Have the children help you sort the animal pictures into two groups: those that hatch from eggs and those that do not. Create a graph or poster of the results of your groupings.
3. Place all materials in one area of the room. Display the graph or poster for reference.
4. On one egg shape, draw any animal that hatches from the egg.

5. Cut the second egg shape in half. Using a paper fastener or two attach the second egg to the first so that it covers the drawing of the animal.

6. Show the children how to "crack" open the top shell to see the animal(s) which hatch from eggs.

7. Place the completed eggs in a basket to be used by all the children.

More to do

Names of the specific animals can be written on each egg.

Related book

Chickens Aren't the Only Ones by Ruth Heller

—*Lyndall Warren, Milledgeville, GA*

Classification of Amphibians   5+

The children will learn to discriminate amphibians from non-amphibians and classify them on the basis of their characteristics.

Materials needed

Basic information book on Frogs/Amphibians with large, color pictures
Set of classification cards depicting amphibians and other animals
Cardboard or other heavy paper
Clear contact paper (optional)
Glue
Scissors

What to do

1. Make a set of classification cards by finding large colorful pictures of amphibians and other animals in magazines. You may be able to find these in "Ranger Rick" and "Your Big Backyard."

2. Cut out the pictures and mount them on heavy paper or cardboard. Cover them with clear contact or laminate if you like.

3. Read over the informational book and become familiar with it. Prepare some open-ended questions to ask the children regarding the book.

4. Read the informational book to the children. Discuss the information and emphasize amphibian characteristics in relation to specific amphibians.

5. In a small group, show the children how to group the animal cards using the classification process you have been discussing.

6. Allow the children to classify cards on their own. Make observations of vocabulary being used and reinforce.

More to do

For older children, print key vocabulary words on cards and use them when discussing the amphibian characteristics. Allow the children to look through magazines and choose their own pictures.

—*Cheryl Collins, Hughson, CA*

Worm Painting

2+

Children increase fine motor skills while exercising their creativity.

Materials needed

Black construction paper
Paint
Yarn
Scissors

What to do

1. Dilute the paint so the yarn can easily be dipped in it.
2. Cut yarn into 6" pieces.
3. Give each child a piece of paper.
4. Make several colors of paint with pieces of yarn available for the children to choose from.
5. The child moves the yarn covered with paint around the paper, imitating the movement of a worm.
6. Let dry.

More to do

Dig up worms and watch how they move on the sidewalk.

Related books

Amazing Spiders by Alexandra Parsons
Amazing Snakes by Alexandra Parsons

Related songs

"I'm Being Swallowed by a Boa Constrictor"
"Eensy Weensy Spider"

—Sandra C. Scott, Vancouver, WA

Shiny Constructions

2+

Materials needed

Several small containers of glue to be shared
Pieces of wood scraps or paper
Food coloring

What to do

1. Pour food coloring into small bottles of glue and shake. Use one bottle of glue for each color desired.
2. Have small pieces of wood or paper in the middle of the table.
3. Children make their sculptures by gluing the wood or paper in any arrangement they wish.
4. The color glue dries in brilliant "shiny" colors.

More to do

Try all color combinations together. They will blend nicely. The glue can also be squeezed on to white paper in designs or a circular motion.

—Patricia Kepner, Norwalk, CA

Helpful Paint Hint +2

This is not an activity but a helpful hint. By using this mixture, paints can easily be removed from children's clothing. This should be mixed a day ahead of use.

Materials needed

16 oz. container of dry tempera
1 cup of dry baby detergent
Warm water

What to do

1. Mix paint a day ahead of use.
2. Mix tempera and enough water to fill the container half full. Return the lid and shake well, mixing thoroughly.
3. Add dry baby detergent and stir from the bottom of the container. Add enough water to fill the container an inch below the top (mixture will swell).
4. Mix and shake ingredients thoroughly.
5. Allow paint to sit several hours; paint will thicken considerably. If paint becomes pasty, add a couple of tablespoons of water.
6. Left thick, the mixture can be used for finger paint or an activity that calls for a thick paint.
7. When thinned with water, the mixture is wonderful for easel painting.
8. This paint mix keeps indefinitely in the refrigerator and smells good too!
9. Best of all, it washes out of clothes in a normal washing.

—Iris Hutchens, Memphis, TN

Toothbrush Painting +2

Children learn to paint different designs using an everyday object.

Materials needed

Old toothbrushes
Paint
Paper
Trays for holding paint
Art smocks

What to do

1. Collect some old toothbrushes.
2. Mix tempera paint a little thick.
3. Place paint on trays with the toothbrushes.
4. Put out paper for painting.
5. Have children put on a smock and enjoy painting with the toothbrush.

—Janice Parks, Stockdale, TX

Stained Glass

2+

Children will experiment with a different medium to make things stick instead of using glue. Through this activity, children explore colors, develop fine motor skills and improve eye-hand coordination.

Materials needed

Thin, colored, plastic sheets—theme paper covers work well
Clear contact paper (at least 2 feet per child)
Scissors

What to do

1. Pre-cut the clear contact paper. Provide two sheets per child making each one at least one foot long. The day before the activity, store the sheets flat under a heavy object to prevent curling.
2. Give each child a sheet of colored plastic and pair of scissors. Have the children attempt to cut the plastic into small pieces. The plastic is usually sturdy enough for even the younger children to cut. Provide assistance if needed.
3. When most of the plastic has been cut, collect the small pieces, mix them all together, and redistribute them so each child gets a variety of colors.
4. Allow time for the children to experiment with the different shapes and colors. Encourage them to overlap their colors to make new colors.
5. Provide one sheet of clear contact paper per child. Encourage the children to try to peel the backing off the contact paper. Assist those who need help.
6. Have the children arrange their colored pieces on the contact paper, sticky side up.
7. When the child has arranged his colored pieces "just the way he wants them," provide another sheet of clear contact paper to lay over his picture, sticky side down. Again, encourage the child to peel off the backing, providing assistance as needed.
8. Trim the edges of the clear contact paper where it did not match, or cut the contact paper into a different shape (e.g. rainbow, triangle, flower, etc.)
9. Hang the "stained glass" in the windows and watch the color reflections. Ask the children "How many colors do you see?"

—Julia A Masury, Derry, NH

Ice Dancing

3+

While the children explore the properties of ice, they will use a new art media to create an original artwork.

Materials needed

Finger paint paper
Dry tempera
Ice cubes
Newspaper
Protective smocks
Cassette/record player
Dancing music of various moods and tempos

What to do

1. Ice cubes should be approximately 1" x 1". A larger piece of ice will not melt quickly enough to dilute paint.
2. Put smocks on children.
3. Cover work area with newspaper.
4. Sprinkle a small amount of dry tempera on finger paint paper.
5. Give the child a cube of ice and tell him that when he hears the music he should make the ice cube "dance" across the paint. The size of the ice cube determines the length of this activity.
6. Start the music.
7. Enjoy!
8. Lay painting to dry and clean up.

More to do

Vary the amount of paint/number of colors used. Show pictures or videos of ice dancing competitions.

Related books

White Snow, Bright Snow by Alvin Tressett
The Snowy Day by Ezra Jack Keats
The Big Snow by Berta Hader

—Brenda Orbaugh, Tyler, TX

Tissue Fireworks

3+

Children grasp patterns and improve their motor integration skills through finger tip exercises.

Materials needed

Black construction paper, one sheet per child
White chalk
Glue
White and colored tissue paper
Scissors

What to do

1. Cut tissue into 1" squares.
2. Draw fireworks patterns on the black construction paper with chalk (three per paper).
3. Give each child one piece of prepared black paper and a container of 1" tissue paper squares and a container of white glue with a squeeze top.
4. Instruct the children to use their finger tips and ball up each square of tissue. Be sure they pick up only one piece at a time.
5. Instruct the children to place glue dots along one line of a firework, and to place the balled-up tissue on the glue.
6. Have them complete the task, using any color patterns they desire.

More to do

Have children draw their own fireworks. Have the children cut their own tissue squares.

—Penny Barsch, Hamden, CT

Texture Bears

3+

In this activity, children express themselves through drawing and creating textures.

Materials needed

Sheets of brown paper
Cardboard circles (various sizes)
Crayons
Glue
Dried coffee grounds
Dried tea leaves
Sawdust
Cotton swabs
Tempera paint
Scissors

What to do

1. Put the textured materials into shallow containers and set them out on the work table.
2. Have the children make circle bears. Give them brown paper and cardboard circles. Instruct them to trace the circles to make the bear's shape (e.g., large circle could be the bear's body, medium circle could be the head, and small circles could be the ears, arms and legs).
3. Show the children how to smear glue inside the outline. (Vary the amount of guidance you provide according to child's ability.)
4. Have the children choose the material(s) they want to use and sprinkle them over the bears. Shake off excess.
5. When the bears are dry, have the children use cotton swabs dipped in tempera paint to draw their facial features.

More to do

Hang a mural or very large poster of a forest scene on the classroom wall and have the children glue or tape on their bears. Make two- or three-dimensional bears from various materials (e.g., clay, dough, popcorn, soap flakes, birdseed) and compare textures. Play a guessing game with textures. Glue materials such as mesh, felt, velvet, foam, bubble packing, textured wallpaper, and dotted swiss onto cardboard bears (two of each material). With eyes closed, children should feel two of the bears and say if they have the same texture. Sing "The Bear Went Over the Mountain."

Related books

Corduroy by Don Freeman
Jesse Bear, Jesse Bear, What Will You Wear by Nancy Carlstrom

—Diane Billman, West Carrollton, OH

Paper Quilt

Children will observe how a patchwork quilt is put together and will use shapes to form their own designs.

Materials needed

Patchwork quilt (for use as an example)
Wallpaper samples (enough to make shapes for a paper quilt)
Large sheets of paper to use for background
Glue or paste

What to do

1. Cut out lots of square and triangular shapes from the wallpaper and set aside.
2. Introduce the activity to the children by showing them the patchwork quilt and asking a few simple questions, such as "Have you ever seen one of these?"
3. Point out the shapes in the quilt without distracting the children too much from appreciating the overall design.
4. After the children have had a chance to examine and feel the patchwork quilt, tell them that they are now going to put some shapes together to make quilt designs.
5. Present the background paper and the wallpaper shapes to the children. Put out the paste or glue. Give each child a sheet of background paper and demonstrate how the shapes can be moved around to create different designs on the paper.
6. Let the children experiment by making different designs. When they are ready, tell them that they can create a permanent design by gluing the shapes to their background paper. Do not change or correct their designs; some will have overlapping edges and other unique features but children should feel that any design they make is fine.

More to do

Do this as a group activity and use one very large background sheet. When the group is finished with the paper quilt and the glue has dried, hang it on the classroom wall for display.

Related books

The Josefina Story Quilt by Eleanor Coerr
Texas Star by Barbara Hancock Cole
Same Johnson and the Blue Ribbon Quilt by Lisa Campbell Ernst

—*Georgia Heald, Iowa City, IA*

Let's Make an Impression

3+

This activity teaches children to identify some impressionist paintings and how to make an impressionist painting.

Materials needed

Pictures of impressionist paintings (i.e., Monet, Renoir, Sisley, Morisot)
Photographs of objects
Art paper
Tempera paint
Brushes
Water

What to do

1. Put up reproductions of impressionist paintings around the classroom.
2. Discuss the paintings and explain the style of painting is called impressionism. These artists painted things the way they looked to them, not exactly as they were.
3. Show children examples of photographs and paintings and discuss the differences. Photographs show the exact item while the impressionist paints the object as it appears to them at that moment.
4. Have the children go outside and look at a tree. Tell them to notice the sunlight on the tree, or the rain, or the snow, or whatever. Ask them to paint that tree when they get inside. Show them how to show atmosphere (sunshine or rain) with swirls of paint greatly thinned with water over the picture. Set these paintings aside.
5. On another day when the weather is different, have them look at the same tree again and make another tree painting. Compare the two paintings with the children.

More to do

Frame the pictures and hang them around the classroom. If available, take the children to a local art museum and have them observe impressionist and other style paintings.

Related book

Linnea in Monet's Garden by Christina Bjork   —*Lucy Fuchs, Brandon, FL*

Corn Shuck Painting

3+

The children will use corn shucks to paint.

Materials needed

Paint
Paper
Unshucked corn

What to do

1. Have children help shuck corn. Discuss the different ways of using the shucks.
2. Explain to them that instead of a paintbrush, you are going to use corn shucks for painting.
3. Discuss the corn shuck painting. Why is this different from a painting with a paintbrush?

More to do

Paint with corn cobs by rolling them across the page. Make a broom with corn shucks. Eat corn on the cob!
                                                                     —*Sandra Acuna, San Antonio, TX*

Tissue Paper Water Transfer Collage

3+

This activity will improve hand-eye coordination, awareness of cause and effect and appreciation of art. Children learn to make choices of shape, size and color and expand their capability to make aesthetic judgements.

Materials needed

Construction paper
A variety of colors of tissue paper
Scissors
Paintbrushes
Small container for water

What to do

1. Cut up different sizes and shapes of tissue paper.
2. Lay out 12" x 18" pieces of construction paper.
3. Have the children cover the construction paper with water using paintbrushes.
4. Ask the children to place the cut up tissue paper on the construction paper.
5. Then brush water over the tissue paper.
6. Help the children remove the tissue paper (the shape and color of the tissue paper will remain on the construction paper and colors will bleed together).

—*Patricia Kepner, Norwalk, CA*

Epsom Salts Painting

4+

Children observe physical change of salts dissolving in water and liquid changing to crystal through a creative art experience.

Materials needed

Dark construction paper
Crayons
Epsom salts
Very warm or boiling water
Measuring cup, bowl and spoon
Paintbrush

What to do

1. Observe frosted windows on a winter day. Discuss the change taking place and why frost forms.
2. Boil two cups of water. Measure one cup of Epsom salts and stir into the boiling water to dissolve.
3. Color pictures with crayons on dark construction paper. Instruct children to press firmly with crayon.
4. When the picture is completed, have the children brush Epsom salts solution over their pictures.
5. Cover the entire paper with numerous coats of solution.
6. Let it dry.

More to do

Cut paper into snowflakes or various shapes.

—*Ruth Lieurance, Colorado Springs, CO*

Tissue Square Leaves

Children gain awareness of changing leaf colors and differences in shapes and names of leaves (oak, elm, maple).

Materials needed

Pre-cut posterboard oak, elm and maple leaves (about 7" x 10")
Tissue squares in fall colors, 1" wide
White glue thinned with water
Brushes and containers for glue
Newspaper
Crayons
Scissors

What to do

1. Pre-cut leaf shapes, cutting enough to allow each child a choice.
2. Cover tables with newspaper for painting and drying.
3. Precut 1" tissue squares in fall colors.
4. Thin glue and pour into containers.
5. Prepare stories, games, objects and activities about fall.
6. Have the children choose his leaf and write his name.
7. Have the children cover half the surface with glue mixture.
8. Apply squares to the glue-covered half, allowing them to overlap and hang over the edges.
9. Repeat with the second half of leaf.
10. Spread glue over the entire surface to seal tissue squares.
11. Allow to dry.
12. Trim off excess tissue to show shape of leaf.

More to do

Go on a fall walk to collect leaves and objects. Use tissue leaves to chart, graph, and classify on the rug or bulletin board.

Related books

A Tree Is Nice by Janice Udry

—Susan Oldham Hill, Lakeland, FL

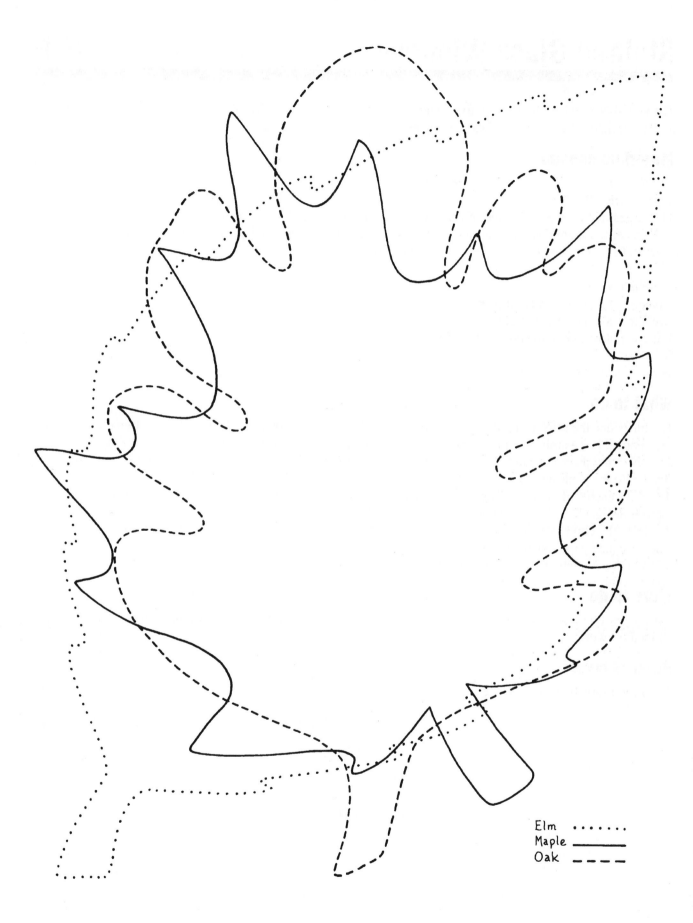

Elm ········
Maple ————
Oak – – – –

Stained Glass Windows

4+

Through this activity, children are exposed to a new art form, become familiar with the art of Marc Chagall and appreciate different ways of expressing creativity.

Materials needed

For the class:
Marc Chagall by Ernest Rabolf
The largest pictures you can find of Chagall's work in various art history books
Pictures of his stained glass windows for the Hadassah-Hebrew University Medical Center
Pieces of stained glass (i.e., window decorations) as examples

For each child:
1 piece of black construction paper
A white crayon or piece of chalk
Various colors of cellophane or tissue paper
Scissors
Tape

What to do

1. Introduce the artist using the book, *Marc Chagall*. Discuss the pictures, having the children tell you what they notice. For example, some characters are floating in the air. Ask why you think the artist did this.
2. Show the pieces of stained glass. Let the children examine the pieces. Explain that there is a "frame" (lead) and the glass inserts.
3. Have each child draw a simple design using the crayon/chalk and black paper. Have child cut out the interior design. This is their stained glass "frame."
4. Help the child to cut out colored cellophane or tissue paper to fill in the design. Tape this on "wrong side" of black paper (side the child did her original sketch on).
5. When complete, hang the "stained glass" artwork on the window.

More to do

Visit a church or other site where there are stained glass windows. Invite a professional stained glass artist to show their work.

Related book

No Good in Art by Miriam Cohen

—Gail Dezube, Vienna, VA

Snow Owl

The children will practice their fine motor skills while cutting and gluing an owl in this extraordinary use of a paper plate!

Materials needed

Large paper plates, one per child
Stapler
Children's scissors
Black buttons (optional)—use only with children old enough not to put them in their mouths
Glue (optional)
Non-toxic black markers or black crayons
Small yellow construction paper triangles, three per child

What to do

1. Fold and staple the paper plate (see figure 1) and cut along dotted lines (see figure 2A), being careful not to cut through the back of the plate. Unfold the wings.
2. Have the children cut fringes on wings, head and tail. (See figure 2B).
3. The children may use a black crayon or marker to make the eyes. If you are working only with older children, they may glue on the black buttons.
4. The children may glue on two yellow triangles for ears and one for the beak. (See figure 3.)

More to do

The owls may be mounted on large tongue depressors to make owl puppets.

Related book

Owl At Home by Arnold Lobel

—*Jyoti Joshi, Framingham, MA*

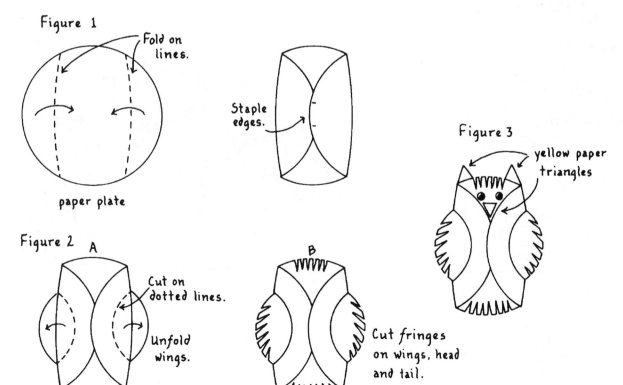

Figure 1
Fold on lines.
paper plate

Staple edges.

Figure 3
yellow paper triangles

Figure 2 A
Cut on dotted lines.
Unfold wings.

B
Cut fringes on wings, head and tail.

Peaceful Doves

These simple birds are fun to construct, and make a beautiful mobile when suspended from a tree branch.

Materials needed

White construction paper, 4"x 6"
Red and orange nontoxic markers or crayons
Scissors
Silver sparkles or glitter
Glue
Hole punch
String

What to do

1. Trace the child's hand onto the white paper with four fingers together and thumb extended away from fingers.
2. Draw an orange beak on the edge of the thumb and have the child cut out entire shape. Offer help with cutting as necessary.
3. Draw a red eye on each side of the thumb.
4. Glue sparkles or glitter on the dove for a festive look.
5. Attach a string through the top of the dove's body for hanging.

More to do

Make many doves, perhaps one by each child in the class, and hang them from a piece of wood for a mobile.

—*Jyoti Joshi, Framingham, MA*

Figure 1

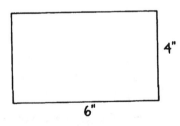

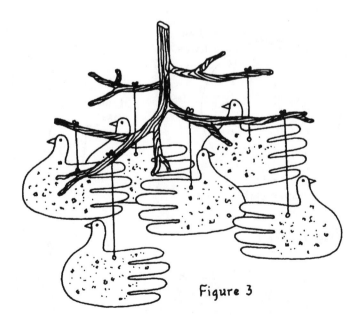

Figure 3

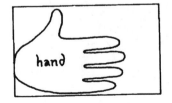

Figure 2

Black Owl

Creating Black Owls is a perfect project for recognizing shapes.

Materials needed

Small paper plates (6" in diameter)
Scissors
Black paint
Paintbrushes
Glue
Small cupcake liners
Black or yellow buttons

What to do

1. Cut the plate at the bottom (see illustration) and save the piece for later use.
2. Paint the paper plate with black paint and let it dry. While the paint is drying, talk with the children about the creatures of the night, their colors, etc.
3. Cut three little triangles out of the piece of the plate that was saved.
4. Glue on two triangles for owl's ears and one for his beak (see illustration).
5. Glue the cupcake liners for the eyes on either side of the beak.
6. Glue buttons inside the cupcake liners.

More to do

Staple an owl (or a family of owls!) on a branch.

Related book

Owl at Home by Arnold Lobel

—*Jyoti Joshi, Framingham, MA*

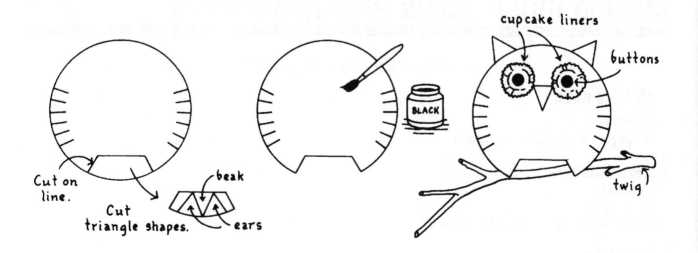

45

Bird Words

3+

The children will, through brainstorming, make up a list of vocabulary that concerns itself with birds and their daily activities.

Materials needed

Feathers (various sizes and colors)
Bird's nest
String
Egg
Map
Feeder
Binoculars
Crayons
Paper for drawing
Blackboard and chalk or chart tablet paper and marker

What to do

1. Show the children each item. Write it on the blackboard or chart table paper.
2. Ask the children to add other things about birds (example: trees) to the list, and write the words on the blackboard or chart tablet paper.
3. For younger children, draw a simple picture next to the words for illustration.
4. Talk about the new words.
5. Encourage the children to make a booklet of drawings of the items they think of.
6. If the children are old enough, have them label the drawings.
7. If time allows, add a simple sentence that is dictated by the child.
8. At outside playtime, encourage the children to look for local birds and their homes. Talk about them at snack time or show and tell.

—Doris-Jane Smith, Katonah, NY

Making Bird Feeders With Paper Rolls

3+

Children sharpen their observational skills and learn about birds as a result of this creative activity.

Materials needed

Hole puncher
Toilet paper tubes, one for each child
Yarn
Bag of bird seed
Peanut butter
Butter knives
Dish pan or similar container for bird seed

What to do

1. Punch two holes opposite each other at one end of each paper tube.
2. Pour bird seed into the dish pan.

3. Spread peanut butter on the entire paper tube.
4. Put the tube in the dish pan and cover it with seeds.
5. Tie yarn onto the tube so the bird feeder can hang on a tree or fence.

More to do

Make extra bird feeders to hang outside the classroom window. Serve trail mix or make sunflower seed biscuits for snack. Do Hap Palmer's "Little Birdies" from *Learning Basic Skills*.

Related song

"Hungry Birdie" (sing to tune of "I'm a Little Teapot"), written by K. Weiss

> *I'm a little birdie,*
> *Hungry as can be,*
> *But I see a bird feeder*
> *On that tree.*
> *I will fly right over,*
> *And eat my fill,*
> *Then I will sing on your windowsill.*

—Joan M. Weiss, Novato, CA

Bird Mobile

3+

This activity will stimulate an interest in birds and in feeding and observing them.

Materials needed

Two wire hangers per child
Yarn or string
Construction paper
Masking tape
Glue
Scissors
Hole punch
Bird pattern (see illustration)
4" x 4" red squares
2" diameter yellow circles
6" blue triangles
14" lengths of yarn (four per child)
8" lenghts of yarn (one per child)

What to do

1. Place hangers at right angles to each other. Tape them together around the hooks (hooks should be parallel to each other) and where they cross each other at the bottom.
2. Trace bird pattern on red and blue 8" x 11" sheets of construction paper folded in half (this allows children to cut two birds at once).
3. Children cut out 2 sets of birds.
4. Punch holes in bird's wings and attach yarn.
5. Attach birds to corners, alternating red and blue birds.
6. Cut out and assemble bird house (triangle roof, square building and circle door).
7. Punch hole in top of roof. Attach yarn and tie to center of hangers.

More to do

Place a bird feeder near classroom windows so birds may be easily observed. Make bird feeders from pine cones and peanut butter rolled in bird seed.Make a chart of the birds that come to your feeder, and how often they come.

Related books

A Year of Birds by Ashley Wolff
Have You Seen Birds by Joanne Oppenheim

—*Barbara Corbin, Cincinnati, OH*

What's in a Bird Nest?

4+

This reading readiness activity allows children to discover the materials used in a bird's nest. It also provides an opportunity to develop an awareness of the environment and enhances the child's view, awe and love of nature and animals.

Materials needed

Bird nest(s)
Posterboard
Glue or tape
Marker
Newspaper

What to do

1. In the fall or winter, when trees are bare, bird nests can be easily found. Ask parents to become "nature detectives" in the hunt for abandoned nests.
2. For the activity, prepare a table or the floor by covering the area with newspaper.
3. Allow a group of children to disassemble the bird nest. After each discovery of the material used, glue or tape the item on the posterboard. The teacher can label each find.
4. The poster can then be displayed on the science table with any leftover portions of nest.
5. Make sure everyone washes hands thoroughly!

More to do

Have the children make bird feeders. String cereal on yarn, tie the ends together and hand for the birds to enjoy! Give each child two ribbons of crepe paper for wings. Play a recording of "Feed the Birds" from "Mary Poppins." Direct the children to move their wings to the music. Give positional directions: above your head, behind your tail, etc.

Related books

The Best Nest by P.D. Eastman
Are You My Mother? by P.D. Eastman
Dead Bird by Margaret Wise Brown
Fly Away Home by Eve Bunting

Related fingerplays

"Five little robins up in a tree"
"Here's a nest for a robin
"I saw a little bird go hop, hop, hop"
"Five little chickadees sitting on the floor"

—Teresa J. Nos, Baltimore, MD

Our Fine Feathered Friends

4+

Children will have an opportunity to examine bird feathers and learn about birds.

Materials needed

Feathers from different birds (contact pet stores or zoos)
Magnifying glasses
Parrot or other pet bird, accompanied by an owner/handler (contact pet stores or local breeders)

What to do

1. Lead a discussion on birds. Ask questions like: Do all birds look alike? How do they move? What do they eat? Why do birds have feathers? What do feathers feel like?
2. Display the feather collection and ask children to describe the various colors and sizes they see. Point out the quill and explain how the feather attaches to the bird's body. Also explain that the "barbs" that attach to the quill help keep the bird warm and dry, and that down feathers usually aren't visible.
3. Allow children to examine various feathers with magnifying glasses. Ask them to draw or describe what they see. Have them feel the feathers to experience their softness and stiffness.
4. Introduce the live bird. Ask the children if they see the downy feathers or quills. Encourage the bird's handler to describe the various parts of the bird (beak, talons, etc.) as well as the bird's personality and habits (tricks it does, favorite foods and toys). Some discussion of where the bird's species comes from and what that climate is like may also be appropriate. Give children a chance to ask questions.

More to do

Have children collect pine cones and make simple bird feeders by coating them with peanut butter and rolling them in bird seed. Go for a walk near the school. Listen for bird songs and look for molted feathers on the ground. Tell children about the quill pens people used to use for writing. Give each child a feather and some paint and encourage them to draw a picture using the quill of the feather. They might also use the other end of the feather as a paintbrush. Ask children to draw a picture of an imaginary bird. Have them dictate a story about their bird and write it neatly on a piece of paper to display with their picture.

Related books

Rain Forest by Helen Cowcher
Why Can't I Fly? by Rita Golden Gelman
Have You Seen Birds? by Joanne Oppenheim

—Kim Arnold, Stow, OH

Robin

4+

The children can paint, cut and glue to create a robin from a paper plate.

Materials needed

Large paper plate
Red paint
6" x 9" brown construction paper
Markers
Scissors
Glue
Stapler
String and dowels or sticks (optional)

What to do

1. Have the children fold the paper plate in half, paint it red and allow it to dry completely. This is the robin's body.
2. On brown construction paper, draw a small circle for the robin's head, a larger circle for his wings and three long strips for the tail (see illustration.) Cut out each of these shapes. Allow the children to cut if they are able.
3. Glue the beak to the head. With a marker, draw an eye on each side. Glue the head to one end of the body near the top fold.
4. Fold the wing circle in half and glue it to the top center of the body fold, so you have a half circle wing on each side of the robin's body. Glue only near the fold so that the tips of the wings can be flapped up a bit.
5. Have the children curl the brown strips by wrapping them around a finger. Glue or staple them to the other end of the body near the top of the fold to finish the robin.

More to do

To make these birds fly, attach a string to the top of the bird and tie the string to the end of a stick or dowel. Take them outside and let the children fly them, but be careful of poking and running. A blue jay is made by painting the body blue and adding a blue paper crown (small fringed triangle shape) to the top of the head.

—Jyoti Joshi, Framingham, MA

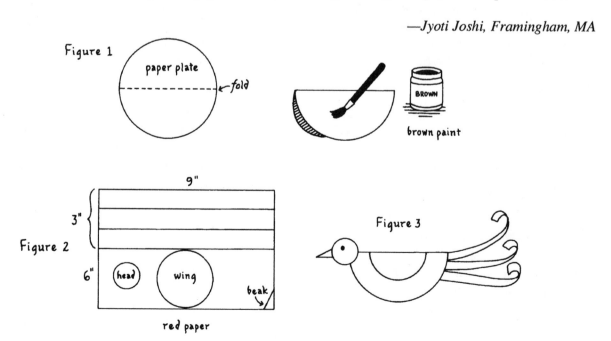

Penguin

A fun and unusual activity, the children create a penguin by tracing different parts of their bodies.

Materials needed

6" x 9" while and black construction paper, one of each color per child
Black and yellow markers
Scissors
Glue or stapler

What to do

1. Trace a child's shoe on the white paper and have the child cut it out. Help those children who need it. This will be the penguin's body (see illustration).
2. Fold the black paper in half and trace the child's hand. Cut out the folded tracing. These will be the penguin's wings (see illustration).
3. Glue or staple the black wings (folded lengthwise) around the penguin's body on each side (see illustration).
4. Draw eyes and beak with black and yellow markers.

More to do

Glue the penguin on blue paper and use finger tips to print with white paint to create snow all around the penguin.

—*Jyoti Joshi, Framingham, MA*

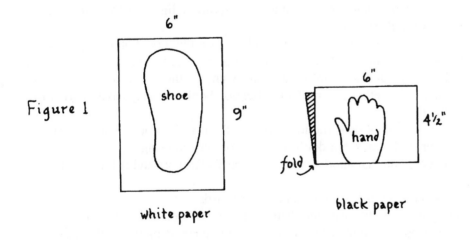

Figure 1

6"

9"

shoe

white paper

6"

4½"

fold

hand

black paper

Staple
black wings.

Dangling Birds

5+

Children will develop fine motor skills through tracing, cutting and manipulating paper in order to assemble dangling birds. They will also learn vocabulary relevant to theme of birds such as indigenous, plumage, migration, etc.

Materials needed

Posterboard, oaktag or cardboard
Stapler
Scotch tape
Various colored construction paper
Scissors
Pencils, chalk, crayons
Bird books and pictures (optional)
String or yarn strips

What to do

1. Cut several strips of posterboard about 1/2" wide, which will be stapled together at ends to form ring. Depending on the size of your posterboard sheets and strips, cut several bird stencils that would fit onto your posterboard ring. Label stencils, e.g. cardinal, starling, crow. You may want to staple rings together ahead of time depending on age group you're working with.
2. Begin activity by discussing with children how lucky we are to be able to see birds almost EVERY day, and that different kinds of birds live in different places all over the world.
3. Tell children that today they can make a few birds indigenous to their area. It means that it lives here naturally. What are some birds you see around your town (city, state) every day?
4. Help them with some names of birds, then restate, "well then these birds are indigenous to (your state)!" Some might not be around right now because they've migrated.
5. If you enjoy using models in order to stimulate interest, show children a simple model of a dangling bird.
6. Assist children in looping their oaktag strip and stapling their strip ends together to form ring.
7. Show children the various stencils of birds and see if they can identify any by their shapes.
8. Allow children to examine the stencils, as well as any bird identification book you may have in order to choose a few favorites they'd like to trace.
9. Allow children to select from various colors of construction paper for their birds. You might suggest checking out appropriate coloring in your bird books, but don't require "correct" coloring.
10. Introduce the word "plumage" and explain that another word for a bird's feathers and coloring is it's plumage.
11. Children can help pass out scissors and pencils for tracing and cutting birds.
12. Once they've traced their bird and cut it out, they can add their own name as well as label their bird, copying labels on backs of stencils if needed. Children can decorate birds plumage using the chalk and crayons.
13. Staple or tape the bird onto the oaktag ring. Fill the ring with birds.
14. Make as many as time allows!

More to do

Take children on a "birdwatch" in your area either before or after activity to reinforce what birds are indigenous to your home state. Repeat this activity using bird stencils of any sort, for example, birds of prey, endangered birds, exotic birds, etc.

Related books

Are You My Mother by P. D. Eastman
Have You Seen Birds? by Joanne Oppenheim
Feathers for Lunch by Lois Ehlert

—*Shirley Rockefeller, Durham, NH*

Wild Ducks

Children develop fine motor control through rolling and shaping. They develop expression through pictures and writing.

Materials needed

Flour
Salt
One bowl
Spoon
Paint
Paintbrushes
Duck cookie cutters
Cookie sheets
Rolling pins
Oven
Construction paper
Were You a Wild Duck—Where Would You Go by George Mendoza

What to do

1. Read *Were You A Wild Duck—Where Would You Go* by George Mendoza.
2. Construct a wild duck using baker's clay. Students can draw the recipe by folding a piece of construction paper into six squares and follow these directions:

Square one: Draw a bowl and write, "Add 2 cups of flour."
Square two: Draw a bowl and write, "Add 1 cup of water."
Square three: Draw a bowl and write, "Add 1 cup of salt."
Square four: Draw a bowl and write, "Stir."
Square five: Draw a cookie cutter and write, "Shape."
Square six: Draw an oven and write, "Bake."

3. Mix up the recipe and give each student a piece of dough to roll out. Let the children use the cookie cutters to make a duck shape.
4. Bake the shapes at 350 degrees for about ten minutes. Let them cool and then have the students paint their "wild ducks."
5. Using the newly created ducks, have the children role play a typical day in their life. Were you a wild duck, where would you go?

—Lori Erickson, Harris, MN

My Body

2+

Here's a simple musical activity you can do without extra preparation or materials that gives children practice in identifying different parts of the body.

What to do

1. Have children sit or stand.
2. Sing the song "My Body" and have the children point to each body part when named. Be sure to go slowly enough, especially at first, that the children have time to do this.
"My Body" (to the tune of "Jimmy Crack Corn")

> *I have two eyes, one nose and a mouth (three times)*
> *Let's all clap our hands! (clap, clap)*
> *I have two arms, two legs and a tummy, etc....*
> *I have ten fingers and ten toes, etc....*
> *I have one head, two ears and a bottom, etc....*
> *I have two elbows and two knees, etc....*
> *I have two eyebrows and two shoulders, etc....*
> *I have two hands and two feet, etc....*
> *I have two wrists and two ankles, etc....*

3. At the end of each verse, everyone claps hands twice.

More to do

Wiggle each body part as you sing about it. As the children become more familiar with the song and the parts of their bodies, sing the song faster and faster, then slower and slower. They will like the changes and the challenge of keeping up.

—Trish Weaver, Raleigh, NC

Balloon Person

3+

In this activity, children will learn to identify body parts and put them together properly.

Materials needed

Balloons—one per child
Construction paper
Tape
String
Crayons and markers
Scissors
Hole punch

What to do

1. Blow up the balloons. These will be the bodies.
2. On construction paper, trace an oval or round head, smaller than the balloon. Also trace arms, legs, feet and hands in a size to correspond to the head. Cut out the body parts for the younger children and allow those who are skilled with scissors to cut out their own.

3. Give the children the heads and have them color in the faces.
4. Have the children tape the head onto the top of their balloon.
5. Have them tape the other body parts onto their balloon in the appropriate places.
6. Punch a hole at the top of the construction paper head of each balloon person. Attach string to the head (reinforce hole with tape) and hang the people from ceiling.

More to do

Add other body features such as yarn or colored string or confetti for hair, ears and clothing. Have kids trace their own hands and/or feet and cut out and add to people.

—Dixie Havlak, Olympia, WA

Beanbag Body Toss

3+

The children learn to identify and match different parts of their bodies by playing this beanbag toss game.

Materials needed

Beanbags
Pictures of different parts of the body, for example magazine cut-outs
Large posterboard divided into sections approximately 5" x 5"
Glue
Marker

What to do

1. Glue six to ten pictures onto various squares on the game board. With the marker, boldly outline each square that shows a picture.
2. Each child in turn tosses a beanbag onto the board. If it lands on one of the pictures, he or she must name that part of the body. Offer help with the naming as needed.
3. The child must then wiggle or move that part of the body.

More to do

For a greater challenge, add a second beanbag and have the child move two parts at once.

—Karen Gassett, Framingham, MA

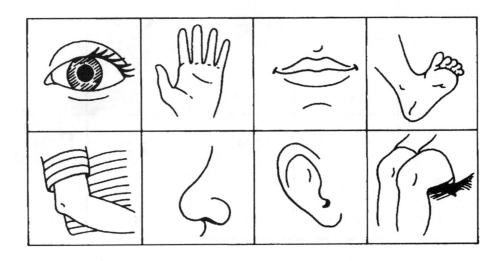

Body Bingo

3+

This familiar game will reinforce the recognition and names of various body parts.

Materials needed

Body bingo cards—4" x 4" grids with pictures of body parts on each square (Place the pictures in different locations on each card.)
Markers (old bingo chips, beans or small stones)

What to do

1. Have the children sit in a circle on the floor.
2. Give each child a card and some markers.
3. Point to a part of your body and name it. Have everyone place a marker on the corresponding part on their card.
4. Let each child take a turn as caller.
5. Callers may call a part that has already been called since the parts may be duplicated on cards. The game ends when a child gets four squares in a row.

More to do

Either before or after the game it is fun to sing the song "Head and Shoulders Knees and Toes."

—Terryl L. Buck,
Yarmouth, ME

The Body

eye	head	foot	arm
ear	mouth	hand	nose
neck	eye	hair	leg
body	hand	toes	fingers

Healthy Teeth

3+

The children will learn about their teeth and the importance of good dental hygiene.

Materials needed

Several old toothbrushes
Yellow paper
White paint
Smocks

What to do

1. Cut large tooth shapes out of the yellow paper (one for each child in the class).
2. Cover the art table with newspaper and put out small cups of white paint.
3. Ask children to describe what would happen if they didn't brush their teeth for a day or two.
4. Have children brush the white paint onto the yellow paper teeth using toothbrushes instead of paintbrushes.

More to do

Make a simple toothpaste puzzle by drawing a picture of a tube of toothpaste (include a squiggle of paste coming out of top) on cardboard. Cut the cardboard into four or more pieces, laminate with contact paper and let the children put the puzzle together. Bring in mirrors so that the children can look at their own teeth.

Related book

Little Rabbit's Loose Tooth by Lucy Bate

—Linda Ford, Fremont, CA

Shadow Tracing

4+

In this activity, the children will have fun with their shadows.

Materials needed

Paper (large sheets)
Pencils

What to do

1. Talk about shadows and what they are.
2. On a sunny day, take pencil and paper outside and help children trace each other's shadows. (You can trace the shadows of the younger children.)
3. Display the shadow tracings and have the children guess who they belong to.

More to do

Trace shadows on the sidewalk using colored chalk. Play shadow tag and have children try to "catch" each others shadows by jumping on them. Compare shadows of different sizes and shapes. Put a pole or stake in the ground. At different times during the day mark the shadow using chalk, string, or smaller stakes.

Related songs

"Me and My Shadow"
"I Have a Little Shadow"

Related books

Bear Shadow by Frank Asch
Shadows Here There and Everywhere by Ron and Nancy Goor

—Linda Ford, Fremont, CA

Growing and Changing   4+

The children will learn to see differences in themselves as their bodies grow.

Materials needed

Photographs of children as infants
Current photographs of children taken by the teacher
Oaktag crib for bulletin board
Craft paper roll or commercially prepared height chart

What to do

1. Send home letters to parents requesting a photo of their child as an infant or toddler.
2. Photograph each child individually in the classroom.
3. Make a large oaktag crib and mount it on the bulletin board.
4. As baby pictures arrive, have the children mount them on the oaktag crib and try to guess "who's who."
5. When all infant pictures have been received, mount the current pictures next to the crib, discussing each in comparison to the child's younger picture. Discuss differences in size and ability of children in general terms, being careful not to single out specific traits of any particular child.
6. Measure off inch marks on craft paper for a height chart (or use purchased height chart) and post it in a convenient place in the classroom. Measure the children using the chart. Note each child's name and the appropriate inch mark and measure them again in a few months.

More to do

Use pieces of yarn to connect the pairs of baby and big child pictures on the bulletin board. Sing the following song (to the tune of "Good King Wenceslaus"):

> *Babies are a chubby bunch,*
> *Some are skinny too.*
> *Eating applesauce for lunch,*
> *Momma holds the spoon.*
> *Baby bottles, diapers, naps,*
> *Riding in the stroller.*
> *We were little babies once, but now we are older.*

Related books

Peter's Chair by Ezra Jack Keats
I Can Do It By Myself by Lessie J. Little and Eloise Greenfield
All By Myself by Anna G. Hines

—Judy Contino, Ozone Park, NY

Body Tracings

This activity will increase children's awareness of their own bodies.

Materials needed

Mural paper or brown postal paper—approximately 3' to 4' wide and as long as the child is tall)
Scissors
Crayons or pastels
Masking tape

What to do

1. Cut out one piece of paper for each child. Tape each piece to the floor or wall.
2. Have the children lie down on (or stand in front of) their papers. Trace the child's entire body on the paper. You might let children trace each other.
3. Encourage the children to finish the pictures by drawing their own faces, hair and clothes on the outlines.

More to do

Use the body tracings to encourage the children to talk about themselves—their likes, dislikes, strengths, weaknesses, hobbies, etc.

—Susan Buchalter-Katz, Lawrenceville, NJ

Who Am I?

In this activity, the children will explore how our facial features make each of us special and unique.

Materials needed

Hand mirror
Large white construction paper
Overhead projector or lamp
Pencils
Marker
Color squares or circles

What to do

1. Set up the projector close to the blackboard. Tape one piece of construction paper to the blackboard. Have the pencil and marker handy.
2. Initiate a discussion about facial features and have each child look in a mirror to study eyes, eye brows, hair, skin, nose, mouth, lips, dimples, etc.
3. Tell the children that you will be making a picture of each of them. Explain that this picture is called a profile because it is a side view of the face.
4. Turn on the projector lamp and turn off the classroom lights. Draw shades or curtains if necessary to darken the room.
5. Have one child stand between the projector and the paper so that her profile fills the paper (some adjusting is necessary due to height differences).
6. Trace the child's profile with the pencil. When you are satisfied, go over it with a dark marker and then print the child's name on the back.

7. Print the following fill-in-the-blank sentences below the profile. Speak with each child and fill in the blanks with their own words.

8. I am a _____.

I am _____ years old.

My skin color is _____.

I have _____ (picture of hair).

I have _____ (picture of eyes).

I have a nice (picture of smile).

Can you guess who I am?

9. You may have the children lightly color in the background of their pictures leaving the profile blank.

More to do

Use these profiles to lead a discussion on similarities and differences among people. Talk about heredity by asking the children to say how much they resemble their parents and grandparents. Without naming the children, hold up profiles and ask the children to guess who the drawings are. You might read the sentences as clues.

Related songs

"It's You I Like" by Mr. Rogers

"Free to Be You and Me" by Marlo Thomas & Friends

"Glad to Have a Friend Like You" by Marlo Thomas & Friends

"Getting to Know You"

Related books

Who Goes to School? by Margaret Hillert

Who Is Tapping at My Window? by Alahambra Deming

—Karen Megay-Nespoli, Massapequa Park, NY

Organ Tunics   5+

Through this activity, children will understand that their body is filled with important organs that do different jobs.

Materials needed

Red, blue, pink, tan, orange, white construction paper

Organ stencils

Body maps

Brown grocery sack or two large pieces of construction paper for each child

Tape

Reference book

What to do

1. Make a map of the organs in the body in proper position and size for a five year old. Copy this onto the front of a bag or a piece of construction paper. Tape front and back pieces of construction paper together to form a tunic or cut paper bag to form a tunic. Make one of these for each child in your class.

2. Make stencils of organs the same size as designed on the map. Use them to cut out organs for each child as follows: Lungs-orange; heart-red; esophagus-white; stomach-pink; liver-purple; pancreas-tan; intestines-

white; kidneys-blue. Prepare each organ with two sided tape or place a loop of tape on the back. Make one set of these for each child in your class.

3. At the time of the activity, show the children an anatomy chart or one of the tunics and talk about what each organ does.

4. Tell them that they each have these organs and that they are in special places in their bodies.

5. Have them put on the organ tunics and the teacher should put one on too.

6. Pass out the organs one at a time to each child. Put the organ on your own tunic in the proper position and have the children do the same with theirs. They could work with a partner.

7. Continue until you have placed all the organs correctly and everyone's body is complete.

More to do

Blow up a balloon and deflate it to show how the lungs work. Invite a doctor to come in and talk about the body.

—Dixie Havlak, Olympia, WA

Six Clowns

2+

The children will practice matching and naming colors as they match hats to clown collars and then help add features to a clown's face.

Materials needed

6 copies of clown pattern/6 hats
1 clown face
Markers or crayons
Felt-back tape
Laminating material
White felt square
Small felt swatches of red, green, blue, orange, yellow and purple
Scissors
Flannel board
Picture of a clown

What to do

1. Color your clowns. Each clown hat and collar should match.
2. Laminate clowns and hats. Put a strip of felt-back tape behind each clown piece and hat.
3. On the white felt square, trace the clown's face. Out of the other felt cut a red nose, an orange mouth, blue eyes and a green collar. The hat may be any color.
4. Show children a clown picture. Ask if they've ever seen one.
5. Say the poem:

   There once were 6 clowns
   Who went into town
   As they took their walk
   The wind began to talk
   Whoo-whoo-whoo

   Well what do you suppose
   Happened to the clowns with the red nose?
   The winds blew and blew
   And away their hats flew

6. While the first verse is being spoken, put the six clowns on the board. During the second verse, place the six hats randomly around the board. When the poem is completed ask children to take turns matching the clown hats to their collars.
7. Place the felt face of the clown on the board. Explain to children this clown is missing parts of his face, but they can help remake his face by using the felt pieces you have. Call one child at a time to add the features of the face.

More to do

Assign each child a color, and have her walk around the room and find something of that color to bring back. Add shapes or numerals to match on collars and hats.

Related books

Of Colors and Things by Tana Hoban

—*Marzee Woodward, Murfreesboro, TN*

Elephant Headbands

2+

Children will use fine motor skills to paint elephant headbands, then engage in fantasy play.

Materials needed

Cardboard tubes from inside paper towel rolls
Posterboard
Paper bags from grocery store (heavy gauge)
Gray paint
Paint brushes
Stapler
Newspaper

What to do

1. Cut headband strips from posterboard and big elephant ears from paper bags ahead of time. Staple one tube (this will be the elephant's trunk) to the middle of each headband and the ears on either side of the tube. Mix gray paint and cover the work table with newspaper.
2. Have children put on smocks.
3. Talk to the children about elephants and where they live. Have they ever seen elephants at the circus? Ask them if they know what color elephants are.
4. Have each child paint an elephant headband with the gray paint.
5. When all the headbands have been painted, set them aside to dry.
6. Have the children try on their elephant headbands and encourage them to pretend they are elephants.

More to do

Have a class circus.

—Susan Westby, Palm Bay, FL

Create a Shape Circus

3+

Children use their imaginations while working with familiar shapes to create their own circus picture.

Materials needed

Light colored paper background sheets, 8-1/2"x11", one per child
Various paper shapes to represent animals and circus items, such as a flowered oval = clown, pink triangle = cotton candy, large red triangle = tent, grey square = elephant, large circle = ring, striped rectangle = tiger or zebra.
Glue

What to do

1. Cut out the various shapes and store them in a compartmented container, such as a muffin tin.
2. Give each child a sheet of background paper.
3. Show a shape and give a description of the animal or item the shape represents.
4. When the children respond with the name of the animal or item, give them the symbol and let them paste it in their "circus" picture.
5. Continue until all the shapes are given out.

More to do

Make a circus obstacle course.

Related books

Curious George Goes to the Circus by Margaret Rey
Circus Fun by Margaret Hillert
Circus by Brian Windsmith

—Judith Aronson, Salem, MA

Under the Big Top   3+

Children practice matching and sorting shapes and animals.

Materials needed

Construction paper—one sheet per child
Many animal forms cut from colorful construction paper
Animal crackers
Glue
Crayons
Scissors

What to do

1.   Cut the animal forms from colorful construction paper. For each child you will need three half-circles, three rectangles, one equal-sided triangle, two unequal-sided triangles, one small flagshaped triangle, one circle, two stars and one seal. You may wish to make each shape used for the tent the same color except for the half circles, which should all be a contrasting color. (See the illustration and pattern on the following page.)
2.   Show the children a prepared tent.
3.   Point out the different shapes and let the children try to name them all. Then show them the precut shapes.
4.   Explain how they may arrange them and then glue them to make their own circus tent. Let them use a crayon to draw a flagpole.
5.   Then show the children the animal crackers. Explain that they may glue them on the picture after they have made the tent.

More to do

Put a number on the top of the paper and have the children try to count out that many animal crackers to glue onto their picture.

Related books

See the Circus by H. A. Rey
The Circus Baby by Maud Petersham
At the Circus by Eugene Booth

—Julie Langhorn, Damascus, MD

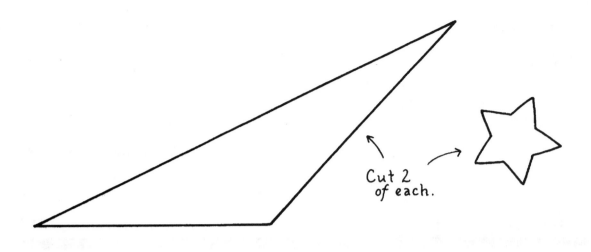

Cut 2
of each.

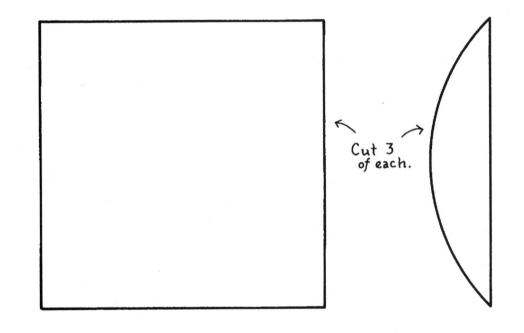

Cut 3
of each.

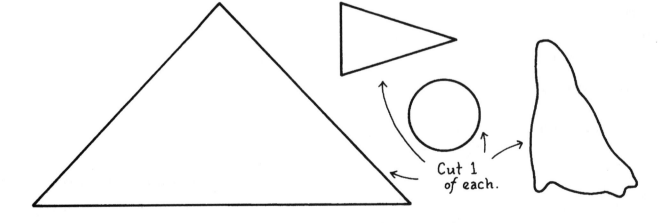

Cut 1
of each.

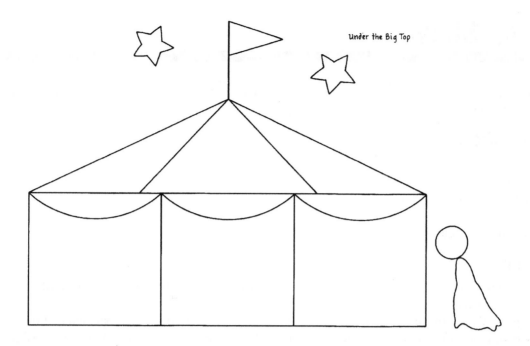

Clown Costumes

4+

This activity develops small motor skills such as cutting, drawing and pasting.

Materials needed

12" x 18" construction paper—2 sheets per child
Markers or crayons
Cotton balls
Elastic
Scissors
Stapler

What to do

1. Fold one sheet of construction paper in half. Trace collar pattern on paper.
2. Open collar. Have children decorate with markers. Glue on cotton balls for buttons if you like.
3. Put collar on over head.
4. Decorate another sheet of paper for hat.
5. Teacher staples into cone shape and staples on an elastic strip to keep hat on.

More to do

Have a circus parade—children march to music and play instruments. Teacher paints clown faces on children. Have clown snacks—ice cream scoop in cupcake paper, cone for hat, raisins or M+M's for face.

Related books

Spot Goes to the Circus by Eric Hill
Curious George Goes to the Circus by Margaret Rey

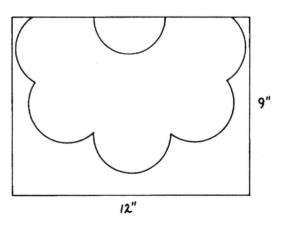

—*Judy Haase, Itasca, IL*

C I R C U S

67

Big Top Show

4+

This learning activity can stimulate the children's imagination, provide visual support for the theme and improve gross motor skills.

Materials needed

Heavy yarn
12 clothespins
Approximately 24 small balloons
Large old sheet
Book or pictures of circus acts

What to do

1. Borrow books on circus acts or pictures of circus performers from the library's picture file.
2. Blow up balloons ahead of time and place them in a garbage bag.
3. Tie yarn to clothespins and hang them from classroom ceiling. If you have a paneled ceiling, loop yarn around the metal bars that support the ceiling panels, so that the clothespins hang down about 18 inches from the ceiling. Space the clothespins to form a large square with some pins in the middle. Attach an old sheet to the clothespins to form a partial tent.
4. Attach yarn to the balloons and tie them together in groups of six to make four long bunches of balloons. Hang one bunch of balloons from each corner clothespin of the "tent." This will help define the area of the tent and create a Big Top effect.
5. For circle time, have the children sit under the circus "tent."
6. Pair the children in teams of two or three.
7. Explain that you want each team to do a circus act. Show the books and pictures from the library. Give examples such as: Lion Tamers act could be one tamer, two lions doing tricks.
8. Give the teams some time to come up with their acts.
9. Now you are ready for your Big Top Show. Have each team perform their acts under the circus tent with you acting as Ringmaster.

More to do

Children can make circus posters advertising their acts. Once you have practiced, invite other classes to come and watch the performance under the Big Top.

—*Joy M. Tuttle, Dublin, OH*

Shoe Monster

2+

Children show they can match their own shoes.

Materials needed

Children's shoes

What to do

1. Have each child take off one shoe and place it in the middle of the group.
2. Have the children cover their eyes.
3. Tell them a shoe monster will come and hide their shoes. Pretend you can hear him coming in the room. Greet him. As you are talking to the monster, hide the shoes around the classroom.
4. Have the children open their eyes. What happened to their shoes?
5. Have children look around the room for their shoe.
6. Have fun! Do it again!

—Melissa E. Kohler, St. Louis, MO

Toddler Shoe Search

2+

The children will practice removing and putting on their shoes, and matching like shoes.

Materials needed

Shoes (just those children are wearing)

What to do

1. Have the children remove their shoes and place them in a line.
2. Arrange the children in a line opposite their shoes.
3. Have the children close their eyes and mix up their shoes (I have found that if I tell the children what I am doing in a lively way they will be less inclined to peek). Add your own shoes or shoes from the dress-up corner if possible, so the last child to search for his shoes will still be challenged.
4. Call one or two children at a time to go up and find their shoes. Keep the other children involved by being an enthusiastic announcer. ("Watch Katie! She has found a red shoe. Is it hers? No, she put it back. She is picking up a pink sneaker. Yes, it is hers! Now she is looking for the matching shoe. And she's found it! Hurray! Everyone clap for Katie!") When the children find their shoes, they should go back to the line and put them on.
5. Repeat until everyone has had a turn. The very last child should be first when you play the game again, as the first player is the most challenged in this game.

More to do

Let one of the children mix up the shoes and/or call names of classmates to claim the shoes. Sing or recite the rhyme "One, Two, Buckle My Shoe."

Related book

Two Shoes, New Shoes by Shirley Hughes

—Joyce A. Hatton, Tillamook, OR

CLOTHING

That's Hats!

Materials needed

Hats of any type for play time
Books about hats
Paper
Crayons and markers
Paint and paintbrushes
Pieces of material, straw and shiny foil
Glue
Puzzles and pictures of hats

What to do

1. Send home a notice to parents that the class will be talking about hats the following week. Tell them you would appreciate any book, record, tape or hat they might have to share with the class. Pin the note to the child's coat. You could even cut their name tags in the shape of a hat, or make the letter in the shape of a hat.
2. If the children have not brought books, be sure you have some on hand. During reading time, read *What's Up in the Attic?* This will lend itself to dress-up play during their free time.
3. Have the children draw a hat with crayons or markers. Some may want to paint a hat. Have a few pieces of material, some straw and some shiny foil (for badges) to add to their pictures.
4. Have puzzles about hats and pictures of hats as well as real hats they can try on in the dress up area. Listen to what the children are saying and how they act with different hats.

—Opal M. Hantke, Maplewood, MN

Mitten Match

Children learn to recognize similar and different objects.

Materials needed

Old wallpaper sample book
Scissors
Marker
Yarn
Two thumbtacks
20 spring-type clothespins

What to do

1. Cut a matching pair of mittens from patterned wallpaper. Make a total of ten pairs, each pair from a different pattern of wallpaper.
2. Make a clothesline on the wall using yarn and thumbtacks.
3. Have the children match mitten pairs.
4. When a match is made, the children clip them to the line with clothespins.

More to do

Have children match paper mittens by letters, numbers or shapes.

Related book

The Three Little Kittens by Paul Galdone

—Charlene M. Roediger, Allentown, PA

Shoe Pair

3+

Children will develop observation skills in this non-competitive matching game.

Materials needed

Large bag
Children wearing shoes

What to do

1. Find an area where the children can sit on the floor with their feet in plain view. If your children are not accomplished at tying shoe laces, you may want volunteers to help with that chore at the end of the game.
2. Have the children sit on the floor and remove one shoe.
3. Place these shoes in the large paper bag.
4. Stand in front of the children. Reach into the bag and pull out a shoe at random. Describe the color and special details of the shoe as you show it to the children. Tentatively match the shoe to obviously wrong shoes, pointing out the differences. Finally, match your choice to the correct shoe, pointing out the similarities. The child whose shoe you picked becomes the next player.
5. Let the child pull a shoe from the bag and have her describe it. Let the child find the mate to the shoe she picked. Very young children may need help from the teacher.
6. Do not let the children put their shoes back on until the end of the game. The game is over when the last shoe has been pulled from the bag and matched to its owner.

More to do

Study the history of shoes. Bring in a shoe last and explain how shoes were made in it. Bring in a large pair of shoes and let the children try to walk in them. (Very young children can keep their shoes on when trying the large shoes. Supervise the children's efforts so they don't fall.) Bring in many different types of shoes ballet, snow, hiking, tap, cowboy, sandals) and discuss their specialized uses.

Related books

Alligator Shoes by Arthur Dorros
Shoes by Elizabeth Winthrop
Story of Shoes by Lucy Strauss

—Christina R. Chilcote, New Freedom, PA

CLOTHING

A Hat Is Not Just a Hat!

4+

Children will be able to make hats of their own by following instructions.

Materials needed

18" x 24" newsprint paper
Paintbrushes
Watercolors or food colors
Glue
Measuring cups
Aluminum pie pans
2" strips of cut material and/or ribbon
Collage materials
Molds for hats (flower pots, paint cans, cooking pots, tempera paint bottles, etc.)
Scissors
Staplers
Water
Who Took the Farmer's Hat by Joan L. Nodset

What to do

1. Read the book aloud to the children.
2. Solicit ideas about other hats.
3. To make hats:

   In a pie pan, mix 2 cups of glue to 1/2 cup of water and stir.
   Lay out one piece of newsprint paper on a flat surface.
   With a paintbrush, spread the glue and water mixture onto the entire surface.
   Place a dry piece of newsprint over the wet surface and smooth it out.
   Place the paper over the mold that you have chosen.
   Tie the ribbon or material around the circumference of the mold. Do not tie it too tight
   because you will need to slip it off to decorate the hat.
   Let dry.
   Gently remove.
   Decorate and design your hat.

4. If you want a farmer's hat, fringe the ends. If you want an fedora, round the edges. If you want a bonnet, scallop the edges. Be creative!
5. When you complete the painting and gluing collage process, the hats are ready to wear!

Related books

A Three Hat Day by Laura Geringer
Jennie's Hats by Ezra Jack Keats

—Patricia Arpino, New York, NY

Flower Garden

This activity teaches color discrimination and shows the children how to compare and distinguish color differences.

Materials needed

Flannel board
Felt squares in different colors
Pipe cleaners
Glue

What to do

1. Cut out some different colored felt flowers (tulips are an easy shape) with matching colored pipe cleaner stems. Also cut bee shapes from the same colors.
2. Arrange flowers on felt board.
3. Have the children place the correct colored bee above the corresponding flower. This may be done by one child or the bees may be passed out to several children and they may take turns.

More to do

This activity may be used as a fun way to test color recognition. Separate colored blocks or crayons into color coded containers. Mix them up and see if the child can arrange them correctly.

—Terri B. Piette, Jarrettsville, MD

Stone Search

This manipulative activity will give children practice in color matching.

Materials needed

48 stones
4 egg cartons
Sand table

What to do

1. Divide stones into four groups of twelve and paint them four separate colors. Paint the egg cartons corresponding colors.
2. Hide the stones in the sand table. Put the egg cartons nearby.
3. As children find the stones, encourage them to fill the corresponding egg carton with the correctly colored stones.

More to do

Older children can work in teams to have "races" to find the stones and fill the cartons. Painting pairs of stones with matching strips or using stickers to match pairs of stones will give children practice in visual discrimination.

Related book

Stone Soup by Marcia Brown

—Ellen Domenico, Ewing Twp., NJ

What Color Is My Apple?

2+

This simple color identification game is fun to play in the fall when apples are in season.

Materials needed

Small basket or bucket
Paper apples in red, yellow and green, covered with clear contact paper

What to do

1. Group the paper apples in three stacks by color and put them in your basket.
2. Talk to the children about how apples grow and about the three different colors. Show them an apple of each color, either real apples or your paper apples.
3. Tell the children that you are going to play an apple game with them, and that you will be singing two apple songs.
4. Give each child an apple from the basket. Give all the children the same color. Sing "Apple On The Tree" (see below) as you hand out the apples.
5. Have the children identify what color apple everyone is holding.
6. Sing "What Color Is My Apple" (see below) using the appropriate color.

More to do

When the children are familiar with all the colors, give them different colored apples. When singing "What Color Is My Apple," choose a color to sing about and ask only the children with that color to hold up their apples.

Related songs

"Apples on the Tree" (to the tune of "Twinkle, Twinkle Little Star")

Apples, apples on the tree
One for you and one for me (Repeat)

"What Color Is My Apple" (to the tune of "The Farmer in the Dell")

My apple is red (substitute yellow and green as necessary)
My apple is red
Hi ho the derry-o
My apple is red

—*Trish Weaver, Raleigh, NC*

Mixing Colors Inside Plastic Bags 2+

In this activity, children learn about smooth textures, color recognition and mixing primary colors.

Materials needed

Shaving cream
Plastic bags with a lock top—one per child
Food coloring

What to do

1. Gather materials for activity.
2. Place 1/2 cup of shaving cream in each plastic bag.
3. Ask each child to put one or two drops of food coloring in their bag.
4. Seal the bag.
5. Have the child mix the shaving cream and food color by kneading the bag.

More to do

You can add different food colors to the bag to show how new colors are made. For example, add red food coloring to a bag of yellow shaving cream to make orange.

—Charlene M. Roediger, Allentown, PA

The Color Box 3+

The children will have the opportunity to practice observation and memory skills by playing with the color box. This is a good way to reinforce individual colors as you introduce them to the class.

Materials needed

Color box: cover a shoe box or any other box with solid-colored contact paper.
4 or 5 objects, all of one color. Using some uncommon items can be interesting for the children.

What to do

1. Introduce your color box during circle time.
2. Take each item out and display it on the floor. Have children name each item and identify the color.
3. Put all items back into the box and replace the cover. Say some "magic words." Ask the children what items they remember from the box. Take each one out as the children name it.
4. Call on a child to put each item back into the box. Repeat the next day, perhaps adding one or two new items.

More to do

Encourage children to bring their own items of particular colors. Have them show their items and speak about them to the group.

—Barbara Gardos, Ardsley, NY

Rainbow Simon Says

3+

This gross motor activity adds a new dimension to a timeless game. It improves color recognition, listening skills and the ability to follow directions.

Materials needed

A colored item for each child, such as various colored beanbags, blocks or streamers

What to do

1. Explain how Simon Says is played if the children are not yet familiar with the game.
2. Give each child a designated colored item. Explain that they are only to follow directions given to "their" color.
3. Play Simon Says in the usual manner, adding a color designation to your instructions. For example, "Simon Says, Blue touch the ground."

More to do

Change the color designations. Example, "Simon Says, Red change with Yellow." Continue until each child has a new color.

Related songs

Parade Of Colors by Hap Palmer (from Learning Basic Skills Through Music, Volume II, Red)

—*Martha Mowry, Forestdale, MA*

Doodly Doo Colors

3+

This is an old game with a colorful new twist. In addition to helping children follow directions and distinguish between left and right, it will also help them identify colors.

Materials needed

Red, yellow, blue and white ribbons cut in 20" lengths, 1 set for each child and 1 set for the teacher

What to do

1. Tie your red ribbon to your right wrist, your yellow ribbon to your left wrist, your blue ribbon to your right calf, and your white ribbon to your left calf. Then adorn the children with ribbons in the same fashion.
2. Form a circle and sing following the directions of the Doodly Doo Colors song (see below).

More to do

Encourage older children to tie the ribbons on each other. Make matching-color shoe boxes for storing the ribbons. After the activity, ask the children to return the ribbons to the appropriate boxes. You could play the game using different colored ribbons and changing the song as necessary.

Related book

Color Dance by Ann Jonas

Related song

"Doodly Doo Colors" (To tune of "Looby Loo" or with chords as noted)

D
Here we go doodly doo (circle to the left)
D   A7
Here we go doodly dight (circle to the right)
D
Here we go doodly doo (circle to the left)
A7   D
Lift up your red on the right (stop and lift red)

Here we go doodly doo (circle to the left)
Here we go doodly det (circle to the right)
Here we go doodly doo (circle to the left)
Lift up your yellow on the left (stop and lift yellow)

Here we go doodly doo (circle to the left)
Here we go doodly dight (circle to the right)
Here we go doodly doo (circle to the left)
Lift up your blue on the right (stop and lift blue)

Here we go doodly doo (circle to the left)
Here we go doodly det (circle to the right)
Here we go doodly doo (circle to the left)
Lift up your white on the left (stop and lift white)

Here we go doodly doo (circle to the left)
Here we go doodly dight (circle to the right)
Here we go doodly doo (circle to the left)
Bow to a friend on the right! (bow to the right)

Alternate "Doodly Doo Colors" (To the tune "Hokey Pokey")

D
I put my red right in (put red in circle)
D
I take my red right out (put it out of circle)
D
I give my red a shake shake shake (shake red wrist)
D   A7   D
And turn myself about (turn around in place)

Chorus:
I do the Doodly Doo and I turn myself around (turn around in place)
That's what it's all about! (clap)

I put my yellow left in (put yellow in circle)
I take my yellow left out (put it out of circle)
I give my yellow a shake shake shake (shake yellow wrist)
And turn myself about (turn around in place)
Chorus

I put my blue right in (put blue in circle)
I take my blue right out (put it out of circle)
I give my blue a shake shake shake (shake blue wrist)
And turn myself about (turn around in place)
Chorus

I put my white left in (put white in circle)
I take my white left out (put it out of circle)
I give my white a shake shake shake (shake white wrist)
And turn myself about (turn around in place)
Chorus

—*Lynda Joyce Davis, Huntington Beach, CA*

Human Dominoes

3+

This fun activity helps children develop color recognition and cooperative play.

Materials needed

3" circles from various colors of construction paper
Masking tape

What to do

1. Cut out enough circles so that each child has two. Make sure there are multiples of each color.
2. Tape one circle on each child's head and one circle on top of each child's shoe.
3. Divide the children into two groups and line up on opposite ends of the room.
4. Choose one child to start and have her lay down in the center of the room.
5. Someone from the next group who can match a color lays down head to head, foot to foot, or head to foot.
6. Continue taking turns until all are matched.

More to do

Play a table top color domino game.

—*Joyce Montag, Slippery Rock, PA*

Crayon Color Match

3+

In this matching game, the children will practice identifying six colors.

Materials needed

Table
Box of six crayons—red, orange, yellow, blue, green and purple
6 cards—each with a different colored square

What to do

1. Spread the crayons out on one end of the table.
2. Place the cards on the other end of the table. Allow the children to help turn them face down.
3. Each player takes a turn by turning a card over and matching the card to the right crayon. The child must identify the color he needs for matching.

More to do

Change the game by varying card and crayon colors. Allow the children to play the game independently or in pairs. For older children, you can write the color names, in the appropriate color, on each color card, so that they may match color names as well.

—*Janet Bradshaw, Newark, OH*

Color Bingo

3+

This activity promotes children's cognitive development through color recognition.

Materials needed

Posterboard or shirt cardboard
Construction paper in orange, green, blue, yellow, brown, black, red, pink and purple
Black marker
Ruler
Clear contact or laminate

What to do

1. To make bingo board, cut a 9" x 9" square of cardboard. Using a marker, divide it into nine 3" squares. Make enough of these for each child in your class. Next, cut out two 2" squares of each color from contruction paper. Glue one of each color on your bingo game board.
2. To make bingo game pieces, cut nine 2" squares of cardboard. Cover each square with a different color of construction paper. Make one set of these for each child in your class.
3. Cover the game board and the game pieces with clear contact paper or laminate if desired.
4. To play the game, give each child a 9" x 9" board and nine 2" squares, one of each color.
5. The teacher calls out a color name or shows a color card.
6. The child chooses the correct color and places it on top of the corresponding color on the board.

More to do

The reverse side of the board and the 2" squares could have stickers of various colors to match, such as "smiley" faces or objects such as a red apple, yellow sun, brown bear, orange pumpkin, pink pig, purple grapes, blue ball, green leaf or black cat. For children who are beginning to learn to recognize colors, each board (or the reverse side) could have just three different colors. Red, yellow and blue should be the first three colors to match.

Related songs

"Baa, Baa, Black Sheep"
"Little Boy Blue"
"Colors/If You Are Wearing a _____ Shirt, Stand Up" by Hap Palmer

—Margaret Connelly, Pocomoke City, MD

Color Game

3+

The children will have fun and get some indoor exercise while playing this musical color identification game.

Materials needed

Construction paper in all basic colors
Recorded music (walking tempo)

What to do

1. Hold up samples of each color and have the children identify them.

2. Explain that the color cards will be placed on the floor with space in between them so that the children can walk among the cards without stepping on them.

3. Tell the children that the music will play and when they hear it stop, they should sit down immediately beside the nearest color card.

4. When the children are sitting by their cards, sing the "Color Song" (to the tune of "Twinkle, Twinkle, Little Star")

> *Who's beside the color blue? (substitute each color that you use)*
> *Please stand up if it's you!*

5. Continue the game until you have called each different color at least once.

More to do

Cut construction paper into a variety of shapes such as circles, triangles, squares, rectangles, stars, etc. Play the game as a shape identification game changing the words of the song as appropriate.

—Trish Weaver, Raleigh, NC

The Color Red

This activity teaches the children to recognize the color red and helps improve listening skills and experience contributing to a group effort.

Materials needed

One red crayon for each child
Masking tape
Long piece of art paper—long enough to cover classroom work table
Storybook of "Little Red Riding Hood"

What to do

1. Collect a bag of red objects.

2. Draw an enlarged version of the the character Little Red Riding Hood on a large piece of art paper.
(This activity works well with eight children in a group. For larger groups, make more than one enlargement to color.)

3. During circle time, pass around your bag of red objects and have each child take out one. Have them tell you what the object is and what color it is. Then collect the objects.

4. Next tell the children that you have a story about a little girl who likes the color red. Then read the story, "Little Red Riding Hood."

5. When the story is done, ask questions to see what the children remember about the story.

6. Invite them to join you at the table where you have taped down the large picture of Red Riding Hood.

7. Pass out the red crayons and ask them to help you to color the picture.

8. When the group is done coloring, put their names on the picture and hang it up on the classroom wall.

More to do

Find different versions of "Little Red Riding Hood" to read or tell to the children. Have the children act out the story. Use felt board story pieces to tell the story.

—Joy M. Tuttle, Dublin, OH

Color Wheel

The Color Wheel allows children to observe how primary colors blend together to form secondary colors.

Materials needed

Three empty medicine bottles with eyedroppers attached to the covers
Food coloring (yellow, blue and red)
9" x 9" square of white posterboard or tag board
Penny
Markers
Clear contact paper
Automatic drip coffee filters
Sponges, paper towels or napkins
Baskets or trays

What to do

1.   Fill the medicine bottles with water. Place several drops of yellow food color in one bottle, red food color in the second bottle and blue in the last.
2.   Draw a 6" diameter circle on the posterboard. Make this circle into a color wheel by tracing around a penny at six evenly-spaced points on the circle. Write the color names above each color in the corresponding color marker.
3.   Cover the posterboard with contact paper.
4.   Place all items in a basket or tray with a sponge for clean-up.
Suggestion: Have two or three color wheels available in the beginning. This is a very popular activity and children should not be rushed through it because others are waiting for a turn. An initial demonstration of the activity is very helpful.
5.   Allow children to drop the drops of colored water in the appropriate circle.
6.   The child can observe the colors blending to make green, orange and purple. They may place a coffee filter on top of the drops to save their discovery. (The principles of absorption can also be discussed.)
7.   The child can then clean up any mess and put all of the items back in the basket or on the tray so another child may enjoy it.

More to do

Children can play with yellow, red and blue water in dishpans in the water table in a much less structured way, in fact this would be an excellent introduction to this activity. Children could also experiment with blending playdough in the three primary colors.

—Barbara Evensen, Ripon, WI

What Do You Get? 3+

Children learn to identify the secondary colors that are produced when two primary colors are mixed.

Materials needed

White paper plates
Cotton swabs
Red, blue and yellow tempera paint
Newspaper

What to do

1. Mix red, blue and yellow tempera paint.
2. Give child a white paper plate and three cotton swabs. Add a small amount of red, blue and yellow paint to each plate.
3. Guide the children in mixing two primary colors at a time to create a secondary color. Continue until all combinations have been exhausted.

More to do

The children may choose to paint a picture using the colors that they have created on their own paper plate. Place primary colors only at the easel in the classroom. Encourage children to mix their own colors as needed.

Related books

The Mixed-up Chameleon by Eric Carle
Colors, A First Discovery Book by Gallimard Jeunesse and Pascale de Bourgoing

Related song

"Colors" by Hap Palmer

—Lyndall Warren, Milledgeville, GA

Shady Dealings 3+

Children sequence colors by shade from lightest to darkest or vice versa.

Materials needed

Paint strips from a hardware store that represent shades of various colors
Small plastic bags
Red, blue, yellow and white tempera paint
Paintbrushes
Small container of water for rinsing brushes
Easel
Easel paper

What to do

1. Cut the paint strips into sections.

2. Place shades of one color in a small plastic bag. Consider the age group of the children to determine how many different shades of color to include. Three or four shades are appropriate for children aged three to five.

3. Prepare several bags so the children can work together in small groups to sequence the strips.

4. Mix tempera paint in red, blue, yellow and white.

5. In a large group activity, demonstrate for the children on the easel with the tempera paint how the shade of a color is changed when white paint is added. Start by painting a small circle of one color and blend in a small amount of white to change the shade.

6. Continue this process several times to produce different shades of the same color. Repeat the process with each of the other colors of tempera.

7. Divide the children into small groups.

8. Give each group a plastic bag of paint chips. Ask them to arrange the colors in order beginning with the darkest. For younger children, the darkest paint chip can be mounted on a piece of white paper to give them a starting point for the activity.

More to do

The concept of creating darker shades using black can be introduced to the group in a similar way. Following these activities, allow children to experiment with shades as they work with finger paints. To increase their awareness, search the classroom for things of the same color and discuss the shades found in these objects.

—Lyndall Warren, Milledgeville, GA

Color Telescopes

3+

Children learn that mixing primary colors produces new colors, and observe their environment through color transparencies.

Materials needed

Cardboard tubes from paper towel rolls—one per child
Colored cellophane in red, yellow and blue
Rubber bands
Markers

What to do

1. Cut cellophane into 5" square pieces.

2. Have the children decorate their paper rolls with markers.

3. Have the children take pieces of colored cellophane, place them over one end of their paper roll, and look through the other end.

4. Encourage children to try color pieces alone and in various combinations. Encourage them to talk about the colors they see and share their discoveries with one another.

5. Let the children choose the cellophane colors that make the color they want for their color telescope. Show them how to hold these pieces over one end and secure them with a rubber band.

6. Encourage children to look through one another's "telescopes" and to take their color telescopes outside to look at nature through colors.

More to do

Use this activity after providing children opportunities for free experimentation mixing colored water, paints or finger paints.

Related books

Planting a Rainbow by Lois Ehlert
Color Dance by Ann Jonas

—Judith Dighe, Rockville, MD

Clothespin Sticker Match

3+

Children will practice matching colors.

Materials needed

Large plastic cups
Spring-type clothespins
Colored dot stickers or white dot stickers and permanent markers

What to do

1. Color each of the dots a different color if using white dots. Stick the dots around the top of the cup with a space between each dot.
2. Color each clothespin one of the colors of the dots.
3. The child(ren) match the clothespins to each of the colored dots by putting a clothespin above each dot. (Since this is such a popular activity, prepare more than one set of cup and clothespins.)

More to do

Use to teach one-to-one correspondence.

—*Margaret Moore, Fairfax, VA*

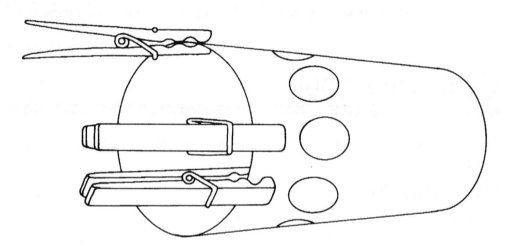

Red Rover, Red Rover Let the Colored Leaves Come Over

3+

This movement activity teaches color recognition, improves listening skills and has the children follow directions.

Materials needed

Construction paper—red, orange, yellow, green and brown
Scissors
Tape

What to do

1. Cut a leaf shape for each child out of construction paper.
2. Teach movements to be used (hop, walk, tiptoe, twirl, gallop, walk backwards, giant/baby steps).
3. Tape a leaf shape on each child.
4. Have each child tell you their leaf color.

5. Group children about 20 feet from you (you can line them up if you want). The same colors don't need to be by each other.
6. Say, for example, "Red rover, red rover, let the yellow leaves twirl over" (You may need to demonstrate).
7. Children with yellow leaves twirl over by you.
8. Continue calling colors and changing movement until all children have gathered by you.
9. Teacher walks to where children started. Repeat game.

More to do

To make this activity different, use colored shapes to teach shapes or letters to teach the alphabet.

Related books

Little Blue, Little Yellow by Leo Lionni

—Kimberle S. Byrd, Grand Rapids, MI

Go Batty 3+

Students identify and match the colors of bat face cards.

Materials needed

Black construction paper
Scissors
Multicolored smiley-faced stickers
Clear contact paper

What to do

1. Cut out 52 or an even number of 5" bats. (Use a stencil or free hand drawing.) Place one colored smiley face sticker on one side of two different bats to make a pair. (Use multicolored dot stickers if you cannot find smiley face stickers.) Cover the bats with clear contact paper.
2. Show the bats to the children. Turn them over and show the different colored faces.
3. Identify the color of each face.
4. Explain the rules. (Note: The game is played like Go Fish.)
5. Pass out 7 cards to each child that is playing. The rest of the cards are spread on the table (colored side down).
6. Each child takes turns asking another if they have a certain colored face (i.e. Do you have a red?). If the child does, he hands over the bat. If the child does not have the color, he says "Go Batty!" The child reaches into the pile on the table and picks up a card. Then it is the next child's turn. The object is to make pairs of colors.
7. The game continues until a player runs out of bats. The child with the most bat pairs wins.

More to do

Have each child make a rainbow book by drawing pictures of a different color for each page in the book.
Have the children make a sponge painting using the different colors while listening to music.

Related books

Who Said Red by M. Serfozo

—Renee Kapusniak, Webster, NY

Eraser Sorting

3+

The children sort and classify erasers and other objects according to color and/or shape.

Materials needed

Small erasers that are the same shape but different colors. Use crayons, clowns, flowers, sunglasses, smiley faces, etc. They are usually sold inexpensively in gross count containers.
Some type of sorting bowl or small clear plastic cups (margarine bowls are great)
Tacky glue
Small basket

What to do

1. Place all objects in a small basket.
2. Take one color of each eraser and attach it to the sorting bowl.
3. Do this to all the different colors so you have on eraser attached to each sorting container.
4. Set the basket and the containers out.
5. Store erasers in plastic bags when not in use. This can be done as an activity to match your theme or unit you are studying for the week.

More to do

Change the erasers to fit holiday themes, for example, ghosts, pumpkins and bats for Halloween, Christmas shapes, Easter bunnies with different colored bows and colored hearts for Valentine's Day! This activity can be done to fit any theme you can find an eraser for.

—Deborah Burton, Irwin, IA

A Visit to the Pet Shop

The children practice identifying pets and their sounds.

Materials needed

Doll
Puppet (pet)
Stuffed animals that could be pets: rabbits, snake, spider, dog, cat, fish, bird, turtle, mouse

What to do

1. Introduce the children to your pet puppet. The puppet questions children about what pets are and what we need to do to take care of our pets: feed them, play with them and give them a home.
2. Show each child a pretend pet. Have the children identify each one and say which they would most like to have as a pet.
3. Tell the following story, presenting each pet as it is mentioned and encouraging children to make the animal sound at the appropriate time:

> "One morning, Ann decided that she would like to have a pet. Her parents said she could if she would care for it. Ann promised she would, so they all drove to the pet shop.
>
> Inside the pet shop, she saw a dog that looked sad. "Would you like to be my pet?" she asked him. The dog barked (children bark), which meant yes in dog talk. She asked a cat the same question, and the cat meowed (children meow), which also meant yes. She asked a slithering snake if he wanted to be her pet. He hissed (children hiss) and slithered on by. Which would be a good pet for Ann? She asked the bird if she wanted to be her pet, and the bird chirped (children chirp). She asked the mouse, and the mouse squeaked (children squeak). What was Ann to do?
>
> Just then a soft, white rabbit caught her eye. She asked the rabbit, "Would you like to come home with me and be my pet?" But the rabbit only sat and looked at her with sad eyes, and Ann knew she wanted the rabbit more than any other animal in the store. She went to the pet shop owner and bought the rabbit and all the items needed to care for it. The shop owner told her how to care for the rabbit and waved goodbye as Ann and her parents left the store. Ann had a pet."

4. Review with the children the sound each animal made.

More to do

Discuss how Ann would need to care for each animal. Using the children's voices and a tape recorder, make a tape of animal sounds.

Related book

Emma's Pet by David McPhail
I'll Always Love You by Hans Wilhelm

—*Marzee Woodward, Murfreesboro, TN*

Getting to Know You

3+

This activity will help small children become more familiar with the older generation and teach them the joy of making others happy.

Materials needed

Audio tape or live music
Cookies
Napkins

What to do

1. Call a local nursing home and arrange a time to bring the children for a 30- minute visit.
2. Teach the children several songs ("Getting to Know You" is a good choice).
3. Talk to the children about what they might see at the nursing home. Mention that some of the people there might not hear or see very well, and might be in wheelchairs. Remind the children that the people in the nursing home were children once, long ago. Emphasize friendliness, smiles and warmth.
4. On the day of the visit, have the children make pictures or cards to pass out to their new friends.
5. At the nursing home, have children sing for 15 minutes and encourage residents to sing along.
6. Have children pass out their cards and drawings.
7. Appoint one or more children to pass out cookies to the residents (check first about dietary restrictions).

More to do

When you return to class, discuss the visit. Ask children to think of some nice things to do on another visit. Perhaps plan another visit (I recommend holidays other than Christmas because nursing homes tend to be busy then and the elderly are often forgotten during the rest of the year).

—*Cathy Chenoweth, Columbia, M0*

Making My House

3+

In this activity children will have an opportunity to improve fine motor skills, work on counting skills and learn about shapes and colors.

Materials needed

Squares and triangles cut from 2" x 4" lumber
Sandpaper
Glue
Poster paint
Paintbrushes
Masking tape

What to do

1. Cut wood into square and triangular shapes. Make a sample house to show the children.
2. Have the children sand the wood. Sandblocks work well.
3. Glue the house and roof together.
4. Add masking tape for the doors and windows.
5. Paint the roof of the house. Let dry.

6. Paint the base of the house. Let dry.
7. Take off the masking tape.
8. Add house numbers if appropriate.

More to do

Make a community out of the houses. Make other buildings in the community (church, school, fire station). Add the buildings to the block area in the room. Use the houses to help the children learn their addresses.

Related books

Building a House by Byron Barton
A House for Hermit Crab by Eric Carle

—Helen Reninger, Bolivar, OH

Democratic Free Time   3+

This activity teaches children about the basic principles of the voting process: that each person has one vote, that voting is done in private, that voting is a way for groups to make decisions fairly and that vote counting must be done by more than one person.

Materials needed

Small booth made from a large cardboard box or a sheet hung up in a corner
Writing surface such as clipboard or tabletop
Crayon
List of names of everyone in the class
11" x 4 1/2" paper
Markers
Shoe box with top
Large version of ballot to use for counting the votes (with the group.)
"I Voted" stickers, if available.

What to do

1. Make the voting ballots on the 11" x 4 1/2" paper by drawing a column of four to five little pictures of favorite free-time activities (e.g., reading: a picture of a book; playing on the playground: a picture of a swing; taking out pets: a picture of an animal, etc.). Place a circle beside each picture. Make enough copies of the ballot for everyone, including some spares.
2. Make a large copy of the ballot on construction paper, chalkboard or marker board for the group to see.
3. Arrange the voting box with a writing surface and crayon.
4. Make the ballot box by cutting a slit in the top of a shoe box. Place this in your voting area.
5. Make a list of all the children in your class for the voting registration form.
6. At election time, gather the children in a circle and explain concept of voting.
7. Explain the ballots and the choices.
8. Have a child come up and help to mark his or her name off the registration form.
9. Let the child go into voter's booth and vote for only one choice by coloring the circle next to the appropriate picture. Limit to 30 seconds per voter.
10. Have children place their ballots into ballot box. Hand them "I voted" stickers if you have them.
11. Let all the children repeat this sequence until everyone is finished. Have two voting booths if the group is large.

12. Select one or two children to help with the vote tabulation. They "read" the vote and you mark it on the big group ballot. If any ballot has more than one vote, you can throw it away if you want.
13. When all the votes are counted, have children tell you which activity won and go do it!

More to do

Visit a real voting booth. Visit a legislature or city government meeting if possible. Vote on other issues, such as which story to read.

—Dixie Havlak, Olympia, WA

Where Does Our Mail Come From?   4+

Children learn about the postal system by mailing a letter home and receiving it.

Materials needed

Used greeting cards
Plain white typing paper
#10 envelopes, one per child
Postage stamps, one per child

What to do

1. Fold the typing paper in thirds so that it will fit neatly into the #10 envelope and cut out pictures from used greeting cards.
2. Discuss how people communicate with each other through the mail. Tell the children that they are each going to make a greeting card for a family member at home and mail it.
3. Have each child choose several greeting card pictures to paste on the middle section of the folded paper. Allow glue to dry thoroughly.
4. Tell the children to decorate their cards with crayons or markers and add their own greetings. You might need to help younger children.
5. Have the children address the envelopes (using the names of family members) or do it for them, emphasizing neatness and the need for a complete, accurate address.
6. Give each child one postage stamp to lick and position in the proper corner of the envelope.
7. The children should insert their cards in envelopes and seal them.
8. Walk the class to the nearest mailbox and let each child mail his (or her) own card.

More to do

Have the children bring their greeting cards back to school after they receive them at home. Discuss how the letter got to their house.Set up a classroom post office (props could include a table, a small scale and a cardboard box with a slot in the side). Provide pencils, stickers for stamps, envelopes, paper, etc. Try to arrange a guided trip through a local post office.

Related books

Where's My Blankie? by Anna Dickson
A Letter to Amy by Ezra Jack Keats

—Judy Contino, Ozone Park, NY

Mail Carrier

Children learn about community.

Materials needed

Shoe boxes
Crayons
Tape
Construction paper or wrapping paper

What to do

1. Have each child bring a shoe box from home.
2. Pass out construction paper or wrapping paper.
3. Help the children design and decorate their boxes.
4. Write each child's name clearly on his box.
5. Line up the boxes in the classroom. Have the children use them to send notes, pictures, drawings or other gifts to each other.

More to do

Talk about communication, the postal service and addresses. Use a United States map to discuss sending letters to relatives living in other states.

—*Cathy Chenoweth, Columbia, MO*

The Letter Carrier

4+

Children learn to recognize their personal information (name and address) while learning about their neighborhood letter carrier.

Materials needed

White envelopes
Crayons
Scissors
Pencils
Construction paper

What to do

1. Discuss with the children the role of the letter carrier. Explain that we mail letters, cards and other important information in an envelope and that the name and address (house number, street, city, state and zip code) on the front of an envelope helps the letter carrier find our homes. Depending on the ability of the group, the teacher may want to address the front of the envelope for each child.
2. Open up the envelopes to make a house. Have the children glue their envelopes (houses) onto the construction paper.
3. Have the children decorate the envelopes to resemble their houses, and fill in the remaining portions of the construction paper to resemble their yards.
4. Collect the pictures, shuffle them, and have the children try to identify their addresses as you read them.

—*Margaret Dubaj, Niles, OH*

Library Fun

4+

Children learn to love books and handle them carefully. They also develop an interest in libraries and the services they offer.

Materials needed

Three small boxes to hold library cards
Construction paper
Library cards made from three colors of construction paper, one for each child
Librarian's table
Selection of books to be checked out, with a sticky note on the inside cover of each book
Stamp and stamp pad

What to do

1. Decorate a bulletin board with book covers, commercial or child-made.
2. Have the children invent a name for the library. Color a banner emblazoned with the library's new name and hang it above the entrance.
3. Cover three small boxes with construction paper (yellow, blue and green).
4. Prepare library cards in yellow, blue and green and put sticky notes in books to be circulated.
5. Arrange books in an attractive library setting.
6. Make three signs: Library is Open, Library is Closed and Return Books Here. Post them in the appropriate places.
7. Limit the number of children using the library by having those with yellow cards play first, blue second, and green third.
8. Choose a librarian and an assistant to sit at the table.
9. Designate a place for books to be returned.
10. Have the librarian stamp both the sticky note in the book AND the child's card.
11. Returned books are replaced on the shelves by the assistant.

More to do

Designate a day for children to bring a favorite book from home. Make a classroom book on chart paper or individual books. Create book covers for imaginary or favorite books.

Related book

I Like the Library by Anne Rockwell

—*Cary Peterson, Pittsburgh, PA*

Block City

Children develop auditory and fine motor skills with this listen-and-do exercise.

Materials needed

Heavy paper, 14" x 20", one sheet per child
Various colored cutout shapes, enough for each child to have a variety
Glue
Block City by Robert Louis Stevenson

What to do

1.   Select several colors of paper and cut into shapes similar to those of building blocks, scaled down to about 1/3 of a block's actual size.
2.   Set out paper, shapes and glue on work area.
3.   Read the book aloud to the children.
4.   Discuss the story with children, inviting them to create their very own block city. Ask if they have built with blocks and tell them they will now "build" with paper blocks and glue.
5.   Demonstrate how to apply a small amount of glue to the back of a shape and apply it to the paper.
6.   Continue applying shapes to construct buildings. Suggest that the children make castles, schools, houses, churches or stores.

More to do

Make a city by lining up the children's pictures.

—Cathy Chenoweth, Columbia, MO

Collections/Antique Shop

The children will sort and organize a variety of collections.

Materials needed

All kinds of collections:
     jars, books, rocks, shells, frames, earrings, music boxes, bears
Play money
Cash register

What to do

1.   Go to a thrift store or antique shop to look for collectibles.
2.   Save or ask parents to send plastic bottles, lids, caps, rocks, shells, etc., a week before the unit.
3.   Set up your collectibles on a table in dramatic play.
4.   Have children sell their collectibles using the register and play money.

More to do

Visit an antique shop. Invite someone who collects something and have her display her collection.

—Sonia Perez, San Antonio, TX

Flower Shop

4+

Children learn about flowers, develop vocabulary and exercise social and interactive skills.

Materials needed

Silk, plastic or real flowers
Cash register
Play money
Phone
Paper
Pencils
Bib aprons
Tissue paper for wrapping bouquets
Bulb catalogues
Orange juice cans for flowers
Long table at the children's height
Posters of flowers
Watering cans

What to do

1. Encourage parents and fellow teachers to bring in any of the materials listed above.
2. Set up props in the chosen area of the room.
3. Read a story about flowers at circle time.
4. After circle time, and after you have read the appropriate book, fingerplay or poem, tell them about the flower shop.
5. Explain that many people buy flowers for many reasons, such as a birthday, an illness, a wedding or an anniversary.
6. Have the children maintain a pretend flower shop with an owner, employees, customers—even a delivery man!

More to do

Using most of the same materials, set up a flower garden with the addition of styrofoam to "plant" silk or plastic flowers, a plastic wheelbarrow, a length of hose with a spray attachment, gardening gloves and straw hats or visors.

Related books

The Reason for a Flower by Ruth Heller
What Is a Flower? by Jennifer W. Day

—*Cory McIntyre, Crystal Lake, IL*

Pounding Block

Each child will practice hitting a nail with a hammer.

Materials needed

Old tree stumps or portable chunks of wood
Roofing nails with large heads
Small hammers

What to do

1. Show the children how to use the hammer in a safe way.
2. Give each child a small box of nails, a hammer and a piece of wood. Supervise closely.

More to do

Have the children create patterns by wrapping rubber bands or colored yarn around the nails they've hammered into their wood.

—Wanda Pelton, Lafayette, IN

Cast Your Vote

Children will understand the basic concept of the voting process, and reinforce math skills such as counting, more/less and graphing

Materials needed

Orange
Apple
Grapes
Banana
Pear
Small blocks (one for each child)
Posterboard—set up to look like a bar graph
Markers

What to do

1. Show children the five choices of fruit and talk about the voting process and casting votes.
2. Give each child one block.
3. Allow each child to place her block behind their favorite fruit. (Each child places the block one on top of each other).
4. After voting is completed, ask, "How many voted for an orange? an apple? (count votes) "Which fruit received the most/least votes?"

More to do

Set out the graph. Count individual votes. Call a child to come up front and color in the number of votes for each fruit.

—Ann O'Donnell/Lauren O'Neill, Abington, PA

Block Play: Building a Town

4+

Children will learn to name different buildings while they create structures from blocks.

Material needed

Building blocks

What to do

1. Look at pictures of towns and talk with the children about various types of buildings (stores, fire stations, schools, houses, etc.).
2. Take the children on a field trip to see buildings in their own town.
3. To begin the activity, divide the children into groups of four or five.
4. Divide the classroom blocks among the groups.
5. Tell each group that they are to build a town.
6. Have each child name a building that they would like to construct. (Some children may spend all their time on one building while others build two or three.)
7. Have children visit all the towns that have been made.

More to do

Use shoe boxes or a variety of big boxes to create individual buildings found in towns. Focus on one or two buildings each week. These buildings could include the post office, grocery store, theater, etc.

—*Gail Heyn, Albia, IA*

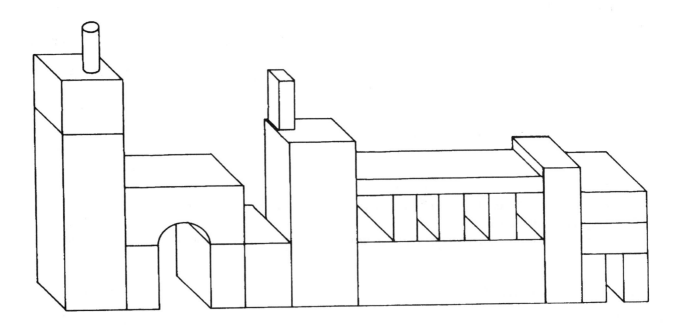

Our Own Newspaper

Children express themselves verbally and see the importance of their words by having a written copy of their work, thus encouraging them to read and think critically.

Materials needed

A newspaper
Paper
Pens
Access to a copy machine
Typewriter, if you decide to type the paper

What to do

1. Be aware that if the children all want to work on the same story, group time can be set aside for this. If everyone has a different idea, stories can be dictated during free play times.
2. Show the children a real newspaper and its different parts such as the masthead, the headlines, the different kinds of stories, and the pictures.
3. Tell the children they can write a newspaper, too, but they need to come up with lots of ideas for stories. Possible stories could be about their class pet, their favorite sports team, or their favorite toys.
4. Write all suggestions down and tell them to start thinking about a story that they made up, a story about their favorite sports team or a story about their favorite toy.
5. Write all suggestions down and tell them to start thinking about what they would like to say. They should also be encouraged to create drawings to go with stories.
6. Allow them to work in small groups if they want. Once all the stories have been dictated, the class can come together and think of a name for their newspaper. Take suggestions and vote on a name.
7. The newspaper can be handwritten or typed and "pasted-up" by the teacher.
8. Run off enough copies for everyone and read it to the class.

More to do

You may want to create follow-up editions. Encourage the parents to share the newspaper with their children.

—*Jessica Mitchell, Oakdale, NY*

COMMUNITY

Brown Bear Bread

2+

During this learning activity, children prepare bread dough and shape it into a bear for baking.

Materials needed

4 cups flour
1 teaspoon salt
8 teaspoons baking powder
1 teaspoon cream of tartar
2 tablespoons sugar
1 cup vegetable shortening
1 1/3 cup milk
Large bowl
2 cookie sheets
Pastry blender or two knives
Oven
Ribbon
Firm paper plates
Plastic bags

What to do

1. Prepare a visual recipe board (rebus chart) with pictures and words describing the recipe step by step.
2. Purchase ingredients in the recipe.
3. Gather all utensils necessary for cooking.
4. Preheat oven to 425 degrees F.
5. Children need to wash their hands. Have the children help you throughout the mixing and kneading process.
6. Grease 2 cookie sheets.
7. Place flour, salt, baking powder, cream of tartar and sugar in a bowl.
8. Cut the shortening into the flour with two knives or a pastry blender until the mixture resembles a coarse meal.
9. Add the milk all at once and stir just until the dough forms a ball around the fork.
10. Turn the dough onto a lightly floured surface and knead 14 times.
11. Divide dough into pieces for each child.
12. Children can make their bear by dividing their dough into rolled "balls" and "snakes" and piecing together a head, two ears, a body, two, two legs and paws. Place the finished bear on the cookie sheet. You may also wish to add raisins for the eyes, nose, mouth and buttons.
13. Bake 15-20 minutes.
14. Remove from oven and cool, then tie a bow around Brown Bear's neck. He will travel home better if placed on a firm paper plate before being placed in a plastic bag.

More to do

The visual recipe board can be used for reading readiness. Recipe ingredients and their nutritional importance can be discussed. Hold a Teddy Bear Day. Ask the children to bring in a favorite Teddy Bear. Discuss their lifestyles, texture, colors, how they differ from real bears and places they live. Make a cave from a box for the Teddy Bears to hibernate in.

Related books

Winnie the Pooh by A. A. Milne

Related song

"The Teddy Bears' Picnic" by Rosenshontz

—*Lauren Brickner-McDonald, Mountain Lakes, NJ*

Rice Cake Creatures

This fun activity allows the children to make special snacks that are good for them.

Materials needed

Miniature rice cakes
Peanut butter
Raisins or currents
Pretzel sticks
Sliced almonds
Thinly sliced carrot or celery strips
Green grapes
Cream cheese
Hand washing station
Plates
Butter knives
Bowls or plates for ingredients
Lots of napkins

What to do

1. Place two rice cakes on each plate and give each child a small knife (plastic works fine). Julienne the vegetables to use as whiskers and cut the grapes in half to be rabbit tails. Put almonds, vegetables, currents and pretzels into several bowls to be shared.

2. Demonstrate a rice mouse to children: spread peanut butter on rice cake, use currents for eyes and nose, half-almonds for ears, vegetables for whiskers and pretzel for tail.

3. Demonstrate bunny to children kids: spread cream cheese on the rice cake, use almonds for ears, currents for eyes, vegetables for whiskers and grape halves for tails.

4. Let the kids prepare their own animals, making whatever creations they choose.

More to do

Any variety of healthy, little ingredients can be used to create any variety of creatures. Apple rounds or small crackers or shapes of bread can be used as the base. Cheese spread and other nut butters can be used as the "fur." Frosting can be use too, but only for special events.

—*Dixie Havlak, Olympia, WA*

What's Cooking?

This activity will introduce the children to a variety of nutritious vegetables and involve them in making soup.

Materials needed

Stone Soup by Marcia Brown (optional)
Crock pot
Chart showing the vegetable soup recipe
3 medium tomatoes
3 stalks of celery with tops
1 medium onion
3 medium potatoes
3 cups of water
1 t. salt
1 t. pepper
3 beef bouillon cubes
10 oz. package frozen peas
Cutting board
Measuring cup and spoons
Sharp knife and table knife
Peeler
Large spoon

What to do

1. Assign children different ingredients to bring from home or provide them yourself. Place all the cooking ingredients and utensils on a low table so children can see and participate. Make the recipe chart and put it where it can be easily seen.

2. Read *Stone Soup* by Marcia Brown. Talk about how the soldiers in the story made their soup and how the class is going to make its soup today.

3. Have the children wash their hands. Allow the children to help prepare the vegetables for the soup. Good tasks for the children are washing and peeling vegetables (if peeler is not too sharp), measuring and adding ingredients, slicing the softer vegetables with the table knife and cleaning up; you should slice the harder vegetables with the sharp knife. Follow these steps, adding each vegetable to the crock pot when it is ready:

Wash, peel, and cut the tomatoes.
Wash, peel, slice and add the carrots.
Wash, slice and add the celery.
Wash, peel, cut, and add the onion.
Wash, peel, cut, and add the potatoes.
Open box and add the frozen peas.
Add the 3 cups of water.
Add 1 t. salt.
Add 1 t. pepper.
Add 3 beef bouillon cubes.
Stir the soup.

4. Plug in the crock pot and cook on HIGH for 4-6 hours. When the soup is ready, pour into bowls or cups and enjoy!

More to do

Ask the children to dictate a story about a class making soup. The story can be illustrated and put in book form.

—Cindy Bosse, Crystal Springs, MS

Pizza Day 3+

The children will learn how to follow a recipe to make a snack to eat. In addition, they will learn roles to play in their dramatic play.

Materials needed

Copy of a pizza recipe. Sample:

    burger buns (split in half) or english muffins
    pizza sauce
    pepperoni (or hot dogs)
    small can of mushrooms (optional)
    sliced american cheese or mozzarella cheese

Spread pizza sauce on one side of a hamburger bun or muffin. Top with pepperoni, mushrooms, and cheese. Ask a grownup to broil pizzas for 5 to 10 minutes, or until cheese melts. You can also bake in an oven for 15 minutes at 350 degrees.

Ingredients listed on recipe

What to do

1. Run off copies of recipe to be taken home with each child. Ask each family to bring different ingredients from home.

2. Cover a coookie sheet with aluminum foil. Lay out buns (or muffins) ready to cover with pizza toppings. Have a piece of paper and pencil beside it to write child's name in the same order pizzas are made on cookie sheet.

3. Explain "Pizza Day" to class. Talk about variety of toppings. Read and explain recipe.

4. Prepare the pizza, following recipe. Cook and eat for snack.

5. Set up dramatic play area. Most pizzerias are willing to give empty cups with lids and cup holder (no straws to avoid mouthing), paper bags, and cardboard to lay pizzas on. Talk about roles in a pizzeria; chef, counter person, and customer. Children can act out different roles.

More to do

Felt Pizza (for 4 year olds and older): Using a round cooking sheet as a guide, cut beige felt in a circle. Have a smaller red felt circle fit inside. Cut both into 8 or 12 slices. Cut reddish-brown circles for pepperoni, yellow strips for cheese, green circles for olives, etc. With this project a child can order a pizza with his choice of toppings.

Related books

Kid Snacks, Healthy Snacks for Kids by Penny Warner
Cookbook for Boys and Girls by Betty Crocker

—*Nancy DeSteno, Fridley, MN*

Sweet And Sour Fruit Flavors 3+

This activity can motivate children to eat healthy snacks, try new foods and learn to distinguish between sweet and sour and reproduce patterns.

Materials needed

Chart paper with "sweet" and "sour" columns
Pictures of sweet and sour fruit
Laminated cards with drawings of "flowers" made out of fruit pieces

Napkins
Scotch tape
Samples of sweet and sour fruits

What to do

1. Prepare chart with sweet and sour column headings.
2. Cut out pictures or make drawings of the sweet and sour fruits the children will taste.
3. Make laminated cards. Arrange some pictures or drawings of different fruits in a flower shape and laminate.
4. Cut samples of real fruit that match the pictures you have gathered for your chart.
5. Have the children wash their hands before beginning this acivity.
6. Read chart headings to group.
7. Let children sample various fruit that are sweet or sour.
8. Have children decide whether to categorize fruit as sweet or sour.
9. Have children tape fruit pictures in appropriate columns.
10. Pass out laminated "fruit flower" cards and have children reproduce the "fruit flowers" by laying real fruit pieces on top of the laminated cards.
11. Congratulate all children on a job well done and allow them to eat their creations.

More to do

Ask the children to bring in various sweet and sour items to make a new "Sweet and Sour" chart. Let the children be creative and design their own fruit flowers on a plate.

—Angela M. Weber, Fairview Heights, IL

Cooking With Literature

3+

The children learn about literature and various concepts that are used during cooking activities.

Materials needed

The Gingerbread Man
1/2 cup shortening
3/4 tsp. salt
1/2 cup molasses
1/2 tsp. baking soda
1/2 cup sugar
3/4 tsp. ginger
1/4 cup water
1/4 tsp. nutmeg
2 1/2 cups flour
1/8 tsp. all-spice
Measuring cups and spoons
Mixing bowls and spoons
Rolling pin and plastic wrap
Cookie cutters
Recipe written in rebus form
Oven or toaster oven

What to do

1. Have all the ingredients and equipment ready. Read the recipe to the children and write it on the experience chart. Have the children glue or tape the corresponding picture next to the word.

2. Talk about the various ingredients. Have the children smell, taste and touch them—how do they taste? how do they feel? Do they taste sweet, sour, bitter, cold, hot, salty? Do they feel smooth, rough, lumpy, wet, dry, oily, mushy?

3. Cooking activities are best done in small groups of five or six children so that everyone can participate and observe what is being done. Several tables can be set up at one time, as long as there is an adult at each table, or several "shifts" can take place to give everyone a chance.

4. Read each ingredient, letting one child measure one ingredient and place it in the bowl. Cue cards can be used to help a child find the right measuring device and/or the correct ingredient.

5. After all the ingredients are placed in the bowl, the children can take turns mixing.

6. Chill the dough for 2-3 hours or overnight.

7. Place the dough on a floured board. Have the children roll it out. Using the gingerbread-man cookie cutters, they can cut out the cookies and decorate them (use raisins, chocolate chips, sprinkles).

8. Bake the cookies at 375 degrees for 10-12 minutes. If using a toaster oven in the room, make sure there is proper safety supervision.

More to do

Do a felt-board story; use puppets to tell the story; do a play; make a recipe book of all the recipes used in school; visit a bakery or factory, use the cookie cutters dipped in paint to make stencils.

—*Lois A. McEwan, Bethpage, NY*

Cinnamon Roll-Ups   3+

This activity will teach the children about food preparation.

Materials needed

Refrigerator rolls found in the dairy section
Butter or margarine
Plastic knives
Cinnamon
Raisins
Sugar
Toaster oven

What to do

1. Give each child one roll of dough. Tell the children to unroll and flatten the dough with their fingers.

2. Have children spread butter or margarine on the top of their flattened dough.

3. Put out small bowls of sugar, raisins and cinnamon. Tell the children to sprinkle all three over the butter.

4. Demonstrate how to roll up the dough so that the butter, cinnamon, raisins and sugar stay inside.

5. Bake in a toaster oven according to package directions for rolls.

6. Let cool and serve!

More to do

Make picture recipe cards for the children to follow when preparing cinnamon roll-ups. Ask the children to retell the steps involved in the recipe. ("What did you do first? Second? Third?) Assign children jobs during clean-up.

Related book

Just Me and My Dad by Mercer Mayer

—Sandra Suffuletto Ryan, Buffalo, NY

Applesauce

3+

This cooking activity develops eye-hand coordination, engages the senses of smell and taste and teaches the children to discuss, plan and share work with others. Additionally, it allows the children to read pictorial and/or written directions.

Materials needed

Electric blender
Spatula
Measuring cups
Spoons and knives
3 large juicy apples
1/2 to 3/4 cup cider or apple juice (add as needed)
1/2 to 1 tsp cinnamon

What to do

1. Assemble cooking utensils, supplies and foods.
2. Provide a pictorial and written applesauce recipe.
3. Core and cut apples into small pieces, place in blender.
4. Add liquid and cinnamon to apples in blender.
5. Blend these ingredients on "High" until smooth.
6. Serve and enjoy.

More to do

Prior to making the applesauce, visit an apple orchard and pick the apples. If an orchard is not available, plan a trip to the grocery store and select apples and purchase remaining ingredients. Some related apple art activities include: apple dolls, apple print or small fingerprint apple trees.

Related books

The Seasons of Arnold's Apple Tree by Gail Gibbons
Rain Makes Applesauce by Julian Scheer

Related song

"Johnny Appleseed"

—Kaethe J. Lewandowski, Centreville, VA

COOKING

Cherry Pie

3+

The children will practice comparing changes that take place when an ingredient is added to a mixture and when the mixture is cooked.

Materials needed

Cherry pie filling
White construction paper
Markers
Flour
Sugar
Milk
Melted butter
Spoon for each child
Cup for each child
Muffin tin(s)
Cooking spray
Measuring spoons

What to do

1. Make recipe cards for each ingredient. Use the markers and construction paper. Use pictures of measuring spoons to show how much of each item is needed. Write out the following recipe:

> *Put 2 tablespoons of flour in a cup*
> *Mix 1 teaspoon of sugar with flour*
> *Add 1 tablespoon of milk to mixture and mix*
> *Add 1 tablespoon of melted butter and mix*
> *Spoon ingredients into prepared muffin tin*
> *Spoon 1 tablespoon of pie filling into middle of batter*

2. Gather the cooking materials.
3. To begin the activity, preheat the oven to 350 degrees.
4. Spray the muffin tin cups with cooking spray.
5. Show the children the cherry pie filling. Discuss and describe how the pie filling looks with the children. Does it look like a real cherry?
6. Pass out cups and spoons to each child. Explain that they are going to make cherry pies for themselves. Show and read the recipe cards introducing the tablespoon and teaspoon measures.
7. Go through the steps of the recipe cards with the children mixing each ingredient. After each addition of ingredients, discuss the changes the children see in the mixture.
8. Bake the pies until golden brown. Serve to the children and discuss the changes that baking the pies made.

More to do

Discuss and taste the differences in maraschino cherries, fresh cherries and cherry pie filling. Tell the story of George Washington and the cherry tree.

Related book

Blueberries for Sal by Robert McCloskey

—Marzee Woodward, Murfreesboro, TN

Olden Days—Making Butter

Children are often fascinated to learn that the pioneers had to make much of their own food. Many of the pioneers had cows for milk, cream, butter and cheese. This multi-sensory activity will give the children the opportunity to experience where butter comes from while using their large muscles to operate the butter churn.

Materials needed

Butter churn—one with a crank handle/gears and a glass container. (Baby food jars with lids could be substituted, just shake.)
2 pints whipping cream
Strainer/spoon/bowl
Small pitcher for buttermilk, the run-off product (fun to taste)
Salt (optional)
Small paper cups/tin foil to cover

What to do

1. Set out materials. Show the children the butter churn and tell them about why and how it was used.
2. Give each child a turn or turns to churn the butter or shake the jars. If you use a churn, it will take about 30 minutes for the butter to harden. It hardens more quickly by the shaking method.
3. Butter will turn a light yellow and be thick when ready. Strain or pour off the liquid. This buttermilk is fun to taste. Use the spoon to gather the butter and press it into a cake. You may mix in a pinch or two of salt to taste, but it is nice to allow the children to experience the pure flavor of the fresh butter.
4. Taste the butter on crackers or bread.
5. Send some home in small paper cups so the children can share the experience of butter making with their families.

More to do

Visit a dairy farm. See cows being milked, and perhaps have a chance to see cream being separated. Bake bread in class to eat with the butter. While churning the butter you can sing.

Related song

(To the tune of "The Mulberry Bush")

This is the way we make the butter
Make the butter
Make the butter
This is the way we make the butter
Churn the butter now.

Related books

The Olden Days by Joe Mathieu
Tales of the American West by Neil and Ting Morris

—*Pamela Schumaker, Minot, ND*

Playdough Design

2+

Children will enjoy the tactile experience of working with playdough.

Materials needed

Ingredients for making playdough: flour, salt, oil, water, and unsweetened powdered drink mix
Cookie cutters
Straws
Scissors
Popsicle sticks

What to do

1. Prepare the playdough. Combine:
    1 1/2 cups flour
    1 cup salt
    3 tablespoons oil
    powdered drink mix
    Add:
    1 cup boiling water.
    Mix and knead until smooth.
2. Distribute the playdough to the children, giving each a generous amount. Encourage the children to make a sculpture or design using the cookie cutters, popsicle sticks and straws (cut up into small pieces).

More to do

Show the children how they can create pinch pots by rolling the dough into a ball and pressing their thumbs into the center, and coil pots by rolling about thin pieces of dough (like snakes) and placing the pieces on top of one another in a circular manner.

—Susan Buchalter-Katz, Lawrenceville, NJ

Create a Creature

2+

Children will use their imaginations to create creatures from playdough and talk about them.

Materials needed

Playdough
Assortment of decorative materials (e.g., feathers, craft sticks, pipe cleaners, buttons, yarn, cotton balls, tiny twigs)

What to do

1. Give each child a ball of playdough. Set out the decorative materials on the table.
2. Tell the children to turn their playdough into a creature and decorate using any materials they wish.
3. Let the creatures sit out for a few days until they harden.
4. At circle time, have children introduce their creatures and tell a little story about them.

More to do

Give children specific ideas for creatures. You might suggest that children make creatures from outer space or creatures from prehistoric days.

—Catherine Shogren, Eagan, MN

Country Clay Hearts

Children enhance their cooking and fine motor skills.

Materials needed

Clay ingredients:
4 cups flour
1 cup salt
1 1/2 cups water
(Mix with hands for 6 minutes, add more flour if too sticky)
Toaster oven
Measuring cups
Spoons
Pot holders
Wax paper
Scissors
Bowls
Thin rope
Heart-shaped cookie cutters
Pencil
Markers
Red and pink paint
Paintbrushes
Smocks

What to do

1. Preset the oven and set out materials on a table.
2. Make clay with class.
3. Give the children cookie cutters. Have them make two hearts and poke a hole near the top of each one. Set them on the wax paper and write the children's names beside.
4. Bake at 350 degrees. Cool.
5. Have the children paint their hearts.
6. Let the hearts dry and string them together with a thin rope. Write the child's name and the date on the back.

More to do

Visit a bakery.

Related rhyme

I have a tiny gift for you.
It's made of paint and clay
It's sent from me to you with love,
For a happy Valentine's day!

Related book

How Spider Saved Valentine's Day by Robert Kraus

—*Ann O'Donnel/Lauren O'Neill, Abington, PA*

CRAFTS

Sometimes I'm Afraid

3+

Children learn to understand emotions, overcome fears and use their imaginations.

Materials needed

12" x 18" piece of paper
Crayons
Scissors
Paste
Markers
Materials such as yarn, buttons, egg carton sections, fabric scraps, feathers, and so on, for each child

What to do

1. If possible, read *Little Toot*. Ask the children how Little Toot must have felt out on the ocean all alone in the dark with the fog horns sounding. Ask if the story scared them.
2. Talk about what might scare them or others.
3. Give each child paper, markers, craft materials, crayons, scissors and paste.
4. Ask the children to draw a big face. Tell them they may decorate it to make a scary mask. Tell them not to be surprised if some turn out to be funny. Rubber bands can be attached so children can wear their masks, or masks can be pasted onto paper bags for the children to wear over their heads. Line eyes up with the child's eyes, then cut them out of the mask and bag before pasting the mask onto the bag.

More to do

Ask the children to bring in creative materials to make another mask. This one can be scary, funny, beautiful or sad. Children can draw things that scare them or things that scare other people.

Related books

Little Toot by Hardie Gramatky
Sometimes I'm Afraid by Sylvia Root Tester
There's an Alligator Under My Bed by Mercer Mayer
You're the Scardey-Cat by Mercer Mayer
Where the Wild Things Are by Maurice Sendak

—*Wendy Pfeffer, Pennington, NJ*

Camera

This activity dispels children's fears of "Picture Taking Day" and improves fine motor skills.

Materials needed

Cardboard egg cartons (one for every three children)
Black paint
Caps from milk bottle or toothpaste tube
Scissors or paper cutter

What to do

1. With tops and bottoms remaining attached, each egg carton must be separated into three sections of four cups (see figures 1 and 2).
2. Paint each section of the egg carton black and let dry completely. This is the body of the camera (see figure 3).
3. Glue on the milk bottle caps for assorted buttons and settings (see figure 4).
4. Now your children are ready to take pictures!

—*Jyoti Joshi, Framingham, MA*

Figure 1 — Cut on dotted lines.

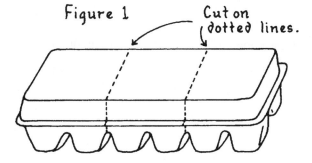

Figure 2

Figure 3

BLACK

Figure 4 — Glue caps.

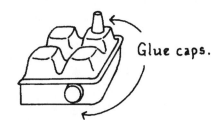

Puzzle Pin

3+

Children learn about textures, colors, sizes, shapes, lines and curves while improving their command of language.

Materials needed

Puzzle pieces from a puzzle with missing pieces
Small pin attachments, purchased from any craft store
Glitter
Small buttons
Sequins
Beads
Any other small item
Super glue, for adults
White school glue, for children

What to do

1. Prepare each item to be used in separate bowl. Place on table.
2. Each child chooses a puzzle piece.
3. With the white glue, allow the children to attach any small items to the front of the puzzle piece. Discuss the size, shape, texture and color of the items chosen.
4. Let the decorated puzzle piece dry.
5. Attach the pin to the backside of the puzzle piece with the super glue. Let dry.
6. Let them wear it with pride or give as a gift!

More to do

Using a puzzle with only a few large pieces, have every child trace and cut out a piece. Later put all the pieces together to show how each piece fits into place.

Related poem

Puzzle piece, puzzle piece,
Where are you?
Puzzle piece, puzzle piece,
What can I do?
I know, I know what's best,
Add a little lace,
And wear all the rest.

Related book

Curious George Goes to the Hospital by H. A. Rey

—*Cathy Bardorek, Norwich, CT*

Balloon Tissue Paper Painting

This activity will provide children with an avenue of self-expression and assist them in developing fine motor skills.

Materials needed

Paper
Tissue paper (all different colors)
Wallpaper samples
Paintbrushes
Scissors
Glue
Water
Blue construction paper

What to do

1. Draw a hot air balloon on a sheet of paper and reproduce it so every child in the class will have one.
2. Cut up tissue paper and wallpaper samples ahead of time if younger children are taking part in the activity.
3. Have older children tear the tissue paper into small pieces.
4. Tell them to brush water over the balloon part of their pictures and place different colored pieces of tissue paper over the wet area.
5. Have children glue wallpaper samples to their balloon baskets.
6. Allow tissue paper to dry and then have children peel it off to see how colors have stayed on the paper.
7. Cut out the balloons or have children cut them out and mount them on blue construction paper or a bulletin board with a blue background.

More to do

You can do tissue paper painting on paper Christmas trees, hearts, shamrocks and hard boiled eggs.

—*Veronica Cavanaugh, Chesapeake, VA*

Pearl Necklace

Children will learn that nature builds beautiful things such as pearls.

Materials needed

1 1/2 loaf of white bread
White glue
Lemon juice
Mixing bowl and spoon
Toothpick
Pearl fingernail polish or slick fabric pearl paint
Yarn
Newspaper or trash bags to cover table

What to do

1. Gather some examples of pearls or mother of pearl for children to examine (mother of pearl buttons). Wear some pearl jewelry.
2. Cover the table with newspaper or trash bags for easy clean up.
3. Make the Bread and Glue dough. Mix together 1 1/2 loaf of white bread with crust removed, 2 scant cups of white glue and 1/2 teaspoon of lemon juice. Mix and knead this very messy mixture. An adult should start this process and the children can help after it has been kneaded for some time.
4. Lay out round toothpicks and colorful yarn long enough to make a necklace and be knotted later.
5. To start the activity, ask the children to take a pinch of dough and mold it to make one large pearl about the size of a shelled walnut.
6. Poke a hole through the "pearl" with the toothpick and let it dry over night.
7. The next day, loosen and remove the toothpick.
8. The children choose a piece of yarn and thread it through the "pearl."
9. Paint half of the pearl with fingernail polish or paint. Let dry. Turn and paint the other side. Let this dry.
10. Knot the necklace and let the children wear them.

Related books

Paddy Under Water by John Goodall
Deep Blue Sea by Bijou Le Tord

—Phyllis Michael, Bristol, VA

Dying Wool   3+

Children learn about wool, from sheep to sweater.

Materials needed

Pictures of sheep, toy sheep
Crude wool
Spinning wheel with spindle
Spun yarn
Wool material in colors
Dye materials
Container with water
Pans to boil water
Red cabbage
Vinegar

What to do

1. Cut yarn in pieces and soak in cold water.
2. Boil the red cabbage in water with a sprinkle of vinegar.
3. Pour colored water in container and keep the yarn in it until cool.
4. While waiting for vegetables to boil, explain the wool process, using the examples at hand: crude wool, spinning wheel, spun yarn and wool material.

More to do

Talk about what farm animals do for us and what they give us.

Related books

A New Coat for Anna by Harriet Ziefert and Anita Lobel
Seasons on the Farm by Jane Miller

Related songs

"Mary Had a Little Lamb"
"Baa Baa Black Sheep"
"Old MacDonald"

—Winny VanGils, Redlands, CA

Class Quilt   4+

The children will learn sharing, cooperation and how to plan together.

Materials needed

Permanent markers
Large index cards
Masking tape
Needles
Thread
Fabric scissors

What to do

1. Cover index cards with muslin. The reason for covering the cards is to ensure that the blocks will all be the same size and the children will have a definite border. The blocks show up better if the children are encouraged to use the markers all the way to the edges.
2. Have the children draw pictures on the fabric-covered cards. A theme could be used (animals, favorite toys, ABC's, favorite activities at school, favorite nursery rhymes, favorite flowers, etc.). Use permanent markers.
3. Take fabric off cards and trim edges to 1/4" seam allowance.
4. Have the children help plan the placing of the picture squares.
5. Sew the squares together.
6. The children can take turns using the classroom quilt at rest time.

More to do

To make a more finished quilt tear shashing fabric in 4 1/2" strips. Set up the sewing machine with even feed foot (special for quilting). Pin and stitch sashing to picture blocks. The children push the foot control while the teacher sews. They can use their hands (which most do) or their feet. They watch the sewing and learn to stop and start quickly at the teacher's instructions. Press seams toward the sashing using a hot iron (done away from the children). Heat each picture block until it is very hot to set the permanent marker into the fabric. After the top is pieced, spread the backing (or whole piece of fabric used for sashing) out on the table wrong side up. Spread batting out and then quilt the top. Spread smooth and pin all three layers together with quilting pins. Sew around each one of the blocks through all three layers. The children take turns pressing the foot control and taking out the pins as the sewing machine comes to them. Quilting pins are extra long pins with a round glass top so they are easy for the children to handle. Let the children help pin the pre-folded bias tape all the way around the quilt. Have the children help sew on bias tape.

CRAFTS

Related books

The Quilt Story by Tony Johnston
The Patchwork Quilt by Valerie Flournoy
Patchwork Tales by Susan L. Roth
The Quilt by Ann Jonas
The Josefina Story Quilt by Eleanor Coerr

—Ann G. Glenn, Memphis, TN

Unique Hats   4+

This activity provides an opportunity to encourage individual creativity while sharing and cooperating with peers.

Materials needed

Paper plates
Newspapers
Craft yarn or ribbon
Glue
Staplers
Tape
Scissors
Assorted decorating materials including cotton balls, rick-rack, feathers, yarn, buttons, stickers, pompons, leaves, sequins
Jenny's Hat by Ezra Jack Keats

What to do

1. Fold and staple newspaper sheets into triangle shaped hats. Punch two holes in each paper plate on opposite sides. Thread ribbon or thick craft yarn through the holes so the paper plate hats can be tied under the chin.
2. Ask the children to bring decorating items to school to use and share.
3. Assemble glue, staplers, tape, scissors and craft decorating materials.
4. Read the book *Jenny's Hat* by Ezra Jack Keats.
5. Discuss why the hat was special. Ask the children to brainstorm ideas for making unique or "one-of-a-kind hats."
6. Show the children the two types of hat bases—the newspaper triangle and the paper plate.
7. Tell children they may choose a base and an assortment of decorations for making their own special hat. Emphasize each hat will be different.

More to do

Hold a hat parade. Take group or individual photographs. Let the children dictate captions for the photos.

Related books

Martin's Hats by Joan Blos
Caps for Sale by Esphyr Slobodkina

—Lois Vogel, Ferdinand, IN

Make an Alligator Purse

Children dramatize a popular rhyme using an alligator purse.

Materials needed

Posterboard
Green construction paper or green paint
Two green pipe cleaners
Glue
Markers
Alligator pattern

What to do

1. Enlarge the alligator pattern to purse size. Transfer to green construction paper or to posterboard which has been painted green and cut two copies.
2. Glue the two shapes together, leaving enough space for purse contents.
3. Add eyes, teeth and other details with markers.
4. Laminate and add pipe cleaners for handles.

More to do

One popular activity used in many whole language classrooms is to rewrite favorite children's books. A teacher might lead a class in a shared writing activity to rewrite the book, *The Lady With the Alligator Purse* by Nadine Bernard Westcott, using a holiday theme such as "The Lady With the Green Shamrock Purse." Take a field trip to the local zoo, making a special visit to the alligators.

Related books

The Lady With the Alligator Purse by Nadine Bernard Westcott
There's an Alligator Under My Bed by Mercer Mayer
Five Little Monkeys Sitting in a Tree by Eileen Christelow

—*Susan Ezzell, Memphis, TN*

Papier-Maché Masks

4+

Children will use their imaginations and fine motor skills to make masks.

Materials needed

Balloons
Papier-mache paste
Newspaper
Pin
Paint
Paintbrushes
Paper towels
Decorating materials (beads, wool, yarn, etc.)

What to do

1. Blow up enough balloons so every child in the class will have one.
2. Purchase or make (from flour and water) the papier-mache paste. Wallpaper paste works well.
3. Have the children cut or tear strips of newspaper, dip the strips in the paste and put them on the balloons, about 3/4 of the way around.
4. Let the balloons dry for 24 to 48 hours.
5. Have the children pop their balloons with a pin and cut the hardened papier-mache around the edges until it is shaped like a mask.
6. Explain that if children want to create faces, they can add a nose, lips, chin, etc., by taking paper towels, soaking them in papier-mache and molding features on the face (same as working with clay). Newspaper dipped in papier-mache combined with strips of dry paper towels will facilitate the drying process.
7. Tell the children they may decorate their masks with paint, beads, wool, yarn, etc.

More to do

Attach string or elastic to the back of the masks so the children can wear them. Display the masks by hanging them on the walls of the classroom. Have children write or dictate a story about the masks they just made.

—*Susan Buchalter-Katz, Lawrenceville, NJ*

Paper Bead Necklaces

4+

Children will improve their fine motor skills as they create their own bead necklaces.

Materials needed

Glue
Water
Brush
Newspapers
Round pencils
Tempera paints
Yarn

What to do

1. Thin the glue with a little water. From newspaper, tear long strips of uneven thickness (3/4" at top and bottom edges, and wider in the middle).
2. Have the children brush glue along one side of the entire strip.
3. Help them place the pencil at one end, slowly roll the strip onto the pencil, and securely fasten the end with a little glue.
4. When the beads are dry, have the children slide them off and make new ones.
5. Show the children how to paint the beads and string them onto pieces of yarn when they are dry to form necklaces.

More to do

Make necklaces for Mother's Day gifts or as costume jewelry for a dress-up corner.

—Manisha Segal, Burtonsville, MD

Picture Frame Weaving   5+

Children will learn something about the weaving process and will increase small muscle coordination.

Materials needed

Wooden 8" x 10" picture frame (glass and back removed)
Push pins
Hammer
Heavy yarn
Masking tape

What to do

1. Lightly hammer six push pins into each 8" side of the frame. Space the pins evenly (about 3/4" apart). Tape one end of the yarn under a top corner of the frame and weave the yarn back and forth around push pins to create the base threads (older children might be able to do this themselves). Tape the other end under a bottom corner of frame.
2. Cut the rest of the yarn into one-yard lengths and put tape on each end.
3. Beginning in one corner, children weave the one-yard lengths of yarn over and under the base threads.
4. In the next row, the process is reversed, going under then over.
5. New threads are started as necessary. Help the children weave in the loose ends and slip the mat off the push pins.

More to do

Demonstrate a small lap weaving loom. Show pictures of large manufacturing looms. Look at woven materials, rugs, etc.

Related book

Charlie Needs a Cloak by Tomie dePaola

—Rachel Stickfort, Newark, DE

CRAFTS

Dinosaur Eggs

3+

This fun-to-make craft activity will allow the children to experience that dinosaurs were reptiles and hatched from eggs.

Materials needed

White construction paper—9" x 12"
White posterboard
Small dinosaur cutouts or stickers
Popsicle or craft sticks
Paste or glue
Crayons

What to do

1. From posterboard, prepare patterns of a 7" x 4 1/2" egg for the children to trace.
2. Give each child a piece of white construction paper.
3. Have small dinosaurs cut out or use stickers on paper.
4. If you have not previously discussed dinosaurs hatching from eggs, read a story or show pictures and discuss.
5. Show the children how to trace around the egg patterns and cut them out. Help with this as needed. The children could color them, if they wish to do so.
6. After the paper egg is cut out, cut an x in the middle or draw one for the older child to cut.
7. Paste little dinosaurs on the end of the popsicle sticks.
8. Have the children push the dinosaur-on-a-stick through the hole as if hatching.

More to do

Have playdough available to make eggs and dinosaurs.

Related books and songs

Dynamic Dinosaur by Melody House Records

—Linda Yuska, Traer, IA

Dinosaur Footprints

3+

Children learn colors and how to make tracks and patterns by printing with a potato.

Materials needed

2 potatoes
Butcher paper
3 or 4 colors of paint
Knife
Small foam meat trays or pie tins

What to do

1. Cut a potato in half, draw a dinosaur footprint inside, and carve around it.

2. Tape a long strip of butcher paper onto the table and set out three or four bowls of paint in small foam meat trays or pie tins (red, yellow, blue, green).
3. Let the children pick up a potato printer and dip into colored paint. Help them scrape some off.
4. Press the printer onto the paper to make a dinosaur print.
5. Allow all the children to make dinosaur tracks on the paper.

More to do

Have children walk through colored paint and across the butcher paper. Compare footprints. Have them make tracks to match a beat which you play on a drum— faster: close together, slower: farther apart. Go to a museum and see dinosaur bones.

Related books and songs

The Popcorn Dragon by Jane Thayer
Dinosaurs by Gail Gibbons
Dinosaur Time by Peggy Parish

—*Darlene Hammond, Syracuse, NY*

Dinosaur Dance

3+

Children will develop gross motor skills and enjoy moving to the music.

Materials needed

Music with a dinosaur theme
Felt (various colors)
Masking tape

What to do

1. Make one set of dinosaur footprints for each child out of felt. Tape footprints (in pairs) around the movement area.
2. Have the children stand on the footprints.
3. Explain that when the music starts they should jump off of the footprints and move around like dinosaurs, but when the music stops they should jump back onto the closest set of footprints.
4. Play this game as long as the children enjoy it.

More to Do

Ask children: Can you stand on top of your footprints? Jump over them? Hop around them? Crawl across them? Sing

—*Linda Westman, Rockford, IL*

Dinosaur Toes and Toenails

3+

Children will develop small muscle coordination and enjoy a nutritious snack.

Materials needed

Whole wheat bread
Soft margarine in a tub
Peanut butter
Safety scissors with metal-edged blades
Butter knife
Toaster

What to do

1. Give each child one slice of bread.
2. Have children use safety scissors to cut several small triangles from the flat end of the bread so the slice resembles a dinosaur foot with toes.
3. Toast the bread.
4. Have children spread their "dinosaur toes" with butter or "mud" (peanut butter). The small triangles become toenails and are eaten plain.

More to do

Print with sponges shaped like dinosaur footprints and dipped in paint. Put paper bags over shoes, secure with rubber bands and stomp around as you listen to music. Sing the "Dinosaur Song" (to the tune of "Ten Little Indians"):

1 BIG, 2 BIG, 3 BIG dinosaurs,
4 BIG, 5 BIG, 6 BIG dinosaurs,
7 BIG, 8 BIG, 9 BIG dinosaurs,
10 BIG DINOSAURS!

Related book

Dinosaurs by Gail Gibbons

—*Jan Clark, Livonia, MI*

Dinosaur Collage

3+

This creative activity complements a learning unit on dinosaurs. Have the children become familiar with dinosaurs by reading stories, singing songs and doing fingerplays about dinosaurs. Show them dinosaur models, pictures and puppets. Then have them make a collage.

Materials needed

Wallpaper sample books
Large, heavy weight paper or tag board (18"x24")—one per child
White glue in jar lids
Popsicle sticks
Children's safety scissors
Newspaper to cover the table

What to do

1. To begin the dinosaur collage activity, cover a table with newspaper.
2. Place a jar lid with white glue and a popsicle stick on the table for each child (this activity works best with six children at one time).
3. Place the wallpaper sheets in the center of the table. Give each child a pair of scissors and a large sheet of heavy paper.
4. Explain to the children that they are going to make a dinosaur collage.
5. Have the children tear or cut the wallpaper into dinosaur shapes.
6. Glue the torn or cut wallpaper to the heavy sheet of paper.

More to do

The children can dictate a story about their dinosaur. The teacher can print this on the page with their collage. Ask the children to name their created dinosaurs "Wallpaperosaurus", "Daycaradon", etc.

Related books

Dinosaurs by Kathleen Daly

Related songs

"Dinosaur World"
"Our Dinosaur Friends"
"If I Had a Dinosaur"
"Rainbows, Stones and Dinosaur Bones"
"What Happened to the Dinosaurs"

—Sharon Conrad-Neustadter, Athens, WV

Dinosaur Hatch 3+

Children will enjoy this art project, where they make pretend dinosaur eggs with baby dinosaurs inside.

Materials needed

Round balloons—one per child
Newspaper strips
Wheat paste
Gray or white paint
Small plastic dinosaurs—one per child
Large pan for the wheat paste

What to do

1. Insert one small dinosaur into each balloon and inflate the balloons to medium size.
2. Tear newspaper into one-inch strips.
3. Prepare wheat paste by mixing 1 cup of flour and 3 cups of water. Stir the mixture over medium heat until it starts to boil. Remove from heat and let cool.
4. Demonstrate how to dip newspaper strips into wheat paste and wrap around the balloon. Encourage the children to completely cover their balloons with wet strips.
5. Let the covered balloons dry for 2 or 3 days.
6. Have children paint the covered balloons with white or grey paint so they resemble eggs.
7. When the paint is dry, prick each with a pin to pop the balloon.

8. Let the children crack their eggs to "hatch" the dinosaurs.

More to do

Encourage children to play with their toy dinosaurs in the block corner, where they can build caves and mountains for them.
Give children dinosaur-shaped cookie cutters and playdough.

Related books

Dinosaur Eggs by Francis Mosley
Dinosaurs, Dinosaurs by Byron Barton
Dinosaurs by Gail Gibbons
The Day of the Dinosaur by Stan and Jan Berenstain

—Karen Arrington, Fort Worth, TX

Dinosaur Dig   4+

Children dig for dinosaur puzzle pieces and learn to make predictions about the whole from examining the pieces.

Materials needed

Large pan or tub
Enough rice enough to fill the pan or tub 3/4 full
Dinosaur puzzle—with at least 8 pieces

What to do

1. Fill tub or pan with rice and bury puzzle pieces in the rice.
2. Speak with class about archaeology, and how we have discovered what dinosaurs looked like. Then, one at a time, let children dig for the dinosaur pieces.
3. As each piece is uncovered, encourage the child to try to fit them together and make a prediction about which dinosaur it is.
4. After all pieces are uncovered, have the child assemble the puzzle with your help as needed.
5. Ask the child to name the dinosaur.
6. The child then hides the puzzle pieces in the rice for the next child.

More to do

Hide a different dinosaur each day. You could also hide pieces of a puzzle, and leave some missing. Let all the children guess the dinosaur and then put the missing pieces onto the puzzle and see which guesses were correct.

—Candi Lavender, Winston-Salem, NC

Dinosaur Dip

4+

Once the children have learned that most dinosaurs ate plants, they'll want to be plant eaters, too. In this activity, they can eat their plants (carrots, celery, broccoli, etc.) with Dinosaur Dip they create by following sequential directions.

Materials needed

Paper cup—one per child
Tongue depressor—one per child
Two metal kitchen spoons
Cottage cheese, low fat
Sour cream, reduced fat
Herbal seasoning
Carrot sticks, celery sticks, and/or other raw vegetable sticks
Step-by-step picture recipe cards—see recipe below

What to do

1. Set up a work area, perhaps a long table divided into work stations by strips of colored masking tape.
2. Place necessary supplies at each work station along with a recipe card showing one step of the process as outlined below:

> Wash hands. *(picture of hands and water)*
> Take a paper cup. *(picture of cup)*
> Place one spoonful of cottage cheese in cup.
> *(picture of one spoon and cottage cheese)*
> Place one spoonful of sour cream in cup.
> *(picture of one spoon and sour cream)*
> Sprinkle herbs in cup. *(picture of shaker bottle)*
> Using tongue depressor, stir well. *(picture of cup with stick, stirring motion indicated by an arrow)*
> Eat with plants. *(picture of carrots and celery)*

3. Tell the children that by following the picture recipe cards they will each have a chance to make their own Dinosaur Dip. Give each child a chance to visit the recipe stations.

More to do

Scientists can tell what dinosaurs ate by their teeth. Plant-eating dinosaurs had flat grinding teeth, but flesh-eating dinosaurs had long, sharp, pointy teeth for tearing. Discuss the types of foods that humans eat, animal and plant. Bring a model of human teeth. Examine the teeth and observe that people have both grinding teeth (molars) and biting teeth (incisors).

Related book

Dinosaurs by Gail Gibbons

—Jan Clark, Livonia, MI

Dinosaur Bookmaking

4+

Children will develop their imaginations and language skills, as well as exercise fine motor skills.

Materials needed

Construction paper—11" x 18"
Markers/crayons
Notebook rings
Hole puncher
If the Dinosaurs Came Back by Bernard Most

What to do

1. Read *If the Dinosaurs Came Back*, a book about a little boy's dream of having his own dinosaur and all the great things they could do together.
2. Ask the children what they would like to do if the dinosaurs came back today.
3. Give the children paper and markers and ask them to draw a picture of something they would do with a pet dinosaur.
4. Go around and ask each child to tell you something about her drawing and write a few lines on the paper.
5. Tell the children you are going to make a book from their drawings. Ask for volunteers to draw front and back covers and make a title page with large, easy-to-read letters.
6. Punch holes in the paper and fasten with notebook rings.
7. Share the book with the class and watch the children's faces brighten as their own pages are read and displayed.

More to do

Set up a rotation so that all the children have a chance to take the book home and share it with their families.

—Linda Westman, Rockford, IL

Dinosaur Hunt

4+

Children learn dinosaur names and facts.

Materials needed

Pictures of dinosaurs mounted on construction paper
Small plastic models of dinosaurs, one per child
Book containing factual information on several dinosaurs

What to do

1. Write a series of clues for the dinosaur hunt (see samples below).
2. Place the pictures and directions throughout your building as suggested by pre-written clues.
3. Hide the small plastic dinosaurs in your room or playroom.
4. Have the first clue slipped under the classroom door or pretend to find it in your room. Follow the clue to find the cut-out (Brontosaurus). Talk about it and read a poem or short passage from a book. On or near the (Brontosaurus), find and read the second clue.
5. Proceed as above to the final clue.

6. Go to your room and place the dinosaur pictures you've found on the floor. Hunt for the plastic dinosaurs (one per child) and match the models to the pictures.

Sample clues

Message slipped under the door:

If we really want to find a really big dinosaur
Let's take a look at (Teacher's name)'s door.

Find Brontosaurus and clue #1:
On our science table if we're in luck.

We'll find a dinosaur with a mouth like a duck.
Find Trachodon and clue #2:

Ankylosauruses had very hard backs.
Maybe one is hiding in our railroad tracks.

Find Ankylosaurus and clue #3:
A Stegosaurus is a funny dinosaur.

Can we find him on the bathroom door?
Find Stegosuarus and clue #4:

Triceratops is very strong.
Maybe he is hiding where our toys belong.

Find Triceratops and clue #5:
Where could Tyrannosaurus hide?

Maybe he wants a turn on the slide.
Find Tyrannosaurus and clue #6:

Did you know that Pterdactyls fly?
We had better look way up high.

Find Pterdactyl and clue #7:
Let's try to find a Dimetron.

He likes toys you can ride on.
Find Dimetron and clue #8:

Now let's see if we can catch.
One dinosaur and then make a match.

Related books

My Visit to the Dinosaurs by Aliki
Giant Dinosaurs by Erna Rowe
Dinosaurs by Peter Zallinger

—*Cary Peterson, Pittsburgh, PA*

Nameosaurus

4+

Children will use their knowledge of dinosaurs and their imagination to create a dinosaur named after themselves. For example, if the child's name is John, then the dinosaur name is Johnosaurus.

Materials needed

Paper
Crayons/markers

What to do

1. Discuss what the children know about dinosaurs. What did they look like? Which ate meat/plants? Which stayed near the water?
2. Have students think "If you could be a dinosaur, what would you look like? What would you do?" Discuss the answers.
3. Help each child to create a dinosaur name for themselves. Print this dinosaur name on each child's sheet of paper.
4. Have markers or crayons in containers ready for use and have each child draw their dinosaur and dictate a dinosaur story to go with their picture.

More to do

Make up a class dinosaur story and record it in a book. Have the children act out the story as the teacher reads it.

Related book

Tyrannosaurus Was a Beast by Jack Prelutsky

—Dianne M. Waggoner, Catawissa, PA

Big Foot Dinosaur   4+

Children compare the size of a young Tyrannosaurus's foot and a child's foot to begin to understand size comparisons of large and small.

Materials needed

Large newsprint or other paper on 3'-4' roll
2' x 3' pattern of Tyrannosaurus foot cut out of cardboard
Crayons

What to do

1. Cut paper into 3'-4' pieces.
2. Find a non-carpeted area or table big enough for papers.
3. Show the children a picture of a Tyrannosaurus Rex dinosaur or a plastic one if available.
4. Ask the children questions to describe the dinosaur (its size, how it moved, etc.)
5. Have the children look at their own feet. Ask them to compare their own foot to the dinosaur's foot. Whose foot is bigger?
6. Show the children the foot pattern of the dinosaur. Tell them scientists believe this is the size of a 3-4 year old Tyrannosaurus' foot.
7. Ask them to trace the pattern of the dinosaur foot onto paper and color it. (The side of a crayon works well for this.)
8. Trace the foot of each child next to the dinosaur foot. Ask the children to compare each footprint.

More to do

Cut several footprints out of brown wrapping paper and tape these to the floor. Ask the children to try to walk, leap, jump or run from print to print. Children could also follow the trail of prints pretending they are following fossil prints like a paleontologist.

Related poem

Apatosaurus, Stegasaurus, Tyrannosaurus too.
Three big dinosaurs with nothing to do.
They went to the river to get a drink and
Before they got back, they became extinct.

—Linda Yuska, Traer, IA

Fossil Hunt

This activity will help children understand fossils and the work of paleontologists.

Materials needed

Large bucket
Plaster of Paris
Water
Small paper cups
Vermiculite
Small plastic dinosaur fossils
Heavy-duty plastic spoons
Mallets
Wooden spoon

What to do

1.   Mix 1 part water, 1 part Plaster of Paris, and 1-1/2 parts vermiculite in a bucket. Pour a small amount in paper cups, one for each child. Add one plastic dinosaur fossil to each cup. Cover fossils with remaining mixture. (Do not pour mixture in drains.)
2.   Let the mixture dry for 1 or 2 days. If it dries too long, it will be too hard to carve.
3.   Peel the paper cup off the dried mixture.
4.   Discuss with the children how dinosaurs might have died. Talk about how we have learned about dinosaurs through their fossils and footprints.
5.   Tell the children that they are going to be paleontologists. Explain that paleontologists hunt for fossils to learn more about dinosaurs.
6.   Have children excavate their "rocks" to look for dinosaur fossils. They can carve with a spoon or use the mallet, when needed. Caution the children to be careful when they are close to their "fossil."

More to do

Create an excavation site in the sand table. Place clean chicken bones in the sand. Provide safety goggles and small brushes for cleaning. Let each child mold a volcano from clay. Add red tissue paper for lava. Make a papier maché volcano. Paint. Add vinegar and baking soda to cause an eruption.

Related books

What Happened to Patrick's Dinosaurs? by Carol Carrick
The Missing Dinosaur Bones by Stan and Jan Berenstein
Whatever Happened to the Dinosaurs? by Bernard Most
Fossils Tell of Long Ago by Aliki

—*Karen Arrington, Fort Worth, TX*

DINOSAURS

Bucky the Recycle Beaver

3+

The students will develop motor skills and an understanding of the need to recycle, while making a recycling bin for home.

Materials needed

9" x 12" white posterboard oak tag
Poster paint or markers
Pencils
Scissors
Glue
Empty one 1/2 gallon milk jugs (paper carton kind)
12" black pipe cleaners
Old newspapers (to cover tables)
Soda can (as demonstration model)
Paintbrushes (if you use poster paint)
Black 1 1/2" pom poms (optional)
Wiggle eyes (optional)

What to do

1. Discuss the need for recycling and how anyone can help.
2. Prepare an example of "Bucky the Recycle Beaver" for use as a demonstration model. Make some patterns of Bucky's face for the children to trace.
3. Have the children trace Bucky's face onto the white posterboard or oak tag (show example).
4. Have the children cut the face out. Talk about scissor safety.
5. Have them paint or use markers to color Bucky's face.
6. Have them cut the 12" black pipe cleaners (three each) in half.
7. Glue the pipe cleaners around Bucky's nose for whiskers.
8. Have them cut milk cartons in half from the bottom up, about 5"- 6" all the way around.
9. Have them take their cut milk cartons and, from the top down, cut two 3" cuts along one side (at the edges of the crease).
10. Have the children glue Bucky's face on the opposite side of the milk carton with the 3" cuts. The original milk carton "bottom" should now be on the top.
11. When dry they can be hung on a garbage can or recycle bin so when you can throw a soda can through Bucky's mouth.

More to do

Have the children make a chart to keep track of how many cans they recycle with Bucky. Have the children glue on the wiggle eyes and pom pom nose.

Related book

50 Simple Things Kids Can Do to Save the Earth by the Earthworks Group

—*Mike Krestar, South Fork, PA*

Our Trash

Children develop the ability to quantify, follow directions, engage in helpful tasks and use a variety of media for self-expression.

Materials needed

Too Much Garbage by Patricia Lauber
Recycling bins

What to do

1. Read the book aloud to the class. Ask the children what they think garbage is. List the answers and compare the differences.
2. Go outside and clean up the playground. Collect the trash and build your own "Mt. Trashmore" in your room. When completed, place appropriate materials into recycling bins.
3. Introduce the idea of reducing unnecessary packaging. Tell your students to re-use plastic containers and paper bags and boxes.

More to do

In order to cut down on unnecessary packaging, eat ice cream cones for a snack because you eat the ice cream and the packaging—the cone!

—*Lori Erickson, Harris, MN*

Oil Slick

Children will see the effect oil pollution has on an immediate environment.

Materials needed

Large tub
Beach objects such as sand, rocks and shells
Water
Used motor oil
Container for disposal of contaminated water
Small objects such as action figures, plastic animals, and marbles
Plastic garbage bag for clean up
Smocks
Rags

What to do

1. Talk to the children about oil pollution and show pictures of oil slicks. Try to find pictures of people cleaning wildlife that has been contaminated. Say that today they are going to make a pretend oil slick and show them the items you have gathered for the activity.
2. Put a large tub outside, in a place where children can easily reach it. Have the children build a "beach" inside the tub with the sand, rocks and shells. Add water.
3. Encourage the children to play at the beach.

4. Pour a little oil on the beach and tell the children that there has been an oil spill. Ask them to observe what the oil does to the beach and to the toys.

5. Have children try to clean up the beach and toys using the rags and clean water.

—*Rosalind Sandler-Sigman, Santa Rosa, CA*

The Balance of Nature

3+

Children will create a cooperative mobile with several life forms from an area of the ocean. As they do this, they will explore concepts of size, weight and position as they relate to the balance of the structure. The teacher will relate this to the balance found in the natural world, in which each element plays a critical role in the survival of others.

Materials needed

Posterboard in several colors
1 dowel (3/8 inch by 36 inches long)
Blue or black yarn
Markers or crayons
A wire coat hanger
Wire paper clips
Hole punch

What to do

1. Precut 10 ocean animals and plants from the posterboard. Be sure to include red seaweed for deep ocean waters, starfish of many legs, turtles and neon colored fish for coral reefs. To prepare the hanger for the mobile, cut two identical 36" x 4" strips of blue to represent the ocean surface. Scallop the top to look like waves. Tape the dowel to one blue piece to stabilize the mobile. Sandwich the coat hanger between the blue surface pieces and staple. Use a hole punch to put holes every two inches in the bottom of the blue piece.

2. Have the children decorate the shapes for the mobile with marker. Both sides will need colors and patterns. Let each child punch a hole for hanging the shape so it will appear to be swimming or growing. This is a good opportunity for the teacher to introduce the patterned neon colors of reef fish, the shapes of fast swimmers, the odd bodies that accompany life in deep water.

3. Tie each shape to a length of yarn. Vary the lengths to correspond to how near the surface the animal or plant might live. Tie the other end of the yarn to an opened paper clip. Set them aside until circle time.

4. Tell the children that everything that is in nature is important. The ocean has a balance of nature with just enough plants, just enough hunters, just enough animals that live on the bottom, just enough swimmers, etc. Ask a child to stand up and demonstrate how to balance with her arms straight out. Put a heavy shell or piece of coral in one hand. Can she still hold both arms level? Point out that the natural balance can be changed by adding or taking away something.

5. Help a child suspend the hanger so that the blue surface is level. Have the children hang the posterboard life forms on the figure so that it remains as level as possible. Discuss why children alternate sides as they hang their shapes on the balance.

6. If necessary, add a small fish to one side or the other to make it completely level and hang the finished mobile in the math area near your classroom balance scale.

—*Caroline Owens, Harrisburg, PA*

Litter: An Eyesore 3+

Children will learn that they can make a positive difference in our environment by participating in a clean-up campaign. This campaign will include actual litter clean-up and designing an anti-litter poster. Through this activity children will also learn the skills needed for teamwork and group participation, such as taking turns, listening to different points of view and compromising.

Materials needed

Contact paper
Posterboard
Marker
Tape or push pins
Litter bags
A littered area
Optional: Polaroid camera and additional litter

What to do

1. Peel back the contact paper and hang it near a littered area using tape or push pins, sticky side out. To emphasize the point, you may wish to add more litter to the area.
2. Hold a group discussion on litter and the effects it has on us and our environment, such as the smell, it's an eyesore, it causes injuries and it hurts the wild life. Explain and discuss the function of waste baskets, garbage cans and litter bags.
3. Explain the activity. Tell the children to gather up the litter in the trash bags and to place a sample of the litter they found on the contact paper.
4. After the litter is picked up, view the area and discuss the difference.
5. Using the contact paper covered with letter, ask the children to help you design an the anti-litter poster. Glue or tape the contact paper on the posterboard and write down the anti-litter message the children agree on.
6. Hang the poster in your room.

More to do

Take before and after pictures of the littered area for comparison. Develop a recycling program.

—Lorene Miller, Fremont, CA

Recycling 4+

This activity will help the children gain a better understanding of recycling and its importance for better living.

Materials needed

Posterboard
Pictures of things that can be recycled—plastic, paper, glass, cans—or actual things
Paste
Tape

What to do

1. On the posterboard, draw the recycling symbol in the middle.
2. Have the children find and bring in pictures/items from home.
3. Glue or tape them onto the posterboard.

More to do

Visit a recycling center. Put out bins in the classroom to separate trash. (Put pictures on the bins to make separating easy.) Organize a recycling hunt on the school grounds or in the neighborhood.

—Lauren O'Neill/Ann O'Donnell, Abington, PA

Ocean Mural   4+

This activity helps children to understand and visualize the wide variety of living things in the ocean.

Materials needed

Large mural paper
White and blue tempera paint
Light colored construction paper
Patterns or stencils of ocean life
Watercolors
Markers
Crayons
Glue
Glitter
Yarn
Tissue paper

What to do

1. Set up a floor area to paint the ocean.
2. Set up areas to make ocean life.
3. Move furniture and cover floor with newspaper.
4. Lay out mural paper.
5. Mix various shades of blue and white paint in small containers.
6. Divide class into small groups and give each group a section of the ocean to paint.
7. Have one group paint waves near the top of the mural paper.
8. Let the ocean dry over night.
9. Hang the ocean on the wall.
10. Put out patterns or stencils of whale, octopus, dolphin, shark, various size and shape fish. You can also make other patterns that children request such as ray, eel, etc.
11. Have the children trace and cut out in one area.
12. Then have children proceed to decorating area to paint, use markers, glitter, etc. Encourage the children to be creative.
13. Let everything dry completely.
14. Let the children decide where to put their creations in the ocean.

More to do

Add seashells that have been traced and decorated, or make them by gluing styrofoam packing pieces to the ocean. Add some torn paper plants to the ocean.

Related books

What's Under the Ocean by Janet Craig
Sea Life by Educational Insights
Whale and Dolphin by Vincent Serventy

—Jennie A. Harrington, Barrington, IL

Recycled Paper Bowls

4+

Children will learn to re-use paper that would otherwise be thrown away to create an artistic and useful object.

Materials needed

Collage box scraps that would normally be thrown away, torn into tiny pieces
Flour
Water
Plastic food wrap
Tape
Bowls (plastic or pottery, smaller bowls are better)
Clear craft glaze

What to do

1. Tear collage scraps into tiny pieces. Approximately two cups of torn paper are needed for each child's bowl.
2. Mix flour and water to form thick liquid.
3. Cover bottom of bowl with plastic food wrap and tape down so the wrap does not come off. This will act as a mold for your project.
4. Take a handful of the scraps and dampen with flour and water mixture (as in paper mache).
5. Press wet paper onto sides of upside down wrap-covered bowl.
6. Continue until bottom and sides of bowl are covered with wet paper. Go approximately 3-4 inches up the sides of the bowl.
7. Allow it to dry, at least 24 hours.
8. Remove the tape from the plastic wrap and pull paper bowl off of plastic bowl.
9. Allow paper bowl to dry on the inside.
10. Teacher can then spray bowls with a clear craft glaze.
11. The result is a beautiful, sturdy, multicolored bowl.

More to do

This multi-colored paper mache could be used for other projects where a form is used.

Related books

50 Simple Things Kids Can Do to Save the Earth by John Javna
A Kid's Guide to How to Save the Planet by Billy Goodman
The Learning Works Earth Book for Kids by Linda Schwartz

—Gail Garfield, St. Louis, MO

ENVIRONMENT

Composting 4+

Children develop the ability to form conclusions from guessing and observation.

Materials needed

Plastic packaging
Lettuce leaves
One shovel
One apple core
Styrofoam pieces
Paper and pencil
The Compost Heap by Harlow Rockwell

What to do

1. If necessary, get permission to dig four holes in the ground. Make sure the secured place is a safe and isolated one.
2. Read the book aloud to the class.
3. Ask your students how long they think it would take for a lettuce leaf, an apple core, a piece of styrofoam and a piece of plastic packaging to decompose. Write down their responses.
4. To add excitement to this activity, go outside and dig four holes in the ground. Drop a lettuce leaf in one hole, a piece of plastic packaging in another, an apple core in the third and a piece of styrofoam in the fourth. Fill the holes with dirt and mark the holes.
5. In one month dig up the four items and compare and contrast the students' guesses with the actual results.
6. Make a compost pile from scraps used in your classroom (apple peelings, banana peels). In the springtime, use the compost to grow flowers or vegetables.

—Lori Erickson, Harris, MN

Great Clean-Up 4+

Children learn to manipulate materials and ideas for unique, helpful tasks. They also reproduce models or demonstrations and seek information by observing, questioning and exploring available materials.

Materials needed

Permission slips for field trip
Glass bottles
Acrylic spray
Tissue paper
Glue
Invitations
It Zwibble and the Greatest Cleanup Ever Created by WereRoss and WerEnko

What to do

1. Get permission from your school to have a "garage sale." It will also be helpful to ask for parents to volunteer their help at the sale. Ask early!
2. Read the book aloud to the children.
3. Adopt a park and clean it up. Invite the children's parents and have a picnic there.

4. Separate the trash found at the park and recycle what you can.
5. Create an "I don't know what to do with it" list of resalable materials from home.
6. After all materials are collected, sort out everything and have a garage sale. Invite parents, other school children, neighbors, etc.
7. With the money collected, buy recycling bins for the school.
8. With the glass bottles found at the park or brought in from home, make vases by using paper scraps.

Directions:
Wash the bottles thoroughly.
Paint glue on bottles.
Place tissue paper on bottles.
Let them dry.
Spray with acrylic spray.
Add water and flowers, if desired.

The children could sell these vases at the garage sale or give them as presents.

—Lori Erickson, Harris, MN

Green Tree

5+

Children learn the value of saving and reusing things and keeping the environment clean for all life.

Materials needed

Large sheets of brown construction paper
Smaller sheets of green or red, orange and yellow construction paper

What to do

1. Cut out a large tree with many branches from brown paper and display it on a bulletin board. Make up a lot of leaves. If it is spring, make the leaves from green construction paper. If it is fall, use red, orange and yellow paper.
2. Throughout the month, have the children do things to "Be Kind to the Earth," such as picking up paper outside, putting scraps in the scrap box to reuse or planting seeds. Write each activity on a leaf and display it on one of the tree's branches.
3. Make sure you find something for each child.
4. As the children become more aware of ecology, the tree will grow.

More to do

Do group environmental activities like planting flowers or a small tree or collecting plastic to recycle. Children love these activities and can't wait to put up another leaf on the "Green Tree."

Related book

Lorax by Dr. Seuss

—Janice Bodenstedt, Jackson, MI

ENVIRONMENT

Leaf Coloring

2+

This activity teaches color mixing.

Materials needed

Paper towels cut out in leaf shapes
Food coloring
Water
Bowls and wax paper

What to do

1. Trace leaf shapes on paper towels and then cut them out.
2. Fill each bowl with water.
3. Together add food coloring to the water until you get the color you want.
4. Hand each child 2-3 pre-cut leaves. Give each of them a piece of wax paper.
5. Each child can choose which colors to dip their leaves in. Leaves can be dipped in more than one color so the colors run together to form new colors.
6. Lay wet leaves on wax paper to dry.
7. Leaves can be mounted on construction paper or hung just as they are.

More to do

Using a large wall and starting in the summer you can put up a large tree and attach the leaves to the branches. As the seasons change, you can change the leaves. During Fall—some can fall to the ground; in Winter—all leaves can fall and become covered with snow; when it is Spring—snow can be removed and leaves can gradually be replaced back on the tree branches.

Related books

Little Blue and Little Yellow by Leo Lionni
Chicken Soup With Rice by Maurice Sendak

Related song

"Here Comes Winter"

—*Tammy Duehr, Guilford, CT*

Leaf Crunch

2+

This sensory experience helps the children exercise fine motor skills.

Materials needed

Empty water table
Lots of fall leaves (somewhat dry)

What to do

1. Collect leaves.
2. Pour leaves in empty water table.
3. Allow the children to scrunch up the leaves with their hands.

More to do

Children can sprinkle the crunched leaves on a cardboard leaf shape with glue to make a leaf mosaic. Allow children to walk on the leaves with their shoes off by putting leaves in a large box on the floor. Have them crawl, roll or safely jump in the leaves.

—Susan Westby, Palm Bay, FL

Apple Picking

2+

The children will learn to discriminate between large and small.

Materials needed

Construction paper
Twelve velcro (1") pieces
Scissors
Glue
Two baskets
Posterboard (optional)

What to do

1. Make a tree (approximately 16" x 20") out of construction paper or draw a tree on posterboard, then mount the tree on a bulletin board or on the wall at children's eye level. Glue velcro pieces to branches.
2. Cut out six large and six small paper apples from construction paper. Glue other half of velcro pieces to apples.
3. Place big and small labels on the two baskets (these might be paper apples with words "big" and "small" printed on them).
4. Randomly place large and small apples on tree branches and put the labeled fruit baskets underneath the tree.
5. Explain to the children that apples come in different sizes. Show them the two baskets and the labels on each.
6. Tell the children that they are to "pick" the apples off the tree and put them in the correct baskets according to size.

More to do

Bring out the building blocks and have children separate them into piles according to size.

Related books

Who Stole the Apples? by S. Heuck

—Renee Kapusniak, Webster, NY

Leaves Are Falling Down

3+

After a walk to see the falling leaves, come indoors and turn hand and arm tracings into a colorful autumn painting! The children will improve their fine motor skills and work with colors in this creative activity.

Materials needed

Easel-size manila paper, one sheet per child
Brown paint, marker or crayon
Paintbrushes
Brown, red, orange, yellow, deep red paint—paint should be thick
Meat trays or other flat pans to hold paint
Cloths or paper towels for wiping fingers

What to do

1. On a sheet of manila paper, trace the child's hands and arms as shown. Extend the fingers upwards to create the tree branches (see figure 1).
2. Have the children paint or color the tree's trunk and branches brown (see figure 2).
3. Have the children dip one fingertip at a time in the paint and then press it all over the paper, especially on the ground (see figure 3).
4. Keep cloths ready to wipe painted fingers.

More to do

Discuss the fall colors of trees, leaves, etc. Look at the trees when all of the leaves have fallen. What part(s) of our bodies does it remind you of? Talk about the uniqueness of our fingerprints. You may want to omit the orange paint and let the children experiment mixing the red and yellow color to make orange.

—*Jyoti Joshi, Framingham, MA*

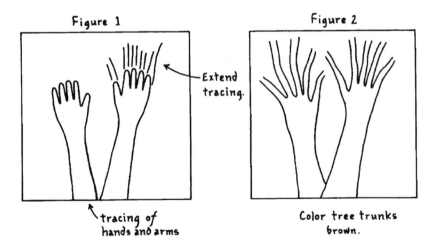

Figure 1

Extend tracing.

tracing of hands and arms

Figure 2

Color tree trunks brown.

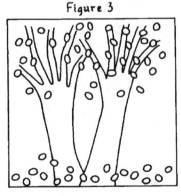

Figure 3

Add finger prints for colored leaves.

Autumn Leaves

Children will learn about autumn and the changes it brings while improving their memorization and motor skills.

Materials needed

Legal-size pieces of plain white paper
Posterboard cut into many different leaf shapes
Scribble cookies (a melted crayon mixture reshaped into half circles)

What to do

1. Introduce the song "Autumn Leaves" (tune of "London Bridge"), and its accompanying movements:

   Autumn leaves are falling down, falling down, falling down. (wiggle fingers, move hands high-to-low)
   Autumn leaves are falling down, red, yellow and brown. (wiggle fingers, move hands high-to-low)
   Rake them up into a pile, into a pile, into a pile. (pretend to rake leaves)
   Rake them up into a pile. Watch me jump inside. (drop to floor)
   Shiny leaves to toss up high, toss up high, toss up high. (pretend to toss leaves)
   Shiny leaves to toss up high to the sky. (pretend to brush leaves from clothes and hair)

2. Sing the song slowly, then repeat, using the gestures, encouraging the children to sing along.
3. Each child may select four or five leaf shapes of their choice. Each child is given one piece of legal-size white paper. Explain they are to cover their leaf shapes with the paper. Demonstrate for the children how to rub the flat edge of a scribble cookie against the paper. The children create their own rubbings.

More to do

Experiment with other rubbing crafts such as tree bark, stone carvings or brick.

—*Christina Chilcote, New Freedom, PA*

Leaf Bookmark

Children develop an awareness of nature and improve fine motor skills.

Materials needed

Construction paper
Contact paper
Leaves
Scissors

What to do

1. Cut construction paper into strips 3" wide and 6" to 8" long.
2. Have the children collect leaves on a nature walk.
3. Place the contact paper on the table sticky side up.
4. Have the children arrange the leaves on the contact paper.
5. Have them choose a strip of construction paper to lay over the leaves.
6. Cut around the edges of the construction paper.
7. The bookmark is ready for use.

More to do

You can use the same process to make place-mats to be used at home or in the classroom.

—*Sandra C. Scott, Vancouver, WA*

Apple Tasting Party   3+

Children will use the sense of taste to describe and appreciate the characteristics of food products made with apples.

Materials needed

Red, green and yellow apples
Samples of apple products: applesauce, apple juice, baked apple, apple pie, apple cake, apple butter
Bread

What to do

1. Begin a discussion on apples and how they grow on trees. Identify the different types of apples and discuss how apples can be used to make other things.
2. Show them the variety of apples and the foods that can be made from apples.
3. Allow each child to have a taste of all the items.

More to do

Flannel board activity—count the apples on the tree. Have the children vote for their favorite kind of apples and make a graph of the responses.

Related books

Ten Apples up on Top by Theo LeSieg

Related song

"Way Up High in the Apple Tree"

—Sandra Acuna, San Antonio, TX

Going Nuts   3+

Children learn about a variety of nuts, develop fine motor skills and learn sorting technique.

Materials needed

A variety of nuts
Variety of nutcrackers or small wooden hammers
Small dish tub
Large bowl
Two small bowls or containers

What to do

1. Fill a small dish tub or large bowl with different types of nutcrackers and nuts.
2. Provide two smaller containers for the children to sort the nut meat and shells.
3. Show the children the uses of the various nutcrackers, how to crack a pecan by squeezing it against another, and how to shell peanuts using your hands.
4. Have the children separate the nut meat from the shells.

5. The following day, fill recloseable bags with the nut meat and have the children crush the nuts with their hands or small wooden hammers. Add the nut meat to a food recipe, such as a fruit bread or muffins.

6. The shells can be glued to paper as a collage or used with clay or playdough for texture.

More to do

If possible, observe squirrels' behavior with nuts. Place some nuts near a tree visible from the classroom and check to see if squirrels will find the treat. Use nuts in counting activities, for example place the number of nuts in each container with the corresponding numeral.

Related books

Squirrels by Brian Wildsmith
The Nutcracker by Hans Christian Anderson

Related song

"Paw Paw Patch"

—Cindi Catlin, San Antonio, TX

Nut Sorting

3+

Children sort and make sets, count and develop language skills.

Materials needed

Assortment of nuts (peanuts, walnuts, chestnuts, coconuts, brazil nuts, almonds, hazelnuts, macadamia nuts) preferably in their shells
Sorting tray with many compartments, or as many bowls as their are types of nuts

What to do

1. Tell the children the name of each type of nut.
2. Ask the children to name the nuts.
3. Put one of each nut in a bowl.
4. Ask the children where the remaining nuts belong.
5. The children sort the rest of the nuts.

More to do

Bring a nutcracker to open the nuts. Eat the nuts during snack time.

Related book

Nutcracker by Hans Christian Anderson

—Nina Marie Sartori-NG, Hong Kong

Leaf Prints

4+

Children will learn the various shapes and colors of leaves.

Materials needed

Three to four different fall leaves (before they turn brittle)
Red, yellow, green and orange paint
Paintbrushes (for each paint)
11" x 9" black construction paper

What to do

1. Mix the four colors of tempera paint.
2. Take the children outside to collect the leaves they will use. They should collect about five each. If there are no trees close to your center, the children can make this a home assignment or the teacher can supply them.
3. Start the activity with a brief talk leaves, how they bud, grow, turn colors and fall from the tree.
4. Once you're back inside, lay newspaper over your table and lay out paints. Since this is a messy activity, wear aprons. Have two children bring their leaves to the table. Each child picks one to paint any way they want using all colors and covering the entire leaf. Then they take the leaf and turn it paint-side down on the large black construction paper. Continue with all of their five leaves, until the construction paper is full of fall colors!

More to do

Make leaf rubbings by putting a piece of paper over a leaf and rubbing with a crayon.

—Deborah A. Cole, Ashtabula, OH

Nature Collage

4+

Take your children on a nature walk in the fall. Allow them to collect natural objects as they go along, and return to the classroom to make a fall collage or mobile from the gathered items.

Materials needed

Construction paper (large size, fall colors)
Non-toxic glue or tacky glue
Small brown paper lunch sacks, baskets or canvas bags the children bring from home
Nature items (found on nature walk)

What to do

1. Obtain the necessary permission for the nature walk in advance. Before you leave the classroom, be sure that each child has a basket or bag for berries, pods, nuts, leaves, stalks, rocks or whatever they discover.
2. As you walk along, point out the trees. Let the children touch the bark and talk about their observations. Is the bark rough or smooth? What color is it? What else do you notice about it?
3. Back in the classroom, have each child arrange and glue their nature items on the construction paper. Children may also draw any other items they remember.
4. Allow glue to dry completely, and display finished pictures.

More to do

Take paper and crayons on the nature walk and have the children do bark rubbings for different trees as the basis for their nature collage. Do this exercise in the spring, or at the beach, or in some other setting. The treasures that are found will be different, and so will the pictures. Instead of making a collage or picture with the found objects, make them into a mobile. Have one small branch available for each child, and tie or thread the nature items onto the branch with string or a needle and thread.

Related books

The Fall of Freddie the Leaf by Leo Buscaglia
The Leaves of Autumn by Ellen M. Dolan
Red Leaf, Yellow Leaf by Lois Ehlert

—*Mary Rozum Anderson, Vermillion, SD*

Flower Bulb Sorting 4+

This is an entertaining, multifaceted activity for the fall. The children will have fun sorting the bulbs by size, matching them with pictures and planting them in a garden or outdoor containers. There's also the wonder of watching them bloom in the spring!

Materials needed

Three or more different-sized sets of spring flower bulbs. For example, crocus, tulip and daffodil bulbs. These may be purchased late summer or early fall.
Laminated pictures of different bulbs which may also show their flowers. Pictures may be cut from old flower magazines, or garden centers may give them to you free.

What to do

1. Place all the bulbs in a pile.
2. Have the children sort the bulbs according to size.
3. Add the different pictures of the bulbs.
4. Have the children match the correct bulb to the appropriate picture. If your pictures show only the flowers (and not the bulbs) the match can be made by size. For example, the crocus bulbs are small and would go with the picture of the small flower. The tulip bulbs are medium in size and would be placed by the picture of a medium-sized flower. The daffodil bulbs are large and would be placed by the picture with a large flower.
5. After your children have had lots of time to practice sorting the bulbs and matching bulbs and pictures, help them plant the bulbs outdoors in a garden or in large containers. Follow the directions for planting you receive when you purchase them.

More to do

The children may also learn the names of the flower bulbs. They may watch the flowers come up in the early spring and bring the pictures outside to compare the pictures to the actual flower.

Related books

Planting a Rainbow by Lois Ehlert

—*Donna M. Banas, Palos Hills, IL*

Fall Poem

5+

Children will become familiar with words and events relating to the fall season.

Materials needed

Language experience paper
Crayons
Metal fasteners
Hole puncher
Several fall poems

What to do

1. Ahead of time, write the following poem on the paper, one line to a page. Punch holes and insert fasteners to make a book.
"Fall Is..." by Dianne M. Waggoner

> *Fall is leaves that fall to the ground.*
> *Fall is pumpkins all around.*
> *Fall is a chilliness in the air.*
> *Fall is coats and sweaters to wear.*
> *Fall is for Halloween coming soon.*
> *Fall is for the huge harvest moon.*
> *Fall is gradually shorter days.*
> *Fall is a squirrel gathering nuts as he plays.*
> *Fall is a lot of things for you and me.*
> *Fall is a beautiful season to see.*

2. Read aloud other poems about the fall. ("Fall" by Aileen Fisher and "Autumn Woods" by James S. Tippett work well.)
3. Discuss the kinds of things that happen during the fall.
4. Tell the children that you have another poem about fall and have written it in a book. Read the poem, "Fall is...".
5. Ask the children what is missing from the book. When they answer "the pictures," tell them they are right and ask for help.
6. Take the book apart and ask for ten volunteers. Give each of the volunteers a page and, if necessary, read the sentence on the page. Tell the children to draw pictures that relate to their sentences. When everyone is finished, put the book back together.
7. Gather the class and reread the poem, holding up each page so everyone can see the picture. Invite the children to read along with you or supply the rhyming word at the end of each line.

More to do

Let students dictate their own "Fall is..." poem or story and then illustrate it. Collect fall leaves and glue them on the cover as a collage.

—*Dianne M. Waggoner, Catawissa, PA*

Just Mom and Me

Children develop storytelling, memory and sequencing skills.

Materials needed

Story "Just Mom and Me" (included)
Flannel board
Felt in a variety of colors: light blue, brown, yellow, red, black, etc.
Yellow yarn
Cool melt glue gun
Ribbon
Scissors
Fabric paint in blue, brown, and red
Posterboard
Colored pencils

What to do

1. Trace the patterns of the characters from standard pattern books onto felt. Make the blanket from light blue, the picnic basket from tan.
2. Cut out all pieces from the felt.
3. Make hair for Mother and Mary Alice. Use a glue gun to attach hair to the flannel board pieces.
4. Cut clothes from other colors of felt. Attach clothes to characters using the glue gun.
5. Add details to the pieces using fabric paints.
6. Make the book from felt. Use colored pencils to draw the cover of the book on posterboard. Glue the posterboard to the felt to finish the story book.
7. Allow all pieces to dry overnight.
8. At circle time, tell the story, placing the flannel pieces on the board as they are introduced in the story.
9. Make the flannel board and the pieces available during free time.

"Just Mom and Me"

This is a story about a little girl named Mary Alice. Mary Alice lives with her mother, her grandmother and her baby brother, Jason. Mary Alice is three years old. She goes to preschool in the mornings. One day, Mary Alice did not want to go to school. At breakfast Mary Alice did not want to eat her pancakes. Mother asked, "What is wrong with you, sweetheart?" Mary Alice didn't say a word. She just sat there with her bottom lip sticking out, looking sad. Then she said, "I don't want to go to school today, mommy." So her mother asked her to drink her juice. Her mother went to the phone to call Mr. Hill, Mary Alice's preschool teacher. Mr. Hill said, "I think Mary Alice is feeling jealous over her baby brother. I think she feels you might love him best. She wants you all to herself." When she was off the phone, she told Mary Alice that they were going to have a together day, Just her and Mary Alice. "But who will take care of baby Jason?" Said Mary Alice. Her mother said that grandma was going to take care of her baby brother while they were gone.

Mary Alice and her mother went off to preschool. Mary Alice's mother was going to be a special helper today at her school. When they arrived at school, Mary Alice showed her mother the finger painting she made the week before, her favorite book and the housekeeping area that she liked so much. That day in preschool they made playdough. Mr. Hill read her favorite story about the three bears, they sang a song about five little monkeys, and they played dress-up, Mary Alice's favorite thing of all. Mary Alice pretended to be a mommy and take care of her baby. At snack time the children had milk and apple slices. Her mother sat at the table with all of Mary Alice's school friends and Mr. Hill. Mary Alice didn't mind that her mom did not sit next to her, because everyone knew that she was Mary Alice's mom.

After school, the two of them went to the park for their picnic. They had peanut butter and jelly sandwiches, juice and yogurt for dessert. They talked about all the fun things they did in school that morning. When Mary Alice and her mother went home, she ran into her room to get her favorite book. She sat down with her baby brother next to her and read the story of the "Goldilocks and the Three Bears" to him. Mary Alice told her mother that her brother was fun to play with. Later that afternoon, Mary Alice asked if she could give her brother his bottle. Mother smiled at the two of them. Mary Alice really did love her baby brother, and now she helps her mother a lot in caring for him.

More to do

Encourage the children to write their own story as a group through dictation.

Related books

All Kinds Of Families by Norma Simon
People In My Family by Bobbie Kalman
Messy Baby by Jan Omerod

—Cory McIntyre, Crystal Lake, IL

Family Banner   3+

The children will recognize different kinds of families.

Materials needed

1 sheet white construction paper 12x18 for each child (I roll it up in a rubber band to make it easier for child to take home)
1 sheet of duplicated directions for each child

What to do

1. Duplicate copies of these directions:
   Please help your child make a family banner.
   Write family name on top.
   Trace each family member's hand and write the name on or under it (Child can do all the tracing or family members can do their own)
   Decorate hands—use crayons, markers, stickers, photos—whatever the family wants.
2. Send home paper and directions.
3. As each child brings in banner, he points to each hand and tells who's in his family.
4. Notice who has biggest and smallest hands in each family.
5. Count how many people in each family.
6. Display the banners.

More to do

Draw a picture and dictate sentences telling what your family likes to do. Role play family activities in the housekeeping area.

Related books

Daddy Makes the Best Spaghetti by Anna Grossnickel Hines
Me Too by Mercer Mayer
All Kinds of Families by Norma Simon

—Judy Haase, Itasca, IL

Taking Care of Babies

Through this activity, children become familiar with the needs of babies and how parents take care of them. This can help children adjust to younger siblings and to satisfy their natural curiosity about babies.

Materials needed

Doll or stuffed animal with legs for each child: they should bring them from home
Tissues
Tape
Baby bottles and toys
Cloth scraps or old wash cloths, etc., for blankets, or kids can bring their own

What to do

1.   Notify parents that the children need to bring a doll or stuffed animal with legs to school with them. Children can also bring in a small blanket for this activity.
2.   Obtain materials to make "blankets" if necessary.
3.   In group, ask the children what little babies can do. Help clarify difference between the abilities of a toddler, an infant and a newborn.
4.   Show the children how to put a diaper on a baby. Use the tissues and tape.
5.   Demonstrate playing with the baby. Help the children select an appropriate toy from those available and show it to the baby. Let the baby "grab" it and "chew" it if appropriate. (No small choking toys should be allowed).
6.   Have the children imitate a baby crying.
7.   Have the children rock and hug and pat their babies and make funny faces.
8.   Discuss feeding the baby. Explain that some children are fed milk from the mother's breast and others are fed by a bottle. Have the children pretend to feed the babies. Let them burp their babies.
9.   Teach the children to swaddle their babies.
10. All together sing a nice lullaby, such as "Rock a Bye, Baby."

More to do

Set up a role-playing area for taking care of babies. Let the children share experiences about baby siblings or bring in their own baby pictures. Have a hospital nursery nurse or nurse-midwife come and talk about newborn babies.

—*Dixie Havlak, Olympia, WA*

Where We Live

Children will learn that there are many different types of homes.

Materials needed

Magazines with plenty of pictures of homes
Glue
Scissors
Construction paper

What to do

1.   Explain to children that they are going on a house hunt.

2. Divide the children into small groups and allow them to cut pictures of homes out of magazines.

3. Have the children glue these pictures on the construction paper to form a collage.

More to do

Go for a walk to look at various houses and discuss similarities and differences. If possible, visit a construction site to see a house being built.

Related song

Peter hammers with one hammer, one hammer, one hammer
Peter hammers with one hammer
All day long.
(Substitute children's names for Peter. Increase the number of hammers to 2, 3, 4 and 5.
Can you think of a way to hammer with 6 hammers?)
At the end sing:
Peter's very tired now, tired now, tired now
Peter's very tired now
Sshh, let's sleep. (children pretend to sleep)

Related books

A House Is a House for Me by Mary Hoberman
People by Peter Spier
Building a House by Byron Barton
Up Goes the Skyscraper by Gail Gibbons

—Linda Ford, Fremont, CA

Say "I Love You" With Coupons

3+

Children learn that a loving, helpful child is greater than any gift.

Materials needed

Crayons
Coupon booklet for each child

What to do

1. During circle time, have children brainstorm about ways to help their family.

2. Write down ideas for coupons and select those you wish to use. Try offers like, "I will take you for a walk," "I will rub your back," "I will clean my dresser," or "I will play with baby brother/sister."

3. Make copies of the coupons (three coupons per page work nicely) for each child, cut apart, assemble them into booklets and staple.

4. Read each page with the children.

5. Have the children color and decorate each page.

6. The children can take them home to give for Christmas or Valentine's Day gifts!

—Cathy Chenoweth, Columbia, MO

Potato Print Family

Each child will make a picture of their family after completing this fun activity.

Materials needed

Potatoes of various sizes
Knife
Paint
Tray
Large construction paper
Markers

What to do

1. Cut potatoes in half, pour paint in a tray and prepare a list of each child's family members.
2. Write the name of the child's family at the top of the paper.
3. Each child will choose the size potato he wants to use to print each member of the family on his paper. Have the child dip the cut end of the potato in the paint and then press it on their paper.
4. The teacher writes the name of the family member under each potato print.
5. Let the prints dry.
6. Let each child draw facial features, hair, arms, legs or whatever he wishes to complete each family member.

More to do

Make a bulletin board display of all the family portraits. Let each child tell you something his family likes to do together. Print the sentence on their family picture.

Related song

"My Family" (to the tune of "The Muffin Man")

I am in a family
Family, family.
I am in a family
And it's lots of fun.
My family likes to go to the beach
Go to the beach, go to the beach.
My family likes to go to the beach
And it's lots of fun!

(Have the children tell you what their family likes to do, and substitute those actions in the song)

—*Mimi Pearson, Trenton, NJ*

FAMILIES

My Clothespin Doll

4+

After hearing their teacher tell this original story, the children will have the opportunity to make a clothespin doll of their very own. Be prepared with extra materials—they will probably want to make more than one!

Materials needed

Clothespins (not the spring kind) at least one for each child
Yarn or corn silk
Fabric scraps, approximately 6" square (draw a 3" circle with a permanent marker on each)
Pipe cleaners
Fine point markers, red, blue or black
White glue or glue sticks
Scissors
A copy of the story "My Clothespin Doll" (included)

What to do

1. Learn the story of "My Clothespin Doll."
2. Gather the children on the circle time rug and tell them the story. Have a basket ready with all the materials you need to make a clothespin doll and make one in front of the children as you tell the story or use a clothespin doll you have made the day before as a prop.
3. After the story, tell the children they can make a doll of their own.
4. Have the materials set out on a table or nearby shelf.
5. Have the children wrap the pipe cleaner around the neck of the clothespin to make the arms. Start at the front, wrap it around to the back, twist it around itself, and bring the two arms back around to the front again.
6. Have them draw a face on their doll with the fine point markers.
7. Glue the yarn or corn silk to the head of the clothespin for hair.
8. Have them choose a piece of fabric for the dress. They can cut out the fabric on the circular line you have drawn.
9. Show them how to cut a hole in the center of the fabric for the doll's head. Fold the fabric in half and then again to form a pie shape. Clip the tip where the folds meet. Open, and it's a dress. Be prepared to do this step for those who can't.
10. Slip the dress over the doll's head and use glue where necessary to hold clothing in place.

More to do

Allow the children to make other dolls with the materials available. Let them be creative with fabric scraps, trims and other throwaways for dressing the dolls. Try to make boy dolls too. Encourage the children, parents and teachers to think of other toys to make. For example, clothespin parachutes, memory games (using scrap wrapping paper) or alphabet bingo.

Related books

May I Bring a Friend? by B. S. Regniers
Best Friends by Mirian Cohen

My Clothespin Doll

In the year 1933, a long time ago, there was a little girl. Her name was Mary. She and her friend Margaret liked to play with dolls. But their parents could not afford to buy such luxuries as toys, because it was a time when a lot of people were very poor and out of work.

Mary told her mother she wanted a new doll. Her mother, knowing there was no money for such things, decided to show the two girls how to make their own little dolls. Mary's mother brought out a basket. In the basket there were clothespins, pipe cleaners, corn silk, cloth scraps, glue and scissors. "First," said Mary's mother, "we need to cut the fabric into circles." Then she said, "Now glue some corn silk to the top of the clothespin." Mary said, "It's beginning to look a little like a doll!" Next Mary's mother took a pipe cleaner and twisted it around the smallest part of the clothespin. "These are the doll's arms," she said. Then her mother picked up the scrap fabric and cut a hole in the center of the cloth. Margaret said, "That must be the doll's dress." "That's right!" said Mary's mother. "Now you can draw a face on the dolls with this pencil." "Look, our dolls are finished!" said Mary. "I think I will name my doll Sara," said Margaret. Mary named her doll Clara. Just then Mary reached over and gave her mother a great big hug and said, "Oh Mommy, thank you so much. This is the best doll ever."

The two little girls played with their new dolls all afternoon, until dinnertime, then the girls put their new friends in the pockets of their dresses.

—Cory McIntyre, Crystal Lake, IL

FAMILIES

Paint the Barn

2+

In this simple activity, all the children will have a chance to help paint the barn.

Materials needed

Big Red Barn by Margaret Wise Brown
Large or medium-size strong corrugated cardboard box with barn doors cut in the front; a large-appliance car-ton such as from a refrigerator is ideal (see illustration)
Red tempera paint
Paintbrushes
Painting drop-cloth
Knife

What to do

1. Read *Big Red Barn* to the children.
2. Explain that they are going to paint their own red barn today.
3. Place the box on the drop-cloth and give the children paintbrushes. Let them take turns painting the barn red. Be sure that everyone has a turn.
4. Talk about how animals live and sleep in the barn as they did in the book.

More to do

Put a small tape recorder and a tape of animal sounds inside the barn after it is dry. Play back farm animal sounds. Have the children listen and identify the animals. If the box is big enough, let the children pretend to be particular animals in the barn. Have them act out the song Old MacDonald's Farm.

Related books

Early Morning in the Barn by Nancy Tafuri
Good Morning, Chick by Mirra Ginsburg
Barn Dance by Bill Martin, Jr. and Jon Archambault

—Peggy Eddy, Johnson City, TN

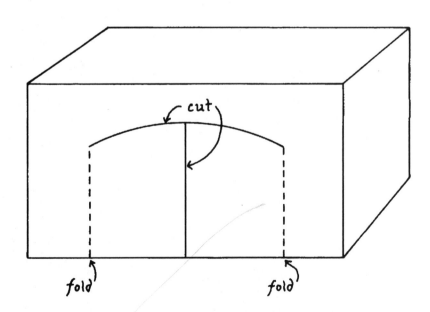

Stick-the-Spot-on-the-Holstein

Children are introduced to the Holstein cow and its black and white coloration.

Materials needed

A large outline of a cow
Black felt "spots"
Masking tape

What to do

1. Prepare a poster with the outline of a cow large enough to accommodate "spots" from every child in your classroom.
2. Tape the cow to a wall in an open area.
3. Cut out irregular black felt "spot" shapes, approximately 3" in diameter.
4. Have the children sit on the floor near the cow poster.
5. Give each child a "spot" with masking tape on the back.
6. Have each child walk up to the cow and place his "spot" on the cow.
7. Comment on where each child places his "spot."

More to do

Have the children use crayons to color on the cow poster, turning it into a mural. Or try stick-the-cotton-on-the-sheep!

Related song

"Old McDonald Had a Farm"
"Did You Feed My Cow?"

Related books

The Cow That Went Oink by Bernard Most
Big Red Barn by Margaret Wise Brown

—Cherie Schmiedicke, Madison, WI

Farm Animals

2+

Children will make farm animals and learn to identify them and the sounds they make.

Materials needed

Paints
Brushes
Crayons
14" x 16" construction paper
Butcher or other large paper
Paper bags
Popsicle sticks
Flour, salt and water for dough
Farm animal patterns

Opaque projector
Books for puppet patterns (below)

What to do

1. Trace animals onto a sheet of paper, copy by machine, and cut up and color for the children to match.
2. Make animals from construction paper. Make two, cut out, glue together, color and add details. Use for single animal hang-ups, mobiles, and for children to identify, color and make puppets.
3. Discuss a different animal on successive days and sing "Old MacDonald" for each new animal. Give the children copies of each animal to color and cut out.
4. Have children paste the cutout animals onto matching shapes.
5. Make puppets, either popsicle stick or paper bag, or both. The children can color, cut and paste these. Sing "Old MacDonald" with children holding up the puppets they made, with one for the farmer.

More to do

Make playdough: 4 cups flour, 1 cup salt and 1 1/2 cups water, and let children make and paint an animal of their choice.

Related books

Paper-Bag Puppets by DeAtna Williams

—*Suzanne Lamy/Barbara Lotesto, Dalton, Il*

Old MacDonald's Mural

Children learn to paint and name farm animals and objects.

Materials needed

Paint of varying colors
Some type of painting tool—brushes, fingers, animal-shaped sponges
Large sheet of paper
Tape
Markers

What to do

1. Tape the large sheet of paper to the wall.
2. Gather your group where the paper has been taped.
3. Begin to tell the children a story while you are drawing a barn: "I have a special friend and he has a very special name, and I think that many of you may know him." (Old MacDonald) The children will guess what you are drawing.
4. When you are done drawing you can then continue to say "There is a special song about my friend who lives on a farm. Can anyone think of what it is?"
5. When the children say "Old MacDonald Had a Farm," explain that the group is going to sing the song. While the group is singing, draw the animals that they are singing about.
6. After the children have finished singing about all the things on the farm (including tractors, cars, ponds and any other creative answers), explain to the group they will get to paint the object that they suggested.
7. Children are given the choice to do other activities while they are waiting for their turn to paint, or stay and watch if they choose.

More to do

Blank paper could be put on the wall the next day with only the markers out, and the children could draw on the mural paper or sing as they wish. Stencils of farm objects and markers could be put out for the children to trace onto paper of varying sizes.

Related book

Old MacDonald Had a Farm by Carol Jones

—*Melissa Browning, West Allis, WI*

FARMS

Farms 3+

Children learn about farm implements, crops, animals and activities and discuss the importance of farming.

Materials needed

Farm books with pictures of implements and animals
Samples of corn, soybeans, wheat, peanuts—or other available crops at various stages of growth
Cage, water, and food as appropriate for visiting animals
Newspapers
Toy farm sets
Miniature farm implements or photos of them (from dealers or catalogs)

What to do

1. Read books about farms. Show pictures of farm animals and discuss how to care for them, what they eat and what they produce.
2. Show miniature farm implements or photos. Tell how they're used.
3. Show pictures of farm buildings—barns, silos, machine sheds, etc. and discuss their use. Tell about special trucks which carry and dump grain with their hoists, and point out there are special grain trains and barges.
4. Have some farm products present and talk about how they are used. Have an ear of corn with samples of corn flakes, corn syrup, corn meal. Soy beans in their pods could have margarine and oil, and wheat could have a loaf of bread.

More to do

Plant corn or bean seeds at school to see them grow. Experiment by planting one in a dark place, giving one scant water, but supplying a third with adequate water and sunshine. Monitor growth. Invite a farmer to bring or loan a baby animal: baby chicks, baby lambs, rabbits or a baby pig. Discuss the correct care of the animal. Have a cage, plenty of papers underneath, water and food. Stress these are babies and need gentle handling.

Related song

"Farmer in the Dell"

—Marilyn Harding, Grimes, IA

Same and Different 3+

Students will learn the definition of the words same and different through the use of sound

Materials needed

Plastic eggs
Different items for inside the eggs, two of each item—for example, penny, safety pin, paper clip, button, anything else small enough to fit into the plastic eggs.

What to do

1. Put items inside eggs.
2. Review where we get eggs from and how it relates to our study of farm animals.
3. Pass out two eggs to each child.

4. Have children discuss the eggs (outside color, sound from the item inside the egg, etc.) See suggestions below.
5. Go around the circle until each student has found a matching sound for his/her egg.
6. To find out if the insides of the eggs match, crack open the egg and dump out the insides.

More to do

Have children make up their own eggs by putting other things into the eggs. Have children make up their own game of same and different. The following is a list of questions to ask the children:

Where do we get eggs from?
What are some of the uses for eggs?
How are these eggs the same? Different?
What do you think is inside each eggs?
Do any of them sound the same?
Do any of them sound different?
Why do you think they sound the same? Different?
What other things do you think we could put in the eggs?
What other things in the community can we say are the same on the outside, but different on the inside? Vice-versa?
Can you point to two things in the classroom that are different?
Can you point to two things in the classroom that are the same?

—*Tammy Urquhart, Seminole, FL*

Cow Milking

3+

The children will learn about farming and foods that come from farms.

Materials needed

2 child-sized chairs
Broomstick or heavy dowel
Yarn or rope
Powdered milk
Rubber glove
Heavy rubber bands
Paper cow head and tail
Farmer's hat
Small stool
Small bucket
Pin
Yellow and brown tissue paper

What to do

1. Position two chairs facing one another.
2. Place broomstick or dowel between chairs. The broomstick or dowel should be at child's eye level when the child is seated. Secure stick with yarn or rope.
3. To make chairs look like a cow, make a cow face and tail out of construction paper. Fasten them to opposite chairbacks.

4. Fill the rubber glove with powdered milk solution. Do not fill to the top; allow room to close the top of the glove (secure tightly with heavy rubber bands).

5. Attach glove to center of stick with heavy rubber bands so it has some bounce.

6. Carefully put SMALL pinholes in fingers of glove. NOTE: This step may be delayed until the lesson is ready for presentation.

7. Place yellow and brown tissue strips on the floor to simulate barn floor. More than one cow may be needed, based on class size.

8. Tell children it's early morning and it's time to milk the cow.

9. Put on the straw hat, pick up the stool and bucket, and say the farmer needs the bucket to catch the milk and the stool to sit on. Go into the "barn" area to the "cow." Sit on the stool, placing the bucket beneath the "udders." GENTLY squeeze a squirt of "milk" into the bucket.

10. Have children take turns playing the farmer.

More to do

Visit a dairy farm.

—Sandra Wallace Kayes, Philadelphia, PA

Goat Mask

4+

Old MacDonald probably had a goat on his farm. Here's a simple craft project that allows the children to practice fine motor skills while making a goat mask. Similar techniques can be used to create other farm animal masks; the class could even perform the song as a musical grand finale.

Materials needed

Large paper plate—one per mask
Cotton balls
Non-toxic black markers or black crayons
Scissors
Stapler
Glue or glue stick
String or elastic cord
Hole punch

What to do

1. Have the children cut off the outer rim of the paper plate. Save this ring. It will become the goat's horns.

2. Using the inner portion of the plate, fold in the two sides to make the goat's head (see illustration).

3. Draw eyes, nose and mouth with the crayons or markers. Older children can do this themselves, but provide a model to guide them.

4. Glue two or three cotton balls on the chin to make a little beard. Stretch and fluff them out a bit with your fingers.

5. Staple or glue the outer rim of the plate on top of the head to make the horns. The tips of the horns can be curled if you like by wrapping them around your finger before attaching.

6. Cut out the eyes using a hole punch or the sharp scissor point. Make a hole on the far sides of the mask to attach the cross-string or elastic cord.

More to do

Cow masks can be made by using the same techniques and materials but use the whole inner circle for the cow's head—do not fold in the sides. Attach the cut rim "horns" at the top but do not curl them. Finish by painting them with appropriate colors. If you are acting out the song, the cows could wear bells around their necks. Note: Young children are sometimes frightened by masks so introduce them carefully.

Related book

Gregory the Terrible Eater by Garrett Christopher

—*Jyoti Joshi, Framingham, MA*

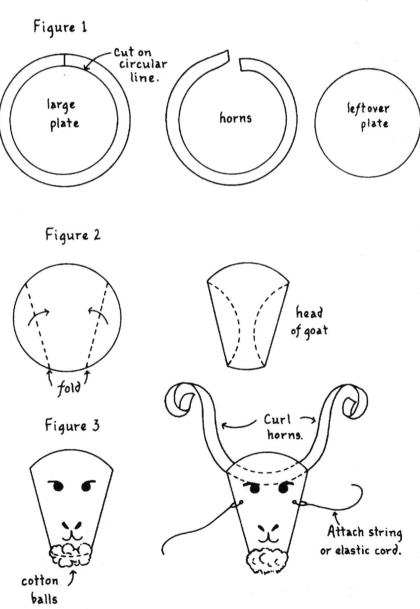

Figure 1

Cut on circular line.

large plate

horns

leftover plate

Figure 2

fold

head of goat

Figure 3

Curl horns.

cotton balls

Attach string or elastic cord.

Duck, Duck, Goose!

4+

In this cutting activity, the children will make a white goose from a paper plate and decorate it with a pretty bow.

Materials needed

Large paper plates—one per child
Colorful ribbons
Orange and black crayons or markers
Scissors
Glue or glue sticks or stapler

What to do

1. Draw two curving lines on the paper plate as shown in the illustration. Notice that section A must be somewhat smaller than section C.
2. Have the children cut out the shapes.
3. To make the head and neck of the of the goose, trim one end of section B (see illustration).
4. See if the children can assemble the pieces as they would a puzzle. You could have a finished model available for them to use as a guide. Section C is the body, section B is the neck and head, and section A is the wing (see illustration). Help those who need help with this. Then glue or staple the pieces together.
Note: When attaching the wing to the body, glue or staple near the top only so that the wing can be raised.
5. Use crayons or markers to color the beak orange and draw a black dot for the eye.
6. Use the scissors to fringe the ends of the tail and wing.
7. Have each child select a ribbon to tie around the goose's neck.

More to do

By choosing appropriate colored ribbons, these could make wonderful holiday decorations or greeting cards—write a little message under the wing!

—Jyoti Joshi, Framingham, MA

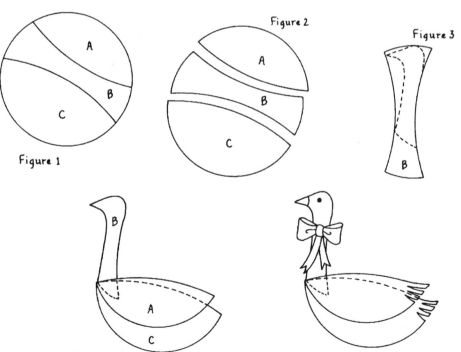

Fruit Picker

This imaginative game will help the children learn to recognize different types of fruits and to identify their shapes and colors.

Materials needed

Chalkboard
Colored chalk
Colored construction paper
Envelopes
Marker
Tape
Magnets or magnetic tape strips

What to do

1. Draw a large tree on the chalkboard.
2. Cut out the different shapes of colorful tree-growing fruits on matching construction paper. For example: red cherries, green apples, yellow pears, orange oranges or pink grapefruits. You may use fruits that are the same color as long as the shapes are different enough to distinguish them, for example, yellow grapefruits and yellow bananas. Have several of each kind so that there will be enough for each child to pick at least one fruit.
3. Stick the fruits on the tree using magnetic tape or magnets.
4. Make an envelope "crate" for each kind of fruit that you put on the tree. Glue an example of the fruit to the envelope and, if you like, label the envelope with the appropriate fruit name. Tape the crates beside the tree.
5. Tell the children that in nature many fruits grow on trees and usually just one kind of fruit grows on each tree. But today, you are going to pick fruit from a magical tree on which many different kinds of fruit can grow. The tricky part will be sorting the fruit so that each kind goes into its own crate.
6. One by one, ask the children to pick a piece of fruit off the tree, say its name, and put it in the proper crate.
7. Continue to do this until they can properly name each fruit, identify its color, and put it in its proper crate.

More to do

Play the same game using a magical bush instead of a tree. Use blackberries, red raspberries, blueberries, figs, etc. With the children's help, make a magical fruit salad for snack which uses the kind of fruits you picked from your magical tree or bush.

Related book

The Very Hungry Caterpillar by Eric Carle

—*Mike Krestar, South Fork, PA*

Stone Soup Day

3+

The children will use their five senses to prepare food items and learn the concepts of sharing and cooperation.

Materials needed

Stone Soup by Diane Paterson
Microwave/microwave bowl or hot plate and pot or crock pot
Microwave bowl
Eating utensils—bowls, spoons, knives
Peelers
2-3 carrots
1-2 potatoes
1/2 pound browned stew meat (optional)
1/4-1/2 onion
Salt/pepper
1 can tomato soup
3-4 bouillon cubes—beef, chicken, or vegetable
1 clean stone
1-4 stalks of celery
1/4 cup of barley
1/2 cup of milk
1/2 cup cabbage

What to do

1. Read the book aloud to the class and discuss the story.
2. Send home a note with each child explaining what and when Stone Soup Day is. Ask each child to bring one ingredient.
3. On Stone Soup Day, have the children help you wash and chop all vegetables. Be sure to be prepared with extra ingredients for children who forget to bring theirs.
4. Place all ingredients in your pot with the stone and cook. Adjust cooking time according to cooking method you are using.
5. While the soup is cooking, you could read the story to the class again.
6. Enjoy the soup for snack or lunch.

More to do

Collect stones for the children to paint. Have children draw pictures of the vegetables that were added.

Related book

Stone Soup by Diane Paterson

—Pamela Schumaker, Minot, ND

Food or Not Food

The students will, when presented with a variety of objects, discriminate objects by sorting them into categories according to their edibility.

Materials needed

Real or "real-looking" replicas of food
Other objects that are not food
Two large containers that will hold the sorted objects and foods

What to do

1. Present the objects one at a time and ask the children to identify them.
2. Have the children sort the objects into separate containers for "food" and "not food."

More to do

The children could be encouraged to think of their own examples of "foods" and/or "not foods." The teacher could help the children focus on specific features of the objects, helping them talk about specific characteristics of foods.

—Barb Lindsay, Clear Lake, IA

Bananas

This art activity will turn a hand tracing into a bunch of bananas.

Materials needed

A bunch of bananas
9" x 12" white construction paper
Yellow and brown paint
Paintbrushes
Marker
Scissors

What to do

1. Talk about how and where bananas grow and point out how they grow as a bunch. Count how many are on the bunch. Ask if anyone has ever seen a banana tree.
2. Trace the child's hand, including a small part of the wrist onto the white paper.
3. Turn the hand tracing upside down and turn it into a bunch of bananas by having the children paint the fingers yellow and the wrist brown.
4. You can have the children who are able cut-out their bunch of bananas if you like.

More to do

Have bananas for snack.

—Jyoti Joshi, Framingham, MA

Grapes

3+

Children often love grapes. Here they'll turn their thumb prints into a big bunch.

Materials needed

A bunch of grapes
Thick grape-colored paint
9" x 12" white construction paper
Shallow paint pans or trays
Green tissue paper
Brown marker
Scissors
Stapler or glue

What to do

1. Show children a bunch of grapes and count them. Talk about how and where grapes grow. Ask if anyone has ever seen a grapevine. Remark that grapes come in different colors.
2. Pour paint into shallow trays, and give each child a sheet of construction paper.
3. Have each child dip a finger or thumb into the paint and press it onto their paper to make grapes. Show them how to group the prints to create a bunch of grapes. Let the pictures dry completely.
4. Using the brown marker, draw stems on the bunch of grapes.
5. Trace each child's hand on green tissue paper and cut it out to make a leaf. Make more leaves as desired.
6. Glue the leaves to the top of the bunch of grapes.

More to do

Older children can use fingers to make each successive row of grapes. They can use one finger, then two, then three and so on, until the top row of the bunch uses all ten fingers. Have grapes for snack.

—Jyoti Joshi, Framingham, MA

Lunch Basket

3+

The children will generate ideas of what foods make a good lunch, make a lunch basket and draw nutritious foods to fill it.

Materials needed

12" x 18" sheets of construction paper
Manila paper
Crayons
Markers
Scissors
Stapler or glue

What to do

1. Cut the 12" x 18" sheets of construction paper down to 12" x 14. " Save the 12" x 4" strips.
2. Have the children think of all the foods they feel make up a good lunch.
3. Encourage them to think of foods from all the different food groups. Chart their ideas.

4. Give each child a 12" x 14" sheet of construction paper and show them how to fold in 3" on all four sides.
5. Cut in 3" on the top and bottom folds.
6. Fold the paper to create a box.
7. Glue or staple the sides together.
8. Fold 12" x 4" strip in half lengthwise to create a handle.
9. Bend and staple handle on top of lunch basket.
10. Have the children draw, color and cut a variety of foods that will make up their well-rounded, nutritious lunch.
11. Place their pictures in their lunch baskets. You may have the children glue them in if you like.
12. The children may take turns describing their lunches to their classmates. Always stress the importance of including different types of foods to make a balanced lunch.

More to do

Create a bulletin board to display the lunch baskets. Classify the food students drew into meats, grains, fruits, vegetables, milk products and snacks. Provide magazines with pictures of food and allow the children to cut them out. Let them remake their "lunches" with different combinations of foods. This could be set up as an independent center activity.

Related books

I Need a Lunch Box by Jeannette Caines
What a Good Lunch by Shigeo Watanabe

—Linda Barrett, Chicago, IL

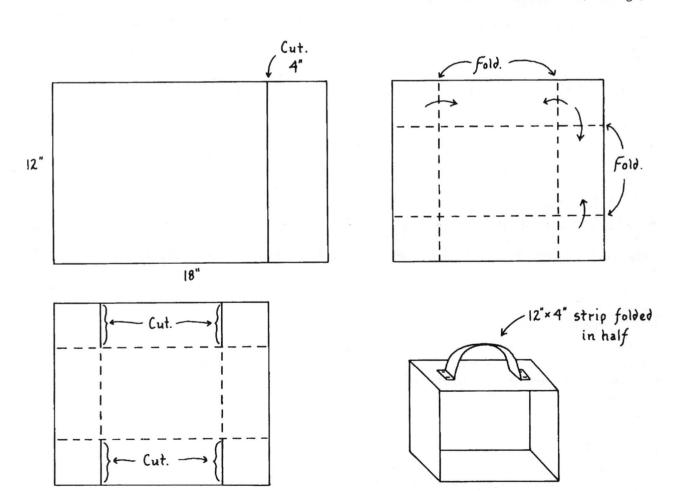

Paper Pizza

This activity engages fine motor skills while encouraging an understanding of sequencing.

Materials needed

White or cream colored paper cut in round "pizza dough" shape
Red finger paint
Scraps of construction paper for pizza toppings (red, green and brown)
Shredded paper
Glue

What to do

1. Pre-cut paper for dough into a pizza sized circle.
2. Prepare red finger paint
3. Talk to the children about creating their own personal pizza.
4. Give each child the paper for the dough.
5. Spoon finger paint onto the paper and have the children spread the "tomato sauce paint" onto their dough. Let the pizzas dry.
6. Let the children tear construction paper scraps to resemble the various toppings they choose to put on their pizza and glue them on top of their "sauce."
7. Squirt glue on top of the pizza sauce and toppings.
8. Sprinkle shredded paper "cheese" on top of the pizza, pressing it down so it will stick.

More to do

Make real pizzas for lunch or snack or visit a pizza parlor. Talk about other things that are round.

Related books

Round and Round and Round by Tana Hoban
How Pizza Came to Queens by Dayal Kaur Khalsa

—Beverly C. Dugger, Johnson City, TN

Before and After Foods

The children will learn to identify the source of favorite foods.

Materials needed

Group 1 foods—handful of peanuts in shell/peanut butter; unpeeled apple/applesauce; unpeeled potato/french fries; handful of grapes on stem/grape jelly; small jar of cream/several pats of butter;
Group 2 foods—a banana; a few lettuce leaves; a glass of milk
Small paper plates
Spoon
Vegetable peeler
Knife
Fork

What to do

1. On separate plates, place several tablespoons of peanut butter, several tablespoons of applesauce, several tablespoons of grape jelly, the pats of butter, and the french fries.

2. Introduce the activity by asking children to name one food they have eaten today. Repeat their answers, using full sentences (Rosa ate cereal. Chuck ate greens...). Then, ask children where the food came from (e.g., the store, the kitchen, the farm, grandma's, etc.).

3. Recap by repeating the foods that children have eaten and where they came from. Then, show the banana. Say, "This is a ___" and let children fill in the blank. Then say, "Yes, this is a banana. A banana grows on a tree. Someone picks it and we buy it at the store. Then we peel it and eat it." Repeat with the lettuce and the glass of milk, asking where the lettuce comes from (garden) and where milk comes from (cow). Point out that bananas, lettuce and milk are ready to eat just as they are. We don't have to do anything special to them before we eat them (except wash the lettuce).

4. Then say, "But not all food comes ready to eat from the garden or farm. Let's look at some other food." Show the peanut butter. Ask what it is and where it came from. If no one can tell you, ask what the peanut butter was before it became peanut butter. If no one guesses, or when someone does, pull out the peanuts. Say, "Peanuts are used to make peanut butter. We take them out of their shells (demonstrate) and grind them up. Then they become peanut butter." Repeat the activity using the other "before and after" foods from Group I. Peel the potato and show how french fries are cut, peel the apple and dice for applesauce, smash the grapes to show how jelly is made, shake the jar of cream to show how butter is made.

5. Ask if anyone knows any other "before and after" foods. Wrap up the activity by naming the "before and after" food pairs.

More to do

Have the children help make one or two of the "before and after" foods. Let them taste the food in the "before" and "after" state and choose the one they like the best. Make two different "after" foods from the same food: grape jelly and grape juice; apple sauce and apple cobbler; butter and whipped cream; mashed potatoes and french fries.

Related fingerplay

"Ten Little Potatoes"

I dug down deep (make digging motion as if holding shovel)
And see what I found
Ten little potatoes (hold up ten fingers and pulse hands)
Hiding underground
Shook off the dirt (make shaking motion with both fists)
Put 'em in a sack (pretend to sling sack over back)
Ten little potatoes (hold up ten fingers and pulse hands)
Carried on my back
Chopped them, cooked them (make chopping motion with one hand on open palm of other hand)
And right before my eyes
Ten little potatoes (hold up ten fingers and pulse hands)
Turned into french fries! (wiggle all fingers when you say fries)

—Andrea Lazzari, Richmond, VA

FOOD

Corn

4+

In this activity the children will create an ear of corn.

Materials needed

An ear of corn
Large paper plate, one per child
Yellow paint
Green markers or crayons
Cotton swabs
Scissors

What to do

1.   Show the children an ear of corn and show how the kernels make rows along the cob.
2.   Fold the paper plate on dotted lines (see figure 1).
3.   Trace part of the child's hand on parts A and B as shown in figure 1 and color them green to make the husk (see figure 2). If you wish, you may use green paper for the hand tracings, cut them out, and glue them around parts A and B.
4.   Open the paper plate. Using a cotton swab and yellow paint, make rows of kernels (see figure 3).

—Jyoti Joshi, Framingham, MA

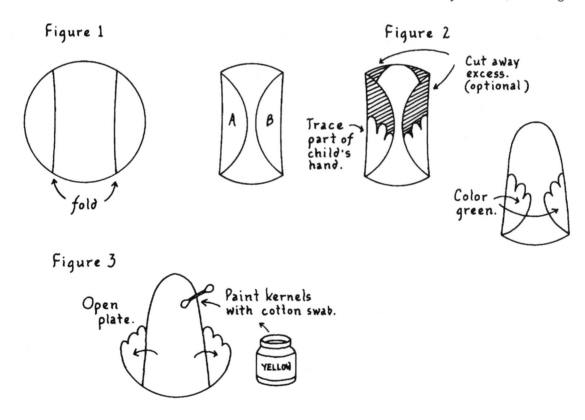

Nutritional Menus

The children will learn that eating a variety of nutritional foods is healthy.

Materials needed

Large pieces of construction paper
Magazines
Glue
Scissors
Crayons
Clear contact paper

What to do

1. Have the children cut out pictures of food that represent the different food groups from various magazines.
2. Take a sheet of construction paper and fold it in thirds to look like a menu.
3. Open the "menu" and lay it flat. Glue pictures that represent a healthy breakfast in the first panel, pictures that represent a healthy lunch in the second and pictures that represent a healthy supper in the third.
4. Fold the menu back into thirds and decorate the outside.
5. Cover with clear contact paper.

More to do

Have the children play restaurant. This can involve role playing, language skills (ordering food), math skills (counting) and social studies (foods from around the world).

Related books

No Peas for Nellie by Chris Demarest
Eating the Alphabet: Fruits and Vegetables From A-Z by Lois Ehlert
The Very Hungry Caterpillar by Eric Carle

—Laura Honkoski, Steger, IL

Let's Make Lunch Week

This activity would be an excellent way to reinforce a study of nutrition by allowing the children hands on experiences with choosing foods to make a balanced lunch. It has the added bonus of involving the parents.

Materials needed

A variety of foods from each food group: cheese chunks, crackers, vegetable sticks, sliced fruit, nut butters, etc.
Napkins
Paper plates
Eating utensils
Cups
A variety of drinks

What to do

1. Choose a time for "Let's Make Lunch Week" and send a note home to the parents to let them know and to explain why you are doing it and how it will work. Also ask that they send particular food items and amounts (which you will assign) with their children each day—but they don't have to send a lunch!

2. When the children arrive each day, gather the foods and sort them into food groups.

3. At lunch time, allow the children to make their own lunches by choosing item(s) from each food group. Vary the selections for each day by assigning different vegetables, fruits, cheeses, etc. daily.

4. Provide a selection of healthy drinks: fruit juice, milk, water, etc.

—Heather Purl, Denton, TX

Good Foods to Eat   4+

The children will explore foods needed for good health and improve their cutting and pasting skills.

Materials needed

12" x 18" piece of manila or construction paper
Pages from food magazines
Paper plates
Scissors
Paste for each child
Laminating material or clear contact paper (optional)

What to do

1. Discuss with the children what they had for breakfast or lunch.

2. Point out the basic food groups needed for good health, for example, protein, milk, grains, vegetables and fruit.

3. Show pictures of foods in each group. Let children tell which foods belong in each group.

4. Have the children paste a paper plate onto the 12" x 18" paper.

5. Let each child choose several magazine pages and cut out pictures of good foods.

6. Have the children choose one picture from each food group and paste it onto their plate to depict a healthy, nourishing meal.

7. Draw a cup of milk or juice, a knife, fork, spoon, etc.

8. Laminate each page. The children may use them as place mats.

More to do

Make a mobile for each food group by cutting out more magazine pictures of foods the children like and are good for them. Make a "good nutrition" person. Children draw a figure with a carrot for a nose, cereal for buttons, strung cereal for a necklace, apple for a head and so on. See how many foods can be on one figure.

Related books

Strega Nona Tomie dePaola
Munching: Poems About Eating by Lee Bennett Hopkins
Cloudy With a Chance of Meatballs by Judith Barrett
Gregory, the Terrible Eater by Mitchell Sharmat

—Wendy Pfeffer, Pennington, NJ

Shopping Lists

This activity reinforces the concept of the basic food groups by having the children create pictorial shopping lists.

Materials needed

Brown butcher paper or paper grocery bags
Magazines and coupons (avoid those for "junk" foods)
Scissors
Glue
Markers

What to do

1. Make yourself aware of the current guidelines which the Dept. of Agriculture recently published for food groups, i.e., the Food Pyramid, and discuss this with the children.
2. Cut out the shape of a paper bag using butcher paper, enough for each child to receive one "bag" for each food group.
3. Using the magazines and coupon inserts, let the children find pictures of foods in the different food groups.
4. Allow older children to cut out their own pictures and assist those who cannot.
5. The children can now divide the pictures into different stacks, one for each food group.
6. Have the students glue their pictures on each of their paper bags, using one bag for each food group.
7. Staple the child's pages together.
8. Make a cover page. Write the child's name and under it the words "Shopping List".

More to do

Take a field trip to a grocery store and have the children look for some of the items on their lists. Parents can allow children to help make shopping lists by drawing pictures or gluing pictures on the list.

—*Nicole Sparks, Miami, FL*

Set the Table For A Balanced Meal

The children will learn how to set a table and to choose a balanced meal.

Materials needed

Paper cups and plates
Eating utensils: forks,spoons,knives—plastic or paper cutouts
Napkins
Food magazines, or photocopies of foods in the basic food groups
Glue
Scissors
11" x 14" construction paper—one per child

What to do

1. Show the children how to properly set the table for a meal, placing the dishes, utensils, and napkins in the proper positions. Also discuss with them how to create a balanced meal by choosing foods from the different food groups.
2. Have the children cut out magazine pictures of various foods in the different groups, or color photocopies of foods.
3. Using the pictures, have the children choose a balanced meal and glue the pictures on the paper plate.
4. Glue the plate in the center of the construction paper.
5. Cut a cup in half lengthwise and glue it to the upper right corner of the paper.
6. Glue on other utensils as if you were setting the table.

More to do

Allow the children to practice setting the table for snack and/or lunch.

—Nicole Sparks, Miami, FL

What Part Do We Eat? 5+

The children will learn to identify the parts of plants we eat.

Materials needed

Various plants we eat (carrots, beets, potatoes, celery, onions, peanuts, greens, etc.)
Flash cards with the name and a picture of the plant on it—home made or store bought
Shoe box
Chart paper
Tape

What to do

1. Identify and discuss the parts of a plant: roots, stem, fruit, flowers and leaves.
2. Show each vegetable or fruit to the children and identify each one. Talk about which part of a plant it is.
3. Make a chart (graph) with columns showing a different part of a plant in each column.
4. Allow the children to take turns picking cards out of the box.
5. Have them identify the plant and decide which part of each plant is the part we eat.
6. Tape the plant card in the proper column of your graph. (Some plants may be placed under more then one part.)

More to do

Have the children actually grow and eat their own fruit and vegetables.

—Nicole Sparks, Miami, FL

Food Storage Center

The children will learn that food is stored in different places.

Materials needed

Large box
Tape
Glue
Old magazines, newspaper or coupons
Scissors
Box cutter

What to do

1. Turn the box upside down.
2. Each side of the box represents a different place to store food. The top of the box is a tabletop. Cover it with contact paper to look like a tablecloth. One side of the box is a refrigerator, another is a cabinet, a third is a deep freezer and a fourth is a storage container for dry goods.
3. Cut large doors in each side of your box. Use small drawer pulls, tacks or attach a string to each door so that you can open them.
4. Tape butcher paper on the inside of the box behind every door.
5. Have the children find and cut out small pictures of food items in magazines, newspapers or coupons.
6. Have the children glue foods in the appropriate storage areas. Note that some foods have more than one storage area. Fruit, for example, can be kept on the table top or in the refrigerator.

More to do

Play "Where do I belong." Place the children in small groups. Put various foods in large grocery bags and give one bag to each group, along with pictures of each storage area. Give the children one minute to place foods in the appropriate area.

—Nicole Sparks, Miami, FL

Food Fun Game

While learning to wait patiently for their turn, the children will also experience various the food groups and learn appropriate serving portions for their age group.

Materials needed

Construction paper—at least nine different colors
Posterboard
Old magazines for pictures
Tape
Glue
Lamination or contact paper
Magic marker
Playing pieces or markers
Spinner

What to do

1. Gather materials. Have the children help you make the game if possible.
2. Cut game board spaces out of five different colors of construction paper and attach to the posterboard, in game board fashion, alternating colors. Use picture of cash register or scanner for finish.
3. Label Start and Finish.
4. Laminate.
5. Cut food card rectangles using colors of construction paper not used for game board. Each color represents a food group.
6. Attach a small rectangle of each of the colors used on the food cards to the spaces of the game board. Keep food groups in close proximity to each other. The food card rectangles will be placed on these spaces during the game.
7. Color and cut food pictures and attach to food card rectangles, keeping food groups on same colored cards. Laminate and cut apart.
8. Make the spinner with different colored spaces using the same colored papers as you used for the game board spaces. Leave a white space and draw a star in it.
9. Obtain playing pieces from an old game or use small objects, for example, buttons, stones, etc.
10. Place the finished game board and playing pieces in a zip lock bag for storage.
11. To play the game:

    Place the color coded food cards on the game board in their appropriate colored rectangles.
    Spin the dial to see who goes first. The first person to land on the star goes first. Play then goes in one direction.
    Spin the dial and move to the color on the board as indicated on the dial.
    If you land on or pass over a small colored rectangle pick up that colored food card.
    Have the child identify the food on the card and then keep that card in their own pile.
    Continue spinning, moving pieces and drawing cards.
    The first player to the cash register at the end of the board is the first person to "check out" of the game.

More to do

Have the children sort their cards and count to find out how many servings of the different foods they have in their pile. Ask questions after the player reaches the "check out" like,"What are the different food groups; how many servings of meats, milk, breads and cereals, and fruits and vegetables do you need; can you tell me some foods in the different food groups?"

Related songs

"Peanut Butter"
"Peas Porridge Hot"
"I'm a Little Teapot"
"Five Little Hot Dogs"

—Sandra Layman, Swanton, OH

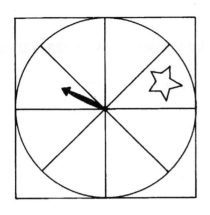

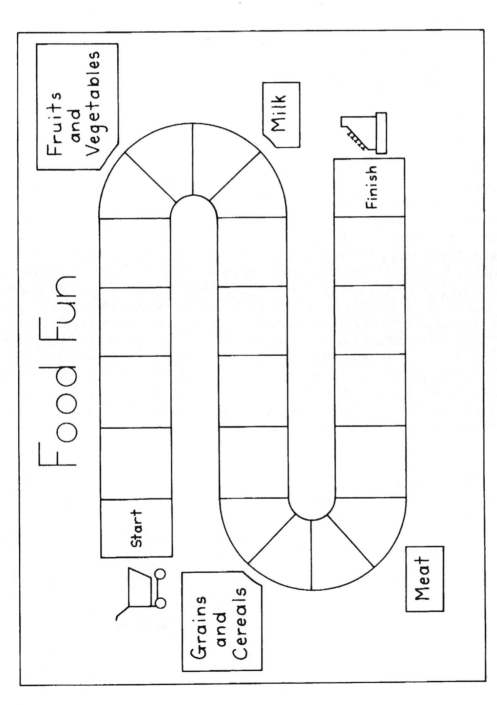

Food Fun

Start

Fruits and Vegetables

Milk

Finish

Meat

Grains and Cereals

Answer Robot

5+

This is a fun and unusual way for the children to work in pairs and practice grouping foods into basic food groups.

Materials needed

Cardboard box—at least 18" x 12"
Craft knife
Markers
Cardboard dials (optional)
Large buttons (optional)
Aluminum foil, (optional)
Index cards in different colors
White index cards
Adhesive circles in the same colors as the index cards
Food pictures
Glue or rubber cement

What to do

1. Use markers and draw a robot on the bottom of the box. Glue on the aluminum foil, cardboard dials and large buttons to make your robot more realistic if you wish. Cut two parallel slits in the box so that the children can reach them when the robot is sitting on a table.
2. Sit the robot box on end on a child-sized table. (You may need to weight the inside bottom of the box with some wooden blocks to keep it from tipping).
3. Prepare food cards by gluing pictures of single items of food to white index cards. Print the name of each food on the card below the picture. To make the game self correcting, choose one color to represent each food group. For example, all the food pictures from the "Dairy Group" would have a blue circle placed on the back of the index card. Other food groups could use different colors and even shapes.
4. Make the answer cards correspond with the color codes of the food cards. For example, use blue cards to print the words "Dairy Group" and add a symbol of pictures of food that are represented by this food group.
5. It takes two children to play this game. One child sits in front of the box and the second child sits behind it. The child in front chooses a food card and slides in through one slot. The child behind the box determines which of the four food groups the pictured food belongs in and pushes the appropriate answer card out the second slot along with the pictured food. The child behind the box can match the colored circle on the back of the picture card with the word card printed on the same color index card.

More to do

The answer card and the picture card which have come back out the slot can be grouped into different boxes labeled for the various food groups.

—*Cathy Falk, Fort Wayne, IN*

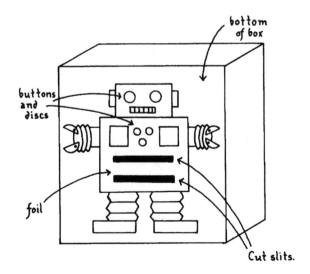

Beanbag Toss

Here's a group game which allows the children to practice following directions and eye-hand coordination. It might be just the thing for a rainy day!

Materials needed

Beanbags (one per child)
Cloth for target (single size bedspread or sheet can be folded to an appropriate size for the age group; target can start big and gradually be folded smaller for older children or as the children become more proficient)

What to do

1. Have children sit in a semi-circle.
2. Put cloth target inside the semi-circle, and explain that the children will try to toss their beanbag onto the cloth.
3. Before handing out the beanbags, demonstrate the game by hold your beanbag, sing the "Beanbag Song" (see below), count to three and toss the beanbag gently underhand. Explain that it is okay if the beanbag misses the target, because that they will have more than one chance. If the beanbags are different colors, explain that they might get a new one each time. Remind the children to remain seated as you toss the beanbags back to them after each try.
4. Give each child a beanbag. Remember to emphasize that they should toss gently after counting to 3, and that it's okay if their beanbag misses the target.
5. Sing the "Beanbag Song," and have the children toss their beanbags onto the target after you count to three. Point out how gently you threw your beanbag.
"The Beanbag Song" (to the tune of "Frère Jacques")

> *I love beanbags*
> *I love beanbags*
> *Yes sir-ree*
> *Yes sir-ree*
> *Watch me throw my beanbag*
> *Watch me throw my beanbag*
> *Spoken: One two three!*

More to do

To make the game more challenging, use a milk crate or other large container as the target.

—Trish Weaver, Raleigh, NC

Fishing Game

2+

Children will enjoy this pretend fishing game.

Materials needed

Light-colored Velcro (a large piece of loop-side and small strips of hook-side with adhesive backing)
Stencils of ocean creatures
Pipe cleaners or plastic hooks (found on new socks or ties)
Fabric scissors
Yarn

What to do

1. Ahead of time, trace ocean creature stencils onto loop side of Velcro and cut out shapes. Wrap the adhesive-backed, hook side of Velcro around plastic hooks or hooks formed from pipe cleaners. Cut yarn into 18-inch lengths and tie to hooks.
2. Set up a "fish pond" in the classroom and let children take turns fishing.

More to do

Use a rocking boat as a spot to fish from.

Related books

Swimmy by Leo Lionni

Related song

"1, 2, 3, 4, 5 Once I caught a fish alive"

—Lillian Hernandez, Ann Arbor, MI

Memory

2+

Children develop visual memory skills by repeating observed actions, picking out matching pairs and taking turns.

Materials needed

Various kinds of gift wrap
Posterboard
Clear contact paper
Scissors
White glue
Pencil
Ruler

What to do

1. Cut the posterboard into two 5" squares. Make ten to twenty pairs.
2. Glue the same gift wrap to two pieces of the posterboard and continue with all the chosen gift wrap. Dry for three hours.

3. Cover both sides with clear contact paper for durability. Use a recloseable bag to store the game in.
4. Show the children the game at circle time, explaining how it is played. Tell them it will be available at one of the tables during free time.
5. Arrange the cards face down on the table.
6. Begin the game by having one child turn over two cards, trying to find a match. If no match was made, the player turns the cards face down again.
7. If a match was made, the player may take another turn. If playing with younger children or for the first few times, the game should go onto the next person, because some children may become impatient while waiting for a turn.

More to do

Make a theme memory game by cutting the posterboard into relevant shapes such as mittens for winter, hearts for Valentine's Day or eggs for Easter. To play with two year olds, place all of the game cards face up and encourage them to look for matching sets.

—Cory McIntyre, Crystal Lake, IL

Milk Jug Drop

2+

This activity will improve children's eye-hand coordination.

Materials needed

Empty half-gallon plastic milk jug
Approximately eight wooden clothespins (without the springs)

What to do

1. Put the clothespins in the jug and screw on the top (do not tighten).
2. Place the jug where the children can reach it. Show them how to unscrew the top, shake the clothespins out and drop them back in one by one. (Allow the children to do as much as they can on their own.)

More to do

Shake the jug when it is full of clothespins and talk about the noise it makes. Substitute wooden spools for clothespins.

—Karen Vettel, Raleigh, NC

Lock and Latch Board

2+

Children will enjoy opening and closing locks and latches and, in the process, will develop eye-hand coordination.

Materials needed

A lightweight board about 2 feet long (shelving board works well)
Various locks and latches and an on/off switch
Felt
Staple gun

What to do

1. Screw the locks, latches and switch onto the front of the board.
2. Staple the felt to the back and sides of the board.
3. Give the board to the children and let them play.

More to do

Put the board away for several weeks then take it out again so children can rediscover it.

—Karen Vettel, Raleigh, NC

Stop and Go Game

3+

The children can practice their gross motor skills while having fun in this endlessly variable game.

Materials needed

3 Cardboard templates: 2-1/2" and 5" diameter circles, 2-1/2" stop sign
25 Manila paper circles, 5" diameter
20 green construction paper circles, 2-1/2" diameter ("go" signs)
5 red construction paper "stop" signs, 2-1/2" diameter
8" manila paper square labeled "Start"
Clear contact paper
Velcro
Markers
Scissors
Optional: Label small green circles "GO" and small red stop signs "STOP"

What to do

1. Cover all playing pieces with clear contact paper for durability.
2. Put small pieces of Velcro on the playing pieces so the small pieces (green circles and red stop signs) will stick to the large manila circles. This will allow you to change the pattern of the small game pieces.
3. Lay out the game pieces as follows: Beginning with the start sign, lay out all 25 large manila circles on the floor in a straight line approximately 5 inches apart, velcro side up. Attach the smaller circles and stop signs to the manila circles, alternating 4 "go" signs and 1 "stop."
4. The children take turns beginning on the start sign and following the road, walking by alternating their feet on each go sign and stopping completely with two feet on stop signs.

More to do

Vary the pattern by adding or subtracting the number of go signs. Hop or jump instead of walking on go signs. Vary the shape of the road layout—instead of a straight line arrange the playing pieces in a U, S or M shape. By changing the small cut-outs, this game has numerous possibilities to both reinforce motor control and emphasize various concepts, such as colors, numbers, shapes or letters. Make cutouts of the concept to be reinforced. Shapes, for example: the children would alternate feet on circles and squares, but stop on triangles.

—Sheila Ach, Syosset, NY

Tick-Tock

3+

The children will learn to listen to instructions while having fun moving to rhythms.

Materials needed

Alarm clock

What to do

1.   Before the game begins, set an alarm clock or kitchen timer to go off at a certain time. Hide the clock somewhere in the room.
2.   Tell the children the object of the game is to find the ticking clock before the alarm goes off.
3.   At the word "Tick," the chidren begin to move around the room listening and looking for the clock.
4.   But when the teacher says "Tock," the children must stop in their tracks. This exercise requires them to listen closely—it's pretty tricky!
5.   The child who finds the clock yells out "Tick-Tock" and brings it to the teacher.

More to do

To extend the activity, play the game with two children at a time. One child is "Tick" the other is "Tock." The children can only move when their name is called. The audience of children may take turns calling out "tick" or "tock."

Related rhyme

My little clock goes tick, tock, tick
My little feet go click, click, click
My little eyes look all around
That little clock will soon be found!

—Edna E. Wallace, Colorado Springs, CO

GAMES

Let's Go Fishing 3+

The children will have fun going fishing, while reinforcing the concept of choice. You could make several different sets of fish for different games. You could have color fish, shape fish or letter fish. You could make each fish different for recognition games, or make several in each set the same to play a simpler matching game. This easy-to-make game is endlessly variable to suit the needs and ability levels of your children!

Materials needed

Child's fishing pole—fishing line and reel or string on a stick, with a strong magnet attached to the end of the line
Fish pond—a child's swimming pool, hula hoop, or other contained area
Magnet
Posterboard fish with hole punched near mouth and hooked with a paper clip. Depending on the concept you wish to reinforce, use colored paper or draw shapes or write letters on each fish
Felt-tip marker
Hole puncher or piercing tool
Paper clips
Bucket or other container

What to do

1. Place all the fish into the "pond."
2. One by one have the children catch a single fish. If more than one is caught, toss all but one back.
3. Reel in the catch and ask the child to identify or match the color, letter or shape. This will depend on the child's ability and on the concept(s) you wish to reinforce.
4. Each caught fish should be returned to a bucket separate from the pond.
5. Allow each child to have at least one turn. As the children become familiar with how to use the game, allow them to play independently or in pairs or small groups.

More to do

You may to wish to involve the children in making fish cutouts. Pictures or stickers may be glued to one side of the fish to make matching games.

—*Cindy Minock, Washington, PA*

Spoon Partners 3+

Children learn about the uses of spoons and match them in pairs.

Materials needed

Pairs of like spoons—enough for each child to have one spoon (ask parents to send in pairs of spoons)
Basket or box

What to do

1. Gather spoons and place in a basket or box.
2. Show each type of spoon and discuss its use (plastic spoon for picnics, wooden spoon for cooking, measuring spoon, medication spoon).
3. Mix up pairs of spoons in the basket.

4. Walk around the children. Have each child take one spoon and hide it in their lap. As you walk around chant (with children) "Spoon, spoon, take a spoon. Then you'll find your partner soon!"
5. After each child has taken a spoon, say "One, two, three, find your partner!"
6. Children look at their spoon and show it to others. Then they move around the room until they find their "spoon partner."
7. The children sit next to their partner when they find him.
8. Repeat the game if desired.

More to do

Have the children line up for an activity when their spoon is described: "You may line up if your spoon is used for cooking." Trace the outline of spoons on cardboard. Children match their spoons to the silhouette.

Related song

"A Spoonful of Sugar" from the movie "Mary Poppins"

—Sarah E. Dill, Madison, WI

Rainbow Toss   3+

Children will learn the colors of the rainbow and improve eye-hand coordination and distance perception.

Materials needed

Posterboard
Markers
Scissors
Tape
Milk bottle caps

What to do

1. Draw a large rainbow on posterboard and laminate it.
2. Tape the rainbow to one end of a table. Put bottle caps in a bowl at the other end.
3. Have the children toss caps at the rainbow. They can try to get one cap on each color, or all their caps on the same color.

More to do

Implement a point system for each of the different colors and keep score.

—Rachel Stickfort, Newark, DE

Up and Down

3+

The children will practice demonstrating the positional terms up and down as they move their bodies and blocks up and down.

Materials needed

2 blocks per child
Index cards
Markers
Pictures of objects that are up (sky, stars, sun)
Pictures of objects that are down (ground, grass, floor)
Flannel shapes
Flannel board

What to do

1. Gather materials.
2. Draw simple shapes on the index cards (or glue on pictures) showing some objects up and some objects down.
3. Sing the following song to the tune of "Put Your Finger On Your Nose."

   Put your hand up in the air, up in the air
   Put your hand up in the air, up in the air
   Like a bird it can fly
   Way up in the sky
   Put your hand up in the air, up in the air
   Put your hand down on the ground, down on the ground
   Put your hand down on the ground, down on the ground
   And let it walk around
   To see what can be found
   Put your hand down on the ground, down on the ground

4. Introduce the words "up" and "down" by having the children model you as you move your body (and various parts) up and down. Label each as you move your body. (Let's raise our foot up in the air; Put your finger down on the ground; Place a part of your body up in the air.)
5. Show the index card pictures. Ask the children to tell you which shape is at the bottom of the picture. Which shape is at the top of the picture. Where is the rectangle in the picture?
6. Show a picture that has various up and down objects. Ask the children to name the objects that are up and to name the objects that are down.
7. Place flannel pictures on the felt board. Put some up at the top and some down at the bottom. Call on one child at a time to remove a flannel picture that is either up at the top or down at the bottom. (You can also ask the child to remove a felt piece and tell you whether it was up at the top or down at the bottom of the felt board.)
8. Pass out two blocks to each child. Ask children to place one block up on their head and the other down on their foot.
9. Ask the children to move around the room and find things that are up and things that are down.

More to do

Go outside and name things that are up and things that are down. Turn on music and pass out scarves. Let the children move their bodies up and down to the music.

Related book

Great Day For Up by Dr. Seuss

Related song

"There Once Was a King Who Had 10,0000 Men"

—*Marzee Woodward, Murfreesboro, TN*

Guess What I Am?

The children will learn how to look for clues in a picture.

Materials needed

Magazines
Glue
Scissors
Construction paper

What to do

1. Cut out a window in the middle of a piece of construction paper.
2. The children will look for large pictures of things in magazines.
3. Paste one picture on a piece of construction paper.
4. Place the cut out construction paper over the picture. Glue only about one inch on the top so that you can flip the top page up.
5. Have each child display their picture. Other children will guess what's under the paper by looking at the small clue in the window.

More to do

Children may make up riddles about their pictures or glue verbal clues.

Related books

Look! Look! Look! by Tana Hoban   —*Linda Wishney, Chicago, IL*

File Folder Games

Children love stickers! This activity uses stickers to help children practice discrimination skills.

Materials needed

Colored file folders
Colored index cards
Scissors
Sixteen to twenty stickers to match your current theme or unit (two sets), for example, cats, bears, tools, trucks, flowers, food, farm animals, etc.

What to do

1. Arrange stickers on the two interior sides of the file folder. Eight to ten stickers will fit on each side.
2. Now stick them on the file folder.
3. Fold the index cards in half and then cut on fold line.
4. Place second set of exact same stickers on index card halves.
5. Laminate or cover with contact paper the cards and the file folder.
6. Store cards in a plastic bag inside the file folder. You can make each file folder game match your current theme or unit.

More to do

Use seasonal and holiday stickers to make file folder games to use with those units.

—*Deborah Burton, Irwin, IA*

The Describing Game

4+

In this simple yet unusual matching game, the children will practice verbal, auditory and observational skills. Emphasize that cooperation between the "describer" and the "listener" will produce successful matches.

Materials needed

Two identical sets of picture postcards, seven cards per set. You can use any kind of postcard—cars, cats, historical places, landscapes, teddy bears—you will just need two of each kind to make two complete sets. Identify each set of cards by placing a colored filing sticker or piece of plastic tape on the back of each set of cards.

What to do

1. Have a child help you demonstrate the new game for the class.
2. Explain that you will be working together to try to match the sets of cards using only words and without looking at each other's cards.
3. Mix the two sets of cards and place them all face down.
4. Ask the child to take all the cards marked with one color while you take all those marked with the other color.
5. Stress that you should not look at each other's cards.
6. Explain that you will be the "describer" first and the child will be the "listener."
7. Take one card and describe what you see pictured on it. Example, "The cat in this picture has long fluffy fur; it is lying on a blue rug and looks like it is ready to pounce on a toy ball."
8. Encourage the "listener" to ask questions if he is unsure which picture you are talking about.
9. When the child feels sure he has guessed the correct picture lay both cards down together between you, face down.
10. Continue describing until all seven sets of pictures have been matched.
11. Turn the cards over one pair at a time to see if they are identical.
12. Note which pairs are correctly matched, stressing that it was a cooperative effort.
13. Turn the cards face down and mix them.
14. Play the game again, this time allowing the child to be the "describer" while you be the "listener."
15. Make the game available in the classroom so that the children may play it with each other.

More to do

Use sets of pictures with content corresponding to classroom units such as planets, insects, foods, etc. Museum shops are an excellent source for appropriate picture postcards. You could also use sets of photographs mounted on tagboard such as photos of your town, your school or of the children themselves.

—Susan J. Jenson, Norman, OK

Cookie, Cookie, Who Has the Cookie? 4+

Children will enhance their observation and memory skills as they play a simple game.

Materials needed

5-10 real or paper cookies
Platter or tray

What to do

1. Gather the children in a circle and tell them that they are going to play a game called "Cookie, Cookie, Who Has the Cookie?"
2. Present the children with a platter of real or paper cookies. You can play this game by focusing on either the number of cookies on the platter or their appearance (shape/color/size/type).
3. Have the children look closely at the cookies. Then instruct them to close or cover their eyes. Take away one or more cookies.
4. Tell the children to open their eyes and look at the platter. Ask them to identify the missing cookie(s) by number or appearance, depending on your focus. (For example, you might ask "How many cookies did I take away?" or "What color cookie is missing from the tray?")
5. Continue playing until the children have achieved a number of successes.

More to do

Make "hand-print kittens." You will need blue, white or orange paint; crayons; a large sheet of paper; and an outline of a kitten's face. Ask each child if she wants to make a blue, white or orange kitten and paint the child's palm, thumb and fingers on one hand with paint of that color. The child should then spread the painted hand and press a print in the center of paper. As the paint dries, have the child draw a face inside the outline of the kitten's head with crayons and then cut it out. Glue the kitten's head to the hand-print body, but make sure the paper is upside down so the fingers become the legs and the thumb becomes the tail.

Related book

The Baby Blue Cat and the Whole Batch of Cookies by Ainslie Pryor

—*Cathlene Hedden, Livonia, MI*

Coupon Game

4+

Children learn how to match things and develop social game skills, including taking turns.

Materials needed

Game board
3" x 5" cards
Pairs of matching coupons
Dice and game pieces

What to do

1.   Cut the product picture from one of each pair of coupons and glue it to random squares on the game board.
2.   Glue each of the other coupons onto a 3" x 5" card. On some cards draw a shopping cart with positive or negative numbers and the matching number of dots. For positive numbers make the dots green; for negative, red.
3.   Laminate the cards and the game board.
4.   Set up the game on a tabletop with game pieces on "Start" and coupon cards face down on the appropriate squares.
5.   Have the children take turns rolling the dice and moving their game piece.
6.   If they land on a purple square they take a card. A coupon card moves them to the appropriate product, and a shopping cart card moves them forward or backward the number of dots on the card.

More to do

Go to a grocery store with coupons for a list of items which the class needs.

—*Rachel Stickfort, Newark, DE*

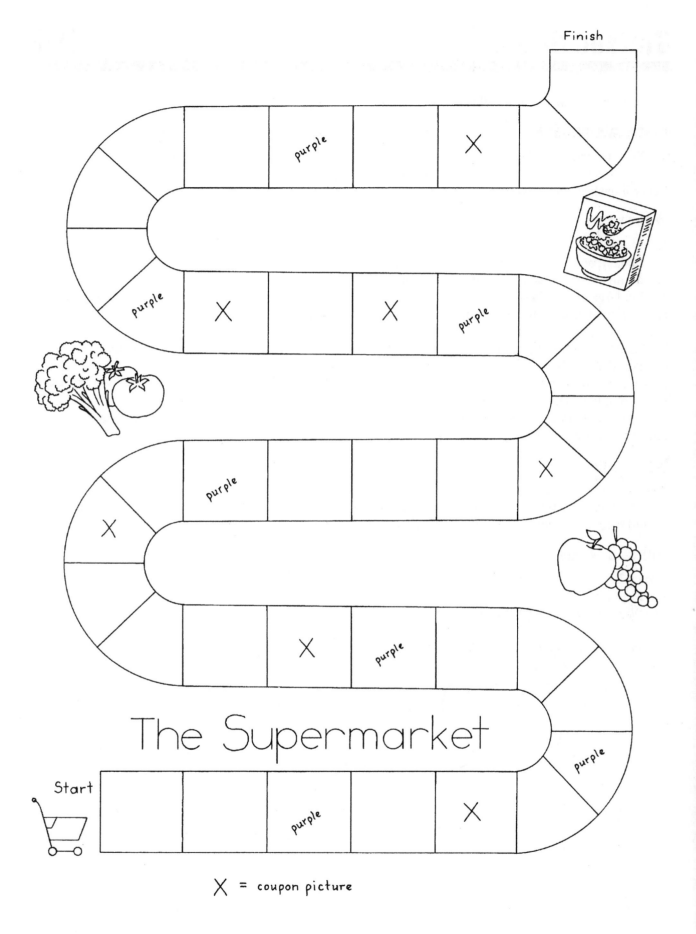

Finish

purple

X

purple X X purple

purple

X

X

purple X

The Supermarket

Start

purple X

purple

X = coupon picture

Tic Tac Bears

5+

Children practice patterning in this enjoyable game.

Materials needed

Tic Tac Toe grids (one large and as many small as needed to accommodate your class)
Tic Tac Bears (large and small bears in two colors—see patterns)
Recording sheet and crayons

What to do

1. Make five large bears of each color (see patterns).
2. Make five small bears of each color for every small grid (see patterns).
3. Laminate bears and grids (decide whether to use velcro or magnets for the large board).
4. Put large grid up in front of your class.
5. Divide the class into two groups.
6. Assign a color to each group.
7. Explain that the object of the game is to be the first group to get three bears of their own color across, down or diagonally.
8. Choose children to come up and place a bear on the grid one at a time. Use whatever selection process works best for you.
9. Allow groups to help their own members (but don't allow negative comments from opponents).
10. Demonstrate score-keeping.

More to do

Give each pair of children a set of small bears, small grid and recording sheet. Demonstrate how children should record the winning pattern on their sheets using the same color crayon.

Related books

Brown Bear, Brown Bear by Bill Martin Jr.
It's Not Easy Being a Bunny by Marilyn Sadler
The Napping House by Don and Audrey Woods

—*Wendi L. Prestridge, Wichita, KS*

Red Wagon Flower Garden 3+

Through this activity, the children will experience the process of germination.

Materials needed

A red wagon
Potting soil—soil that readily absorbs moisture is best
A plastic garbage bag
Flower seeds

What to do

1. Buy the necessary materials.
2. Line the red wagon with the garbage bag.
3. Put in potting soil.
4. Let children plant seeds.
5. Have children care for the garden, by watering and taking it outside to get some sunlight.
6. After the seeds have sprouted, you can transfer them to an outside garden so the children can continue to see them grow.

More to do

Discuss what plants need to grow (sun, air, water). Experiment by giving some plants water and others no water or do the same with sunlight. Instead of planting flowers, plant vegetable seeds and then replant in your garden.

Related songs

"Growing" by Hap Palmer

—*Kelly Barnett, Norwalk, CA*

Building the Yellow Brick Road 3+

Many teachers plant gardens with their children. Here's a fun and practical way to encourage the children to respect the planted areas—build a yellow brick road through the garden!

Materials needed

Patio blocks or flint stones (number will depend on length of path)
Yellow paint—choose an outdoor latex that will be durable and cleans up with soap and water

What to do

1. Design the route of your path. A gently curving path is particularly nice. Step along the path area (using child-sized strides) to get an idea of how many stones or blocks you will need.
2. Outside, have the children help you paint the top side of each stone. Let the stones dry completely.
3. Bring the stones to the garden. Lay them along the pathway. You may want to have the children help dig a bed in the soil to secure each stone.
4. The path will be fun for children to walk on, and keep your plants and flowers safe, as well.

—*Ruth Schoepp, New Brunswick, NJ*

Planting a Garden

3+

Children use imagination to learn how seeds become plants.

Materials needed

Pictures of the process of a seed growing into a plant or
  a seed
  a pot of dirt
  a live flowering plant

What to do

1.   Explain the process of a seed growing into a plant. If you have them, show pictures of seeds and plants. Be sure to explain that plants need water and warmth and light to grow and live.
2.   Tell the children that they will act out a plant's growing process as you sing.
3.   Have the children curl up in a seed shape. Sing "The Flower Seed Song." to the tune of "Ten Little Indians"

> *One little, two little, three little flower seeds*
> *Four little, five little, six little flower seeds*
> *Seven little, eight little, nine little flower seeds*
> *Planted in my garden. (Tap each "seed" as you count)*
> *Water those seeds and watch them grow (sing three times—"water" children)*
> *In my flower garden.*
> *The warm sun helps the flowers grow taller (sing three times—children slowly rise up)*
> *In my flower garden.*
> *Watch those flowers sway in the breeze (sing three times—children sway back and forth)*
> *In my flower garden.*

More to do

After you have a full-grown garden of flowers, fill an imaginary vase with water and pretend to "pick" the flowers and put them in your vase. Use your imagination in deciding how you could act out this part.

—Trish Weaver, Raleigh, NC

Planting Bulbs

3+

The children will learn how bulbs develop.

Materials needed

Bulbs: Tulip, Crocus, Gladiolus, Daffodil, Onion
Shovel
Mulch
Ruler

What to do

1.   Talk about things that grow—people, animals, plants, insects.
2.   Show and discuss the bulbs: tulip, crocus, daffodil, gladiolus and onion.
3.   Show difference in sizes.
4.   Show pictures of the flowers.

5. From each different bulb show where the roots, stem and skin is.
6. Cut one bulb in half to show the beginning of the plant inside.
7. How deep do we have to plant them? Show 6" (tulip and crocus) 10" (gladiolus).
8. Prepare the soil with mulch.
9. Dig the holes.
10. Plant bulbs right way: roots down, stem up.
11. Put in bone meal.
12. Cover.
13. Water regularly.
14. Wait a long time until spring! Its worth it!

More to do

Talk about seedlings, saplings and trees. Or the parts of a plant: roots, stem, flower and leaves. Or the parts of a flower: petals, pistil, stamen, pollen, calyx and corolla. Or the parts of a leaf: stem, vein and tip.

Related books

Planting a Rainbow by Lois Ehlert
The Reason for a Flower by Ruth Heller
The Tiny Seed by Eric Carle
Trees by Harry Behm and James Endicott

Related songs

"Springtime Is Coming"
"Because It's Spring"
"In the Leafy Tree Tops"
"Popcorn Popping"

—*Winny Van Gils, Redlands, CA*

Garden Collage

3+

The children will choose what they want in their gardens, then paste the objects on paper.

Materials needed

Paper: any size, but large is best for younger children
Magazines with flower or vegetable pictures
Paste/glue
Markers
Crayons
Scissors

What to do

1. Cut paper to desired size.
2. Put glue and paste in containers easily handled by young children Place markers, crayons, scissors and pictures on table.
3. Talk to children about gardens. See what their idea of a garden is and what is grown in a garden.
4. After hearing the children's comments and discussing gardens, show the children pictures of flowers and vegetables.
5. Discuss what they would grow in their garden.

6. Talk about the rows and how people plant their gardens.

7. Have the children choose what they would like in their garden from the garden catalogs and make a collage.

8. Some children will be able to draw rows for their gardens.

More to do

Talk about colors of the flowers and vegetable. A field trip to a garden might be fun. Have the children plant their own garden on the playground or in the classroom. Role play how a plant grows, if it is watered and if it is not.

—Jane Hibbard, Archbold, OH

Growing Radishes

3+

The children will learn how plants grow by watching and documenting the growth in their own radish garden.

Materials needed

An area available for planting close to the classroom and a water source (a long row beside a wall or fence would be ideal)

Packets of radish seeds

Gardening tools, adult and child-sized if possible

Water hose or watering can

Magnifying glass(es)

5" squares of posterboard or construction paper for plant drawings

Greens and salad dressing

What to do

1. Recruit older children and/or adult volunteers to help you dig and turn the soil for the garden. Have the children remove grass and weeds from the turned soil.

2. Rake the soil into a mound-like row.

3. Show the radish seed packets and the actual seeds to the children. Draw a picture of the packet and the seeds on one of the 5 inch square papers. Go out to the garden and give each child several seeds to plant about 1/2 inch deep and 1/2 inch apart (or as directed on the packets).

4. Water the row.

5. Watch the garden each day and pull weeds as necessary.

6. When plants are about an inch tall, thin so that remaining plants are approximately an inch apart.

7. Let children handle and observe the plants that were removed. Provide magnifying glasses. Bring a little plant inside. During circle time, draw a simple picture of what the little plant looked like, with the children providing their observations to guide your drawing, or have the children draw the radish on their own.

8. Continue weeding and watering the garden as needed.

9. After a week, remove a radish plant from the row and observe its progress. Again, bring it inside and draw it with the children's help, or have them draw it themselves. Repeat in one and two weeks.

10. When radishes mature (approximately 30 days), the children can pull them from the soil and wash them. Make a final radish drawing.

11. The class can then assist in making a large green salad with sliced radishes included. Top with salad dressing and enjoy! If the radishes are very spicy, you might try slicing them paper thin with a vegetable peeler.

More to do

Laminate your series of radish drawings or cover each with clear contact. Tell the story of your radish garden and place each drawing in its proper place in the sequence of the story. A ledge or chalk rail works well to hold them as you speak. Make these drawings available to the children so they may tell the story and sequence the pictures on their own. Grid a piece of paper into six areas numbered one through six. Label the blocks in the following manner:

We grow radishes
Seeds
Roots
Stems and leaves
Mature radishes
Salad

Duplicate the master and have the children illustrate each block using your drawings as a guide (display your drawings in sequence). Have them cut out the blocks and assemble their own little book, We Grow Radishes. If you had them make periodic drawings of the radishes, bind those into a similar book. Have them design a beautiful cover. Offer help as needed.

—Carol G. Taylor, Pineville, LA

Zucchini Squash Plants   4+

Children follow simple directions to learn about raising plants and the changes in each stage of the plant's growth.

Materials needed

Spoon
Potting soil
Squash seeds
Paper cups
Large tray
Water and sunlight

What to do

1. Place materials on a large tray.
2. Have each child scoop two to three tablespoons of soil into her cup.
3. Have them put their seed on top of the soil and cover lightly with more soil.
4. Place the plants in sunlight.
5. Lightly water the plants each day.
6. Have the children observe the plant's growth, first daily and then weekly.

More to do

Explain to the children some of the changes that take place during the growing process. When the plants are big enough to be planted outside, prepare a space ouside in the playgournd or send them home with instructions.

—Karen Gassett, Framingham, MA

Seed Wheel

4+

The children can practice their observational skills by matching real seeds, and the seed wheel makes it fun. This is an excellent activity to complement a gardening unit in the spring.

Materials needed

12" cardboard circle (can be obtained at pizza shop) divided into 12 equal pie-shaped wedges using a black felt marker
12 different kinds of seeds, flower or vegetable
12 wooden spring clothespins
Tacky glue

What to do

1. Glue one seed in the middle of each section of the cardboard circle and label that section with the name of the seed.
2. Glue an identical seed to the top of the snapping end of one clothespin.
3. Continue Steps 1 and 2 until you have 12 different seeds on the circle and 12 matching seeds on the clothespins.
4. Read the children a story about seeds (see Related books below for suggestions).
5. Let the children look at seeds and seed packets.
6. Show the children the seed wheel and clothespins. Tell the children that they are to match two seeds that are the same by clipping a clothespin onto the section of the seed wheel that matches.

More to do

Put out a bowl of mixed seeds (don't use very tiny ones) and let the children sort them. Make several seed wheels using different kinds of seeds. Store each wheel with its own clothespins, and allow the children to use them independently.

Related books

Where Does Your Garden Grow? by Augusta Goldin
How a Seed Grows by Helene Jordan
How Does My Garden Grow? by William and Elizabeth Benton
What Shall I Put in the Hole That I Dig? by Eleanor Thompson
The Riddle of Seeds by W. Hammond (Teachers' Information Book)

—*Yvonne Thompson, Ashtabula, Ohio*

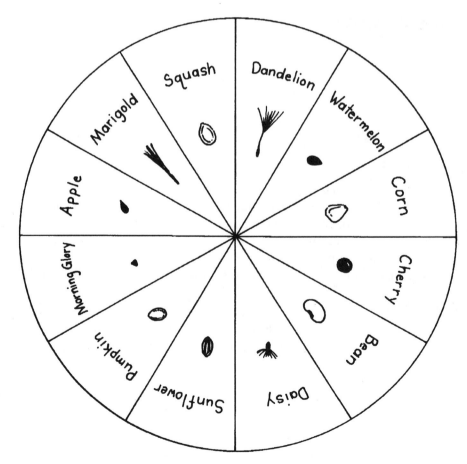

Planting Graph

4+

What can you learn from gardening? How about graphing, sorting and counting skills, finding the most, least, longest, shortest and same to name just a few things!

Materials needed

Empty seed packets—from class seed planting project or from parents
Posterboard
Markers
Glue
Small pictures of children

What to do

1. Draw a graph. Glue empty seed packets on tops of columns. Each child tells kind of seed they planted and glues his picture in the proper column.
2. With the children, find longest and shortest column.
3. Count how many children planted each seed.
4. Which seeds did we plant most/least of?
5. Do any columns have the same number?
6. Did we plant more corn or carrots?

More to do

Compare sizes, shapes and color of seeds. Eat vegetables for snack. Compare plants as they grow. Take a trip to a greenhouse to see plants.

Related books

The Carrot Seed by Ruth Kraus
The Tiny Seed by Eric Carle
Growing Vegetable Soup by Lois Ehlert
The Mouse and the Potato by Thomas Berger
Pumpkin, Pumpkin by Jeanne Titherington

—Judy Haase, Itasca, IL

GARDENING

Changeable Art 3+

This activity promotes working together while providing an endlessly variable classroom activity.

Materials needed

Piece of wood 12" x 24" or larger
Nails—approximately 30
Felt pieces—assorted shapes and colors
Hammers
Hole punch
String

What to do

1. Cut felt into different shapes.
2. Show the children how to carefully use the hammer and nails.
3. Give a small group of children a space on the floor to work.
4. Let them hammer nails half way into the wood. Cover wood piece with nails.
5. Have some children punch holes (one hole per piece) into the felt pieces.
6. Slide pieces of felt onto nails.
7. Two or three pieces of felt can fit on each nail.
8. Hammer two nails near the top of the wood piece. Add string and hang.
9. Children can change the felt shapes around whenever they want to.

More to do

Provide five baskets for felt pieces. Ask the children to put one color in each basket.

—Lynne R. Saunders, Philadelphia, PA

Murals 3+

This activity encourages both creativity and group cooperation.

Materials needed

Large sheet of white or brown mural paper or postal wrapping paper
Pastels, crayons and/or markers
Masking tape

What to do

1. Tape a 4' x 10' piece of paper to the blackboard. Place crayons on a chair or on the blackboard edge where they are readily available.
2. Ask the children to select a theme or title for the group picture (e.g., Winter Fun, Our Class, Monster Mischief). A vote may be taken to select the best title.
3. Instruct the children to design a picture related to the theme. Everyone draws part of the picture until it is completed. If the class is small, the children can all draw at once, or they can work on the mural one at a time.

More to do

When the mural is completed, have the children talk about how they felt working as a team. The class might decide as a group where to hang the mural and/or what to do with it (e.g., should it be left up, given away, or cut up so participants can keep their own drawings?).

—Susan Buchalter-Katz, Lawrenceville, NJ

Tube Art

3+

This three-day activity teaches cooperation, stacking, balancing, relational and size concepts. As we work we talk about tall and short tubes and placing tubes "in front of," "behind," "on top," "next to," and "in between."

Materials needed

Paper tubes from toilet paper, paper towels, or wrapping paper
A big sheet of hard styrofoam, wood, or heavy cardboard for a base
Lots of glue
Paint and glitter

What to do

1. Cover the table with a big sheet of plastic for easy cleanup.
2. Place the base on the table where the children can reach it.
3. Place the tubes, glue pots and brushes on the table with easy reach.
4. Day one: Instruct the children to use lots of glue. As they work, discuss the different learning concepts mentioned above. Younger children tend to paint the whole tube with glue and forget to place it on the base. They need to be reminded to place their tube on the structure. Younger children have to be shown how to stack.
5. Day two: When the structure is dry, let the children paint it. After children are done painting, you may want to finish it off with a can of spray paint.
6. Day three: Drizzle on glue and add glitter.
7. Name your structure.

More to do

This activity can be used to teach about various seasons or holidays. For a winter structure, paint white, add stale marshmallows and green construction paper trees. For Halloween, paint orange, add fake cobweb netting and black spiders. For Valentines Day, paint pink and add hearts. For Easter, hide construction paper Easter eggs on structure.

—Joyce A. Nelson, Lafayette, CA

Friendship, the Perfect Blendship

4+

The children learn to interact positively with each other and to express themselves in a creative manner.

Materials needed

Large piece of art paper (to fit the top of a table)
Collage materials (scraps of paper, fabrics, lace, ribbons and aluminum foil)
Buttons
Sequins
Glitter
Scissors
Glue
Crayons or markers

What to do

1. Tape the large piece of art paper to a low table in your room. Assemble the art materials in the middle of the paper so that children standing around the table can all reach them.
2. Tell the children "We are going to make a friends collage. We'll share all of the things that we use."
3. Allow the children to draw and glue on the papers, using all of the collage materials available on the table.
4. Encourage individual expression and remind the children that they are to share all of the materials as friends would. Talk about how fun it is to work together on a project.
5. When using the glue, make sure the children spread it thinly. Blobs of glue weigh the paper down and make it hard to hang.
6. When the children feel they have sufficiently decorated the papers, allow them to make glue dots, lines and squiggles all over the creation. Give each child a container of glitter and shake, shake, shake. Encourage the children to keep the glitter on the paper.
7. Allow time for drying. Then remove the tape, gently shake off the excess glitter onto the table and collect it to save for another project. Hang your creation on the wall for all to enjoy. When showing to visitors, be sure to emphasize that it was made by a group of friends.

Related books

It's Mine by Leo Lionni
I Sure Am Glad to See You by Martha Alexander
Want to Play? by Marissa Moss

Related songs

"Won't You be My Friend?" by Hap Palmer
"Friends on the Floor" by Hap Palmer

—Virginia Jean Herrod, Columbia, SC

Togetherness Flag

The children will work together to make an American flag.

Materials needed

Red, white and blue paint
Paintbrush
Paint trays
Sheet of paper—2' x 3'

What to do

1. On the large sheet of paper, draw lines for stripes and paint a blue square in the upper left corner.
2. Have the children fill in the bottom stripe by dipping their hands in the red paint and pressing them end to end within the lines of the stripe. Using the white paint, have them make a white stripe just above it the same way.
3. Continue until you have all 13 stripes filled with hand prints.
4. Have the children dip their fingertips in paint and make "stars" in the blue square.

More to do

Have children make our country's very first flag the same way and explain why it looks different from the flag we have today.

—Joyce Wildasin, Hanover, PA

Hamster Maze

The children will learn to solve problems by working together.

Materials needed

Blocks
Hamster or gerbil

What to do

1. Each child picks up two or three blocks.
2. Explain that the blocks will be used to build a maze for the hamster to run through.
3. Begin building the maze by placing your block in the center of the group.
4. One by one, have each child add their blocks to the maze structure.
5. When the maze is finished, evaluate your work and predict if it will work. Will the hamster be able to run through it? Are there any spaces that the animal could fit through and escape? Are there any loose blocks that could fall and hurt the animal?
6. Place the hamster in the maze. Observe the animal's actions to test predictions. In order to encourage the hamster to move, place some food in the maze.

More to do

Talk about other ways to build the maze (different shapes, higher walls). Use found materials in addition to the unit blocks, such as tongue depressors or cardboard boxes. Build mazes for cars, balls or other motion toys.

—Anne Marie Schweiss, St. Louis, MO

GROUP PROJECTS

Castle Creations

4+

The children will practice their fine motor skills and exercise their imaginations as they create a castle from recycled materials. The children can engage in a cooperative effort to build a "class castle," or each child can build on his or her own creation.

Materials needed

"Junk"—for example, gift wrap or paper towel tubes, plastic tops from medicine bottles, paper cupcake containers, toilet paper tubes, small boxes, cones, spools, or oatmeal boxes (ask children and parents to help collect)
Large heavy piece of cardboard or box covers
White paint (other colors optional)
Glitter
Straws
Foil
Scissors
Nontoxic white glue
Tape

What to do

1. Pour the glue into a shallow tray or pie plate.
2. Have the children dip the objects in glue and attach them to the cardboard to create a castle. Use box covers if each child is creating his or her own castle.
3. When the glue is completely dry, paint the castle white and sprinkle with glitter while the paint is still wet.
4. Decorate the city with flags made of straws and foil. Use tape to attach the flags to the highest points of the castle.

More to do

Create other constructions—a space station, a skyscraper or an entire city.

—*Jyoti Joshi, Framingham, MA*

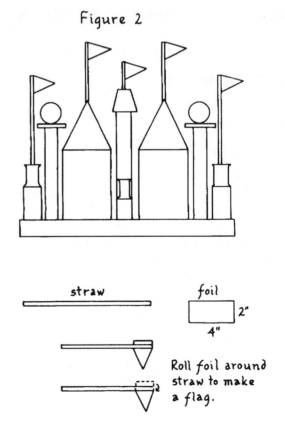

Figure 2

Figure 1

balls

caps   paper towel tubes

lids

spools

cone shapes

toilet paper tubes

oatmeal boxes   shoe box lid

straw

foil

2"

4"

Roll foil around straw to make a flag.

Spelunk! 4+

Children learn about exploring caves in a wonderful rainy day activity.

Materials needed

Sheet or parachute
Climbing structure, tables, chairs, etc.
Tunnel
Large boxes

What to do

1. Place a sheet or parachute over a table or climbing structure and let the children climb in and out and through the "cave."
2. Block off one end of a tunnel and pretend it is a cave. Put a sheet or towel over it to make it darker.
3. Cut the ends off of big boxes and stick them together so the children can crawl through them.
4. Make an obstacle course of different types of terrain a spelunker might encounter. Some types would be steep, bumpy, wet, muddy, narrow, or so small that they would need to crawl.

—Michelle Erlich, San Diego, CA

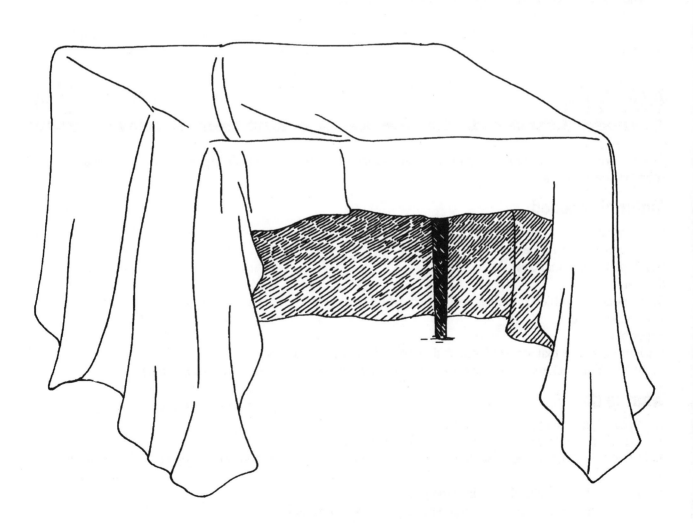

Brushing the Alligator's Teeth 3+

When teaching oral hygiene, have fun and practice fine motor skills by brushing the alligator's teeth as well as your own!

Materials needed

Cardboard egg carton—one per child
Old toothbrushes
White and black paint
Toothpaste (optional)

What to do

1. Turn the egg carton upside down. The egg cups are the alligator's teeth.
2. Using the white paint and toothbrush, have the children "brush" the teeth. You can mix a small amount of toothpaste into the paint for a more realistic smell if you like.
3. Put the black paint out and see if anybody gets the idea to use it to make cavities.

More to do

Play a recording of Hap Palmer's "Brush Away Tooth Decay" and talk to the children about recommended techniques for tooth brushing. Let them practice these on the alligator.

—Jyoti Joshi, Framingham, MA

Mr. Yuk 3+

The children will practice identifying substances that are poisonous and sorting non-poisonous substances from poisonous ones.

Materials needed

Green spray paint
Green construction paper
Black permanent markers
Scissors
Small poisonous objects, such as nail polish, white out, markers or aspirin
Two paper plates
Paper bag
Various groceries that are food; others that are poisonous substances
Eight Mr. Yuk stickers (available for a nominal fee from your local poison control center)

What to do

1. Spray paint paper plates green. Let dry.
2. Use marker to draw Mr. Yuk's face on one paper plate.
3. Staple the plates together with the Mr. Yuk drawing on the front. Cut off the top half of the rear plate to make a pocket.
4. Put small poisonous objects into the pocket.
5. Place other poisonous and non-poisonous objects in a paper bag.

6. Present the Mr. Yuk paper plate puppet. Discuss what he stands for: that any object Mr. Yuk is on is poisonous.
7. Remove poisonous objects from the puppet. Name them and discuss why they are poisonous.
8. Present paper bag of groceries. Remove one item at a time.
9. Ask children "Can I eat this?" If the answer is yes, put it in a food pile. If not, place it next to the puppet and put a sticker on it.
10. Give each child two stickers to place on poisonous objects in their homes.

More to do

The lesson can be extended by letting children trace and cut out green construction paper circles and draw on Mr. Yuk's features with black markers.

—Marzee Woodward, Murfreesboro, TN

Syringe Painting

3+

This imagination-oriented project introduces the syringe to children in a non-threatening way.

Materials needed

Paint—can be made by mixing:

4 cups of flour
2 cups of salt
food coloring
water to the desired consistency

Paper
Syringes without needles (use eyedroppers if syringes are unavailable)
Cups or paint containers

What to do

1. Make the paint and pour it into the cups or paint containers.
2. Add food coloring for desired colors.
3. Place one syringe with the needle removed in each paint container, or give each child her own syringe.
4. Give each child a piece of paper to paint on and have him paint with the syringe.

More to do

Discuss how the syringe works and have the children share their experiences of receiving shots. Introduce other medical equipment such as a stethoscope, thermometer or blood pressure cuff.

Related books

A Trip to the Doctor by Margot Linn
My Doctor by Harlow Rockwell
Going to the Doctor by Fred Rogers

—Michelle Barnea, Dover, NJ

Medical Collage

3+

The children will examine objects they may encounter in a doctor's office or hospital.

Materials needed

Large piece of heavy paper, light cardboard or posterboard
Medicine cups
Surgical masks
Bandaids
Tongue depressors
Glue
Syringes without needles
Plastic gloves
Gauze
Any other medical supplies
Markers or crayons (optional)

What to do

1. Discuss the various objects with the children. Allow them to share their own medical experiences.
2. Allow the children to create a class collage out of the medical supplies. Use it as part of a bulletin board unit display which might include dictated experience stories.

More to do

Allow the children to use appropriate medical supplies for dramatic play.

Related books

A Trip to the Doctor by Margot Linn
My Doctor by Harlow Rockwell
Going to the Doctor by Fred Rogers

—Michelle Barnea, Dover, NJ

Operation Cast

The children can assist with a "real doctoring" activity.

Materials needed

Casting material (available from an orthopedic surgeon) or use plaster of paris and white gauze
Stuffed animals

What to do

1. Send a flyer home announcing the activity. Ask children to bring a stuffed animal to school on the day of the activity.
2. Designate an operating table and choose a stuffed animal patient.
3. Comfort and converse with the patient and make a diagnosis. Have the animal's owner be your assistant.
4. Cut a piece of casting material and let the child wrap it on the animal.
5. Place animals in a "recovery area" so casts can dry.
6. Continue until all the patients have been cared for.

More to do

Set up a hospital in your drama area or visit a hospital. Ask a doctor to visit and speak to your class.

Related book

Maybe a Bandaid Will Help by Anna Hines

—*Dianne Bonica, Tualatin, OR*

Fire Safety

3+

This fingerplay can supplement a discussion on fire safety.

Materials needed

Burnt wood

What to do

1. During group discussion time, explain to the children the hazards of playing with matches. Hold a burnt piece of wood and tell the children that this is what happens when there is a fire in the house. Lead them in this fingerplay:

> *Ten brave firemen sleeping in a row, (fingers curled to make sleeping men)*
> *Ding dong goes the bell, (cup hand to ear to hear bell)*
> *And down the pole they go. (With fists together make hands slide down)*
> *Off on the engine, pull out the hose, (hold nozzle-fist-to direct hose)*
> *When all the fire is out, so-o-o slow.*
> *Back to bed, and in a row. (curl all fingers again for sleeping men)*

Related books

Fire! Fire! by Gail Gibbons
Curious George by H.A. Rey
Changes, Changes by Pat Hutchins

—*Kathleen Shea, West Brookfield, MA*

Finger Cast Puppets

4+

Children are often fascinated by casts. Here they will get to help make and wear one besides turning it into something fun to play with.

Materials needed

Cotton roll or gauze
Casting plaster (can be purchased at medical supply stores or donated by a local hospital or physician)
Water
Shallow bowls or cups
Colored markers
Medicine cups or felt to make puppet hats or clothing (optional)

What to do

1. Cut casting plaster into 2 inch wide, 3 inch long strips (approximately).
2. Divide cotton or gauze into square pieces, large enough to be wrapped around each child's finger.
3. Place water in shallow receptacles such as small bowls or cups.
4. Give each child a piece of cotton or gauze and three or four strips of casting plaster.
5. Have each child wrap the cotton or gauze around one of their fingers and hold it in place.
6. Instruct the children to take a strip of plaster and soak it in water for a few seconds, remove it from water and wrap it around the cotton or gauze on their finger. This may be difficult for them to do by themselves so have them work in pairs (doctor/patient) or with an adult.
7. Repeat until the child has covered the entire finger. Three strips should be sufficient.
8. Have children wet another finger with water and smooth out the small holes in the plaster and create a solid surface.
9. Allow three to five minutes for the cast to dry and then slide it off the child's finger.
10. Let children decorate their "puppets" with markers. Small medicine cups or other materials can be used for hats if desired.

More to do

Discuss the differences in the textures of the materials (rough versus smooth, dry versus wet, soft versus hard). Discuss the experiences of the children or their relatives who may have had casts.

Related song

"Put Your Finger in the Air"

—Michelle Barnea, Dover, NJ

What Makes Our Bones Strong

4+

The children will observe what would happen to our bones without the mineral calcium that we get from dairy products and broccoli.

Materials needed

Vinegar
Two bones (chicken/turkey leg or wing bones)
Two glass jars with lids

What to do

1. Explain to the children that vinegar is an acid and can soften bones by dissolving the calcium in them.
2. Pour vinegar into one of the jars and drop in a bone. Place another bone in an empty jar. Put lids on both jars.
3. Let the bones sit for four to seven days (turkey bones will probably take longer), until the bone in the vinegar begins to get soft.
4. Take out both bones and let the children feel the difference between them.
5. Tell them that the acid in the vinegar removed the calcium from the bone, making it soft. Ask what they think our bodies would be like if our bones were soft like this.
6. Discuss the importance of calcium-rich foods like milk, dairy products and broccoli in our diets and how they help strengthen our bones.

More to do

Cut open the soft bone and examine the marrow (soft brownish material) inside. Discuss the function of the bone marrow in making red and white blood cells.

Related books

The Skeleton Inside You by Phillip Balestrino

—Kathy Schauff, Laurel, MD

Sneeze Experiment

4+

This fun activity will allow the children to experience how germs spread when we cough and sneeze.

Materials needed

Spray bottle filled with colored water (food coloring)
White tissue paper
Those Mean, Nasty, Dirty, Downright Disgusting but Invisible Germs by J. Rice

What to do

1. To introduce the concept of germs, read the book aloud to the children.
2. Discuss the concept of germs. Emphasize that germs are invisible and can make us sick. Explain to the children that we can acquire germs outside, in the bathroom, from our pets or from someone who is sick.
3. Show the spray bottle to the children and explain that it contains colored water. When we spray the water it's like sneezing except that the water bottle doesn't spray germs.
4. Spray the water onto the tissue. Tell the children that the colored marks on the paper are to show us what happens when we sneeze.
5. Allow the children to spray the "sneeze germs" on the tissue paper. Encourage discussion, emphasizing that hand washing kills germs.

More to do

This activity may be extended to an art activity. Have several spray bottles of colored water and enough tissue paper for each child to do a picture. This can be a table, floor or easel activity. You could end this activity with a discussion of the proper way to wash hands and have the children practice. Teach song below.

HEALTH & SAFETY

Related song

To the tune of "Mulberry Bush":

This is the way we wet our hands,
Wet our hands, wet our hands.
This is the way we wet our hands
When we're killing germs.
This is the way we rub with soap...
This is the way we rinse our hands...
This is the way we dry our hands...

—Patricia L. Stash, Pontiac, IL

Safety

4+

This activity focuses on learning the need for safety with strangers and when crossing the street.

Materials needed

Black construction paper cut into 4" x 12" rectangles—one per child
Three circles of construction paper, red, green and yellow—one set per child
Scissors
Pencils
Paste

What to do

1. Pre-cut the construction paper for younger children. Five and six year olds can trace a pattern of the circle and cut it out themselves.
2. Discuss safe and not safe situations with the children. Read them a book such as *Never Talk to Strangers*.
3. Teach the children the refrain: "No, no, I won't go! I will tell someone I know!" Have them hold their hands up in front of them up when chanting the refrain.

When the crossing guard is not at the busy street corner, you say...(refrain)
When someone you don't know offers to give you money or candy, you say...(refrain)
When a stranger offers to give you a ride home, you say...(refrain)
When a friend wants you to take a shortcut home, you say...(refrain)
When the stoplight is RED, you say...(refrain)

4. Have the children make stoplights by pasting the circles on the black rectangle.

More to do

Send the stop light and a copy of the chant home with each child and have them say it with an adult. Take a walk around the neighborhood and discuss safe and unsafe situations.

Related books

Never Talk to Strangers by Irma Joyce
Berenstain Bears and Strangers by Jan and Stan Berenstain

—Barbara Saul, Eureka, CA

Phone Home

4+

The children will develop an awareness of phone numbers and telephone etiquette.

Materials needed

Pre-cut phone shapes out of construction paper—one per child
Small paper plates—one per child
Ink pads
Crayons
Model toy phone (optional)
Glue or paper fasteners

What to do

1. Make the phone shapes from construction paper.
2. Discuss different types of telephones (colors, shapes, etc.) with the children. Point out the different parts of the telephone and encourage them to describe each part and its functions. Telephone etiquette and safety rules can also be discussed.
3. Have the children color a telephone.
4. Glue the paper plate to the center of the telephone to represent the dial. These can also be attached at the center with a paper fastener so that they will turn.
5. Have each child stamp their finger print around the edge of the dial where each number should be. When this is dry, you can help them fill in the corresponding number at the center of each fingerprint.
6. At the bottom of the telephone, write each child's telephone number. Above each number, ask the child to make a stack of thumb prints to represent each digit in their own telephone number. (For example, above the number five, the child would place five thumb prints, above the number two, there would be two thumb prints, etc.)
7. During free time, place a play telephone and all of the children's telephone creations together and have them practice "calling" all of the numbers.

—Margaret Dubaj, Niles, OH

HEALTH & SAFETY

Wrapping Presents   3+

Children improve fine motor skills while participating in this universally popular activity.

Materials needed

Used wrapping paper, ribbon and boxes gathered from celebrations such as birthdays, Hanukkah, Mother's/Father's Day, Chinese New Year and Christmas
Tape
Scissors
Writing utensils
Construction paper (for card making)

What to do

1. Collect a variety of used gift wrapping materials in a large bag or box including paper, ribbons and small gift boxes. The children can also be encouraged to donate used wrapping goods.
2. Display the wrapping materials on a table or shelf for children's easy access.
3. Provide tape and scissors for wrapping.
4. Show the children how to wrap a sample "gift."
5. Writing utensils and construction paper can be added if children are interested in making greeting cards.
6. The materials can be reused over and over again as the children give presents to other children and adults in the classroom.

More to do

Older preschool children may participate in helping sort the wrapping materials with the teacher before the actual wrapping begins. Dramatic play props can include wrapping materials to enhance multi-cultural celebrations.

Related books

Christmas by Peter Spier
The Christmas Box by Eve Merriam
Sheep in a Shop by Nancy Shaw

—Nancy Schwider/Janis Ditchfield, Glen Ellyn, IL

Birthday Celebration   2+

This activity helps each young child feel special on his birthday.

Materials needed

Birthday card
Birthday hat
Treasure chest
Tablet and colored pencils
Stuffed animals

What to do

1. In a decorated box (the "treasure chest"), place a tablet and colored pencils for the child to receive as presents. Hide the treasure chest in the classroom.
2. Give the birthday card and hat to the birthday child.
3. Have everyone sing Happy Birthday (most young children can sing this song).
4. Tell the birthday child to search for the Treasure Chest. Give clues if necessary.
5. Show the child the stuffed animals and ask if he or she would like to pick one to keep for the day (perhaps to take home and return the next day).

More to do

Other children in the class might make birthday cards. Prepare and enjoy a birthday snack.

Related books

Shoes From Grandpa by Mem Fox
Happy Birthday, Sam by Pat Hutchins

—Alvera Bade, Beatrice, NE

Birthdays! Birthdays! 3+

This activity will help children develop a positive self-image and realize that our skills grow as we grow.

Materials needed

Large piece of paper
Scissors
Crayons
Paste
Small candles
Collage materials for each child

What to do

1. Hang a chart in your room showing all the children's birthdays or draw a cake on the calendar whenever a birthday occurs.
2. On the child's birthday or half birthday (for summer children) talk about how old the birthday child is during your calendar activity or circle time. Discuss all the things we can do as we get older.
3. Give the birthday child a large piece of paper, scissors, crayons, candles and collage materials. Ask the child to draw a large circle for a cake (help younger children).
4. The child may color the "cake" then decorate it with crayons, lace, flowers, ribbons and so on. Paste a candle on the cake for each year. Write on the paper, "_____ is __ years old."

More to do

Children may draw something they can do this year that they couldn't do last year. Label the page, "Now I Can....". Ask senior citizens to come in and tell about their childhood and their birthdays as they grew up.

Related songs

"You're Growing" by Fred Rogers on *Won't You Be My Neighbor?*

—Wendy Pfeffer, Pennington, NJ

Halloween—Spider's Web Game   3+

The children will have a chance to practice gross motor skills in the classroom while playing this Halloween game, a wonderful party activity.

Materials needed

Black yarn

What to do

1. Set a large piece of furniture or gym equipment in the center of your classroom or gym.
2. String the yarn from the equipment to other outlying equipment in the room to form a large spider web covering the game space. Wrap the yarn around table legs, chairs, or shelves, and keep returning to the center. Be sure that your strings vary in height.
3. Have children, from one to three at a time, take turns moving in and out of the spider's web, trying not to get stuck!

More to do

Hang small spider rings or plastic bugs from various points in the web for children to retrieve as they move about the web. Hide a tiny plastic fly somewhere and challenge them to "find the spider's dinner."

Related song

"The Great Big Spider" (to the tune of "Eensy Weensy Spider" but substitute the words Great Big Spider)

—Sandra Suffoletto Ryan, Buffalo, NY

Halloween—Melt the Witch   3+

Children will improve gross motor skills while playing a fun Halloween game.

Materials needed

Moveable chalkboard
Colored chalk
Sponges
Bin of water

What to do

1. Draw a witch's head or whole body on the chalkboard (make sure witch is not too scary looking).
2. Place the board in an area where it will stand alone and not fall over.
3. Fill the bin with water and sponges.
4. Have children stand close enough to the board to be able to hit it accurately with a wet sponge. Place water bin and sponges near this spot.
5. Tell children to take turns throwing wet sponges at the witch to try and "melt" her away. (As the witch becomes wet and water drips down the board, it will appear as if she is melting.) Be sure that children are squeezing out the sponges before throwing!

More to do

Draw other Halloween characters on the board, or let the children draw them, and repeat the activity.
Sing "The Witch's Brew" song:

Stirring and stirring and stirring our brew
oooooooooo oo ooooooooooo oo
Stirring and stirring and stirring our brew
oooooooooo oo ooooooooooo oo
Tiptoe, tiptoe, tiptoe, BOO!

—*Sandra Suffoletto Ryan, Buffalo, NY*

Halloween—A Charlie Brown Halloween   3+

Children use descriptive words to expand their vocabulary.

Materials needed

It's the Great Pumpkin, Charlie Brown
Prepared figures
Song printed on chart paper

What to do

1.   Write the following song on chart story paper.
"Sitting in the Pumpkin Patch" (to the tune of "London Bridge Is Falling Down")

Sitting in a pumpkin patch.
Pumpkin patch, pumpkin patch.
Sitting in a pumpkin patch,
Waiting for the Great Pumpkin.
I think I see him in the sky,
In the sky, in the sky.
I think I see him in the sky.
Is it the Great Pumpkin?
It's just a _____ passing by,
Passing by, passing by.
It's just a _____ passing by,
Not just the Great Pumpkin.

2.   Prepare cutout figures, such as a green goblin, black cat, orange pumpkin, spooky bat, ugly witch, white ghost or red devil.
3.   Read the book aloud to the children.
4.   Sing the song to the children, pointing to the words.
5.   Describe the figures to the children. Talk about the descriptive words.
6.   Teach the children the song.
7.   Select children to pick figures to sing about.
8.   Sing the song, each time choosing a different child to select a figure to sing about.

More to do

Allow the children to make their own figures and use descriptive words to describe them. Write the words in large print and have the children "read" their words and show their figures. Make a bulletin board with the figures.

Related books

Cranberry Halloween by Wende and Harry Devlin
Clifford's Halloween by Normal Bridwell
Arthur's Halloween by Marc Brown

—Debbie Chaplin, Hot Springs, VA

Halloween—Pumpkin Mosaic   3+

Children practice fine motor skills through an art activity.

Materials needed

Paper plates
Hole punch
Glue
Scissors
Yarn
Black, orange, green construction paper

What to do

1. Cut out different faces from black construction paper (happy, sad, angry, scared).
2. Give each child a paper plate and a piece of orange construction paper.
3. Have the children rip the construction paper into small pieces.
4. Let the children cover the paper plate with glue and cover the entire plate with the orange pieces.
5. When they are finished, let the children glue on a face of their choosing. You may want to lay them out on a table beforehand.
6. Let the children cut out a stem from your green paper and glue it on.
7. Punch a hole in the top and the children can string the yarn through.

More to do

Ask children to give a situation that corresponds with the face they chose. Example: "The pumpkin saw a witch fly by and that's why he's got a scared face." Visit a pumpkin patch.

Related books

How Spider Saved Halloween by Robert Kraus

—Lauren O'Neill/Ann O'Donnell, Abington, PA

Halloween—Sewing a Spider's Web

Children improve their fine motor skills and practice number recognition and sequencing while sewing a spider's web.

Materials needed

Cardboard rectangles or large meat trays (approximately 8" x 6") with ten holes punched around the edges, one per child
Black or orange yarn
Childproof plastic needles
Number lines from one to ten (as needed)

What to do

1. Around the rim of the cardboard or tray, write the numbers from one to ten out of sequence (see illustration).
2. Thread the needles with yarn and knot the end. If possible, have the children do this.
3. Begin the first stitch at number one (sew up from behind, so the knot will be on the back) and make each stitch to the next number in its proper sequence through ten. This will make the spider's web. Have number lines available (taped to the table or in some way displayed in the work area) for those who need them.

More to do

Make a spider out of black construction paper and put it inside the web.

Related books

Be Nice to the Spiders by Margaret Graham
The Very Busy Spider by Eric Carle

—*Jyoti Joshi, Framingham, MA*

Figure 1

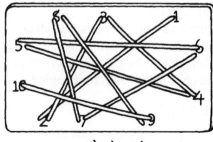

Thread yarn through numbers.

Figure 2

spider's web

Halloween—Pumpkin Windsock

4+

Children will make a Halloween decoration and learn about the value of recycling.

Materials needed

Empty 12 oz. frozen juice cans
Orange, green and black construction paper
Orange streamers
Glue
Green yarn
Hole punch
Black markers
Scissors

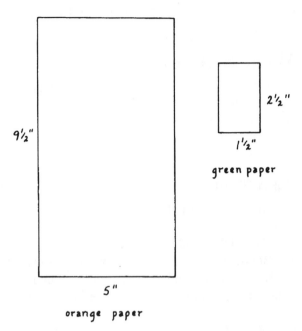

9½"

5"

orange paper

2½"

1½"

green paper

What to do

1. In advance, cut out the bottoms of empty juice cans; draw 5" x 9 1/2" rectangles on orange construction paper and 1 1/2" x 2 1/2" rectangles on green construction paper; and cut five 30" pieces of orange streamers and one 25" piece of green yarn for each windsock.
2. Have the children cut out the orange and green rectangles.
3. Give each child in the class the materials she will need to make the windsock (one juice can, one orange and one green rectangle, five pieces of orange streamer and one piece of green yarn). Put out markers and glue.
4. Tell the children to put glue along the 5" edge of the orange rectangle and wrap the rectangle around the juice can to cover the surface. Smooth down the glued end to anchor the wrap in place.
5. Have the children glue the green rectangle to the inside of one end of the can so that it sticks up like the stem of a pumpkin.
6. Show the children how to draw a Jack-O-Lantern face on the side of the can directly below the green stem using black markers.
7. Tell the children to glue one end of each orange streamer to the inside of the bottom of the pumpkin can. Make sure they use all five streamers and cover the bottom perimeter.
8. Punch two holes opposite each other (left to right) on top side of can, approximately 1/2" down from top edge.
9. Tell the children to thread green yarn through holes and tie ends into a knot, for hanging.

green stem

green yarn

hole

juice can

orange streamers

More to do

Have children parade outside holding their windsock streamers. This works best on a windy day.

—Kathryn Daelhousen, Leominster, MA

220

Thanksgiving—Tom Turkey's Feathers

Through this activity, children learn to recognize, match and name colors.

Materials needed

Large piece of posterboard
Scissors
Assorted colors of construction paper
Markers
Masking tape

What to do

1. Draw a turkey on a large piece of posterboard. Give him approximately 15 to 25 feathers in assorted colors.
2. Cut out an equal number of feathers (all the same size) from a piece of posterboard. Color one side of the feather to match each feather on the turkey.
3. Hang the turkey on a poster, wall or blackboard at the children's level.
4. Place the cut-out feathers in a pile color side down.
5. Have the children choose a feather from the pile one at a time. When a child picks a feather, ask what color it is. If the child does not know, other children can help.
6. Put tape on the plain side of the feather and let the child place their feather on a feather of the same color on the turkey poster.

More to do

The children can count how many feathers there are of each color. After all the feathers have been placed on the turkey, you can reinforce color recognition by asking each child to find or take off a certain color feather. For older children, color words can be written on cut-out feathers. Children can read the color word when they pick a feather and then place on the correct color on turkey.

Related books

Sometimes It's Turkey, Sometimes It's Feathers by Lorna Balian
Thanksgiving Day by Gail Gibbons
Color Dance by Ann Jonas
Do You Know Your Colors? by J.P. Miller and Katherine Howard

—*Janet Shearer, Manville, NJ*

Thanksgiving—Trick That Turkey

The children will develop auditory/listening skills during this activity.

Materials needed

Card table or other small table
Sheet or blanket
Picture of a turkey

What to do

1. Cover the table with the sheet to make a "turkey house." Tape or pin the turkey picture to the front of the turkey house. Gather the children in front of the turkey house.
2. Explain that you have made a turkey house, and discuss what animal might live there.
3. Explain that a turkey only comes out of his house when you call him the right way, leading the discussion to the idea that the turkey will only come out when he hears "gobble, gobble."
4. Establish the basic rule of the game by asking, "Will the turkey come out if we say 'moo' . . . 'oink' . . . 'tweet-tweet?'"
5. Ask or select a child to be the turkey. This child goes into the turkey house, with a reminder that the turkey only comes out when he hears "gobble, gobble." You may want to ask the child, "Will you come out if we say 'meow?'"
6. Now it is time to trick that turkey! Elicit suggestions from the group as to what animal noise they should make in order to trick the turkey. Remember to be quiet so the turkey doesn't know you are trying to trick him.
7. Make three or four "incorrect" animal noises, before finally deciding that you just can't trick the turkey. Call him the right way by saying, "gobble, gobble."
8. Give the turkey a big hand for being so hard to trick.
9. If a turkey should be tricked, coming out at the wrong time, talk to the turkey. "Turkey, did we say 'gobble, gobble'? Get back in your house. You are such a silly turkey." You may then want to reinforce the rule by questioning the turkey once again.

More to do

Substitute another animal for the turkey.

—LouAnn Kaletka Gayan, Ottawa, IL

Thanksgiving—Handy Turkey 4+

Children will have fun with this Thanksgiving activity, while improving their fine motor skills.

Materials needed

6" x 9" construction papers, different colors
Markers
Scissors
Glue or stapler

What to do

1. Trace shoe on brown paper and cut out to make the turkey's body.
2. Trace hand with fingers spread apart on other colors of construction paper and cut out to make feathers.
3. Glue or staple feathers onto turkey's body.
4. Draw or make a waddle, eyes and beak from the leftover scrap paper.

More to do

Staple the turkey to a lunch bag to make a puppet.

—Jyoti Joshi, Framingham, MA

Hanukkah—Menorah Game

Children will learn about Hanukkah and practice skills such as number recognition and counting.

Materials needed

Posterboard or oaktag
Markers
Clear contact paper

What to do

1.   Make the game. Cut four playing boards (8" x 8") from oaktag and on each, draw nine squares of equal size. Draw the Star of David in the middle square and number the other squares one through eight. Cut 36 small square cards (the same size as the squares on the playing board) from posterboard. On 32 of the cards draw a menorah and add candles to match the numbers on the playing board (e.g., four menorah cards will show one candle, four will show two, four will show three, etc., up to eight candles). On the remaining four blank cards draw the Star of David. Color the cards and boards and cover with clear contact paper.
2.   Play the game. Hand out the boards to four children and place the small cards face down on the table. Children take turns picking a card and placing it on their boards. If they pick a menorah card, they match the number of candles in the menorah to the number in the square (a card showing two candles in the menorah is placed over the number two square); if they pick a Star of David card they put it in the middle square. If they pick a card they already have, they should put the card at the bottom of the pile. The game continues until one or all of the children have their filled their boards.

More to do

Talk about Hanukkah with the children before playing the game. Bring a menorah into class and light one candle for each day of Hanukkah.

Related books

The Story of Hanukkah by Amy Ehrlich
I Love Hanukkah by Marilyn Hirsch
The Chanukkah Guest by Eric A. Kimmel

—*Janet Shearer, Manville, NJ*

Hanukkah—Menorah Match-Ups

Children learn to match colors and patterns.

Materials needed

1 or more Hanukkah menorahs
1 set of patterned cards
1 or more 44-count boxes Hanukkah candles (assorted colors)

What to do

1.   Fill one menorah with a single color or simple pattern of candles. Leave the remaining menorah(s) unfilled for use by the children.

2.   Introduce both the menorah and this activity to your children as a group. Show the children your candle-filled menorah.

3.   Traditionally, the first candle in the menorah is placed on your right as you face the menorah. New candles are added to the left. However, it might be wiser to start at the left for this activity.

4.   As the children face the menorah, point to the first candle. Help the children identify the color by name.

5.   Invite one child to locate another candle of the same color in the candle box. Help the child place the new candle into the second menorah. The candle's color and placement should match those of the first candle in the original menorah.

6.   Continue until the second menorah (the children's menorah) is filled to match the first menorah.

7.   Children may work on subsequent candle patterns independently. Several children may work on this at the same time, depending on the number of menorahs available.

More to do

If only one menorah is available, prepare a set of ten or more pattern cards. Use blank 6" x 8" index cards to draw menorahs. Use colored markers to match those of your candles and fill the menorah with pictures of candles. To be certain that you have a sufficient number of candles of each color, lay out a set of candles and copy the arrangement of the set onto the illustrated menorah on the card. Vary the colors or patterns on the cards. There are many types of Hanukkah menorahs. Invite a Jewish parent to visit your classroom and show how the menorah is filled and lighted.

Related books

Chanukah Is.... by Martin Lemelman
Rainbow Candles: A Chanukah Counting Book by Myra Shostak

Related song

"By the Window (Where You Can See the Glow From My Menorah)"

—*Marji E. Gold-Vukson, West Lafayette, IN*

Hanukkah—Menorah   4+

Children learn about the Jewish holiday of Hanukkah.

Materials needed

10" x 12" blue and yellow construction paper
Eight white paper strips or stickers plus one strip longer than the others, per child
Cotton balls, nine per child
Orange paint
Cotton swabs
Markers
Scissors
Glue

What to do

1.   On the yellow paper, trace both of the child's hands with thumbs overlapping. Outline only the fingers, not the palms or wrists.

2.   Cut the tracing and glue it onto the blue paper.

3. Glue eight white strips for candles on all fingers but the thumbs. The center candle sits in both thumbs and should be taller than the other candles.
4. Glue cotton balls to the candles as flames.
5. With cotton swabs, paint the tips of the cotton balls orange.

More to do

Discuss with the children the importance of different cultures.

—Jyoti Joshi, Framingham, MA

Christmas—Holiday Wreath

2+

This activity teaches spatial relations.

Materials needed

Pasta (any shape)
One can of green spray paint
Two circles from green tag board or posterboard for each child
6" of thin red ribbon tied into a bow for each child
8" thin red yarn for each child
Instant camera and film for photographs of each child
Glue
Hole punch

What to do

1. Cut out two circles per child from tagboard or posterboard.
2. Cut out a circular center of one of the circles. (The lid of a one pound coffee can is a good size.)
3. Cut the ribbon into 6" lengths and the yarn into 8" lengths.
4. Take an instant photograph of each child.
5. Give the children posterboard wreath shapes and ask them to glue pasta to their own wreath. After glue dries, help each child spray paint the pasta. Let it dry.
6. Next, help the children put a photo of themselves in the hole and glue it on the back posterboard circle.
7. Place a red ribbon bow at the bottom of the wreath.
8. Punch a hole at the top and thread with red yarn. Hang the wreath.

More to do

Other frames can be made with tongue depressors and decorated with acorns or miniature pine cones. Heart shapes from red poster board could be used at Valentine's Day or pink for Mother's Day. Sea shells could be used rather than pasta and left natural.

—Marjorie Schwickrath, Reston, VA

Christmas—Christmas Presents 2+

Children improve their visual perception by identifying toys of different sizes.

Materials needed

Large and small boxes
Toys that fit each box
1 pillowcase

What to do

1. Put the toys in the pillowcase. Tell the children it's just like Santa's bag.
2. Let each child pick a toy from Santa's bag.
3. Each child decides what box the toy should go in and puts the toy in it. (Depending on ability the child can chose between all the boxes or just two of your choice).
4. Continue with each child.

More to do

Have two different-sized dolls, combs or other objects, and discuss sizes. Have the children identify the toys before putting them in boxes.

—Susan Westby, Palm Bay, FL

Christmas—Recycled Paper Ornaments 2+

By making this special holiday decoration, children learn the basic concepts of recycling and that even they can help recycle.

Materials needed

Carton-sized box of shredded paper
Large plastic or metal bucket
Warm water
Liquid starch
Large wooden spoon
School glue
Colander
Glitter
A few metal cookie sheets or trays
2 aluminum pie tins
Paper clips (one per child)
Wood screws (one per child)
Letter to families

What to do

1. Prepare for this activity at the beginning of December. Gather materials. Ask a local company to save carton-sized box of shredded paper for your class.

2. Talk to the children about garbage and the problems it creates for our environment (no room for it, spoils our drinking water, pollutes the air, etc.) Talk a little about recycling. Ask if there are ways that the children's families help to recycle things.

3. Show the children the box of shredded paper. Tell the children that we will recycle this into holiday tree ornaments instead of throwing it away and creating more garbage.

4. Have the children help put the shredded paper into the bucket. They may tear the shredded paper into smaller bits.

5. When the bucket is three-quarters full, slowly add water and have the children take turns stirring the mass with a large wooden spoon.

6. Pour in one cup of liquid starch and continue to add water until the water is about 1" above the level of the paper.

7. Stir the paper and water mixture occasionally for the next two days. Add more water if the mixture seems dry.

8. For the activity, have each child take a handful of the pulpy mass and squeeze the excess liquid back into the bucket. Tell the child to make a big "meatball" shape (about the size of a baseball).

9. As each paper ball is created, place it on the metal tray to dry.

10. When all of the pulp has been made into paper balls, be sure not to pour the remaining liquid down the drain. Strain it in a colander first. Otherwise the bits of paper will clog the drains.

11. Let the paper balls dry for about one week. A faster way to dry them is to put them into a low oven (about 225 degrees) until they are dry.

12. When dry, put one wood screw into each paper ball allowing the screw head to be exposed about 1/4 inch.

13. Put a pie tin containing glue and another container containing glitter on the table.

14. Have the children roll the ball in the glue and then the glitter.

15. Place the finished piece on the metal tray to dry.

16. After a day or two, bend paper clips into an "S" shape and attach one end to the exposed screw head so that the glittered ball can be hung as an ornament.

More to do

Send a note home with ornament explaining the activity and how the children have learned about recycling. Brainstorm different ways the class could re-use things such as empty milk containers, plastic bags, paper bags, cardboard, etc.

Related books

Christmas Tree Memories by Aliki

—*Marjorie Debowy, Moriches, NY*

Christmas—Santa, Santa, Walk Around 2+

Children will enjoy a simple game with a Christmas theme.

Materials needed

Santa hat
Small box wrapped as Christmas gift

What to do

1. Have the children sit in a circle.
2. Pick one child to be "Santa." Have the child put on the Santa hat.
3. Santa carries the present and walks around the outside of the circle while the rest of the group chants, "Santa, Santa, walk around, Santa put the present down!"

4. Santa puts the present down behind a seated child. That child picks up the present and tries to tag Santa, who runs around the circle to the empty place and sits down. If Santa is tagged, he must do it again. If Santa reaches the empty space without being tagged, the child holding the present puts on the hat and becomes the Santa.

5. The game continues until all the children have had a turn.

—Mary Paciocco, Appomattox, VA

Christmas—Handy Holiday Wreath $3+$

Here is a way to make a holiday wreath using tracings of the children's hands. This would be an excellent project for the whole class to work on together.

Materials needed

10" x 12" green construction paper
Red buttons or bottlecaps, or a red marker
Scissors
Stapler
Glue

What to do

1. Trace the children's hand prints onto the green paper. You will only need one hand tracing from each child for a class wreath, but each child could make her own using seven or eight personal hand tracings.
2. Have the children help you cut out the hand prints.
3. Staple all the hand cut-outs together in a circle, palm-to-fingers (see illustration).
4. For berries, glue the red buttons or bottle caps around the wreath, or draw them in with the red marker.
5. Use your class wreath as a door decoration or as the centerpiece of a holiday bulletin board display.

—Jyoti Joshi, Framingham, MA

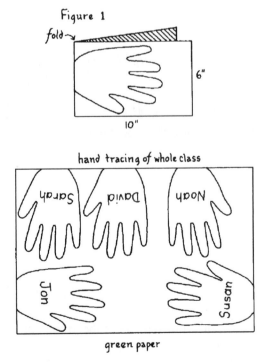

Figure 1

fold

6"

10"

hand tracing of whole class

Sarah David Noah

Jon Susan

green paper

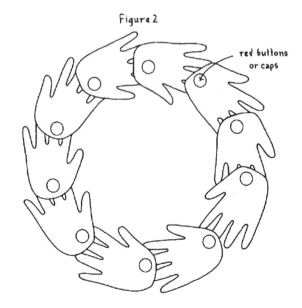

Figure 2

red buttons or caps

Christmas—
Rudolph the Red-Nosed Reindeer

Children learn about animals and nature through a creative experience that improves their fine motor skills.

Materials needed

6" x 10" brown construction paper
Two small twigs or black construction paper
Red pompons, one per child
Black buttons (optional)
Sparkles or glitter
Markers
Scissors
Glue, stapler or tape

What to do

1. Trace shoe on brown construction paper and cut out.
2. Unless using small twigs for antlers, trace hand on folded black construction paper, making sure the fingers are separated, and cut out (see figure 1). You now have one shoe and two hand cut-outs.
3. Glue the hand cut-outs (or tape twigs) on either side of the top of the shoe cut-out.
4. Glue buttons or draw eyes, glue a red pompon for the nose, and draw a mouth.
5. Glue sparkles on the nose to make it twinkle (see figure 3).

Related book

Rudolph the Red-Nose Reindeer

Related song

"Rudolph the Red-Nose Reindeer" by Barbara Shook Hazen

—Jyoti Joshi, Framingham, MA

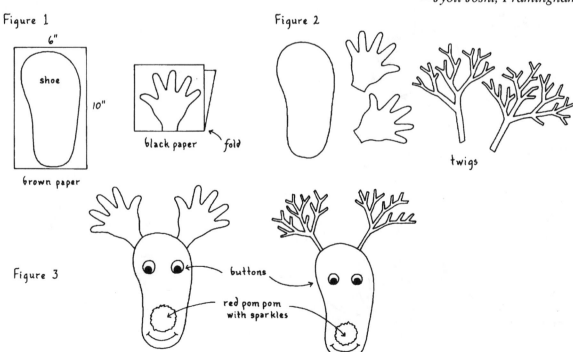

Figure 1
6"
shoe
10"
brown paper
black paper
fold

Figure 2
twigs

Figure 3
buttons
red pom pom
with sparkles

Christmas—Santa Pocket

3+

Children learn about sharing and giving and to recognize shapes.

Materials needed

9" diameter paper plates, two per child
9" x 12" red construction paper
Red pompons, one per child
Black buttons, two per child
Cotton balls
Markers
Scissors
Stapler

What to do

1. Cut one plate in half and staple it on top of the other plate.
2. Cut a triangle shape out of red paper for Santa's hat and staple it to the plate.
3. Glue cotton balls all over half of the plate and one cotton ball on the tip of Santa's hat.
4. Use buttons for eyes and a pompon for a nose, or draw them with markers.

More to do

Use Santa pocket to store holiday cards. For St. Patrick's Day, make a green hat instead of red.

—*Jyoti Joshi, Framingham, MA*

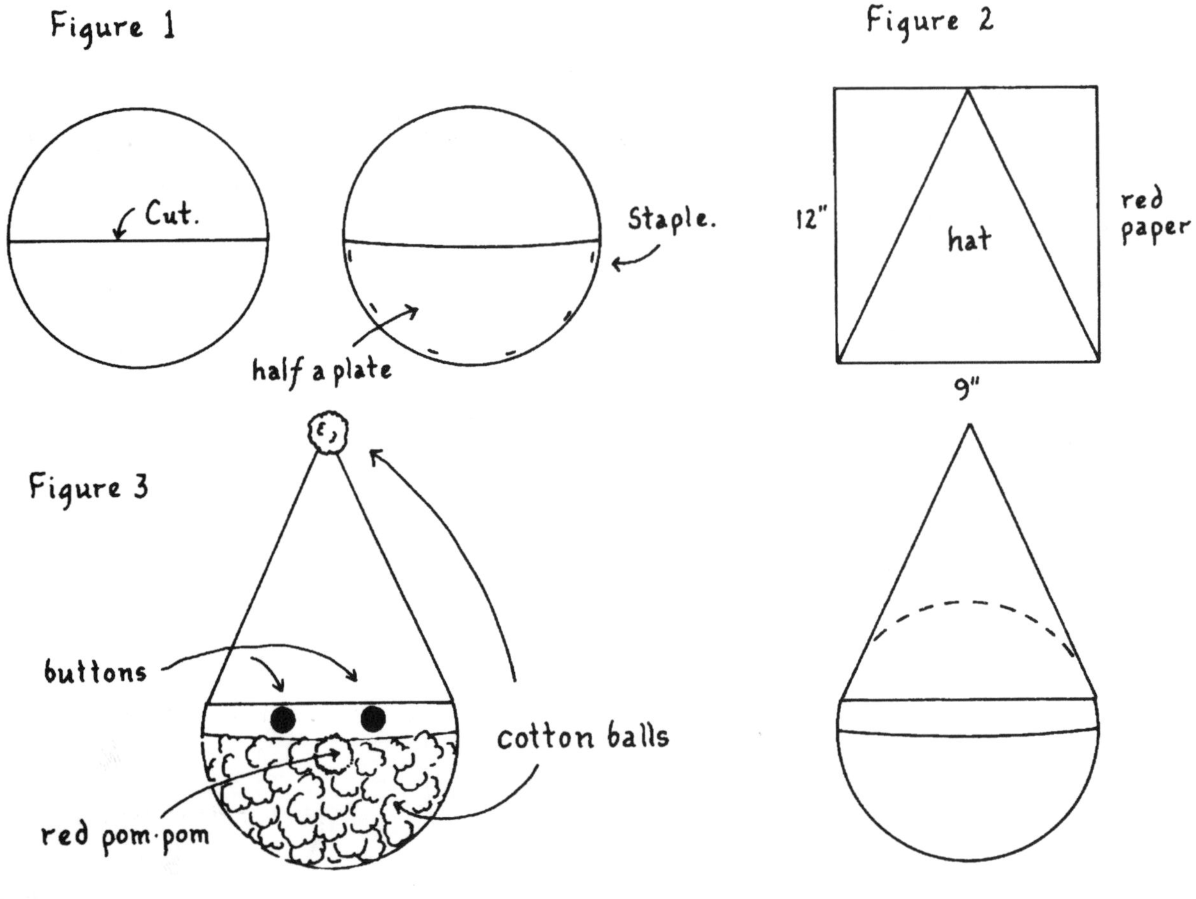

Figure 1

Cut.

Staple.

half a plate

Figure 2

12"   hat   red paper

9"

Figure 3

buttons

cotton balls

red pom·pom

Christmas—The Nutcracker

Children will experience how a nutcracker works and learn about different kinds of nuts.

Materials needed

One or more nutcrackers (invite children to bring in nutcrackers from home)
Nuts (assorted varieties)

What to do

1. Separate nuts by type and place them in labeled containers.
2. Demonstrate how to safely use a nutcracker to open a nut.
3. As children crack the nuts, talk about what different nuts are called and ask children to describe how they look and taste inside. Enjoy the nuts at snack time.

More to do

Bake banana nut bread or some other favorite recipe using nuts. Show an old-fashioned nutcracker (like the one in Tchaikovsky's "The Nutcracker" ballet). Read the story of the Nutcracker and play musical selections from the ballet. Use nuts for classification and counting activities. Make Christmas tree decorations by painting walnuts gold and stringing a thread through the top.

Related books

The Nutcracker Ballet by Deborah Hautzig

—Jane Gordon, Fountain Hills, AZ

Christmas—Egg Carton Christmas Tree

This activity gives the children an opportunity to work in a group.

Materials needed

Approximately 50 paper egg cartons
Glue
Green paint
Decorations (children would make)

What to do

1. Glue six egg cartons together to form the tree base. Continue to stack and glue using fewer cartons on each level. Allow to dry.
2. Paint green, add decorations

More to do

Leave the tree up after Christmas and remove the decorations. Add hearts for Valentine's Day or eggs for Easter.

—Lynne Saunders, Philadelphia, PA

"Christmas Joy" Photo Gifts

3+

The children will develop motor skills, creativity and self-esteem while creating a special holiday gift for their parents.

Materials needed

Pre-cut cardboard "JOY" backgrounds (see illustration)
Close-up individual photographs of children
Red and green tempera paint and brushes
Glue
An assortment of small decorative items: pieces of rick-rack and holiday ribbon, pretty buttons, glitter or confetti
Metallic cord or ribbon for hanging

What to do

1.   Tell the children that they are going to make a special holiday gift for their parents or someone else who is special to them.
2.   Give each child a cardboard "JOY" background to paint. Tell the child to completely cover the background with either red or green paint. Let dry.
3.   Put out an assortment of decorative items for the child to glue onto the background. Let dry.
4.   Tape each child's picture to the back of her background so that the child's face is displayed within the "O" of "Joy."
5.   Punch a hole in the top and add metallic cord or ribbon for hanging.
6.   Write the child's name and the year on the back of the gift (older children can do this themselves).

More to do

Give children wrapping paper and have them wrap their gifts. Give children holiday-shaped sponges or cookie cutters and tempera paint to make prints on colored tissue paper.

Related book

Merry Christmas Mom and Dad by Mercer Mayer

—Cynthia DeGilio, Arcadia, FL

Christmas—Glittering Pine Cones

Children make a beautiful tree ornament from natural items.

Materials needed

Large pine cones (approximately 6" long)
Glue in a bottle
Glitter in several different colors
Box lid (to hold pine cones while glittering)
Glue gun
Red or green velvet ribbon

What to do

1. Gather the materials and place them on the table.
2. Have each child select a pine cone and hold it over the box lid.
3. The children squirt glue over the entire pine cone.
4. Have each child select color(s) of glitter and sprinkle over the pine cone.
5. Allow glitter to dry at least 24 hours.
6. Make a loop from the ribbon and use the glue gun to attach it to the bottom of the pine cone. Allow another 24 hours to dry to make sure the ribbon is secured to the pine cone.

More to do

If children live in a section of the country where pine cones are plentiful, go on an outing so children can search for their own pine cones to decorate.

—Janet K. Nobles, Tulsa, OK

Christmas—Egg Carton Tree

Children learn about math, numbers, sharing and how to have a creative experience while using fine motor skills.

Materials needed

Styrofoam egg cartons in different colors
Posterboard
Glitter
Scissors
Glue

What to do

1. Cut egg cups from all egg cartons for a total of seventeen egg cups (see figure 1).
2. Glue one egg cup one inch from the top in the center of the posterboard.
3. Immediately beneath the single cup, glue two more, one on either side. Continue the pattern with a row of three, four, and five (see figure 2).
4. Ask the children what shape has been made.

5. Glue the two remaining egg cups vertically to form the trunk of the tree.
6. Put glitter on the tree for a festive look (see figure 3).

More to do

Use a toilet paper or paper towel tube dipped in paint to print rows of increasing size in the pattern indicated above. Use hand prints similarly. Use a footprint for the tree trunk.

—*Jyoti Joshi, Framingham, MA*

Figure 1

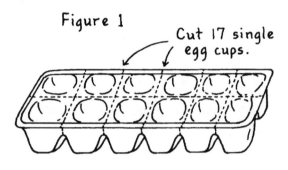

Cut 17 single egg cups.

Figure 2

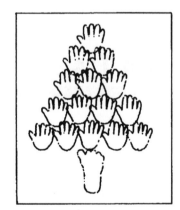

Start 1" from top.

Add glitter.

Figure 3

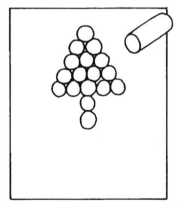

tube painting

hand and foot prints

See-Through Christmas Tree

Children will enjoy making a beautiful Christmas decoration for their classroom.

Materials needed

Green butcher paper
Wax paper squares (6" x 6")
Crayons
Grater
Small containers (one for each color of crayon shaved)
Travel iron
Newspapers

What to do

1.   Cut out a large Christmas tree shape from green butcher paper. (Its size will depend on where you want to display it; a large sunny window is an excellent place.)
2.   Sketch ornament shapes on the tree (balls, bells, angels, stars) and cut them out so each shape becomes a hole in the tree.
3.   Shave crayons and put shavings in separate containers according to color. (A small hand-held grater works best but remember that crayon shavings leave permanent stains on plastic graters.)
4.   Cover the work surface with newspapers.
5.   Plug in the travel iron. (These small, lightweight irons are ideal for crayon melting; children can use them with supervision.)
6.   Give each child two pieces of wax paper. (For safety reasons, allow only one child to do this activity at a time.)
7.   Tell the children to choose the colors of shaved crayon they want to use and place them on one piece of wax paper.
8.   Have the children cover the crayon shavings with another square of wax paper and iron the two together so that the crayons melt in the middle.
9.   Tape the shaved crayon picture to the back of the tree behind the cut-out areas, so the colors shine through when lighted from behind.

—Janet K. Nobles, Tulsa, OK

Bulletin Board Christmas Tree

Children will practice cutting circles and use basic shapes to create a Christmas symbol. The exercise will also reinforce quantitative concepts.

Materials needed

Aluminum pans from individual pot pies (the number will vary according to the size tree you wish to make)
Aluminum foil
Colored construction paper
Scissors
Thumb tacks

What to do

1. Trace, cut out and place a construction paper circle in the bottom of every pan.
2. Leaving room for a star, fasten one of the pans near the top of the bulletin board, placing the thumb tack in the center of the colored circle.
3. Fasten two pans below the first in the same fashion to make a second row, spacing them evenly on each side.
4. Continue to make new rows, adding one pan to each row, forming a triangle to fit your bulletin board. Leave space for a trunk—a rectangle cut from the brown paper in proportion to your tree.
5. Make a star from the aluminum foil and fasten to the top of the tree.

More to do

Number the rows and circles. Ask the children: "How is each row different? Which rows have more circles? Which rows have fewer?" You may want to make packages—squares and rectangles of various sizes. Play a guessing game—what might be inside each one? This will give the children an opportunity to relate size and shape of objects to the various squares and rectangles.

—*Mary Jo Shannon, Roanoke, VA*

Kwanzaa—Light the Kwanzaa Candles   4+

This simple holiday-time activity will allow the children to learn about an African cultural tradition with which they might be unfamiliar. The harvest festival known as Kwanzaa is celebrated from December 26th until January 1st in many African-American communities.

Materials needed

Seven cardboard toilet tissue rolls covered with construction paper: three red, three green and one black
Red, green and black construction paper candles the same height as the toilet tissue rolls (made by cutting the paper to size, rolling it around a pencil, securing the ends with tape, and slipping the pencil out) one per child
Yellow construction paper to make candle flames for each candle

What to do

1. Discuss the meaning of Kwanzaa and how it is celebrated (see below).
2. Put the covered cardboard rolls on a hard, flat surface in this order—three red, one black, three green.
3. Hand out the candles and tell the children that we are going to light the Kwanzaa candles.
4. One at a time, have each child tell the class the color of his or her own candle and place it in the matching candleholder.
5. After all the children have put their candles in the holders, the yellow flames should be visible.

More to do

Discuss with the children that learning about other cultures is interesting, helpful and fun.

Kwanzaa

Kwanzaa comes from the Kiswahili word "kwanza" which means "first." The essence of Kwanzaa is a true appreciation of Black people, building a sense of community and supporting common values.

DAY	PRINCIPLE	MEANING
December 26	Umoja	Unity
December 27	Kujichagulia	Self-determination
December 28	Ujima	Collective work and responsibility
December 29	Ujamaa	Cooperative economics
December 30	Nia	Purpose
December 31	Kuumba	Creativity
January 1	Imani	Faith

There are seven symbols of Kwanzaa:

SYMBOL	SYMBOLISM
Mkeka (straw mat)	Foundations upon which all else rests
Kinara (candle holder)	Original stalk from which we all come—African ancestors
Mishumaa saba (7 candles)	Nguzo saba—seven principles
Vibunzi (ears of corn)	Children—an ear for each child
Kikombe	Unity cup
Mazao (crops)	Fruits of our labor
Zawadi (gifts)	Rewards for our achievements

Lighting ceremony—Light one mishumaa each day symbolizing the principle of that day. Begin with the black candle, which represents the first principle, Umoja (unity). Each day after alternately light the red and green candles. After each lighting, discuss with the children the principle of the day.

—Brenda Hankins, Louisville, KY

Martin Luther King, Jr. Day— Friendship Circle

4+

This activity helps the children understand the principles that Martin Luther King believed in and his dream for all people to join hands and be friends.

Materials needed

Very large sheets of newsprint (at least 24" x 24"); one per child
Tempera paint in various colors
Paper towels

What to do

1. Place paper towels in shallow containers. Pour paint of one color into each container.
2. On large sheets of paper, lightly draw a large circle as a guide to help younger children.
3. Let each child pick one color of paint to use.
4. Have the first child begin by placing her hand in the chosen color of paint and then making a hand print on the paper of each of her classmates.
5. The next child picks a color, and repeats the above procedure.
6. Repeat so each child in class has a turn, forming a circle of hand prints.
7. If necessary to complete the circle shape, children may add additional hand prints.

8. When paint is dry, names may be added alongside the hand prints.

More to do

Talk about sharing toys, taking turns, and peaceful problem-solving, emphasizing the importance of discussion and cooperation. Discuss prejudice.

Related book

A Picture Book of Martin Luther King, Jr. by David Adler

—*Sally Lipke, Cape Girardeau, MO*

Martin Luther King, Jr. Day— "I Have a Dream" 5+

The children listen to the dreams Martin Luther King, Jr. had for the world and decide on a dream that would make the world a better place.

Materials needed

Material on the life of Dr. King
A copy of the "I Have a Dream" speech (optional)
Pages with "My dream for a better world" printed on them
Crayons or markers

What to do

1. Print "My dream for a better world" on a page or have it duplicated.
2. Read a book, show pictures, show a film or listen to a tape about the life and dreams of Dr. Martin Luther King, Jr.
3. Discuss the dreams Dr. King had for a better world.
4. Have the children dictate their dreams to the teacher, and write the dictation on the prepared pages.
5. Let the children illustrate their dreams.

More to do

Discuss other people and their dreams. Discuss how the students could make their dreams come true.

Related books

Martin Luther King, Jr. by Margaret Boone-Jones
Martin Luther King Day by Linda Lowery

—*Elaine Root, Garland, TX*

Chinese New Year Celebration

Children will develop an awareness and respect for another culture as they participate in a celebration of the Chinese New Year and experience Chinese food.

Materials needed

Musical instruments or noise-makers
Paint
Markers
Construction paper (green)
Scissors
Long piece of paper (as long as a bulletin board or wall)
Electric wok and utensils
Food for stir-fry: water chestnuts, broccoli, celery, rice, stir-fry seasoning, shrimp or chicken, baby corn
Paper plates and spoons

What to do

1. Introduce the concept of the Chinese New Year and compare the celebration to New Year's Day. Talk about how the Chinese celebrate with a parade and good things to eat. Point out China on a map or globe. Explain that dragons in China are good luck and that today the class is going to make its own good luck dragon.
2. Let the children watch you as you draw a dragon head at one end of the long paper. Have the children put their hands in green paint and press them down on the paper to make the dragon's feet. Continue on the dragon's back to make his scales. Draw a line around the palm prints.
3. Cut out a face hole. Cut the claws, ears and tail out of green construction paper; cut yarn for the beard and long ears.
4. Let the children cut up the vegetables with a plastic knife. Pre-heat the wok with oil and have the children gradually add the ingredients while you cook. Enjoy a Chinese meal.
5. Walk around the classroom or school with noise-makers or musical instruments. (Explain that on New Year's, the Chinese people make lots of noise to scare away nasty things like bad ghosts.)

More to do

Attach long poles or sticks to the large wall dragon and parade around the room or school. Let the children make their own individual dragon puppets out of paper bags. Have the children count all the hand prints on the dragon costume.

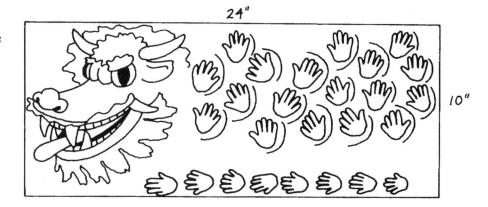

24"

10"

Related books

Lon Po Po by Ed Young
Tikki Tikki Tempo by Arlene Mosel

—*Teresa Jarmuz, Alden, NY*

Chinese New Year's Day

5+

The children will learn about Chinese culture and identify the name of the year according to the Chinese.

Materials needed

Placemats that list the names of the years in the twelve-year cycle (available from Chinese restaurants).
Tangerines
Fortune cookies

What to do

1. Chinese New Year's Day varies from year to year (depending on the new moon), but is usually in early February. Find out the date and the type of animal for the current year and begin to plan your Chinese New Year celebration.

> *1994—Dog*
> *1995—Boar*
> *1996—Rat*
> *1997—Ox*
> *1998—Tiger*
> *1999—Rabbit*
> *2000—Dragon*
> *2001—Snake*
> *2002—Horse*
> *2003—Sheep*

2. Before your celebration explain to the children that not everyone celebrates the New Year on January 1. Tell them that you are going to celebrate the Chinese New Year and you would like them to wear the color red for the occasion since this is the color for happiness in China. (Also send a note home explaining your plans to the parents.)

3. The day of the celebration, put a picture on the chalkboard or bulletin board of the animal which is associated with the current year.

4. Tell children about the name of the animal of the year and the qualities of such an animal. You may also talk about the animal of the year they were born.

5. To celebrate the holiday, distribute fortune cookies, explaining that these were invented in the United States but are served in Chinese restaurants. Have the children make some little slips of good fortune such as "Good luck!" and "I like you." Put them in a box. Have each child draw one out.

6. Complete the celebration with a snack of tangerines, the way the Chinese would do. Oranges and tangerines originally came from China.

More to do

Read some stories from China, for example, Chinese fairy tales. Play some Chinese music.

Related books

The Story About Ping by Marjorie Flack and Kurt Wiese
The Chinese Word for Horse and Other Stories by John Lewis

—Lucy Fuchs, Brandon, FL

Valentine, Valentine, Red and Blue

2+

Children enjoy a simple tag game with a valentine theme.

Materials needed

One red and blue valentine

What to do

1. Have the children sit in a wide circle on the floor.
2. Pick one child to carry the valentine.
3. The child with the valentine walks around the outside of the circle while the rest of the group chants, "Valentine, valentine red and blue, I have a valentine just for YOU!"
4. As soon as the child with the valentine hears the word "you," he puts the valentine down behind the closest child. That child picks up the valentine and tries to tag the valentine giver, who runs around the circle to the empty place and sits down. If the valentine giver is tagged, he must give the valentine away again. If the valentine giver reaches the empty space without being tagged, the child holding the valentine must now give it away.
5. The game continues until every child has had a turn to give away the valentine.

—Mary Paciocco, Appomattox, VA

Valentine's Day—Heart Scepter

2+

Children use recycled materials to create heart scepters.

Materials needed

Styrofoam trays
Egg cartons
Scissors
Glue
Glitter
Aluminum foil
Tape
Newspaper

What to do

1. Cut out heart shapes from styrofoam trays and long strips from the tops of egg cartons.
2. Cover the table with newspaper and put out all the materials.
3. Have each child take a styrofoam heart and decorate it using glue and red glitter.
4. show the children how to cover the cardboard strip with aluminum foil or cellophane and secure with tape. Staple the hearts to the covered cardboard strips.

More to do

Make crowns to go with the scepters and encourage the children to engage in imaginative play.

—Patricia A. Webb/Barbara Howard, Norwich, NY

Valentine Magnets

3+

Children will practice small motor skills and gain self-esteem as they produce a lovely valentine gift for family members.

Materials needed

Sheets of stiff red cardboard (or styrofoam)
Heart patterns
White or silver doilies
Individual photos of children
Magnet strips
Glue
Scissors

What to do

1. Have the children trace heart patterns on red cardboard or styrofoam and cut them out (you may need to help the younger children with this step).
2. Tell the children to glue a doily to the front of their cardboard hearts.
3. Hand out the individual photos and have the children glue them on top of the doilies.
4. Let the children snip magnetic strips and glue them to the back of their hearts.

More to do

Have each child tell you one or two things she loves about a family member. Write the words on a sticky label along with the date and child's name. Have the child apply the label to the heart, under the photo. Encourage the children to experiment with surfaces that attract and repel the magnetic strips.

Related song

"I Wish You a Merry Love Day" (to the tune of "I Wish You a Merry Christmas")

I wish you a happy love day
I wish you a happy love day
I wish you a happy love day
From my heart to you!

—Ellen Domenico, Ewing Twp., NJ

Valentine's Day—Musical Hearts Game

3+

Children increase their vocabulary for Valentine's Day with "love, hug, share and heart," improve their skills in sharing and helping and enhance their ability to follow directions and rules.

Materials needed

Large paper hearts taped to the floor
Record or tape of music

What to do

1. Cut several large hearts out of roll paper. Make each one large enough for a few children to stand together on it.
2. Talk to the children about sharing with friends, helping, and ways we show we care, like hugging.
3. Explain that you are going to play a game like Musical Chairs.

4. When the music plays, the children move or dance around the hearts on the floor. When the music stops, each child finds a heart to stand on.

5. Explain that there will not be enough hearts for each child, so they will need to share with their friends. Also, sometimes it may seem like there is not enough room on the heart for any more friends, but if they try very hard, they can probably help their friends find a spot on the heart. They may have to help by holding onto their friends or "hugging" them so they won't fall off the heart.

6. Stop and start the music as in Musical Chairs.

7. After a few rounds, take one heart away each time you stop the music. Continue until only one heart remains and all the children are touching part of the heart.

More to do

Have children discuss creative ways to help their friends; some children may find unique ways to get on the heart, such as putting their hands on it or touching it with their elbow. Have children take turns controlling the music or choosing which heart to take away.

Related song

"Love Somebody, Yes I Do"

—Sandra Suffoletto Ryan, Buffalo, NY

Valentine Game   3+

This activity promotes group cooperation and allows children to identify numbers and exercise in place.

Materials needed

Red construction paper
One beanbag (red and/or heart shaped is good)
Marker
Clear contact paper

What to do

1. Cut out large (dinner plate size) heart shapes. Cut an amount your children will be able to count. Write a different large number on each heart. Cover each heart with clear contact paper.

2. Explain to the children that you have hearts with numbers written on them. Hold them up, one at a time and have the class identify each number. Next, put the hearts, face up, in a bunch on the floor. Do not over-lap.

3. Show the beanbag to the children. Demonstrate how they can gently toss the beanbag so that it lands on one of the hearts. (If the beanbag lands on the floor, let the thrower identify the heart closest to it.) Ask the child throwing the beanbag to identify the number and suggest a way of moving "in place" (i.e. jumping, twisting, bending arms, etc.).

4. Now the class will, all together, count aloud as they do the chosen movement the number of times shown on the heart.

5. Continue the activity until each child has had a turn to toss the beanbag and suggest a way of moving.

More to do

Instead of letting each child think of a movement, have a basket of small paper hearts available with different ways of moving written on them. After the child throws the beanbag and identifies the number, let him draw a small heart from the basket. The teacher can read it to the class. Continue the game as before.

—Trish Weaver, Raleigh, NC

An Owl Valentine

The children will practice their fine motor skills while cutting and pasting to make this unusual owl valentine.

Materials needed

12" x 9" blue or red construction paper, one piece per child
8" x 8" brown construction paper, 2 per child
Markers
Scissors
Glue or glue sticks

What to do

1. On the brown paper, draw and cut out two large heart shapes. They should be the same size. Children may do the cutting.
2. Glue one brown heart on the blue or red paper.
3. Fold the other heart in the center so that the tip covers the top of the heart (see illustration).
4. Glue the folded heart upside down on top part of the other heart (see illustration).
5. Draw the eyes and color in the beak with markers.

More to do

Have each child dictate a short Valentine's Day message and write it on the inside folded part of the owl's beak. When you lift the beak, you can see the message.

—Jyoti Joshi, Framingham, MA

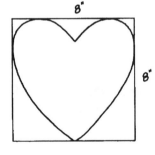

Figure 1

2 pieces brown paper

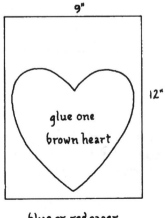

Figure 2

glue one brown heart

blue or red paper

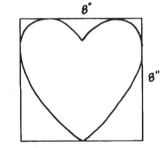

fold one brown heart

Figure 3

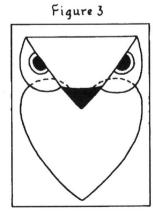

Valentine's Day—Ladybug's Family

These heart-shaped ladybugs make a cute Valentine's Day card, and the varying sizes allow the children to order them from largest to smallest.

Materials needed

12" x 9" red and white construction paper rectangles, one per child
Non-toxic black markers or black crayons
3" strips of black construction paper approximately 1/4" wide, five per child
Glue or glue sticks
Scissors
Pencils (unsharpened)
Crayons
Pebbles (optional)

What to do

1.   Fold the red construction paper in half and cut out several hearts of varying sizes (see illustration). You can show the older children how to draw the half heart on the fold and let them cut out themselves. These will be the ladybugs' shells.
2.   Give the ladybugs black dots on their red shells.
3.   Fold the white paper in half to make a card and glue the ladybugs on the front. You could have the children order them from large to small or vice versa. Show the children how to curl the antenna (black strip) by wrapping it around a pencil. Glue one to each lady bug.
4.   Write a message inside or allow children to decorate the inside with crayons or more lady bugs. They could have a trail of large to small ladybugs travelling all over the card!

More to do

Ladybugs can also be made from flat pebbles. Collect various sizes with the children, enough so that each child can have his or her own little family. Have the children wash and dry them, paint them red, and add small black dots. These could be paperweights or houseplant decorations.

Related book

Grouchy Lady Bug by Eric Carle

—Jyoti Joshi, Framingham, MA

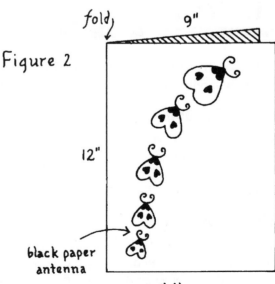

Figure 2

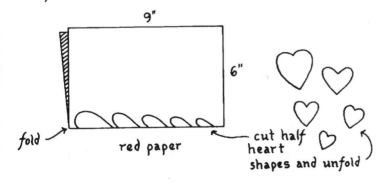

Figure 1

Valentine's Day—Heart Game

4+

The children will use their large muscles and have lots of fun as they play this game—lively entertainment for Valentine's Day or any day!

Materials needed

Construction paper, preferably red or pink
2 dice

What to do

1.   Have the children help you cut twelve large hearts out of construction paper and number them from two to twelve.
2.   Write a message on the back of each heart. The message might say, for example, "make a funny face," "tell a joke," "sing a song," "pretend you are a bird [or another animal]," "cry like a baby," "say something nice to a friend," or "hug your teacher." You can keep the messages on the valentine theme or you can vary them.
3.   Place all the hearts on the floor in numerical order. Make sure that the numbers are visible and the messages are face down.
4.   Let the children take turns rolling the dice and turning over the heart that bears that number. Read the messages and encourage children to act them out.
5.   Continue until all children have had a turn.

More to do

The game is endlessly variable by changing the messages on the backs of the hearts. You could play it as a detective game, drawing pictures of objects in your room on the backs of the hearts and having the children find the objects and bring them to the circle. This eliminates the need for reading. Ask everyone to do ten jumping jacks and have them feel their heartbeat.

—*Jyoti Joshi, Framingham, MA*

St. Patrick's Day Treasure Hunt

4+

Children will learn about St. Patrick's Day and will practice listening to clues and following directions. This activity will reinforce the meaning of words such as over, under, behind, etc.

Materials needed

Green construction paper
Treats or small prizes
Gold foil
Basket or small pot

What to do

1.   Before St. Patrick's day, introduce the children to the holiday by telling them about Leprechauns and their pots of gold. Read or tell them a story about Leprechauns, such as "The Boy and the Leprechaun." Point out that Leprechauns will do anything to protect their pots of gold, but that they always have to tell the truth. Ask them to wear green on St. Patrick's Day for luck.

2.   In preparation, cut shamrocks out of green construction paper. Write messages on them from the Leprechaun. The first message should be: "Dear boys and girls, I stopped by your room and left a special little surprise for you, but you will have to be very smart to find it. My first clue is—look under the table." Make other shamrocks with clues (e.g., above a window, beneath a shelf, behind the door, near the record player, inside the wastebasket, between some books, among the blocks) leading to the basket of treats and hide the shamrocks around the room. Note: The actual places where clues are hidden will depend on the room and its resources. The clues can be made more challenging by being more general (e.g., look under something with four legs, look behind something that opens and closes, look above something you can see through).

3.   Wrap individual treats or prizes for the children in gold foil and place them in the basket. Hide the basket wherever your last clue tells the children to look.

4.   Before the children arrive, mess up the room a little by putting a few things upside down, backwards, or in the wrong places. Put the shamrock with the Leprechaun's first message in an obvious place.

5.   When the children arrive, let them discover the mess that the Leprechaun has made. The children will have fun straightening it up. Then read aloud the message on the first shamrock. Ask one child which table she thinks it might be under and have that child go and check. Proceed this way with different children taking turns until each clue is found. Try to involve all the children in the class and continue until they find the pot of gold.

More to do

Serve green foods at snack time. Let the children experiment with paints to create different shades of green. Provide many different items that are green for a collage (e.g., paper, fabric, glitter, painted pasta). Sing the song "Michael Finnigan."

—Rayne P. Reese, Glendale, MO

Easter—Let's Match Our Eggs   2+

The children will practice their visual discrimination skills by matching pairs of Easter eggs and placing them in a basket.

Materials needed

Six to seven pairs of paper eggs approximately 3" tall, of different colors or decorated with different patterns
Easter basket

What to do

1.   Lay all the eggs on the floor or on a surface where the children can see and touch them. One by one, hand a child an egg and ask the child to match it with another egg that has the same color or design.

2.   Give as many chances as needed for the child to find the matching egg.

3.   Once a match is made, put the pair in the Easter basket.

More to do

Vary the colors or designs to make different sets of matching eggs. The designs can become more complicated or similar to make matching more challenging. You could use pairs of actual hard boiled eggs for an interesting change.

—Kelly Stuart, Richmond, MO

Easter—Egg Match

3+

Children will match like patterns.

Materials needed

Posterboard
Pastel markers

What to do

1. Cut out sixteen eggs, each about 4" in length, from the posterboard.
2. Draw a unique pattern on each (no two eggs should have the same pattern).
3. Cut all the eggs into two pieces using different configured lines for each one (so only halves with matching patterns can actually be put together). Laminate the pieces.
4. Mix up all the pieces and lay them out on a table.
5. Have the children come up, one at a time, and find two matching halves.

More to do

For each egg, write the same number on the back of both halves for self-checking. Decorate hard-boiled eggs. Make egg puzzles with more than two pieces.

—Rachel Stickfort, Newark, DE

Easter—Scrambled Eggs

3+

The student will be able to identify and match colored halves of paper eggs.

Materials needed

Construction paper (different colors)
Markers/crayons
Contact paper (optional)

What to do

1. Cut out about twenty 5"-long eggs from colored construction paper, using as many colors as possible. Then cut the eggs in half in a zigzag pattern, making sure that all eggs are cut exactly the same way so halves are interchangeable. (You might photocopy an egg pattern on white paper and hand out to students to color, then collect and cut out.)
2. Mix up the egg halves and place on the floor or on a bulletin board at children's eye level.
3. Tell the children that you have some scrambled eggs that need to be put back together before the Easter Bunny comes to town.
4. Have the children come up, one at a time, and find two halves of the same color, then identify the color for the rest of the class.

More to do

Have a plastic egg hunt using eggs that have different colored tops and bottoms. Once everyone has an egg, tell the children to switch one egg half with someone else to make both halves of their egg the same color. Put the construction paper eggs together with different colored tops and bottoms, then have the children remake them so both halves match.

Related books

Is it Red? (Is it Yellow, Is it Blue) by Tana Hoban

—Renee Kapusniak, Webster, NY

Mother's Day Bath Salts

3+

Children will mix and blend primary colors to create secondary colors and produce a Mother's Day gift.

Materials needed

Epsom salts
Food coloring
Bath oil (scented)
Baby food jars
Colored spiral ribbon
Sandwich bags

What to do

1. Have each child pour some Epsom salts into a sandwich bag.
2. Put out the food coloring and let the children pick the colors they would like to use to tint the Epsom salts. Explain how new colors can be created by mixing other colors together.
3. Have the children add the food coloring to the Epsom salts and then seal and shake their bags until the salts are the desired color.
4. Give children the bath oil and have them add several drops to the Epsom salts in the bag and shake some more to scent them.
5. Hand out the colored ribbons and help children tie them around the neck of their baby jars.

More to do

To promote language development, have each child fill in an open- ended sentence: "I love you, mommy, because...". Write the child's quote on a sticky label with the date and child's name. Have the child apply it to the bottom or side of jar.

—Ellen Domenico, Ewing Twp., NJ

Grow a Plant for Mother's Day

3+

Children help to start a new plant as a beautiful Mother's Day gift.

Materials needed

Sharp knife for the teacher
One or more mature begonia plants
Clear glass or plastic containers, one per child
Aluminum foil
Masking tape and markers
Potting soil—use a professional mix, or mix your own using equal parts garden soil, peat moss and sand
Peat pots, one for each child
Plastic spoons
Water and pitchers for pouring
Florist's foil for covering pots (optional)

What to do

1.   Discuss how plants grow by absorbing water mixed with plant food through their roots. Explain that parts of plants can grow new roots all by themselves, if they have water.
2.   Show children the roots of the old plant and cut slips from the plant, removing about 4" of each stem. Carefully remove the lower leaves from each slip, leaving 1" of bare stem.
3.   Give each child a container to fill with water.
4.   Cover filled containers tightly with foil.
5.   Let children punch a hole in the center with a pencil and insert the bare stem of a plant slip.
6.   Put children's names on containers, making sure the name only covers one side of the container so they can watch the roots develop.
7.   Place containers in indirect sunlight, in a place where the children can watch. Allow several weeks for root development.
8.   When the roots are well-developed, transplant into peat pots filled with potting soil. The children can fill the pots with soil using the plastic spoons.
9.   Make a hole in the center of the soil using a pencil.
10. Pour some water into the hole.
11. Carefully remove the baby plant from the container and insert the roots into the hole.
12. Use the spoon to gently push soil around the stem.
13. Transfer name-tape from clear container to peat pot.
14. Place pots in a waterproof tray near a window. Water frequently to keep the peat pot moist.
15. Pots may be decorated as gifts by placing them on squares of florist's foil large enough to gather around the pots.

More to do

Make Mother's Day cards to attach to the plants. Let children dictate the sequence of steps involved while you transcribe a chart.

—Mary Jo Shannon, Roanoke, VA

Mother's Day Coupon Holder   4+

Children will use small motor skills to create a useful gift.

Materials needed

9" x 12" sheets of posterboard or tagboard
Hole punch
Yarn
Brad fasteners
Decorating materials (stickers, paints, markers, crayons, etc.)

What to do

1.   Have the children position their tagboard sheets in front of them so that the shorter sides are at the bottom and top.
2.   Show them how to fold up the bottom end to about 3" below the top end and then fold down the remaining 3" over the bottom part to make a flap.
3.   Tell them to punch holes up and down both sides. Explain that they should not punch the flap itself.
4.   Give each child a piece of yarn and demonstrate how to tape one end into a "needle" and how to tie a large knot in the other end.

250

5. Have the children sew up one side at a time, either in a wrap-around or up-and-down fashion. Make sure they use a separate piece of yarn for each side and knot off at the end.

6. Demonstrate how to push a brad fastener through the pocket and the flap from the inside out so it can be opened and closed on the outside of the flap. You might punch holes in the pocket and flap ahead of time to make passage of the brad easier.

7. Encourage the children to decorate and label their coupon holders.

(TIP: When doing this project with younger children, fold the posterboard, punch holes and prepare the yarn ahead of time.)

More to do

Have children create their own coupons for special chores or tasks (e.g., doing dishes, folding laundry, setting the table) that can be given as gifts to family members. Children could use pictures instead of words to show what coupons are for. Have the children count out real money (coins) to match the amount shown on a coupon.

Related books

Something for Mom by Norma Sawicki
Hooray for Mother's Day! by Marjorie Sharmat
Mother, Mother, I Want Another by Maria Polushkin
Happy Mother's Day by Steven Kroll

—*Lona Parker, Hunstville, AL*

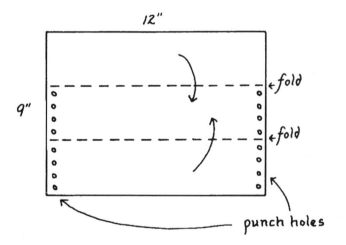

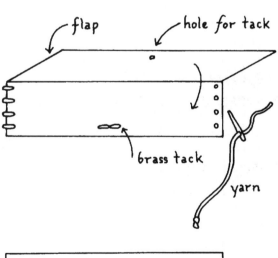

Mother's Day— Mouse and Cheese Bookmark

4+

The children will have fun making these little mice, and the bookmarks make a lovely Mother's or Father's Day present.

Materials needed

6" x 9" pieces of gray or white and yellow construction paper Tiny pink construction paper hearts (for mouse ears)
Chalk or marker
Scissors
Glue
6" pieces of yarn, one per child

What to do

1. Fold the gray and yellow construction papers in half. Draw half-heart shapes on both. Have the children cut out the shapes (see illustration).
2. Glue the pink heart upside down on the front side of the gray heart. This will be the mouse's ear. (See position on the illustration.)
3. Draw an eye and whiskers on the front side of the mouse and glue the yarn partly inside the folded gray heart.
4. Punch holes all over the yellow heart (the cheese) and glue it under the mouse.

—*Jyoti Joshi, Framingham, MA*

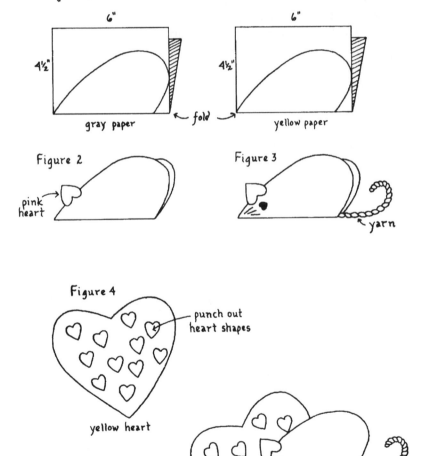

Figure 1
6"
4½"
gray paper
← fold →
6"
4½"
yellow paper

Figure 2
pink heart

Figure 3
yarn

Figure 4
punch out heart shapes
yellow heart

Mother's Day—A Butterfly Gift

Here's a chance to turn a beautiful springtime butterfly into a lovely and useful gift for mom or dad!

Materials needed

Spring clothespins, one per child
Tissue papers cut into three sizes—10" x 5", 9" x 4", 8" x 3"—in three different spring colors, one of each size per child
Pipe cleaners, one per child
Glue or glue sticks
Scissors
Magnets or magnetic tape, one per child (optional)
Markers

What to do

1. Fold the tissue papers in half and draw a heart shape with an open bottom on the fold (see illustration). Cut out the hearts. These are the butterfly wings.

2. Have the children glue the shapes together **only** at their centers in descending order, with the largest on the bottom and the smallest on the top.

3. Hold the clothespin so that the opening end is at the bottom. Draw the design for the body of the butterfly on the clothespin. Glue it to the center of the wings.

4. The children then twist the pipe cleaner around the underenath part of the clothespin and bend it up for antennae (see illustration).

5. If using magnets, glue one or attach a strip of magnetic tape to the back of the clothespin. These make useful and colorful refrigerator magnets.

—Jyoti Joshi, Framingham, MA

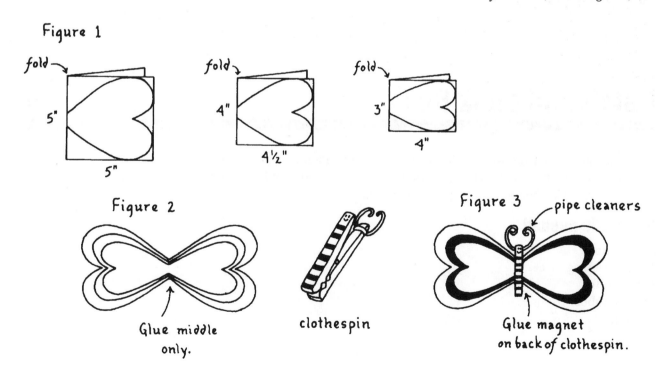

Figure 1

fold   5"   5"

fold   4"   4½"

fold   3"   4"

Figure 2

Glue middle only.

clothespin

Figure 3   pipe cleaners

Glue magnet on back of clothespin.

Butterflies

2+

Children will develop an awareness of primary colors and the symmetry of butterflies.

Materials needed

12" x 18" sheets of construction paper
Pipe cleaners
Liquid tempera paint in primary colors
Bowls
Plastic spoons or eye droppers

What to do

1. Fold construction paper in half and cut into butterfly shapes. Put out paints in bowls with a spoon or eye dropper in each.
2. Show children pictures of butterflies and point out how the colors on butterfly wings are symmetrical (i.e., the same on both sides).
3. Have the children open their butterflies and put drops of paint on each wing. Tell the children to fold their butterflies again, press them with their hands, and open.
4. After the paint is dry, have children fold pipe cleaners in half. Staple them to the butterflies to make antennae.

More to do

Have children glue collage materials on their butterflies. Go on a nature walk and look for butterflies. Order a butterfly kit so that children can observe a chrysalis change into a butterfly.

Related book

The Very Hungry Caterpillar by Eric Carle

—Frances Archibeque, Albuquerque, NM

Catch and Look Box

3+

Now you can catch and observe bugs without squishing them by hands or smashing them by nets. You only need to make one box (although the children will want more). Send home the directions so parents can make them at home. This box has a high parent approval rating.

Materials needed

Milk cartons
Nylon stocking pieces
Sharp knife
Tape or rubber bands
Scissors

What to do

1. Cut a window in the bottom of the milk carton.
2. Cut carton on three sides so it will bend open.
3. Cover window with part of a nylon.
4. Open to collect insect, close to observe, then open to release.

(I believe that this same idea could be applied to a plastic (permanent) box with hinges and a screen on both ends. With a latch/hook to close for study.)

—Linda Ann Hodge, Minnetonka, MN

The Very Hungry Caterpillar Becomes a Butterfly

3+

After hearing the story of how a caterpillar becomes a butterfly, the children can use their imaginations to act out the stages to musical accompaniment.

Materials needed

The Very Hungry Caterpillar by Eric Carle

What to do

1. Read the book and show the children the pictures that illustrate each stage of development. (Note: chrysalis, not cocoon, is the correct name for that early stage in the development of a butterfly.)
2. Encourage the children to make their bodies into the same shapes. For the chrysalis, they can put their arms up over their heads and clasp their hands together. Explain that they are hanging from a limb.
3. Sing "I Want to Be a Butterfly" and have the children act it out verse by verse.

"I Want to Be a Butterfly" (to the tune of "Shortening Bread")

> *I want to be a butterfly, butterfly, butterfly*
> *I want to be a butterfly (flap wings while singing)*
> *Just for fun!*
> *First I'll be the egg,...etc. (roll up in a tiny ball)*
> *Next I'll be the caterpillar,...etc. (stretch out on tummy and wiggle)*
> *Then I'll be the chrysalis,...etc. (pretend to hang from branch)*
> *Now I'm a butterfly,..etc. (flap wings and fly in place, or if space allows, around the room)*

More to do

As a special treat, eat butterfly-shaped crackers for snack. Obtain or make a set of cards which show the butterfly's stages of development: tiny egg, caterpillar, chrysalis, butterfly. Allow the children to mix them up and then order them in the proper sequence.

—Trish Weaver, Raleigh, NC

Fingerprint Ants

3+

The children will develop fine motor skills, while learning about ant farms and the physical characteristics of ants.

Materials needed

Newspaper
9" x 12" construction paper
Clean, sifted sand
Stamp pad, or sponge with black tempera paint
Crayons
Glue

What to do

1. Cover tables with newspapers.
2. Discuss the physical aspect of ants and ant farms with the children.
3. Have the children draw two wavy lines across the construction paper for the ants' tunnel.
4. Have the children put ants within the wavy lines by placing three fingerprints end to end, using the stamp pad or sponge with paint.
5. Add antennae and legs with crayons.
6. Spread glue everywhere except inside the wavy lines.
7. Use spoon to sprinkle sand over glue.
8. Tap off excess sand.

More to do

Watch a live ant farm.

Related book

The Ant and the Elephant by Bill Peet

—Joyce Montag, Slippery Rock, PA

3-D Spider Web

3+

The children will learn about spiders while developing fine motor skills.

Materials needed

The Very Busy Spider by Eric Carle
Black construction paper
White glue in "squeeze" bottle

What to do

1. Cover a table with newspaper and dress the children in their smocks.
2. Read *The Very Busy Spider* to the children during group time. Let each child feel the raised effect of the spider web in the book. Talk about how the children think the web was made that way. And what shape the web is.
3. Tell the children that they can make a spider's web that will feel the same way.
4. Pass out construction paper and glue bottles to children at the table.

5. Encourage the children to squeeze the glue bottles over their papers to form lines (like a web).
6. When dry, the glue will feel like the raised web in the story.

More to do

Provide the children with felt animals who were in the story to use at the flannel board to retell the story themselves. (provide pieces of yarn for the web) Count the numbers of animals who visited the spider. Which was biggest? Smallest?

Related books

The Very Busy Spider by Eric Carle
Spider's Web by Barrie Watts and Christine Back
Be Nice to Spiders by Margaret Bloy Graham
The Adventures of Spider by Joyce Cooper Arkhurst

Related songs

"The Eeensy, Weensy Spider"
"The Spider Web"
"Spin, Spin Little Spider"

—Michelle Therrie, Pittsfield, MA

Crayon Shaving Butterfly

3+

Children learn about changes in size, shape and color in an exercise which develops hand-eye coordination.

Materials needed

Iron
Wax paper
Newspaper
Black construction paper
Cheese grater
String
Hole puncher
Various color crayons (chunky crayons are easier to handle)

What to do

1. Cut the butterfly bodies from black construction paper (see pattern).
2. Cut wax paper about 2" larger than butterfly pattern (Two pieces are needed per butterfly).
3. Trace the butterfly with a permanent marker onto the wax paper. Only one traced wax paper is needed for each butterfly.
4. Preheat iron.
5. Lay out newspaper.
6. Place one piece of wax paper on the newspaper (piece with the butterfly outline).
7. Allow the child to choose various color crayons to grate on the cheese grater.
8. Spread the shavings within the butterfly outline.
9. Place paper butterfly body in the proper area.
10. Cover with second piece of wax paper.
11. Cover with newspaper.

12. Iron over the butterfly area until shavings are melted.

13. The teacher can cut out the butterfly on the outline.

14. Punch a hole for string in the head.

15. Tie with a loop of string.

16. Hang the butterfly in a window and watch the colors gleam!

More to do

Children can lie on the floor and move slowly like a caterpillar. They can pretend to wrap into a cocoon; by sitting all curled up. When the "cocoon" opens, the children become a butterfly. Obtain caterpillars for captivity. Watch them as they go through the stages from caterpillar to butterfly.

Related book

The Very Hungry Caterpillar by Eric Carle

—*Anne Bonsted, New Hartford, NY*

Busy Bees

3+

The children will do the work of honey bees, building a hive, making honey, laying eggs.

Materials needed

Unit blocks
Yellow easter grass (honey)
4-5 lunch bags—stuffed and painted white
White paint
Paintbrushes
Newspaper
Large construction paper flowers
Flannel board cross section of bee hive
Flannel board
Yellow construction paper
Scissors
Black pipe cleaners
Stapler

What to do

1. Stuff four or five lunch bags with newspaper, staple the open end shut, paint them white and allow to dry. These are bee eggs.

2. Make flowers from construction paper large enough to stand on.

3. Prepare flannel board pieces as described above from pellon or felt.

4. Make bee hats for every child participating by cutting out headbands from yellow construction paper and stapling on black pipe cleaners. Ball the pipe cleaners at the end if you wish.

5. At group time, using the flannel board, explain to and show the children that honeybees have jobs. Queen bees lay eggs in the hive so that new bees will grow in the colony. Worker bees gather nectar and put it in the hive. Tell the children that they will have a chance to work like bees in a hive in the block area. Ask them to "fly" to the edge of the blocks.

6. Put on a bee hat and explain that people playing there will wear one today.

7. Build the hive (three or four cells), laying blocks around in a hexagonal pattern like a real hive. Have the children help.

8. Lay paper flowers around the block hive. Place yellow easter grass (honey) in center. Put eggs (paper bags) in the area, as well.

9. Explain the bee work again, this time acting it out.

10. Let the children enjoy their "bee" work.

More to do

Explain that each cell serves a purpose: some are for honey, some are for eggs, and so on. Let the children make their own eggs at the art center.

—Judi Mooney, Bear, DE

Dancing Spider 4+

Materials needed

Black construction paper 9" x 12" (one per child)
Extra long rubber bands
Children's scissors
Chalk
Gummed reinforcers
Ruler
Ice cream pail lid
Tape
Extra black construction paper for legs
Stapler

What to do

1. Using chalk, trace ice cream pail circle onto black construction paper, one per child. Take ruler and chalk one dashed line 4" to the center of the circle. This will be the body of the spider. (The center line when cut and overlapped will give the spider a "back".)

2. Pre-cut lots of legs on the paper cutter.

3. On the table put: black paper with circle pattern, scissors, gummed reinforcers (eyes), chalk (to write name), tape and pile of "legs."

4. Teacher supervises use of stapler, extra long rubber bands and a pair of children's scissors.

5. Children cut out the circle and along the dotted line.

6. Children add eyes, using gummed reinforcers.

7. Children count out legs and tape them on.

8. Children cut open rubber band, overlap the slit and staple the rubber band to the middle of the back of the spider (with adult help).

9. Spider will bounce from her web.

More to do

Show children how to fold up the legs like accordion. Spider will dance a lot more. Practice spatial words using the dancing spider.

—Linda Ann Hodge, Minnetonka, MN

The Caterpillar   4+

The children will create a caterpillar.

Materials needed

Egg cartons, 1 for every two children
Scissors
Green paint
Paintbrush
Black marker
Black pipe cleaners, 1 for each child

What to do

1. Cut the egg cartons in half lengthwise so that you have 6 egg cups in a row.
2. Have the children paint the egg carton. Let it dry.
3. Using a black marker, draw eyes.
4. Make two small holes in the carton above and between the eyes, and slip a black pipe cleaner through the holes. Twist it together and bend to make antennae.

Related book

The Very Hungry Caterpillar by Eric Carle

—Jyoti Joshi, Framingham, MA

Butterfly Kite   4+

In this lovely springtime activity, the children will use a special technique to create a butterfly kite which has the same pattern on both wings just like a real butterfly!

Materials needed

Egg cartons, 1 for every two children
Green paint
Paintbrush
Black marker
Black pipe cleaners, 1 for each child
Large size finger painting paper (about 24" x 36"), one per child
Finger paints—bright colors
Scissors
Markers
Glue
Hole puncher
Yarn or string

What to do

To make the butterfly's body:

1. Cut the egg cartons lengthwise, making two rows of 6 egg cups.
2. Have the children paint the egg carton. Let it dry.
3. Using a black marker, draw eyes.
4. Make two small holes in the carton, above and between the eyes, and slip a black pipe cleaner through the holes. Twist it and bend to make antennae.

To make the butterfly's wings:

1. Fold the paper from side to side and draw the butterfly wing shape on the outside (see illustration).
2. Unfold the paper and have the children make a design with finger paints only on one side of the inside of the paper.
3. Press the blank side of the paper onto the design and gently unfold it again. Sometimes the paper sticks so be careful. Show the children how they now have identical designs on both wings.
4. Let butterfly dry completely.
5. Fold the paper again and cut out the wing shape.
6. In the middle of the wings, glue the butterfly's body.
7. Punch two holes in the wings and string the yarn across. Tie a length of yarn or string to the midpoint of this cross-string to make a kite (see illustration).

—Jyoti Joshi, Framingham, MA

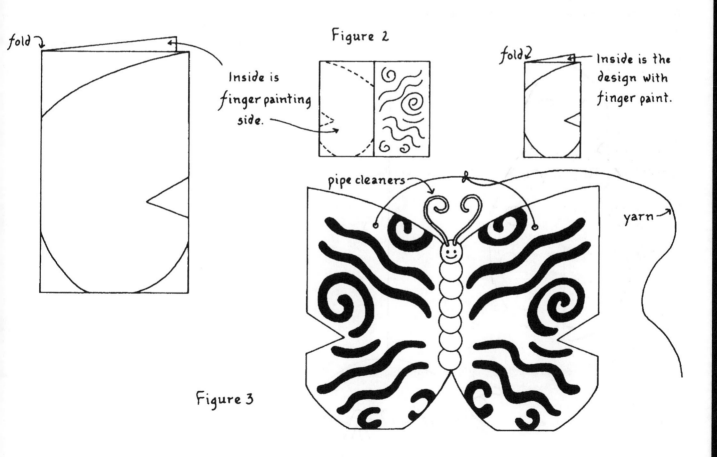

Figure 2

fold

Inside is finger painting side.

fold

Inside is the design with finger paint.

pipe cleaners

yarn

Figure 3

3-D Spiders

Materials needed

Old file folder
Scissors
Construction paper
Paper punch
Stapler
Pipe cleaners
String
Cotton balls
Markers

What to do

1. On old file folders draw spider shapes. Spiders have two sections to their bodies (a head and an abdomen).
2. Cut out and cut a slit half way up the abdomen.
3. Fold point A over point B to form a domed shape back.
4. Punch 4 holes on each side (spiders have 8 legs) and 2 holes for jaws. Take out staple.
5. Make several so that more than one child can work at a time. Let the children trace their own spiders and the places where they will punch the holes. They may need help forming and stapling the body. Let them attach pipe cleaners for legs and short pipe cleaners for jaws. Give each child 2 cotton balls on which they can put 4 dots with markers on each "eye". (spiders have 8 eyes). Attach a piece of string in the peak of the domed back. The spiders can now be hung from their "webs."

—*Patricia Wildenburg, Richland, WA*

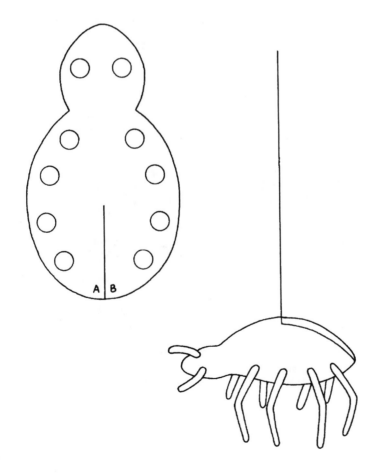

Bumble Bee

Children learn about science and insects, reduce their fear of bees, identify shapes and colors, and improve fine motor skills through a creative experience.

Materials needed

Yellow pom-poms (two per child)
3" pipe cleaners (one per child)
4" x 4" black construction paper
Black marker
Glue
Scissors

What to do

1. Draw two pairs of wings on the black paper and cut them out (see figure 1).
2. Staple the wings one on top of the other. Glue two yellow pom-poms between the wings for the body.
3. Attach the pipe cleaner to make antennae (see figure 2).
4. Draw black horizontal stripes on the pom-poms.

—*Jyoti Joshi, Framingham, MA*

Figure 1

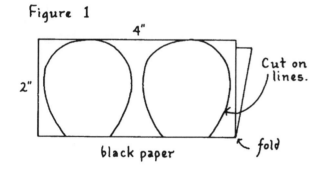

black paper

black wings

Figure 2

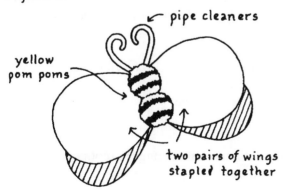

pipe cleaners

yellow pom poms

two pairs of wings stapled together

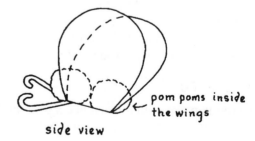

pom poms inside the wings

side view

INSECTS

Symmetrical Insects 4+

The children will begin to understand the meaning of the word symmetry.

Materials needed

Pictures of insects cut in half lengthwise (save the other half)
Small mirrors

What to do

1. Look at pictures of whole insects and noting that their bodies are symmetrical. Introduce this word giving other examples. Show examples of some things that are not symmetrical.
2. Let children experiment with placing a mirror beside a half picture of an insect body so that the reflection in the mirror makes the insect's body symmetrical.
3. Give children both sets of half insects and have them match them to make a whole symmetrical body.

More to do

Use a flannel butterfly body and wings mounted on a flannel board. Supply pairs of various colored flannel shapes that can be placed on the wings. Children work to make two wings that are symmetrical.

—Glynn Garner, Leawood, KS

Lady Bug 4+

This activity teaches the children circle recognition and cutting skills.

Materials needed

Red and black construction paper
Scissors
Glue
What to do
1. For each child trace a 6" diameter circle on red construction paper and a 3 1/2" diameter circle on black construction paper. Cut 1/2" black strips six inches long for back of bug and 1/4" strips 2 inches long for antennae.
2. Have children cut out the 6 circles you have traced.
3. Have children glue the 1/2" stripe down center of red circle with 4 small circles on either side of stripe.
4. Have children glue black head circle on lady bug, overlapping slightly.
5. Roll antenna strips around fat pencil to curl and glue on head for antennae.

More to do

Use round paper with red and black paint on the easels. Call attention to round things in room or ask children to identify them. Examples—doorknobs, buttons, tables. Have circles on flannel board.

Related book

The Grouchy Ladybug by Eric Carle

Related rhyme

Lady bug, lady bug, fly away home
Your house is on fire, your children all gone,
All but one whose name is Ann,
And she crept under the pudding pan.

—*Donna Jackson, Richland, WA*

A Caterpillar Becomes a Butterfly   4+

By using their illustrations, the children will enact how a caterpillar becomes a butterfly.

Materials needed

Paper
Markers
Scissors
The Very Hungry Caterpillar by Eric Carle

What to do

1.   Make a caterpillar which will be small enough to fit through the holes in the children's drawings. Draw a chrysalis and a butterfly.
2.   Read the book *The Very Hungry Caterpillar* to the children.
3.   Have each child draw one of the items that the caterpillar ate; encourage each child to fill up the whole paper. If you have a lot of children, you may want to assign them the drawing of the chrysalis and the butterfly also.
4.   Cut a hole in each drawing large enough for your caterpillar to fit through.
5.   Have the children gather at circle time and read the book again. This time use their drawings as illustrations. Have each child pull the caterpillar through their drawing as it's their turn to be "eaten." Then have the caterpillar disappear behind the chrysalis and pull out the butterfly.

More to do

Laminate each picture and put it together to make your own class book that the children can use whenever they like.

—*Suzanne Sanders, Cherry Hill, NJ*

The Three Little Pigs

2+

This activity will build vocabulary, demonstrate the number concept of 1-3 and provide texture discovery.

Materials needed

The story "The Three Little Pigs"
Straw or hay
Sticks
Brick

What to do

1. Have a large space prepared for children to role play.
2. Read "The Three Little Pigs". Pass around hay, sticks and a brick at appropriate times during the story. Explore and discuss textures and differences in the materials being passed around.
3. Have children recite together repetitive parts of the story while you read. (i.e., "Little pig, little pig, let me come in..."). Encourage voice changes when wolf speaks and when pig speaks.
4. Let the children role play the story while you re-read the story.
5. Allow children to recite their own version of the story.

More to do

Take turns blindfolding each child with scarf. Let them touch the straw, sticks and brick. See if they can identify them without seeing them. Cut out house shapes from poster board. Let the children glue hay and sticks to houses. Red aquarium rocks can be used to make the brick house.

—*Terri Garrou, Morganton, NC*

Goldilocks and the Three Bears

2+

This learning activity builds the children's vocabulary, introduces the number concept 1-3 and the size concept of small, medium and large.

Materials needed

Bowls and spoons (small, medium, large)
Towels or mats (small, medium, large)
Buttons of various size
Lids of various size
Containers of various size

What to do

1. Have a large space available for role play.
2. Read story "Goldilocks and The Three Bears." Have children recite together repetitive parts of story. Encourage voice change when Papa Bear, Mama Bear and Baby Bear speak.
3. Set up bowls and spoons, chairs and towels. Allow children to role play the story.
4. Allow children to recite their own version of story.
5. Put buttons, lids, pots and containers out in groups. Have children arrange each group in order from smallest to largest.

More to do

Cut out bear shapes (small, medium and large) out of cardboard or meat trays. Punch holes around edges. Let children lace colored shoe strings or ribbon around bears. Make oatmeal. Have brown sugar, honey, raisins, cinnamon, etc. available for toppings.

—Terri Garrou, Morganton, NC

A Kangaroo? 3+

The children will use listening skills to enjoy the story *What Do You Do With a Kangaroo?* They can then predict which animal will appear next in the story. Finally they will record or dictate the answer to the question, "What would you do with a kangaroo?"

Materials needed

What Do You Do With a Kangaroo? by Mercer Mayer
Tape recorder
Empty cassettes
Paper
Pencils

What to do

1. Gather the children for story time. Read the book aloud to the children. After the first few pages, ask the children to predict what the next animal might be.
2. After the story, ask the children to record or dictate what they would do with each of the animals in this story.
3. Ask them which animals they would like to stay, and which ones they definitely would not want to stay.

More to do

Have the children draw a picture of how their room might look if all the animals stayed.

—Angelica Lewis, Wichita, KS

Teddy Bear Picnic 3+

Children will improve their listening and memory skills.

Materials needed

The Teddy Bears' Picnic by Jimmy Kennedy
Big sheet of lined paper
Pencil or marker
Food
Picnic basket and utensils
Blanket
Teddy bears

What to do

1. Send home a note to parents asking them to send in certain food items and a teddy bear with their child.
2. Read *The Teddy Bear's Picnic*.
3. Ask the children to recall what the bears did and ate on their picnic.
4. Write each child's name on the sheet of paper and what she recalled about the story.
5. Set up your own teddy bear picnic in the classroom or outside if it is a nice day

More to do

Take pictures at your teddy bear picnic and make your own teddy bear picnic book.

—Christina Casey, Malvern, PA

Magic Mirrors   3+

Students will build language and thinking skills while observing the world through different-colored filters.

Materials needed

Posterboard
Florist's cellophane or tinted plastic food wrap
Scissors
Glue

What to do

1. Cut mirror shapes from the cardboard. Glue cellophane over center opening, as seen in illustration.
2. During circle time introduce mirrors.
3. Children first name the colors, then are given chances to view the world through the colored lenses.
4. Set up discovery center with the "mirrors."

More to do

Discuss and act out feelings while looking through the mirrors. Example: blue can make you feel sad. An experience chart can be added for older children. Combine two primary-colored mirrors to make secondary colors. Example: blue and yellow make green.

—Susan Forbes, Holly Hill, FL

Play and Language

Children enjoy story time through the use of hand made puppets.

Materials needed

Paper bags
Hand stamp and ink pad
Construction paper shapes for animal faces
Paste
Crayons
Markers

What to do

1. Make the story mitt puppet. Place a closed bag, bottom-side up, on your work space. On bottom part of the bag, paste a face. The mouth will be in the fold of the bag. Paste the eyes and nose on the face. Fold ears on the dotted line and paste on the outside fold of the bag; fold the legs on dotted line and paste them to the bag. Practice using the puppet by slipping your hand inside the bag and moving the head section as if it is speaking.
2. Use the story mitt puppet at story time.
3. You can have the children make their own story mitt puppets.
4. Gather all the materials for puppet making. Outline or cut out shapes for the puppet faces from construction paper. If children are old enough, they can cut out their own features.

More to do

Have the children use their own puppets to act out a story you read to them.

—Madeline Currier, Elk Grove Village., IL

Old West Role Play

As children relive parts of cowboy life through this activity, they will develop a greater appreciation and understanding of history.

Materials needed

Cow stencil
Five cows per child
Red napkins or tissue paper for bandannas
One paper grocery bag per child
Old train car (to hold cows after they are rounded up)
Canned pork and beans
Biscuit dough
Hot cocoa ("coffee")
Sticks
Red and orange construction paper (scraps of each) for fire
Cowboy story or song books
Paper plates and plastic spoons

What to do

1. Cut tissue paper into triangles or squares big enough to go around the children's neck. Cut grocery bags into vests. Use the cow stencil to trace and cut out enough cows (brown, tan and black) for each child to have five. Make a train cattle car out of an old milk carton if some other toy train is not available.

2. Prepare biscuit dough (if not store bought).

3. Hide cows all over classroom or outside play area when the children are not there.

4. Make a fake fire out of some sticks and shredded pieces of orange and red construction paper.

5. When it is time for the activity, read a cowboy book or tell kids about cowboys in the old west and how they had to round up cows and move them from the ranches to where the trains could take them back East. Explain the cowboys had to wear special clothing to protect them.

6. Have the children put on vests and bandannas if they want.

7. Send them on a "round up" to find the cows.

8. Have them put the cows in the train car to "ship back east."

9. Have the children help make biscuits.

10. While the biscuits are baking, have the children sit around a campfire and sing cowboy songs or listen to cowboy songs or stories. Heat up the beans at the same time.

11. Serve beans and biscuits and "coffee" for snack.

More to do

Study life in pioneer times: set up a pioneer home with dress up clothes, tub for washing clothes, making butter or bread, old-fashioned toys or slates, reading by candlelight, etc.

—*Dixie Havlak, Olympia, WA*

Special Friends

The children will learn to share feelings with the children's parents and friends, and to see and hear words being written and read to.

Materials needed

Basket
Stuffed animal
Notebook to write down each child's story on what they did with their special friend

What to do

1. Place the animal ("special friend") in the basket.
2. Each child in the class takes turns bringing the basket home with the special friend.
3. The next day, the teacher reads to the class, what the child did with the special friend the night before.

More to do

The child can draw pictures about the events he did with the special friend, and talk the pictures as well as read what he did the night before.

—Rebecca Yahm, Otis A.N.G.B., MA

Let's Make a Telephone

The children will make telephones and talk to their friends with them.

Materials needed

Round tin cans
Sturdy string
Scissors
Nail
Hammer

What to do

1. Using the nail, hammer a very small hole in the center of the lid (of each can). Give each child a pair of cans and a piece of string about 6'-8' long.
2. The children will then put each end of the string into each hole (on the two cans) from the outside of the can towards the inside.
3. Help the children knot the ends of the string in each can.
4. Each child can pick a partner to talk to.
5. Have each child hold a can and move apart so the string in between the cans is held taut.
6. The pair can talk on the "telephone" they just made. The listener just places her can around her ear.

More to do

The children can play a game of "Guess and Decipher." They guess what their partner just said to them on their new telephone.

—Manisha Segal, Burtonsville, MD

Western Wear/Equipment

4+

What a way to learn language skills! This exciting activity will help develop vocabulary, dramatic play skills and observation skills.

Materials needed

Western wear catalogs
Dramatic play items (horse can be made from old broom handle)
Large sheet of paper
Markers
Pictures cut from western catalog
Clear contact paper
Felt
Velcro pieces
Empty fabric bolt

What to do

1.   Cut out western items from the catalogs to be used for group display. Cover an empty fabric bolt with felt to create a felt board. Prepare picture items by covering with clear contact paper. Attach velcro pieces on back to use on felt board.
2.   Display the items as group time begins. As the children come to the group answer any questions they may have about the items you have displayed.
3.   Introduce the activity with an "I Spy" game. ("I spy something you wear on your head. Marsha, can you come up and help me spy it?")
4.   Then, one at time, display the cut out items on the felt board as you let children predict their function. Record some of these predictions.
5.   After the children have made their predictions, explain that they will have an opportunity on their own to use these items to write a story about themselves wearing or using these items. Write the sotry just as they tell it, grammar usage and all.
6.   Now is the time to introduce your dramatic play items. You may want to model and show your wild wild west side!
7.   Set your limits on group usage of the dramatic play items.
8.   Put out dramatic play items and let them create their own scenarios!

More to do

Plan a Western dress-up day. Eat a meal similar to one eaten on the trail. Have bails of hay for tables or seats. Invite a guest to talk about caring for horses. Demonstrate how to use a lasso. Ask the guest to play guitar and sing some old west songs. Borrow a real saddle and display it safely for children to climb on and to pretend (maybe set on bail of Hay).

Related song (fingerplay)

"Five Little Cowboys/Cowgirls"

> *Five little cowboys got dressed to ride.*
> *The first one said, "I need my hat for outside."*
> *The second one said, "I need my boots to complete my suit."*
> *The third one said, "I need my rope to use I hope."*
> *The fourth one said, "I need my bandanna with a banana."*
> *The fifth one said, "We need chaps to cover our laps."*
> *So, the five little cowboys got ready to go*
> *And they hit the trail so I am told!*

—Merry Carol Kelly, Tallulah Falls, GA

A Kangaroo Without a Pocket?

The children will use listening skills to enjoy the story of *Katy No Pocket*, then practice making decisions.

Materials needed

Katy No-Pocket by E. Payne
Aprons with pockets
Different animals to put inside pockets

What to do

1. Gather the children for story time. Read the book aloud to the children. Be sure to discuss Katy's feelings about her lack of a pocket. Before you reach the end of the story, ask the children how they would help Katy with her problem.
2. After the story, invite the children to take an apron with pockets and choose from the items inside a few objects to put in their own pockets.
3. If they wish, they can fill their pockets with other classroom items. Be sure to remind the children to empty their pockets before they leave for the day.

More to do

Have the children act out how they think Katy felt when she had no pocket. Have them act out how they think she felt when the man gave her the apron. Sing the song Katy made up on the way to the city.

—Angelica Lewis, Wichita, KS

Rhythm Language

Children will practice sounding out one- and two- syllable words.

Materials needed

Pictures of objects with one- or two-syllable words
Construction paper or tagboard

What to do

1. Mount pictures on construction paper or tagboard cut to the size of flashcards.
2. Place the cards face-down in the middle of the circle.
3. Each child takes a turn selecting a card from the pile, reciting the word the picture represents and taping or counting out the syllables.

The child selects a picture of a flower.
The child says "flower."
The child taps and counts the number of syllables "1, 2."

More to do

Ask the children to also identify the color of the object.

—S. Lorna Zemke, Manitowoc, WI

Cookie Cookbook

4+

Children develop language skills in this activity.

Materials needed

1 recipe from each child
Off-white construction paper
Cookie pattern
Crayons

What to do

1. Ask each child to bring in their favorite cookie recipe. (Send a note home to the parents about this activity.) Type or copy each recipe onto the cookie pattern. Have a blank copy of the cookie pattern for each child.
2. Ask each child how they make cookies.
3. Ask questions: How much flour would you use? What else do you put in it? Then what do you do?
4. Write down what each child says in quotes on the blank cookie pattern.
5. Let each child make cookies on the construction paper. Use this as the cover.
6. Use staples or a paper punch and string to put the book together.

More to do

Make a class cookbook instead of individual ones. Make a class recipe, then make some cookies using a real cookie recipe.

Related book

Milk and Cookies by Frank Asch

Related song

"Ten Little Cookies" (to the tune of "Ten Little Indians")

> *One little, 2 little, 3 little cookies,*
> *4 little, 5 little, 6 little cookies,*
> *7 little, 8 little, 9 little cookies,*
> *Ten cookies in my mouth!*

—*Susan Armfield, Leominster, MA*

Flannel Board Story Box

4+

Children develop language and social skills and an appreciation of books, stories and storytelling.

Materials needed

Cigar box, or any box with a flip top, one per child
Black felt
Paint
Crayons
Contact paper
Glue
Scissors

What to do

1. Teachers can make the boxes and allow the children to use them with flannel board stories or each child can make their own box.
2. Have children decorate the outside of boxes with paint, crayons, colored contact paper or medium of their choice.
3. Glue a piece of black felt to the inside of the flip top.
4. Provide children with their favorite story flannel board characters and shapes to use on the flannel board story box. Pieces can be conveniently stored inside the box and won't get lost.
5. Sit back and enjoy the children's creative variations of their favorite stories.

More to do

Teacher-made flannel board story boxes can be put in the language arts interest area, along with story pieces for independent play by the children. Numbered fingerplays such as "Five Little Monkeys" can be made into flannel board pieces and used on the box to practice pre-math skills.

Related books

The Very Hungry Caterpillar by Eric Carle
The Very Busy Spider by Eric Carle
The Little Old Lady Who Swallowed A Fly by Ladybird Books
The Mitten by Jan Brett
Brown Bear, Brown Bear by Bill Martin Jr.

—*Michelle Therrie, Pittsfield, MA*

A Silly Cookie Story

4+

Children will develop sequencing skills and practice following verbal directions.

Materials needed

If You Give a Mouse a Cookie by Laura Joffe Numeroff
Objects from the story: picture, puppet or drawing of a mouse, cookie, empty plastic tumbler, straw, mirror, child scissors, whisk broom, sponge, bed (doll size), book (any title), paper and crayons, pen, tape

What to do

1. Gather the children into a circle and explain that you are going to read a funny story about a mouse who gets a cookie and the adventure that happens after that. Tell them that they should listen carefully because they will play a game when the story is finished.
2. Read the story.
3. Distribute objects from the story (children may share objects if necessary).
4. Tell the children to place the objects on the floor in front of them and to listen carefully as you read the story a second time. Explain that they are to hold up their objects when they hear them mentioned and put them back down on the floor as the mouse continues on his journey.

More to do

Draw a cookie jar on a large sheet of paper. Have the children "fill" the jar with cookies by dipping sponges or cookie cutters in paint and pressing them inside the outline.

—*Cathlene M. Hedden, Livonia, MI*

What's in the Box   4+

This activity helps improve listening and language development skills.

Materials

One shoe box
Holiday wrapping paper
Ribbon
Small items to place in the box (at least one per child)

What to do

1. Wrap the top and bottom of the box separately. Put the items (candy, small toys, stickers, etc.) in the box. Tie the box shut with the ribbon.
2. Bring the box to circle time.
3. Tell the children there is something for everyone in the box.
4. Shake the box several times.
5. Ask the children what they think might be in the box. Have each child take a guess.
6. Tell the children that at the end of the day we will open the box to see if anyone guessed right.
7. Shake the box throughout the day (this is a good attention getter at transition times).
8. At the end of the day, review some of the guesses. Open the box and share what's inside with the class.
9. Put something different in the box each day for a week.

—*Brenda Hankins, Louisville, KY*

Using Descriptive Words   4+

This activity asks the children to use descriptive words and add them to their vocabulary.

Materials needed

Geraldine's Blanket by Holly Keller
A favorite toy from home

What to do

1. Read the book *Geraldine's Blanket* by Holly Keller to the children.
2. Send a note to the parents and ask each child to bring in a favorite toy from home.
3. Before the activity, read the book to the children again. Ask the children to describe Geraldine's blanket.
4. Sit the children in a circle. Put all the toys brought from home in a pile in the center of the circle.
5. Describe a toy to the children. After the description is given, ask the children to tell you which toy has been described.

More to do

After the children have seen the teacher model the activity, have the children take turns describing the toys.

Related books

William's Doll by Charlotte Zolotow
Corduroy by Don Freeman
Laura Charlotte by Kathryn Galbraith
Alexander and the Wind-up Mouse by Leo Lionni
Ira Sleeps Over by Bernard Waber

—Debbie Chaplin, Hot Springs, VA

Poetry Dramatization   4+

Children use their bodies and imaginations to act out original poems.

Materials needed

Large poster or chart paper
Markers or crayons

What to do

1. Write the poems listed below on a separate sheet of poster paper, chart paper or large construction paper. (The print should be large enough for the students to see. You may choose to do one poem a day or both on the same day.
2. Tack the poems to the wall.
3. You can begin by asking students if they recognize any letters, sounds or words in the poem. Ask them to come up and point to the part that they recognize.
4. Read the poem you have chosen and sweep your hand under each line. Ask the children to help you read it again. (They usually read from "memory".) "Read" the poem several times to help the children become familiar with it.
5. As the poem is read again, ask for volunteers to act it out.

More to do

Ask the children to help illustrate the poems by drawing on the paper that has the poem written on it.

Related poems

"Cat"
> *Fancy, furry feline,*
> *Slinking about my house.*
> *It's dinner time for her you see,*
> *She's looking for a mouse.*

"Mouse"
> *Mischievous, merry mouse,*
> *Scampering across my floor.*
> *He won't be dinner for any cat,*
> *He's running to the door.*

—Dianne M. Waggoner, Catawissa, PA

I Am a Monster

4+

This activity combines fine motor control, creativity and free expression.

Materials needed

Large pieces of paper (as large as student)
Crayons or markers

What to do

1. With the children, talk about monsters including their features, what they eat, their size, etc.
2. Have each child lie on paper on the floor.
3. Draw around the child.
4. Have the children turn this silhouette into a monster by added details such as claws, bones, big eyes, etc.
5. Hang up the finished monsters!

More to do

This can be a great language activity for students describing their individual "monsters." This is also useful for motivating question/answer dialogue between students.

—Sherril Scott, Hermitage, TN

Money Bag

3+

Money Bag helps the children become familiar with different kinds of coins and their value.

Materials needed

Small brown bag (3.5" x 6.5") for each child and teacher
Pennies
Nickels
Dimes
Quarters

What to do

1. Place a penny, a nickel, a dime and a quarter in each bag.
2. Distribute one bag to each child.
3. Let each child explore what is in the bag.
4. Remove one coin from your bag. Ask the children to find the same type of coin in their bag. It may take more than one try to find the correct coin.
5. Talk about the coin's value and texture.
6. Continue until all four coins have been discussed.

More to do

This activity can be adapted to older children by placing different coins (silver dollar, half dollar) in each bag. Coins from other countries can also be discussed.

—Connie White, Athens, GA

Musical Money

3+

Children will learn to identify coins while gaining skills in hand-eye coordination.

Materials needed

Paper or plastic cup
Quarter
Dime
Nickel
Penny
Tape recorder
Music cassette

What to do

1. Seat the children in a circle.
2. Put a coin in the cup and pass it around.
3. Play music while the children pass the cup around the circle.
4. When the music stops, the child holding the cup must remove the coin and identify the coin.
5. Put a different coin in the cup each time. Continue play until all children have had at least one turn.

More to do

This game can be played as a counting game using pennies only. Put a number of pennies in the cup and pass it around. The child who has the cup when the music stops then counts the number of pennies in the cup.

Related books

The Purse by Kathy Caple
Peter and the Penny Tree by Thomas James
From Gold to Money by Ali Mitgutsch

—Mary Rozum Anderson, Vermillion, SD

Coins   4+

Here's a simple song to help children learn to recognize different coins and their value.

Materials needed

Pennies, nickels, dimes, and quarters—enough to give each child one coin
"The Coin Song" (see below)
A Piggy bank or other type of coin bank

What to do

1. Show each coin to the children and tell them its worth. Review several times.
2. Sing "The Coin Song" and hold up the appropriate coin as you sing about it.
"The Coin Song" (to the tune of "Shortening Bread")

> *A penny is one cent, one cent, one cent*
> *A penny is one cent,*
> *I know that!*
> *A nickel is five cents, etc....*
> *A dime is ten cents, etc....*
> *A quarter is twenty-five cents, etc....*

3. Give one coin to each child. Sing "The Coin Song" again. After each verse, have the children with the appropriate coins bring them up and deposit them in the bank, one by one. Continue to sing the appropriate verse as they do this. Sing the other verses and have the children with those coins put them in the bank. Continue until all coins are collected.
4. You can redistribute the coins and continue play for as long as the children are interested.

More to do

With a small group, give each child a handful of different coins. Sing any one of the verses of "The Coin Song," but instead of "I know that!" substitute "(Child's name) has (number)". Allow the child to fill in the blank by telling you the number of coins that were just mentioned that he or she has.

—Trish Weaver, Raleigh, NC

Piggy Bank

The children will love making these useful piggy banks. This activity complements a study of money, but also makes a nice gift.

Materials needed

Paperboard salt container or other canister with pour spout, one per child
Single egg cups (cut from an egg carton)
Black buttons or large round black stickers
Pink paint
6" black pipe cleaners
Pink construction paper cut in 2" squares
Scissors
Glue

What to do

1. Glue the egg cup to the bottom of the salt box on the end opposite the pour spout. This will be the pig's nose.
2. Paint the whole pig pink and let dry completely.
3. While painted box is drying, cut the pink construction paper square diagonally to make triangles. Then cut a small slit in the base of each triangle. Overlap the edges along the slit and staple to make ears.
4. For eyes, glue buttons or apply stickers on each side of the face above the nose.
5. Glue the two ears on top of the head.
6. To make the tail, first poke a small hole in the other end of the canister with a scissor or nail. Then curl the pipe cleaner around a finger or a pencil and insert it.
7. The spout is for putting money in the piggy bank.

—Jyoti Joshi, Framingham, MA

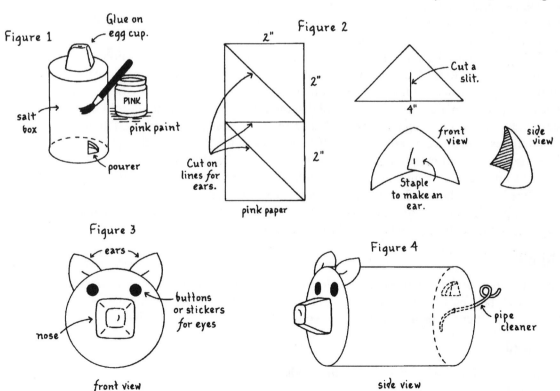

Let's Go Shopping

4+

The child will learn to identify penny, nickel, dime, quarter and half dollar (or desired coins for age level) and match these same coins to a picture of them on the game board.

Materials needed

Spinner—made from a 6"-8" oaktag circle, brad and safety pin or a commercial blank spinner

Pictures or stamps of coins—penny, nickel, dime, quarter, half dollar

A "coin box"—small box

Plastic or paper coins

Six game boards—six pieces of 9" x 12" oaktag or posterboard

Master change card—one piece or 9" x 12" oaktag or posterboard (optional)

What to do

1. The idea of this activity is to match and identify coins.
2. Locate a commercial spinner or make your own. To make a spinner, section a 6"-8" oaktag circle into five wedges. Paste or stamp a sample of each coin in a separate wedge of your circle. Push a brad through the loop end of a large safety pin and put it through the center of the circle. If using a commercial spinner, mark off sections with different coins as described above.
3. Purchase plastic or make paper coins. Place them in the small box which has been labeled "coin box."
4. To create game boards, use six pieces of 9" x 12" oaktag or posterboard. Mark these into four 1/2" x 4" sections—with a total of six sections per board. Cut pictures of items children like (toys, clothes, furniture, etc.) from magazines or catalogs. Glue one of these pictures to each section of the game boards. Under each item, glue one, two or three coins that will stand for the cost of this item. Write the cost (the amount of the coin value) below. (For this game, the costs are not accurate, for example, a stuffed bear might have a dime pasted underneath, a shirt might have a quarter and a nickel.) During the game you might remind the children they are "pretend shopping" and discuss the actual cost of some of the items shown.
5. A "Master Change Card" is made on a 9" x 12" piece of oaktag. This card shows various coin values (for example, a dime is equal to two nickels; a nickel is equal to five pennies).
6. Each child chooses a game board—or play in teams of two players to a board.
7. If necessary to chose a first player, start the spinner around and the first person to spin a penny is the "first" player. After this the play proceeds to the right.
8. The "first" child spins the spinner. Whatever coin the spinner lands on, the child will name that coin and choose it from the "coin box". He places it on a matching coin on his game board. (Whether the coin on the board or the spinner is heads or tails up does not matter.)
9. The play continues to the right with each child spinning, naming and placing coin on his board.
10. If an item has all the coins under it covered, then the child has "purchased" that item.
11. Play continues until all coins are covered on a card and all the items "purchased". The first child to cover all of his coins wins, but all children have purchased something by this time.
12. If a child spins a coin he cannot use, for example he has all of his dimes covered and he spins a dime, he may look at the Master Change Card and use the coin box to exchange his dime for two nickels, or one nickel and five pennies; coins which he may still need on his card. (Some children may have some extra coins if they have made change. You can call them a bonus at the end!)

More to do

Have the children make their own shopping card by cutting out items they would like from a catalogue or magazine. Let them paste on one or two coins for the cost and help them write the cost below. Write shopping lists or a letter to Santa for items they would like.

Related books

Peter and the Penny Tree by Thomas James and Dodie O'Keef

26 letters and 99 cents by Tana Hoban

—*Martha Warren, Fairmont, WV*

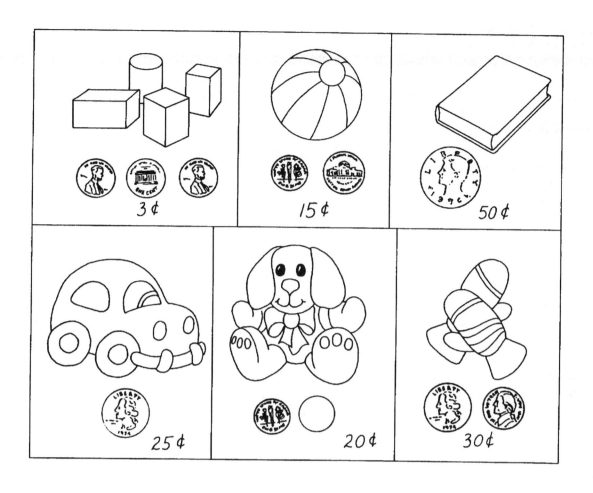

3¢ 15¢ 50¢

25¢ 20¢ 30¢

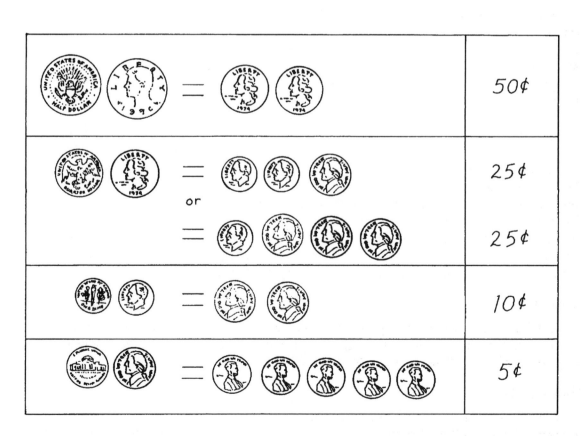

	50¢
	25¢
	25¢
	10¢
	5¢

Money Pots

5+

In this activity, children will become acquainted with the appearance and value of different coins.

Materials needed

Two pots
Ten of each coin (penny, nickel, dime, quarter)

What to do

1. Show children the coins and explain their different values. Let the children practice identifying the coins and naming their values before playing this game.

2. This is a game for two players. Give each child a pot with 20 coins (five of each) inside. Start the game by having both players reach into their own pots and pick a coin without looking. The two players should compare coins and decide which one has the highest value. The player with the coin of the highest value gets the other player's coin. If both coins are of the same value, they are placed on the table and two new coins are drawn; the player with the coin of highest value gets both coins from the last drawing as well. Play continues until the pots are empty, and the child with the most coins wins.

More to do

Have the children figure out the total value of the coins they drew during the game.

—Lona Parker, Huntsville, AL

Turkey Trot Races

This activity will help improve the children's gross motor skills and coordination.

Materials needed

Paper plates (2 or more)
Yarn
Glue or tape
Construction paper (various colors)
Large carpeted area

What to do

1. Cut feather shapes out of construction paper and glue or tape around the edges of paper plates. Make two holes across from each other near the center of each plate and push yarn through the holes so the plate can be tied around a child's waist.
2. Tie the plates around the waists of two or more children so that the feathers are in back and the tie is in front.
3. Tell the children they are going to pretend to be turkeys. Show them how to walk in turkey position: on their knees and with their hands under their arms.
4. Have the children do the turkey walk to a designated spot and back again when you say "Go." Make sure everyone gets a turn.

More to do

Play a record at 78 speed to encourage the children to move faster. Let the children trace and cut the feathers and attach to plates. Have the children knee walk around obstacles. Sing the following songs:
"Fat Turkeys Song" (to tune of "Did You Ever See a Lassie?")

Oh, gobble, gobble, gobble,
Fat turkeys, fat turkeys.
Oh, gobble, gobble, gobble,
Fat turkeys are we.
We walk very proudly and gobble so loudly,
Gobble, gobble, gobble, gobble, gobble.
Oh, gobble, gobble, gobble,
Fat turkeys are we.

"Turkey Feathers Song"

With a wobble, wobble, wobble,
And a gobble, gobble, gobble.
All the turkeys spread their feathers on Thanksgiving Day.
When they see the farmers coming,
All the turkeys start a running,
And they say you cannot catch us on Thanksgiving Day.

—Sandra Suffoletto Ryan, Buffalo, NY

MOVEMENT

Can You Climb Like a Monkey? $2+$

The children practice moving their bodies as animals by singing and acting out various animal movements.

Materials needed

Pictures of various animals

What to do

1. Gather pictures of farm animals, wild animals, domesticated animals, etc.
2. Show the children the pictures of the animals. As each picture is shown, have the children name the animal and talk about how each one moves. Encourage the children to show each other how the animals move.
3. Sing the following song to the tune of "She'll be Comin' 'Round The Mountain" for the children, using one of the animals to act out the moves:

> *Can you climb like a monkey?*
> *Can you climb?*
> *Can you climb like a monkey?*
> *Can you climb?*
> *Can you climb like a monkey?*
> *Can you climb like a monkey?*
> *Can you climb like a monkey?*
> *Can you climb?*

4. Sing the above verse again, encouraging the children to participate. You can sing other verses and substitute other animals and their corresponding movements.

More to do

Ask the children to bring an animal picture from home to talk about or provide magazines before the group gathers and ask the children to find pictures of animals.

Related book

Just Me by Marie Hall Ets

—*Marzee Woodward, Murfreesboro, TN*

Ball Kicking $2+$

This activity teaches children to kick a ball while sitting.

Materials needed

One large ball for each group of eight children
Masking tape

What to do

1. Make an "X" with masking tape where each child will sit in a circle. Allow enough room for their legs to move freely without interfering with other children.
2. Have each child sit on an "X."
3. Ask the children to stay on their mark. This makes the game easier and more enjoyable.

4. Explain that no hands are to be used. Children having difficulty with this rule may be asked to place their hands at their sides.

5. Ask the children to kick the ball using only their feet and legs. They don't need to kick the ball directly to another child, just close enough so another child can reach it.

6. Place the ball in front of a child to start the game.

7. When the children get restless, make the game more challenging. Ask them to lie on their stomachs, propping themselves up on their elbows with feet facing the circle. Now it is more difficult to kick the ball.

8. Have the children cool down; put away the ball; ask the children to lie down and place one hand up at a time shaking it loose; repeat with legs; ask each child to breath deeply five times; stand up and shake whole body.

More to do

Replace the ball with a balloon. While the children are lying down, ask them to use their arms and hands.

—Sylvia Behnk, Chomedy Laval, Quebec, Canada

Making Imaginary Applesauce

3+

Once you have had the experience of making real applesauce with your children, make it again—but let the children be the apples!

Materials needed

Masking tape (optional)
Song, "Making Applesauce" (see below)

What to do

1. Make a large circle on the floor with the masking tape. This will be your cooking pot. Have the children sit in a circle around the pot.

2. Walk around the outside of the circle singing the first verse of the song and each time you sing "cut," touch a child on the shoulder. These children become the apple pieces and go into the pot and take a seat. Continue until all the children (apple pieces!) are in the pot with no core, seeds or stems.

"Applesauce Song (to the tune of "The Mulberry Bush")

> *This is the way I cut the apples, cut the apples, cut the apples,*
> *This is the way I cut the apples,*
> *Making applesauce.*
>
> *Now I'll pour the water on, the water on, the water on,*
> *Now I'll pour the water on, (pretend to pour water on the children)*
> *Making applesauce.*
>
> *This is the way the apples cook, the apples cook, the apples cook*
> *This is the way the apples cook, (pretend to stir the children)*
> *Making applesauce.*
>
> *Now I'll stir the cinnamon in, etc....(pretend to sprinkle cinnamon on the children)*
> *Now I'll stir the apples 'round, etc.... (pretend to stir the children)*
> *Now it's cooked and it can cool, it can cool, it can cool,*
> *Now it's cooked and it can cool,*
> *I've made my applesauce. (Sing this verse quietly.)*

3. As you sing the Applesauce Song, add the ingredients one by one and stir the apples using a very large (imaginary) spoon! Have the children act out each part, boiling and bubbling in the beginning and becoming mushy by the end.

4. When the song is done, tell the children to be very still while the applesauce is cooling. Taste your delicious children!

More to do

Make and enjoy real applesauce for snack.

—Trish Weaver, Raleigh, NC

Leaf Dance   3+

This learning activity exercises large muscles allowing the children to move freely in creative dance. Additionally, the children will see the creation of the color orange by combining red and yellow.

Materials needed

Heavy black marker
Scissors
Large sheet of plain newsprint or classified ad section of newspaper
Red tempera paint
Yellow tempera paint
Medium-sized brushes
"The Gentle Sea" by Hap Palmer
Record or tape player

What to do

1. Using the marker, draw the outline of a large simple leaf on the paper. Make one for each child. Cut out the leaf or have children with good cutting skills cut out their own leaves.
2. Have each child use red and yellow paint to paint the giant leaf. Paint only one side of the leaf and allow to dry overnight.
3. Gather children together in a large open area such as a gym.
4. Tell the children that they are going to use the leaves they painted to participate in a leaf dance.
5. Play the record or tape of "The Gentle Sea" by Hap Palmer and have the children to listen to the music. Explain that when the music goes up, they may want to toss their leaf into the air. When the music goes down, they may want to fall to the ground with their leaf. When the music seems to twirl, they can twirl around.
6. Give each child a leaf.
7. Once again start a record or tape and let the dance begin!

More to do

You might like to choose a classical recording such as a waltz or "Autumn Leaves" by Roger Williams to do another dance.

—Gail Heyn, Albia, IA

Goldilock's Walk

This activity develops large muscle skills such as walking, running, leaping, jumping, hopping and crawling, and helps the children learn to follow directions.

Materials needed

Hoops or bicycle tires
3/8" diameter rope
Balance beam
Tunnel
8' ladder if available

What to do

1. Make a path on the floor with your materials. For example, you could arrange four tires in the path, then lay out rope, four more tires, a tunnel, balance beam and finish with four more tires. If you have a playhouse, this path could be arranged to lead to the playhouse. The arrangement can be varied and should take into consideration the age and ability of the children.
2. At various active playtimes allow the children to experiment using the materials to be placed in the "path."
3. Tell the story of "Goldilocks and the Three Bears" a few times allowing the children to retell it.
4. After the path has been set up tell the children they will each have a turn to be Goldilocks walking to the home of the three bears. Example: "Hop through the tires, tiptoe on the rope, walk in the spaces of the ladder, crawl through the tunnel, walk sideways on the balance beam and turn around and come back." Instructions can be the same for everyone or individual for each child participating depending on age/ability.

More to do

Allow a path to be set up during play for the children to use in their own way. They must follow safety rules established by the teacher. Pretend to be the bears walking down the path. Low notes on the piano represent Papa, middle C represents Mama, and high notes are for Baby Bear. After children are introduced to this, have them try to figure out which bear they are to be by listening to the notes.

—*Irene A. Tegze, Waldwick, NJ*

How Can We Get From Here to There?

The children will explore problem-solving strategies and creative movement while practicing their gross motor skills in this game based on a nursery rhyme!

What to do

1. Assemble the children in a sitting group and recite the rhyme "Trot, Trot To Boston" several times, until the children can say it with you.

    Trot, trot to Boston,
    Trot, trot to Lynn.
    Trot, trot to Salem,
    And back home again. (substitute names of your neighboring towns)
2. Review the meaning of trot and ask a child to demonstrate.
3. Ask individual children to stand and show other ways to use their feet to get to Boston. For example, run, hop, gallop, slide, jump.

4. Ask children to get to Boston (or other city) without standing up and using their feet. For example, crawl, roll, move on knees, crab walk, somersault.

5. To bring the group together again when you are ready to stop, ask the children to: "Trot, trot to circle and all sit down."

More to do

Add to the problem-solving possibilities. Can they still jump with both hands on some part of their bodies? How many different ways can they can hop? Can they hop in place? In a circle? Hands on hips? Holding their opposite foot? What other ways can they hop? Have children draw a picture of themselves moving in their favorite way and share their picture with the class.

Related book

This Is the Way We Go to School by Edith Baer

Related song

"Now Tall, Now Small" from *Wee Sing* by Pamela Conn Beall and Susan Hagen Nipp

—Margery Kranyik, Bridgewater, MA

Bubble Fun   3+

This learning activity is designed to improve eye-hand coordination, balance and gross motor skills like bending, jumping and hopping.

Materials needed

Bubble mixture and wand

What to do

1. Purchase or make the bubble mixture. Mix:
   1 Tablespoon liquid detergent
   1/2 teaspoon sugar
   4 oz. of water
2. Have the children form a circle, preferably outside. Demonstrate how to burst the bubble by poking it with your finger. Move around the circle blowing bubbles and letting the children burst them.
3. Ask someone to pop the bubbles by clapping both hands together. Move around the circle blowing bubbles and let each child clap to pop them.
4. Demonstrate stomping the bubbles and have the children do the same.
5. Have the children jump high up in the air to bat the bubbles with their hands. Blow the bubbles well above their heads.
6. Instruct the children to raise one foot, then hop on a bubble when it lands.
7. Have the children pretend that their feet are stuck to the ground. Continue blowing bubbles and tell them to lean, bend and stretch without falling over to pop the bubbles.
8. Tell children to burst the bubbles using only their knees, elbows, wrists and other body parts.

More to do

Let children help you make homemade bubble juice. Do bubble blowing on a windy day and let children watch how the wind carries the bubbles away in one direction.

—Cindy Bosse, Crystal Springs, MS

Monkey See, Monkey Do

This activity will enhance gross motor skills.

What to do

1.   Learn the following rhyme:

> *Monkey see, monkey do*
> *Monkey smiles when he looks at you.*
> *Monkey see, monkey do*
> *Monkey waves when he looks at you.*
> *Monkey see, monkey do*
> *Monkey (walks, hops, skips, runs, etc.) when he looks at you*
> *Monkey see, monkey do*
> *Monkey yawns when he looks at you. Good night!*

2.   Practice the actions that go with the rhyme before you actually chant it for the children. Fingers can outline a big smile on the face for the first verse. Other actions are self-explanatory. The final verse will slow down the activity, and the children can stand still or sit down at "Good Night!"
3.   Chant the rhyme slowly the first time, making sure that the children imitate your actions.
4.   Chant the rhyme more quickly after that and encourage the children to move and chant along with you.

More to do

Have the children suggest the action verb in the rhyme and what the action would look like. Have the children substitute another zoo animal's name for "monkey" and suggest an action to go along with it.

Related books

The Curious George series by H.A. Rey
Gorilla by Anthony Brown
The Pippo Series by Helen Oxenbury
Five Little Monkeys Jumping on the Bed by Eileen Christelow

—*Christina Chilcote, New Freedom, PA*

Velcro Obstacle Course Lines

In this activity the children will develop gross motor skills and coordination.

Materials needed

Masking tape

What to do

1.   If your movement area is an indoor carpeted space you can create lines, shapes, patterns, numbers or letters for the children to move on with the masking tape.
2.   Provide an additional challenge to the children by asking the children to move over the design in a certain way. For example:
   tiptoe
   crawl
   heel-to-toe walk
   gallop

Other directions to consider are march, hop, skip and walk on your knees.

More to do

Older learners can combine actions, moving while doing other actions: ex. walking and swinging arms, marching and clapping, walking sideways and snapping fingers, etc.

—Bev Schumacher, Ft. Mitchell, KY

Balancing Beanbags   3+

Children locate body parts in this gross motor activity.

Materials needed

One beanbag per child
Music for movement, walking rhythm (record, piano)

What to do

1. Gather children in an open area with room to move.
2. Explain that they will each receive a beanbag and will be moving around the room when the music is playing.
3. As the music plays the teacher names a body part for the children to place the beanbag on and try to balance it as they move.

More to do

As children become more adept at balancing and moving, the music can be sped up or varied in rhythm. Children may take turns calling out parts.

—Marni White, Casper, WY

Shadows   3+

Children learn about body movements, while exploring how the body blocks sunlight or an indoor light.

Materials needed

White sheet
Long rope, or two lengths of twine
Safety pins
Duct tape
Reading lamp

What to do

1. Fold the top edge of the sheet around the rope and pin together with safety pins. Tie rope tautly to opposite walls and tape the bottom edge of the sheet to the floor to make a smooth, tight screen.

2. Or, tie a loop at one end of each length of twine. Insert a safety pin through a loop and one corner of the sheet. Tie, pin or tape the length of twine to the ceiling. Repeat this procedure with the other corner of the sheet. Tape the bottom edge of the sheet to the floor to make a smooth, tight screen.
3. Shine the lamp on the back of the sheet.
4. Have one or two children go behind the backlit sheet.
5. The children can dance, twist or shadow-box.
6. The rest of the children will notice the shadows cast on the sheet and their size, height and actions.
7. Discuss how shadows do the same thing individuals do.
8. Class may "direct" the performing children's actions.
9. Take turns allowing other children to create moving shadows.

More to do

On a sunny day, go outdoors to investigate the height and width of shadows at various times of the day. Ask if we can see our shadow at night when the sun is gone. How?

Related books

Bear Shadow by Frank Asch
Shadow by Marcia Brown
Shadows: Here, There and Everywhere by Ron Goor

—Linda Barrett, Chicago, IL

Blanket Dancing   3+

Materials needed

Variety of blankets, one per child
Music with varied tempo

What to do

1. Gather the blankets together or have the children bring theirs from home. Show and discuss different textures and sizes of blankets.
2. Give each child a blanket.
3. Turn on the music.
4. Encourage the children to move the blanket on their head, shoulders, hands, feet, legs, arms, up over their head, behind their back or "find their own way."

More to do

Make a quilt by gluing pieces of material together. In dramatic play, have a fabric store with a variety of different fabrics and material books.

Related book

Ruby by Alison Lester

—Sandra Acuna, San Antonio, TX

Color the Movement

4+

The children will practice basic movement skills (walking, jumping, hopping, skipping, etc.).

Materials needed

Color strips of construction paper of basic colors (red, blue, green, orange, purple, etc.)
Recorded music

What to do

1. Cut the strips/paper evenly into large enough pieces (minimum size is 4" x 5 1/2" or larger) so they can be readily seen while the children are moving.
2. The teacher has children make a circle and he/she stands in the middle of it.
3. Assign a certain movement to each color (use only two to three colors at first)
4. The teacher plays a recording and asks the children to move as designated by the color shown.
For example:
> *Green—walk*
> *Blue—hop*
> *Yellow—run*
5. In order to move smoothly from one movement to another, it may be necessary to designate one color as the "STOP" color. For example:
> *Red—stop*
This will prevent chaos or children bumping each other!

More to do

Teacher can divide class into two "teams," each taking turns on a movement as the color is shown. As children become more skilled, teacher can flash colors more rapidly to determine if children can keep the beat and move smoothly from one basic movement to another.

—S. Lorna Zemke, Manitowoc, WI

Kangaroo Broad Jump

4+

Children will enhance jumping skills and compare theirs to a red kangaroo's.

Materials needed

Tape (or flags), to mark the jumping line and the children's distance.
Enough rope or string for each set of partners to have 25 feet

What to do

1. Mark off the jumping line with tape or flags.
2. Have the children choose partners, taking turns standing on the jumping line.
3. Show the children how to broad jump. Explain they should not bend their knees too deeply.
4. Partners on the jumping line broad jump and then wait for their spot to be marked.
5. Have the other partner stand at the jumping line with one end of the 25 foot string.
6. Have the jumping partner hold the opposite end of the string. Have him walk with the string in the direction they jumped until the string is pulled tight, and note how far they jumped on the string.
7. Let the remaining partners take a turn.

8. Explain to the children that the string represents the length of one jump of a red kangaroo.

Related books

Norma Jean, Jumping Bean by Joann Cole
Animal Jumpers by K. Lilly

—Angelica Lewis, Wichita, KS

Kangaroo Tag

4+

Children will enhance their jumping skills by participating in a revised version of tag.

Materials needed

Whistle

What to do

1. Gather all the children in a circle, preferably outside.
2. Show the children how to do a kangaroo jump (arms close to chest, palms facing downward, knees slightly bent).
3. Tell the children that they are going to play kangaroo tag and explain that the mother kangaroo (the child who is "it") is searching for her babies (joeys). When the mother kangaroo tags a joey, that child then becomes the mother and tries to tag someone else.
4. Stress the important rules: kangaroos jump but do not run; tagging should be done in a gentle way; and everyone must stop when the whistle is blown.
5. After all the children understand the rules, ask someone to volunteer to be the mother kangaroo (you might offer to be the mother first).
6. Play the game. If the children become too tired or too wound-up, blow the whistle and take a rest.

More to do

Change the rules and have the children hold hands after being tagged so that the whole group becomes the mother kangaroo and must jump together. The game ends when all the children are holding hands.

Related book

Norma Jean, Jumping Bean by Joann Cole

—Angelica Lewis, Wichita, KS

Preschool Olympics

MOVEMENT

Children will develop and strengthen gross motor skills and perceptual/motor skill while building self-esteem.

Materials needed

Pictures of Olympic events
Small table
Chairs
Scooters
Balance beam
Masking tape
Balls
Large blocks
Tumbling mat

What to do

1. Discuss the Olympics with the children and show them pictures of some Olympic events.
2. Have the children do some mock Olympic activities in the classroom but avoid making them competitive. The following are a few suggestions:

    Balancing on one foot for several seconds, then hopping on one or both feet from one point to another.
    Walking on a low balance beam or masking tape line and jumping off the end in victory stance.
    "Ski jumping" off a low table (make sure it is stable) and landing with bent knees.
    "Bob sledding" on a scooter by following a curved course marked with tape on the classroom floor.
    Tumbling on a gymnastics mat, doing somersaults and cartwheels.
    Playing ball games that involve bouncing, throwing and catching.
    Following an obstacle course (e.g., large blocks to crawl under and around, rows of chairs to crawl through, book stacks to step over).

3. After all children have had the opportunity to participate over several days, present ribbons to everyone. Parents may be invited to the ceremony.

More to do

As an art project, have children decorate Olympic medals made from gold and silver paper glued to cardboard. Punch a hole in the top of each medal and thread through a string. These medals can be worn by everyone.

—Rayne P. Reese, Glendale, MO

Fun With Opposites 5+

Children learn about opposites and improve their gross motor skills through movement and exploration.

What to do

1. Use an area in which children can move comfortably, sitting or standing.
2. Review the concept of opposites with the children by asking questions: "What is the opposite of long? high? empty?" Ask the children about other opposites.
3. Say to children: "Let's find opposites with our bodies. Raise your hands up in the air, place them down on the floor. Touch the front of your body, touch the back of your body. Stretch as high as you can. Bend as low as you can. Make your face look happy. Make your face look sad. Can you do something slow? How about fast? Find something hard. Find something soft. Now take a deep breath and look at me."

More to do

Give everyone beanbags. Ask children to use their bodies and place them high, low, over, on, off, up, down, front, back. Try the activity with partners, placing a beanbag on each other.

Related books

Over and Under by Catherine Matthias
Push, Pull, Empty, Full by Tana Hoban

Related music

"Opposites" from *Getting to Know Myself* by Hap Palmer

—*Margery Kranyik, Bridgewater, MA*

MOVEMENT

Exploring Sound Through Music   2+

Through this activity, children learn the concept of loud and soft.

Materials needed

"Soft and Loud Song" by Hap Palmer
Audio tape of alternating soft and loud music
Rhythm instruments for all the children
Wooden spoons
Pot lids
Empty coffee cans with plastic lids
Chopsticks
Bells, or anything else that makes a sound
Tape player or record player

What to do

1. Locate a copy of Hap Palmer's song or record your own tape of alternating soft and loud musical selections.
2. Gather rhythm instruments or materials for homemade instruments. Make sure all the children have something to play.
3. Familiarize yourself with the music you have chosen.
4. Have music ready to play.
5. Hand out the instruments and demonstrate how they work. Remind children to keep quiet while they are waiting.
6. Demonstrate soft and loud sounds.
7. Play the song and help the children learn when they need to play soft and loud. You may want to repeat the activity several times. Be prepared for some loud performances!

More to do

Have the children march slowly when they play the music softly and move quickly when they play loudly. Have the children change instruments.

—*Rahnna Peck, Southbury, CT*

Dance Along Songs   2+

This activity allows children to express enjoyment of music through dancing.

Materials needed

Four kinds of music (e.g., orchestral, rock, folk, piano)
Tape recorder
Scarfs

What to do

1. Select appropriate music from four distinct categories. Record the music on tape and color code the tapes according to the type of music.
2. Invite children to dance with you in a spacious area of the room.

3. Tell the children you will be playing several kinds of music and that they may dance any way the music makes them feel. Provide scarfs as an additional mode of expression.
4. Play one type of music.
5. Dance by yourself and say what the music makes you want to do (i.e., skip, bounce, rest, etc.).
6. Play each of the different types of music and talk with the children about how the different music made them feel like moving.

More to do

Make a "Music I Like" chart. Along the top of the chart, list the categories of music you will be playing, and in a vertical column down the left side of the chart, list the children's names. Tell the children about the various kinds of music and how each has its own distinct sound and rhythm. Emphasize that everyone likes and dislikes certain kinds of music. After playing each selection, ask the children if they enjoyed it. If they say yes, have them place a smiley face or other decal in the appropriate square. Have the activity arranged in a quiet area of your room to help the children concentrate. Pillows to sit on are helpful.

—Brian Wenzell, East Lansing, MI

Dancing in Paint

2+

Children develop artistic expression and a feel for rhythm.

Materials needed

Large bedsheet or piece of fabric
Kitchen serving tray, for paint
Tempera paint (add liquid soap to it for easy cleaning)
Dishpan filled with warm soapy water
Towels
Record player

What to do

1. Tape fabric to floor.
2. Place the paint-filled tray at one end of the fabric and the dishpan of water at the other end.
3. Play music.
4. Have the children step into tray of paint, making sure all pant legs are rolled up.
5. The children then step onto the fabric and dance to the music as long as they wish.
6. When they are finished, have them step into the pan of water.
7. Assist them in washing and drying off feet.

More to do

Try different kinds of music—classical, jazz or rock.

—Charlene M. Roediger, Allentown, PA

High in the Sky, Low on the Ground

3+

Children practice comparing and making high and low sounds by listening, labeling and using musical instruments.

Materials needed

One instrument per child (tambourines, bells, triangles, shakers, tone blocks, or drums)
Step xylophone and mallet
Flannel board
Flannel worm and bird

What to do

1. Make a worm and a bird from flannel material.
2. Introduce the activity by using the worm and bird on the flannel board. Ask how birds move, where they fly, how worms move, and where they crawl.
3. Demonstrate how our bodies can move high and low. Have the children practice stretching high and low.
4. Music also has sounds that are high and low. Demonstrate this with your voice. Have the children practice also.
5. Sing high and low sounds. Have the children move their bodies up and down according to whether the notes are high or low.
6. Musical instruments can make high and low sounds like our voices. Demonstrate by playing a high note and a low note on the xylophone.
7. Using the step xylophone, have the children listen to various notes played and identify them as high or low sounds.
8. Call on one child at a time to play a high or low note.
9. Hide the xylophone from the children's view and play notes. Have the children compare them. Which one is higher? Which is lower?
10. Show and play musical instruments you have collected. Name each one.
11. Give each child an instrument. Call on two children at a time to play their instruments. Compare sounds as high or low. Continue until all have had a turn.
12. Have the children play all low sounding instruments play. Have all high-sounding instruments play.

More to do

Play a variety of musical sounds. Have children label each as low or high sounds. Encourage children to move their bodies up and down as the musical pieces move up and down with high or low sounds.

—Marzee Woodward, Murfreesboro, TN

Beanbag Rhythm

The children will learn how to listen to the rhythms of music and will practice following simple directions.

Materials needed

One beanbag per child
Recorded music
Large plastic detergent bottles
Drum sticks (cut 1/2" diameter dowel sticks into 9" lengths)
Masking tape

What to do

1. If you don't already have beanbags, you can make them in the following manner:
   Cut brightly-colored corduroy or muslin cloth into different shapes. A rectangle might measure 4" x 5."
   Sew the sides together but leave an opening at one end.
   Fill the bags with dry beans until they are half full.
   Sew the ends closed.
2. Show the children the beanbags. Describe the different shapes and colors.
3. Give each child a beanbag. Let the children get acquainted with them. Let them feel the bag and toss it back and forth in their hands.
4. Ask the children to walk holding a beanbag in outstretched hand. They may then alternate their hands.
5. Beat the detergent bottle "drum" with the dowel stick in a moderate tempo while the children walk and march.

More to do

The children put the beanbag under their chins and walk or march to the beat of the drum. Later, they may do this to recorded music. As the children become efficient in their walking and marching, ask them to put the beanbag on their heads, under their arms, or on their shoulders as they march. They may also try carrying the beanbags between their upper and lower arms at the elbow. Still later they may put the beanbags on their feet, behind their knees or on their stomach or back. Ask the children for suggestions as to where to place their beanbags.

—*Angelina Yoder, Barium Springs, NC*

Tone Color

Children will learn to play rhythm instruments and to select appropriate instruments to represent animal sounds.

Materials needed

Various rhythm instruments, one set per child (e.g., rhythm sticks, tone blocks, jingle bells, triangles, cymbals, various types of drums)
The Little Red Hen, a picture book

What to do

1. Have each child select a rhythm instrument.
2. Ask the children to name their instruments and describe how they are made.

3. Arrange the children in groups according to the kinds of instruments they select (e.g., instruments made of wood, instruments that jingle, instruments that clang).

4. Suggest to the children that they tap the wooden rhythm sticks and tone blocks to the "cluck" of the hen as you read the story.

5. Have the children decide which group should play for each of the animal sounds in the story.

6. Read the story and have the children play their instruments each time their characters speak.

More to do

Reread the story and have different groups of children chant the characters' words. Sing "Red Hen's Song" by Carmen Ravosa. Sing "Old MacDonald Had A Farm" and "Cat Goes Fiddle Dee Dee," using characters from the story. Use the instruments to accompany other stories such as:

The Brementown Musicians
Farm Concert
There Was an Old Lady Who Swallowed a Fly
Chicken Little

Related books

Bread, Bread, Bread by Ann Morris

—*Kay McAlpine, Lima, OH*

The Old Woman Who Swallowed a Fly   3+

Children learn a fun, silly song along with some concepts about the food chain.

Materials needed

Words and music to the song "There Was an Old Woman Who Swallowed a Fly"
Marking pens
Old woman puppet clothing, or any sort of flannel-type material to wrap around your arm
Small animal props representing the animals in the song (a fly, a spider, a bird, a cat, a dog, a goat, a cow, and a horse)

What to do

1. Construct a prop puppet using a scarf and a doll's dress as shown in figure 1.

2. Using a red marker, color the outside edge of your hand from the tip of the index finger to the tip of the thumb.

3. Turn your hand into the puppet's head and face by curling the fingers into a semi-fist as shown in figure 2. Complete the face by using either blue or brown markers to make eye dots just below the index knuckle (a black marker can also be used to make pupils and eyelashes).

4. Put the puppet's clothing on your hand.

5. Sing and teach the children the song, "There was an Old Woman Who Swallowed a Fly," and have the old woman puppet swallow the appropriate animal prop as it is introduced in the song.

More to do

Allow the children to color their hands and lead the group in song.

Related books

There Was an Old Woman Who Swallowed a Fly by Ladybird Books

—*Leslie Kuehn Meyer, Vermillion, SD*

Figure 1   Step 1

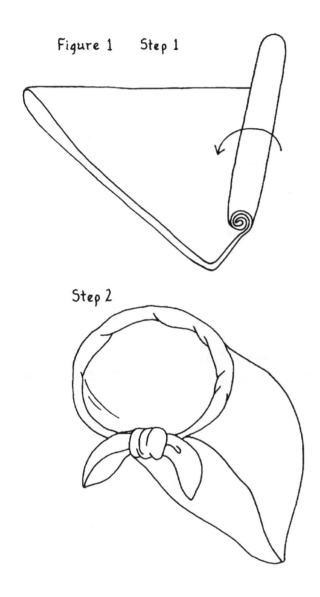

Figure 2

Step 2

Step 3

Insert hand here.

Finished puppet

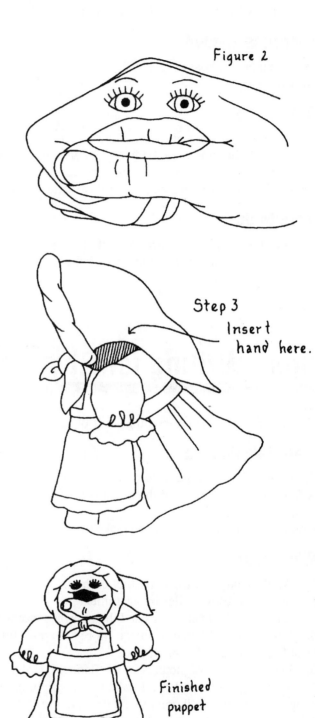

Dancing Angels/Pounding Hooves

3+

This activity introduces children to classical music and helps them identify how music makes them feel.

Materials needed

Cassette tape of classical music
Cassette player

What to do

1. Put the music on and let the children's imagination take over.
2. Ask the children to use body movements to show how the music makes them feel.
3. Make up stories about the music (e.g., angels floating on clouds to slow graceful music and horses with pounding hooves running over the hills to loud echoing music).

More to do

Research the story behind each piece of music you play and what the composer had in mind when he wrote the music. Tell the children that story and ask them if they think the composer was feeling happy or sad or angry.

—Sylvia Stillwell, Madison, CT

Song Writing for Rhythm Instruments

4+

Children develop the pre-reading skills of symbolic representation and sequencing.

Materials needed

Rhythm instruments (purchased or homemade)
A few copies of pictures of the instruments (simple, 3"x 4" line drawings work best)
Flannel board
Sandpaper (or other materials to make the instrument pictures adhere to the flannel board)

What to do

1. Apply sandpaper to the back of each instrument picture.
2. Sort pictures into piles by instrument.
3. Introduce the instruments and their corresponding pictures to five or six children.
4. Give each child an instrument. More than one child may have the same instrument, but try to have at least four or five different types.
5. Put a sequence of pictures on the flannel board.
6. Tell the children, "When I point to each picture, the person holding the instrument will play (or shake or bang) it once. Then I'll point to the next picture and the person with that instrument will play it one time, and so on."
7. Do this several times with different arrangements. Then ask a child if he would like to make a sequence and lead the band.

More to do

After the children understand that they are making songs by the order of the pictures, you can ask some leading questions: How should you show that you want the person to play loud or soft? How can you show if you want everyone to stop? Find a way to preserve the children's compositions. Make smaller versions of the pictures and give the children sheets of paper on which to glue the pictures in the sequence they had chosen.

Related songs

"Homemade Band" by Hap Palmer

—Barbara A. Fitzsimmons, Newton, MA

Beethoven Brush Art   4+

Children learn about different tempos and moods of music.

Materials needed

Paints (many colors)
Paintbrushes
Paper
Record player/cassette player
Music by Beethoven

What to do

1. Instruct the children to paint to the music tempos, encouraging them to be creative.
2. Start the music.

More to do

Use crayons instead of paint. Have the children use one color at a time, changing when the music changes or when you call out, "Change!"

—Elaine Payne, Plantation, FL

What Does That Music Sound Like?   4+

Children learn that some composers write music to create a certain picture or mood.

Materials needed

Several musical recordings that evoke strong images. (Moussorgsky's "Pictures at an Exhibition," Tchaikovsky's "Nutcracker Suite," and Richard Rodgers' "Carousel Waltz" are good choices.)

What to do

1. Explain to the children that you are going to play some music and that they should close their eyes and try to imagine what the composer was thinking.
2. Play the music a second time and encourage them to move around and act out what they are hearing.
3. If they listen to "Carousel Waltz," ask if they can see the horses moving up and down? What else does the music make them think of?

—Jessica Mitchell, Oakdale, NY

Making Horns

4+

The children will enjoy making their own musical instruments and discovering what sounds they can produce.

Materials needed

Cardboard tube, one per child
Construction paper
Crayons or markers
Clear contact paper
Wax paper
Thick rubber bands, one per child
Scissors

What to do

1.   Give each child a cardboard tube and have her choose materials to decorate the outside of it.
2.   Cut a piece of contact paper large enough to cover the child's design and overlap the lip of the tube. Fold the contact paper inward over the lip.
3.   Cut the wax paper 1" larger than the diameter of the end of the tube. Pull wax paper tightly over the end of the tube and secure with a thick rubber band.
4.   Use scissors to cut slits in the wax paper and then cut one or two finger holes in the tube itself, near the wax paper end of the tube.
5.   Have the children sing or hum "do-do-do, re-re-re,..." into the open end of their horns.

More to do

Play follow the leader by repeating the leader's sound. Discuss the feeling of vibration when air is blown into the horn. Discuss different types of sounds the children produce, and their qualities.

Related books

My Five Senses by Aliki
Song and Dance Man by Karen Ackerman

—Evelyn Metoyer Williams, Los Angeles, CA

Color Match Musical Notes

In this activity, children learn to match a colored note letter to a colored keyboard color and to play a tune.

Materials Needed

Copy of London Bridge music score for each child
Copy of piano keyboard for each child
7 different colored stickers or markers
Piano or organ keyboard

What to do

1. Write each note at the top of the keyboard in a different color (G, A, B, C, D, E, F).
2. Glue a corresponding color sticker at the bottom of the keyboard.
3. Color the notes of the music score to correspond with the colors you have used for each note.
4. Play the tune for the children on the piano or organ keyboard.
5. Call out the colored sticker or note letter as they are played, and let the children touch the appropriate note on their pretend keyboard.

More to do

This activity can be used for other songs.

—Sheila G. Wood, Arlington, TX

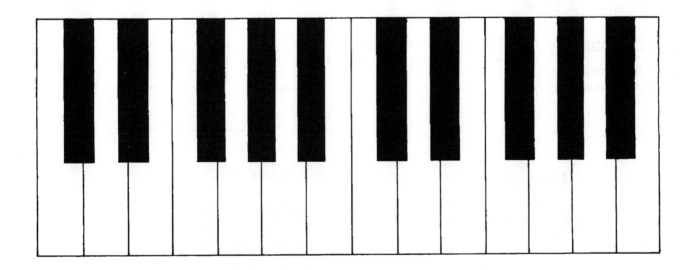

Totem Pole

3+

Children learn about other cultures while improving their fine motor skills.

Materials needed

Paper towel or gift wrap tube
Brightly colored construction paper
Brown paint
Markers
Scissors
Stapler or glue
Small objects (optional)

What to do

1. Paint the cardboard tube with brown paint and let it dry completely.
2. Trace child's hand and foot on several pieces of construction paper and cut out the shapes. Allow the children to do the cutting when possible.
3. Draw designs and glue other small objects on the shapes.
4. Glue the shapes onto the brown tube. (See illustration).

—Jyoti Joshi, Framingham, MA

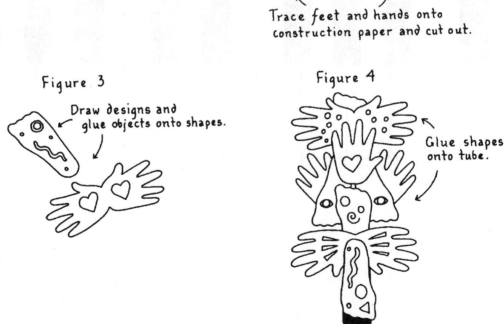

Figure 1

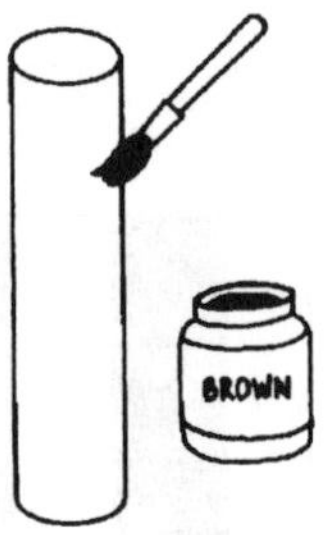

Figure 2

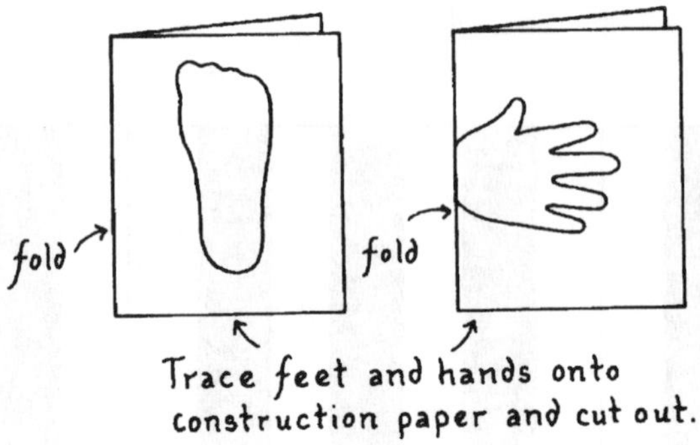

Trace feet and hands onto construction paper and cut out.

Figure 3

Draw designs and glue objects onto shapes.

Figure 4

Glue shapes onto tube.

Indian Sand Painting

The children will have fun making Indian designs in this unusual way.

Materials needed

Crayons
Medium grain sandpaper, 6" x 4"—one per child
Toaster oven or school kitchen electric oven
Construction paper
Double-stick tape or glue

What to do

1. Cut colored construction paper into 9" x 6" rectangles.
2. Using crayons, have the children draw Indian designs on their sandpaper.
3. Set oven on broil. One at a time, carefully place each colored sandpaper on the oven rack, directly below the element. (Caution: Do not use gas oven because of fire danger from direct flame. Supervise children carefully during this step.) The children can observe the melting process through the open oven door. Melt for approximately three to five seconds or until the crayon appears wet and glazed. Remove and cool.
4. Mount sand painting on colored construction paper, using double-stick tape or glue.

More to do

Use the Indian designs to decorate headbands, oatmeal-box drums, paper tepees or canoes. Using Indian symbols, draw a story as created and dictated by children in the class.

Related book

The Legend of Indian Paintbrush by Tomie dePaola

—*Teri Schmidt, Silverton, OR*

Pocahontas

This activity will teach the children about a famous Native American peacemaker.

Materials needed

Large sheets of drawing paper
Small sheets of construction paper in various colors
Strips of brown construction paper, 1" wide
Markers and/or crayons

What to do

1. Draw an oval (for a face) on each sheet of drawing paper.
2. Cut feathers from various colors of construction paper.
3. Read a story about Pocahontas. Explain that she was a princess among her people (Native Americans) and that she made peace between her people and the colonists when they came to America.
4. Pass out the face outlines you have made. Have the children add the features to the face of Pocahontas. Let them put a headband and feathers on her head.

More to do

Talk about Native Americans. What kind of houses did they live in? What kind of food did they eat? What kind of things did the Native Americans teach the colonists?

Related books

Pocahontas by Jan Gleiter & Kathleen Thompson
Pocahontas by Ingri & Edgar Parin d'Aulaire

—Laura Honkoski, Steger, IL

Canoes

4+

Canoes were important to many Indian tribes.

Materials needed

Manila paper
Markers
Crayons
Hole punch
Yarn
Plastic needles

What to do

1. Give each child a folded piece of manila paper.
2. Place the canoe pattern (see illustration) on the fold. The older children can trace and cut out the canoe; younger children will need help with this step.
3. Each child decorates her canoe with markers or crayons.
4. The teacher punches holes in the ends of each canoe, and the children stitch them closed with yarn and plastic needles.

—Elaine Commins, Atlanta, GA

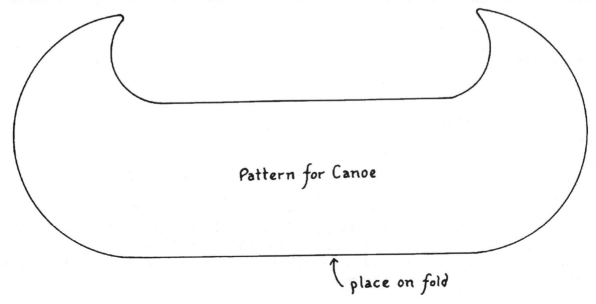

Pattern for Canoe

place on fold

Native American Tepee

This activity introduces young children to one type of housing used by the first Americans.

Materials needed

Paint
Paintbrushes
Crayons
Markers
Scissors
12" x 18 " pieces of cardboard or posterboard
Manila paper
Straws
Stapler

What to do

1. Cut out one or two tepee patterns (see illustration) from the cardboard or posterboard.
2. Each child traces a pattern on manila paper, cuts it out and decorates it with paint, markers or crayons.
3. The teacher staples three straws to the center of the straight edge of the cutout (see illustration). Fold and staple together to form a tepee.

More to do

Research different Indian crafts and how they were used. Share this information with the children, using samples when available. Talk about the kinds of clothes Native Americans wore and what they wear today; the various tribes and where they lived, then and now; Indians today and the way they live and work. Invite guests who can add to the quality of this unit.

—*Elaine Commins, Altanta, GA*

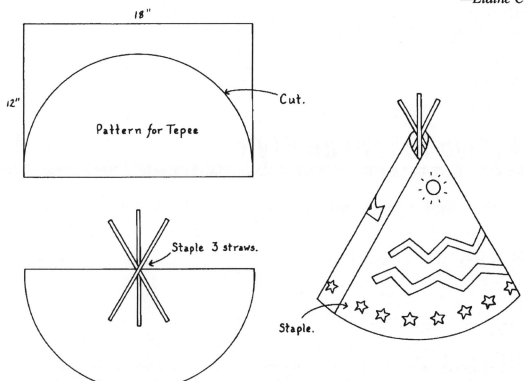

18"

12"

Cut.

Pattern for Tepee

Staple 3 straws.

Staple.

Weaving

4+

Weaving is an Indian craft that children will enjoy.

Materials needed

Manila paper
Scissors
Marker
Colored construction paper

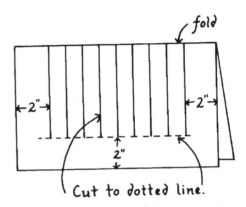

What to do

1. Fold the pieces of manila paper horizontally (the long way).
2. The teacher draws evenly-spaced guide lines on the folded piece of paper. The guide lines should be drawn to within 1 1/2" to 2" from the lower edge.
3. Each child cuts along the guide lines, being careful not to cut to the edge. Younger children will need help with this step.
4. Using two or more colors, the teacher cuts out 12" strips of paper to be used for weaving. The older children can help with this step, especially if you draw lines to cut along.
5. The children unfold their paper and weave one color strip at a time in and out of the slits. Strips are inserted alternately over and under the paper.

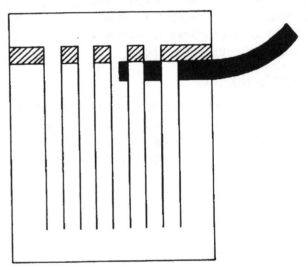

—*Elaine Commins, Atlanta GA*

Kick Ball/Native American Style

4+

Through this activity, children cooperate with partners, practice eye-foot coordination and learn about Native American culture.

Materials needed

Rock
String
Outdoor play area

What to do

1. Talk with the children about the ways Native Americans hunted for food a long time ago. Speed in running was very important. This helped them catch the animal they were chasing. Many of the children's games centered on running and accuracy. Cooperation was also important because it was more important to work together than to end up with nothing to eat.

2. Have the children help you make a ball by wrapping the rock with string until it is a reasonable size. Secure the end of the string by tucking it inside the ball. Explain that Native Americans made everything they used, including toys.

3. Plan and mark out an easily identifiable course. For example, around the perimeter of the play yard.

4. Let the children pick their partners.

5. While other children are playing, one pair of children work together and take turns to kick the ball the entire distance of the course.

6. The course should be long enough that the children will have plenty of opportunity to take turns and help each other and will feel a sincere sense of accomplishment by making it to the finish line!

—Barbara M. Reynolds, Pomona, NJ

Triangular Tepee

4+

This is a versatile activity which can be used to teach young children about one kind of Native American dwellings.

Materials needed

Three long poles to form the skeleton of the tepee
A large white sheet
Stapler
Markers or tempera paints

What to do

1. Gather painting and decorative materials for the tepee and set aside.

2. To make the tepee, set the poles up and tie them together with string or yarn at the top. With the children's help, cover the poles with the sheet and secure with staples.

3. Tell the children that some Native Americans lived in tepees and that they liked to decorate their tepees with art work.

4. Allow the students to decorate the tepee by drawing or painting on the cloth.

5. Now enjoy the tepee! It can be a special place to read or play or just sit and relax!

More to do

Have a rain dance around the tepee. Sew beads on the sheet as extra decoration.

—Lisa M. Lang, Parkersburg, WV

Making Indian Necklaces

4+

In this activity, the children learn part of the process that Native Americans used in making and decorating their clothing.

Materials needed

Earthen clay (may be purchased—self-hardening clay)
Feathers (bird, chicken, rooster or duck)
Any of the following:
   Acorns or nuts (with small hole drilled through)
   Popcorn
   Bells
   Beads
   Yarn

What to do

1. Gather desired materials to string on necklace.
2. Cut yarn to appropriate lengths for children's necklaces.
3. Let children make clay balls. Poke hole through middle. Stick 1-3 feathers in each bead. Each child could make 1-4 "beads." Let dry overnight.
4. Knot yarn and tie a bead on one end. Wrap other end in tape so yarn won't fray.
5. String items on yarn. Follow a pattern, e.g., bead, acorn, bell, clay bead—repeat.

Related book

Children of the Earth and Sky by Stephen Krensky

—*Mary L. Barron, Lafayette, LA*

Setting up a Home for Worms

Children develop observation and cooperation skills, plus an awareness of nature.

Materials needed

Aquarium
Plants
Soil
Water and bowl
Gravel
Worms
Worm books

What to do

1. Read a book about worms and look at worm pictures.
2. Meet the worms. Have the children name them.
3. Help the children prepare a home for the worms—clean the aquarium, arrange gravel, put in soil and add water.
4. Visit with the worms, then put them in their new home.
5. Discuss how to care for the worms.

—Kim Anderson, Elberfeld, IN

Worms

This activity helps children become familiar with earthworms in a fun and natural way.

Materials Needed

One earthworm per child
One paper plate per child

What to do

1. Purchase earthworms. (They are sold by the dozen at bait shops.) Store the worms in the refrigerator until ready to use.
2. Seat the children at a table.
3. Talk to the children before the activity and explain that earthworms are safe to touch and that they must be handled gently.
4. Give one paper plate to each child.
5. Place an earthworm on each plate. You can use a spoon to handle the earthworms.
6. Encourage the children to touch the worms. The children can pick up the worms and watch them stretch and wiggle.

More to do

While the children are examining the worms, name the worm's body parts and have the children repeat the names. When you are finished with the activity, have the children carry their plates outdoors and let the worms go. Everyone can say "good bye" to the worms as they wiggle their way back into the ground!

—Susan M. Myhre, Bremerton, WA

Snipping Grass

2+

Children use gross and fine motor skills in an art-related experience.

Materials needed

Large sheet of white butcher paper
Masking tape
Green paint
Paintbrushes
Art smocks
Clean-up bucket of soapy water and towels
Scissors or snippers

What to do

1. Mix the paint.
2. Prepare the clean-up water.
3. Tape the butcher paper to the floor and wall.
4. Give each child a paintbrush and let them paint the entire sheet of paper with green paint.
5. Have the children clean the brushes in the soapy water and put them up to dry.
6. After the paper has several minutes to dry, tell the children that they are going to make it look like grass by using scissors or snippers to cut the paper.
7. Using the scissors or snippers, let the children practice their snipping skills by cutting several inches straight into the top and bottom of the paper.
8. The teacher can then cut the entire paper in half through the middle and have a long row of grass.
9. Mount the "grass" on a wall for a display.

More to do

Make paper flowers, bugs or caterpillars to put in your grass. Older children can use pencils or curl the grass strips.

Related Books

Childs Garden of Verses by Robert Louis Stevenson

—*Beverly C. Dugger, Johnson City, TN*

Lily Pads

2+

Children create a life-like lily pad that can be used in a pond.

Materials needed

Green construction paper
White typing paper
Light colored paint
Dark green paint (darker than the construction paper)
Small paintbrush
Toothpicks
Lily pad and flower petal patterns
Glue

What to do

1. Cut lily pads out of green construction paper and flower petals out of white typing paper.
2. Have children paint one or both sides of several flower petals with light colored paint. Flower petals should curl as they dry.
3. Use toothpicks to paint dark green radiating lines on a lily pad.
4. When the lily pad is dry, glue the flower petals around the center of the lily pad.

More to do

Talk about other plants that are found in, on or around a pond.

—Leslie Kuehn Meyer, Vermillion, SD

Worm Watch

3+

Children are fascinated by worms. In this activity, they will have the opportunity to build a worm farm in the classroom and observe earthworms at work.

Materials needed

Clean gallon jug and/or individual pint jars
Small rocks or pieces of a broken flower pot for drainage
Several types of soil/sand
Decaying leaves and grass
Dark paper or fabric
Spray bottle
Worm food such as corn meal, green leafy vegetables, grass cuttings, potato peelings, bread crumbs, or small amount of coffee grounds (two tablespoons every other week)
Damp cloth
Earthworms (from your garden or bait shop)

What to do

1. After collecting several types of soil, put small rocks or broken flower pot pieces in the bottom of the jar. Begin putting in layer upon layer of soil until jar(s)/jug is 1/2 to 3/4 full. Avoid using all hard and compact soil, and do not mix different types of soils together in one layer.
2. Place a few decaying leaves/bits of food on top.
3. Get earthworms and put into jar(s). A gallon jug can hold a dozen earthworms.
4. Keep the soil moist by misting daily. Discard any moldy or smelly foods. Cover the top of the wormery with a damp cloth. This will help keep the soil moist and the earthworms cool. Be sure to keep the wormery in a cool place with no direct sunlight.
5. Cover the jar/jug with black paper or fabric to create darkness, which will stimulate the worms to tunnel and mix layers of soil. If you use light, sandy soil on top, you will soon see it mixed with lower soil layers.
6. Use a dim light when observing the work and activity of earthworms.
7. After a few weeks, you may see a thin layer of dark earth on top. This pure, rich humus is soil made by the earthworms and is good for gardens.
8. Remember to return the earthworms to a garden after the experiment.

More to do

Experiment to find out which kinds of leaves your earthworms seem to prefer to eat. Record findings. Experiment with the benefits of earthworms to growing things. Take two plants of the same species, age, and size. Plant them in two identical pots with identical soil layers. Add a few earthworms to one pot (two to four, depending on size) and none to the other. Put pots side by side and water equally and simultaneously. After a month or two, there should be a difference in the sizes of the plants. The plant whose pot contained earthworms should be taller, bushier, and healthier looking.

Related books

Naturewatch by Adrienne Katz

—Carolyn Jackson, Portland, OR

Nutty Mobile 3+

Children will create a lovely mobile out of nature objects.

Materials needed

String
Sticks between 12" and 16" long
Leaves
Acorns, assorted nuts
Pine cones
Scissors
Tack
Bags

What to do

1. Prior to doing the activity with children, collect sticks long enough to support the items for the mobiles and cut pieces of string in different lengths.
2. Give the children small bags and take them on a nature hike. Tell them to collect nature objects such as leaves, acorns, pine cones, nuts, and dried bark. Return to the classroom.
3. Help the children tie their objects to the strings for hanging. Poke holes in the leaves using a paper punch or scissors and wrap string securely around other objects.
4. Give each child a stick and demonstrate how to tie the items to the stick in a balanced way.
5. Tell the children to tie another string in the middle of stick. Hang the mobiles from the ceiling by tacking the ends of the middle strings to the ceiling.

More to do

Have the children paint the nature objects or sprinkle them with glitter before tying them on.

Related books

Drawing From Nature by Jim Arnosky

—Dana Musch, St. Paul, MN

Snails

To learn through movement and song snail anatomy, habits and movement.

What to do

1. Sing the following to the tune of "I'm a Little Teapot" to introduce the activity.

   I'm a little snail
   And I can crawl
   Here is my house
   It fits me all
   Whenever I get scared
   I curl up small
   Then out I pop
   Antennae and all!

2. When the children learn the song have them "become" snails by doing the movements while singing the song.

More to do

Make playdough snails. Roll dough like a snake then roll up and add pipe cleaners for antennae. Let harden, then paint. Have empty shells of varying sizes available in science area for free exploration. With living snails, have snail races so children have a sense of their movements and speed.

Related books

The Snail's Spell by Joanne Ryder
The Biggest House in the World by Leo Lionni

—*Mindi Shelow, Flushing, NY*

Shell Snail

Children will learn what snails look like.

Materials needed

Clam shell or scollop shell
S-type styrofoam
Glue
Sequins

What to do

1. Attach shell to styrofoam so that it looks like snail head.
2. Glue one sequin on each side of head.

More to do

Show various sizes and kinds of snail shells. Show picture of snail. Pretend to crawl like snails.

—*Mary Brehm, Aurora, OH*

Worm Farm

3+

Children learn how earthworms live and move.

Materials needed

Aquarium or other clear container
Loose soil
Worms
Plants
Shovel

What to do

1. Take the children outside to an area with rich soil and lots of worms. Tell the children that they are going to dig for earthworms and then create a similar habitat in the aquarium so the earthworms can be observed for several days.
2. With the shovel, turn up several clumps of soil and let the children capture worms. Put soil in the aquarium and have the children add the worms. Then add some plants from the site.
3. Back in the room, keep the aquarium slightly damp and encourage the children to watch the worms crawl and make tunnels.
4. After several days, return the worms to their natural habitat and explain how their digging keeps the soil loose and better for the plants.

—Cindy Bosse, Crystal Springs, MS

Dirt Day

3+

Children develop observation skills while learning about what things are found in dirt.

Materials needed

Shovels
Spade
Spoons
Water table or individual plastic tubs
Sand, gravel, topsoil, and clay-based dirt
Magnifying glasses
Paper cups
Water
Poster or paper
Marker

What to do

1. Announce the date of Dirt Day with a big poster. Request that children wear old play clothes and bring extras to have on hand.
2. Empty the water table or set out several plastic tubs.
3. Have separate containers of sand, gravel, topsoil and clay-based dirt.
4. Label a paper cup for each child.
5. Have books and field guides about rocks and minerals available.

6. Take the children outside with shovels, spoons and a garden spade.

7. Choose a spot and dig up a large spadeful to bring back to the classroom. Allow the children time to explore the hole with their digging tools.

8. Bring a shovelful of dirt inside and place it in the empty water table (or in a few plastic tubs). Let the children comb through the dirt.

9. Record comments and observations on a large poster or individual work sheets. Ask, "Are there any living creatures? Rocks or stones? Any surprises (nails, glass, bones, etc.)? If earthworms or insects are found, encourage gentle observation for a short period of time. Discuss their role in the environment, then bring a few children along to release the creatures outside.

10. Rocks, stones or pebbles discovered in the course of observation can be assembled in the science center as the beginning of a rock collection. Ask for other contributions.

11. Allow children to add water to the dirt and observe changes.

More to do

Make bricks by packing mud into the bottom half of cut-off wax milk cartons. Allow to dry in the sun and carefully peel off cartons. Talk about adobe houses.

Related books

How to Dig a Hole to the Other Side of the Earth by Faith McNulty
A Hole Is to Dig by Ruth Krauss

—*Sharon Dempsey, Pomona, NJ*

Tree Bark Rubbing 3+

Tree bark rubbing is a great way for children to become familiar with tree bark consistency, density, texture and color. This activity can also improve eye-hand coordination.

Materials needed

Sheets of paper
Color crayons
Trees or samples of different tree bark

What to do

1. Peel the paper off several crayons. Gather other necessary materials.

2. Lead a group discussion on trees including the different parts, the roots, trunk, bark, branches and leaves.

3. Demonstrate the activity. Place a piece of paper on the tree's trunk and rub a color crayon, using the whole side, over the paper.

4. Let the children create their own bark rubbings.

5. Discuss the differences in the pictures and tree barks.

More to do

Pin up and display the rubbings. Extend the group discussion to the role of our trees: shade, beauty, homes for animals, wood and its contribution to clean air.

—*Lorene Miller, Fremont, CA*

Nature Wreaths

3+

Children participate in the wonders of nature through hands-on experience.

Materials needed

Paper plates
Glue
Objects from nature
Small lunch bags (brown paper bags)

What to do

1. Cut out the center of paper plates. Make enough for each child.
2. Take a class "wonder walk." Hand out the paper bags and ask the children to collect nature items such as dried grasses, pine straw, wild flowers, leaves, etc.
3. Give the children a wreath shape and a small cup of glue.
4. Have children glue all the objects they found onto the wreath.

—Cynthia Burnett, Atlanta, GA

A Tree Is Nice

3+

This activity provides a fun art project that displays the children's creativity.

Materials needed

One white T-shirt provided by each child
Sponges cut into small shapes
Fabric paints (green, brown, orange, red)
Fabric pen

What to do

1. Put a piece of cardboard inside each shirt.
2. Provide flat trays for paint and sponges (muffin tins work well).
3. Have children dip sponges in the brown paint and apply to the shirts to make the tree trunk.
4. Children can add leaves by using sponges dipped in a variety of colors.
5. Write "A Tree is Nice" on T-shirts.
6. Hang to dry.

More to do

Adopt a tree on or near your school's grounds. Eat, sing and tell stories around it. Take pictures. Talk about saving trees. Explore trunk, leaves, etc. Plant a tree in school yard or nearby park.

—Lynne Saunders, Philadelphia, PA

Build a Pond

Children create their own science center and learn about things that make up a pond.

Materials needed

Blue paint
Sticks of varying lengths and thicknesses
Sand
Small rocks
Cardboard soda case (from the grocery store)
Paper or plastic bags

What to do

1. Clear off a table that can be used as the "pond" for at least one week.
2. Take children on a nature and collecting walk. Give each child a bag for collecting sand, rocks, shells and sticks (varying in length and thickness) to use for the turtle pond. Avoid dirt, grass or leaves because these items will decay and smell after only two to three days.
3. Back in the classroom, arrange the collected items in the cardboard soda cases. These will become the pond's shoreline.
4. Set aside some thick sticks to use as floating logs.
5. Allow children to paint the surface of the science table blue. For a ripple effect, dribble some dark blue and white paint on the table and lightly swirl these colors in with the original blue paint to create a marbled look.
6. Allow the paint to dry, add the shoreline, and place the "logs" in the pond.

More to do

Use the pond as a science center to teach children about many of the components found both above and below the pond's surface. You might add models of turtles, frogs, flying insects, water insects, fish, snakes, ducks, lily pads or other aquatic plants.

—Leslie Kuehn Meyer, Vermillion, SD

Over in the Meadow

Children learn about meadows and the many animals they sustain by creating a miniature meadow setting.

Materials needed

Twigs
Pine branches
Grass
Leaves
Sand
Soil
Rocks
Pine cones
Pans of water
Manila paper

Markers
Pencils
Clay
Pipe cleaners
Feathers

What to do

1. Cover a table with newspaper.
2. Have the children collect some of the items from their yard or on their way to school. You could collect some of these items ahead of time to make sure you have a variety of materials.
3. Discuss the children's familiarity with the meadow habitat. Yards, parks, and vacant lots have similar attributes (trees, grass, rocks, puddles, insects).
4. Supervise small groups of children as they arrange sand, soil, water trays, twigs, pine cones and rocks on the table.
5. Have the children create a meadow animal with clay, or color and cut one out of paper. Place their animals in the meadow scene.

More to do

Go on a trip to a meadow.

Related books

Over in the Meadow by Ezra Jack Keats

—Linda Barrett, Chicago, IL

Snail Race   4+

This activity allows the children to observe living creatures and discover the characteristics of the snail.

Materials needed

Five or six garden snails
Six small sticky dots of different colors
Flat surface for the race (a clear plexiglass or glass top table is ideal)
Clock, sand timer or other measure of time

What to do

1. Gather five or six snails from the garden and place them in a can or box with leaves, grass, etc.
2. Mark a 1' circle on your table surface with masking tape or draw a 1' circle on a large piece of paper to place on the viewing surface.
3. Divide the class into four, five, or six teams, depending on the size of the group. Explain that each team will have a snail which it will "race." Brainstorm facts that the children may know about snails. Predict how long it will take for a snail to move out of the circle.
4. Let each group choose a snail and a small sticky dot of different colors. They may want to name their snails. Place the sticky dot on the top of the snail's shell.
5. Place all the snails in the middle of the circle. Set the timer, sand clock or stopwatch. Have the children gather around and observe the snails as they move. The first snail to go out of the circle is the "winner." Record the time. Continue observing for second, third, and fourth place winners. Record the times of all the snails.

6. Make a chart with each team's color and winning time.

More to do

Create a classroom home for the snails in a terrarium and continue your discussion of snails. Compare how snails move in relation to other animals. Discuss the spiral on the snail's shell—look for other spirals in nature. Practice drawing or tracing a spiral.

Related books

The Biggest House in the World by Leo Lionni
The Story Snail by Anne Rockwell
Snail's Spell by Joann Ryder

Related song

"Hello, Little Snail" (to the tune of "Twinkle, Twinkle Little Star"):

> *Hello, hello little snail,*
> *You leave behind a silver trail.*
> *In your shell you move so slow,*
> *What is it that makes you go?*

—Jean Bickert Gold, Sacramento, CA

Sunshine and Moonlight   4+

Through an art project, children will learn more about the differences between day and night.

Materials needed

Blue, black, and yellow construction paper
Scissors
Glue stick

What to do

1. For each child, draw a sun and clouds on a sheet of blue paper and a crescent-shaped moon and stars on a sheet of black paper.
2. Have the children cut the shapes out of the blue and black paper to create day and night scenes. (They can cut up through the paper to reach the shape if it's easier for them.)
3. Glue the blue day scene on one side of the yellow paper and the black night scene on the other side. The yellow will show through the holes in the blue and black paper to create night and day scenes.

More to do

Cut out shapes of other objects that are seen in the day and night, such as trees, birds, and owls, etc.

Related books

Where Does the Sun Go at Night by Mirra Ginsburg

—Dana Musch, St. Paul, MN

Pollination of Flowers

To teach the children how bees pollinate flowers.

Materials needed

Small 3" circle or egg-shaped styrofoam ball
One pipe cleaner or chenille stem
Construction paper (to cut out facial features of the bee)
Cooking flour (or corn starch—about 1/2 cup)
A sheet of butcher paper (or large poster paper)
Markers

What to do

1.   Prepare the butcher paper or posterboard by drawing flowers about 4" to 5" round, with a round center about 2" in diameter. Color the flowers appropriately, leaving the center blank.
2.   To make the bee, cut the pipe cleaner into 2 1/2" pieces and insert into the bottom of the egg-shaped styrofoam ball. Cut out wing shapes, and draw facial features with a marker. Glue the wings into place.
3.   Sprinkle a little flour in the middle of each flower. Show the children how the bee lands on the pollen in the middle of the flower and gets the pollen on his legs, and how he then carries that pollen to the next flower and mixes it with that flower's pollen.

More to do

Each child could make her own bee — and you could have a class of busy bees!

—Jacqueline Smallwood, Royersford, PA

I Spy Soil

Children identify the properties of soil in the school yard.

Materials needed

Trowel
Bucket or box
Outdoor area suitable for digging
Blackboard and chalk or chart tablet and markers

What to do

1.   Take the children for a walk around the school yard, playing "I Spy." Encourage them to listen carefully for you to say that you spy some object. Children who think they see what you named may raise their hands and make a guess.
2.   When the class is out and is in a position to view some soil, say, "I Spy some soil." When a child correctly identifies some soil, use the trowel to scoop some up for closer inspection.
3.   Ask them about the properties of soil. What words would describe it?
4.   Move to another site and repeat the I Spy. Look at another sample, thus allowing other children to have an up-close look. Ask them how this soil sample differs from the last one.
5.   Scoop up enough soil for everyone to have a portion.
6.   Bring the children back into the classroom.

7. Ask them about the soil they observed outside. Review some of the properties of soil by having students name them again. List them on the board.
8. Experiment with more soil the following day.

More to do

Start a soil property book and list the properties of soil. Make a picture of a plant in soil. Using a manila folder, open the folder and draw a horizontal line across the middle of it. Draw a plant above the line and its roots below the line. Apply glue around the roots with a cotton swab or with fingers. Sprinkle soil over glue and dump excess on newspaper. Take remaining soil back outside to be recycled. Enjoy a realistic picture of what a plant looks like when it is growing outside in soil.

Related books

In My Garden by E. Cristini and L. Puricelli

—Twyla Sherman, Wichita, KS

Borrowing Bags and Sharing Trays 4+

Children learn about nature conservation through borrowing and sharing.

Materials needed

Large styrofoam trays, at least 8" x 10", one per child
Brown paper sandwich bag, one per child
Marker
Play sand, one cup for 15 children (about 20 lbs.)
Corn seeds, 2 cups for 15 children
Wild bird seeds, 2 cups for 15 children
Blueberries, 1 pint for 15 children
1/4" colored paper scraps, 1 cup for 15 children
Colored wool or yarn scraps, 1 cup for 15 children
Dried leaves or grass scraps, 1 gallon for 15 children
Name labels

What to do

1. Write "borrowing bag" on each brown bag.
2. Put styrofoam trays out on table.
3. Arrange remaining materials in containers on the table.
4. Write each child's name on a label.
5. Ask children what animals might live outside. What do the animals do when children see them? Do they fly away or hide?
6. What are some ways to make friends with shy animals? Suggest sharing some treats. Discuss some things that animals might like.
7. Suggest they can make sharing trays with items in containers.
8. Let each child cover the bottom of the tray with sand (one cup per tray) and then add seeds and other treats. Put name tags on the trays. Leave room for the animal to stand in the sand.
9. Carefully take the trays outside and leave them for 30 minutes.
10. Take the children for a walk. Give each one a borrowing bag to collect what animals have used, such as a chewed leaf or twig or a nutshell or piece of wood that has holes bored into it.

11. Return to the trays. Did any animals take anything? Are there animal tracks in the sand? Do you know what animals came?

12. In the classroom, point out that sharing treats with animals can help us learn about them and even shy animals try new treats.

13. Remind children that the objects in the bags belong to the animals and should be returned to where they belong.

More to do

Have children draw and share pictures or tell stories about something they learned from this activity. Leave the sharing tray on the window ledge for a few days and record what animals come.

Related book

How To Be A Nature Detective by Millicent Selsam

Dorothee Goldman, Chevy Chase, MD

Tree Houses   4+

This activity allows children to use motor skills, reuse discarded items, plan ahead and then follow the plan.

Materials needed

Any discarded items originally made from trees
Glue
Staples
Tape
Scissors

What to do

1. Discuss the types of items that are made from trees. Ask families and local businesses to donate any trash that is made from trees (such as boxes, paper, tubes).

2. Gather the items.

3. Have children draw their plan for a house. They can draw either an exterior or an interior view.

4. Ask the children to sort through the items for shapes that will complete their house.

5. These items are then glued, stapled, or taped together to make the house.

6. Decorate the house by coloring and attaching discarded paper items.

More to do

The class could use large boxes and paper to make one big house. They could plan and create a house from a story or from their own imaginations.

—Lona Parker, Huntsville, AL

Monkey Line

Children develop fine motor skills while learning to order numbers.

Materials needed

Colorful, laminated monkeys numbered 1-10
Clothespins and clothesline

What to do

1. Glue each monkey to a clothespin mouth-end up so it can easily be clipped to a clothesline.
2. Tie the clothesline across the room, at a height accessible to the children.
3. Explain to the children they will clip the monkeys on the rope from one to ten, or from ten to one, or they could fill in blank spots in between already-clipped monkeys, such as 1___5_7__10.
4. Monkey Line can be used in small group instruction as well. Give each child a monkey and ask him to come up and clip his monkey on in order.
5. After all monkeys are clipped on, have the children close their eyes and either remove one or mix them all up. The children correct mistakes.

More to do

Monkey Line can be used to teach the alphabet. Adapt idea to go with other units of study: Kites in spring, mittens in winter, or leaves or apples in fall.

Related book

Caps for Sale by Esphyr Slobodkina

Related song

"Monkey See, Monkey Do"

Related fingerplays

"Five Little Monkeys Swinging in a Tree"
"Five Little Monkeys Jumping on the Bed"

—Shirlayne Schmidt, Lincoln, NE

Number Lotto

Children learn to recognize visual symbols, relate amounts to number symbols and develop eye-hand coordination.

Materials needed

Four to six sheets of 11" x 7" posterboard
Fabric paints
Colored glue
Felt-tipped markers
Clear contact paper
Stencils
Scissors
Ruler

What to do

1. Divide posterboard into six equal sections. Go over all lines with a black marker.
2. Print the name of each number below each numeral on spaces of the game board. Use one color for each game board. Number one side of the board one through six, and the other five through ten.
3. Cut the game pieces from the other sheets of posterboard, six pieces per sheet. Using fabric paints or other materials mentioned above, draw symbolic representations of each number on the board—five stars for "5," four moons for "4."
4. Cover the game boards with clear contact paper. If you used marker on the game pieces, cover them as well.
5. Set the game out during free time.
6. The children begin the game by matching the game pieces to the squares on game board.
7. This game can be played on an individual basis, or as a group game. If it is being played as a group, be sure not to emphasize winners and losers. When a child completes his card, say enthusiastically, "We have another winner."

More to do

Do the same with the alphabet. Use one letter of the alphabet in each square. Make game pieces with pictures, each starting with a different letter of the alphabet. Or with colors in each square print the color words. On the game pieces glue or draw pictures, objects that match the color words on the game board.

Related books

Six Little Ducks by Chris Conover

—Cory McIntyre, Crystal Lake, IL

Number Puzzle Cards

3+

Children increase eye-hand coordination and counting skills.

Materials needed

Colored posterboard
Scissors
Markers
Contact paper

What to do

1. Cut the posterboard into ten 5" x 8" rectangles.
2. On one half of each card, write a number between one and ten. On the other half draw the corresponding number of dots, stars, hearts or nutshells.
3. Cut each card in two, using a different combination of curves and angles so no two pieces could be mistakenly matched.
4. Lay all the pieces out on a table. The children can match by counting the number of dots, stars, hearts or nutshells on one piece, and finding the numeric equivalent on another. They can check their match because of each puzzle's unique configuration.

More to do

Make number books to reinforce the recognition of each number.

Related book

Berenstain Bear's Counting Book by Jan and Stan Berenstain

Related songs

"Three Little Ducks"
"Five Monkeys"

—Sandra C. Scott, Vancouver, WA

Number Hunt

3+

This activity will introduce number identification through matching and recognition.

Materials needed

Ten envelopes
2" x 2" square pieces of paper
Marker

What to do

1. Write the numbers 1 through 10 on the front side of envelopes. Write numbers 1 through 10 on the small squares of paper. (Make sure there are several of each number to ensure each child may find a range of numbers.

2. Display the numbered envelopes (on the floor, table or stapled to the wall). Make sure the envelopes are within easy access.

3. Hide the numbers. Make sure children can find them easily. This activity should not frustrate the children.

4. Discuss the activity with the children. Ask them to find the numbers and then place them in the corresponding envelopes.

5. Demonstrate the activity.

6. After all the numbers have been found, empty the envelopes and discuss the numbers and how they match.

More to do

Use the same activity for an alphabet hunt.

—Lorene Miller, Fremont, CA

Matching Bears

3+

In this activity, children learn to match a bear with a written number to a bear with the corresponding number of stickers.

Materials needed

Construction paper
Stickers—large and small
Marking pens
Contact paper or laminator

What to do

1.   Cut out ten bears from construction paper. A set of five will be used for numbers; the other half will be used for stickers. (A set with more numbers can be made for older children.)
2.   Draw faces on each bear.
3.   Write the numbers 1 - 5 on the tummy of the first five bears. Place the corresponding number of small stickers on those bears under each written number.
4.   On the second set of bears, use the large stickers and apply 1-5 stickers on the tummy of each bear. Do not write a number on these bears.
5.   Have a child match a bear with the number to a bear with the corresponding number of stickers, until all the bears are matched.

More to do

This activity can be used for circle time; add a magnetic strip on the back of each bear. Place the bears with the numbers in a sequence and count. Hold up a bear with a number, and have the children hold up the appropriate number of fingers.

—Margie Moore, Fairfax, VA

Count the Cars

3+

The children learn numbers by counting familiar objects.

Materials needed

Construction paper
Scissors
Crayons
Pencils
Markers

What to do

1.   Cut out a house shape and several car shapes for each child. Draw the house with an attached garage, large enough to hold some of the cars you have cut out. (If children are old enough, you may want to outline the house and cars and have them do the cutting.)
2.   Choose a number you want to teach the children. Have the children draw that number of windows on their house or that number of people in the house, etc.
3.   Give the children the same number of cars and have them "park" them in the garage.

4. Have the children decorate the house and cars.

More to do

Change the number you are using and repeat the activity. Count to the number you are studying on an abacus.

—Tamar Andrews, Los Angeles, CA

Fingerplay: Five Little Candy Canes   3+

In this activity, children will practice counting from one to five through a fingerplay.

Materials needed

Flannel board
White and red felt for candy cane shapes

What to do

1. Make five candy canes by cutting white felt into candy cane shapes, approximately 1" x 4". Cut five red strips, approximately 1/2" x 1" long, and glue on white felt.
2. Memorize the following fingerplay:

> *Five little candy canes*
> *Hanging from a Christmas tree.*
> *The first one said: "Children really do love me."*
> *The second one said: "Santa's coming here tonight."*
> *The third one said: "Christmas is such a delight."*
> *The fourth one said: "Look, it's Santa that I see."*
> *The fifth one whispered: "Santa's resting by our tree."*
> *So very, very softly, the candy canes did say,*
> *"Have a very Merry Christmas and a Happy Holiday."*

3. Introduce activity to children and recite the poem.
4. Recite the poem again while putting the candy canes on the flannel board.
5. Have children do the fingerplay as you point to each candy cane on the board.
6. Have children count candy canes and number of stripes on each candy cane.
7. Repeat the fingerplay and take candy canes off the flannel board as each verse is said.

More to do

Have each child make five candy canes out of red and white construction paper.

—Dorothea Hudak, Stow, OH

Let's Count

This activity will reinforce counting and memory skills.

Materials needed

Beanbag or ball

What to do

1. Have children sit on the floor in a circle.
2. Ask one child to choose a number (lower than or the same as the number of children in the group) and say it. This becomes the "special" number.
3. Start the game. Pass the ball or beanbag around the group and have each child call out a number beginning with "one" and continuing in numerical order until the special number is reached.
4. Stop the game and have the last child choose another special number. Continue playing until everyone has had a turn.

More to do

Use number "riddles" to choose a number for the counting game. For example, ask "How many fingers do you have?" Then count to 10 as the ball or bag is passed around.

—Brenda Miller, Olean, NY

Buzz Buzz

The children will develop pre-math skills.

Materials needed

White posterboard or oaktag
Scissors
Contact paper or laminating film
Colored markers
Pencils
Glue

What to do

1. Copy the illustrations, color them and glue them to the posterboard or oaktag. Cut them out and, if you really want them to last, laminate them.
2. Place the three hives on the table in front of the children. Hold up two bees and say "These bees went buzzing over to this hive, looking for a nice place to live." Lay the bees on one hive.
3. Hold up one bee and say, "This bee decided to go buzzing over to this hive." Lay the bee on another hive.
4. Hold up three bees and say, "These three bees thought that this hive looked like a nice home." Lay the bees on the remaining hive.
5. Indicate the three hives. Ask which of the hives has the most bees on it. If the children have difficulty, count the bees on each hive and ask again.

More to do

You can extend this activity by playing a version of the game "Pin the Tail on the Donkey". Make extra copies of the bees and have the children color and cut them out. At the same time, draw a large version of the hives on three pieces of posterboard, color them and cut them out. Mount the hives on a wall right next to each other at the children's eye level, put a piece of rolled up masking tape on the back of each bee and you're ready to play. Play should proceed as a normal game of "Pin the Tail on the Donkey" would. Blindfold each child in turn and have them pin their bee on any of the three hives (whichever one they can "find" in the dark). After each child has had a turn, have them count the number of bees that landed on each hive. Then ask again, "Which hive has the most bees on it?" To simplify this activity for younger toddlers, reduce the number of hives used to two. You also might want to eliminate use of the blindfold, since young children do not often enjoy not being able to see.

Related books

One Two Three: An Animal Counting Book by Marc Brown
Count and See by Tana Hoban
1 is One by Tasha Tudor

Related songs

"We All Live Together" by Greg and Steve's Number Rock
"Countup, Countdown" by Hap Palmer
"Flight of the Bumblebee" by Rimsky-Korsakov

—Virginia Jean Herrod, Columbia, SC

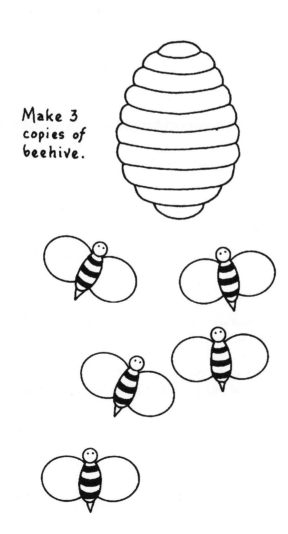

Make 3 copies of beehive.

Numbers

4+

The children will learn to count ten objects.

Materials needed

Ten sorting containers
Ten craft sticks (popsicle size)
Marking pen
Counting materials such as assorted buttons, assorted beans, colored macaroni, beads, etc.

What to do

1. Take a marking pen and place the numeral 1 at the top of the stick.
2. Under the one place one dot.
3. Continue with all the numbers, making sure to place the correct number of dots under the numeral.
4. Place one stick in each of the sorting containers.
5. Set out counting pieces in a basket with the containers.
6. The children can then place the appropriate number of counting pieces in each container either by noticing the numeral itself or by counting the dots.

More to do

You could also print the numeral word on the stick to expose the child to the written form of numbers.

—Deborah Burton, Irwin, IA

Pots of Gold

4+

Children count and add groups of objects when they participate in this activity.

Materials needed

Coins or paper coins
Cups
Paper
Crayons or markers

What to do

1. Make sure children have previous exposure to counting activities.
2. Hide coins in the classroom for children to find and then count.
3. Provide piles or cups of coins for counting.
4. Ask children to count coins and then draw like amounts on a piece of paper.
5. For children ready for the concept of addition: Have two groups of coins to count. Record amounts. Then combine groups and count again. Record final amount.

More to do

Have children set out coins to match written numerals.

—Lona Parker, Huntsville, AL

Road Blocks, a Counting Game

Children practice counting and matching colors.

Materials needed

2 2" x 26" posterboard strips
4 toy cars, no more than 2" long
2" or 4" rectangular box or piece of wood
Colored die
Markers
Glue

What to do

1. Divide the two posterboard strips into thirteen 2" squares.
2. Place them across each other, intersecting on the seventh square on both strips. Glue at that midpoint.
3. With the red marker, color one square on each of the four extending arms. Repeat this process with the blue, yellow, orange, purple, and green. Place the wooden block on the blank center square.
4. The game can be played by up to four people. Each player chooses a car to be her playing piece, and places it at the tip of one arm of the game board. The object is to get to the "parking garage"—the wooden square at the center of the board—by moving one square at a time.
5. The players take turns rolling the die. If the color of the die matches the color on the square ahead of the players' car, she is allowed to advance to the next square. Players cannot skip squares.
6. The first player to reach the "parking garage" wins!
7. Explain the game to the children in small groups to allow everyone the time and space to play. After everyone is accustomed to the rules, leave the game in the play area to be enjoyed by all.

More to do

Instead of coloring the squares number them one through six, and roll a numbered die to move.

—*Judith Dighe, Rockville, MD*

Number Puzzles

4+

Children learn to recognize numbers and solve puzzles.

Materials needed

Various colors of construction paper
White 8 1/2" x 11" paper
Black marker

What to do

1. Cut out large numerals, one through nine, from sheets of colored construction paper. Use a different color for each number.
2. Outline the numbers on the white paper.
3. Glue a small piece of the same color construction paper to the outlined number.
4. Laminate all pieces. Cut the colored numbers into 4 or 5 puzzle pieces.
5. Children must find all the correct colored pieces and reconstruct the number on the outline.

More to do

To make the activity more challenging, make all the numbers the same color. This activity can also be done with letters.

—Rachel Stickfort, Newark, DE

Planes Up High

4+

Children will learn that the numbers 4, 3, 2 and 1 are less than 5 by participating in a rhyme.

What to do

1. Before doing this with children, memorize the words to "Planes Up High":

   5 little airplanes flying high,
   Up through the clouds and in the sky.
   All of a sudden 1 fell down,
   Now fly like a plane and touch the ground.
   Only 4 planes remain,
   Flying through the clouds of rain.
   1 got too wet and had to quit,
   3 planes left to finish it.
   1 got tired and went on home,
   2 more airplanes all alone.
   Another got tired and took a rest.
   The last plane left passed the test!

2. Work with five children at a time. Encourage the children to fly like airplanes. As you say the verse, touch the child that is to leave the "sky" and have him fly away.
3. Change the children in the group until every one has had a turn.

More to do

Start with 10 kids and take away 3 at a time.

—Lydia Brown, Lexington, KY

Teaching Numbers Using Playdough

Children use playdough while learning numbers.

Materials needed

Washable wallpaper squares or plastic
Markers
Playdough
Scissors
Plastic knives

What to do

1. Write the numbers one through ten on washable wallpaper squares (try to use plain-colored wallpaper).
2. Each child can take one numbered square from the sequence, or a full set from one to ten can be made for each child.
3. Have the children roll playdough into snakes and mold over numeral. They can also roll balls to put over dots.

More to do

Substitute letters (capital and lower case), names of children or shapes.

—Shirlayne Schmidt, Lincoln, NE

Monkey Face Finger Puppets

Children have fun while developing language, counting and fine motor skills.

Materials needed

White construction paper circles (2" diameter), five per child
Crayons
Transparent tape
White paper

What to do

1. Give each child five white circles to draw monkey faces.
2. Put transparent tape on the back of each monkey face. The children stick them on their fingers.
3. With the children following, count on your fingers from zero to five and back to zero.
4. Sing and act out the following fingerplay, using puppets:

   Five little monkeys swinging in the tree,
   Teasing Mr. Alligator you can't catch me,
   You can't catch me. (put hands together sideways to look like alligator's mouth)
   Along came Mr. Alligator quiet as can be. Snap! (open and close hands)
   Four little monkeys swinging in the tree.

Continue until no more monkeys are swinging in the tree.

—Tina Burno, Springfield, MA

The Number Train   4+

Children will practice counting out small characters to correspond to the number on the side of the train cars.

Materials needed

10 shoe boxes
Index cards
tape
55 small characters, animals, etc.

What to do

1. Ahead of time, write the numbers 1-10 on index cards and tape one card to the side of each shoe box.
2. Arrange the boxes in numerical order to form a "train."
3. Set out the small characters and assign each child a train car (box). Tell the children to look at the number on the side of their train car and put that many characters inside. (You might want to demonstrate by picking a car and putting in the correct number of characters.)

More to do

Attach the boxes to each other by punching holes in the ends and tying them together with string. Tie a string to the first box and let the children pull the train around the room. Let them use their imaginations to create a depot, bridge and tunnel from objects in the classroom.

Related books

Trains by Byron Barton
The Little Engine That Could by Watty Piper

—*Rebecca Mattis, Ellicott City, MD*

Doggie, Doggie, Count Your Bones   5+

By counting bones, the children will increase counting skills.

Materials needed

Flannel board
Flannel cutout of dog, dog house and 10 bones

What to do

1. Teacher may begin by putting dog, doghouse and bones on the flannel board, counting as she does so.
2. Teacher may then say "Doggie, doggie, count your bones. How many did I put near your home?"
3. Child will then count the bones and answer the teacher.
4. Child and teacher may take turns saying the poem, and counting.
5. Poem may be changed to "Doggie, doggie, count your bones. How many do you have in your home?"
6. Teacher may let child put bones on board and say "Doggie, doggie, count your bones. How many did I put near your home?" (For beginning children only use five bones, then increase slowly.)

More to do

Collages of dog pictures cut from magazines may be made. Science area may have a selection of clean bones for children to study. This game may be introduced at small group time, then the flannel board may be left out for children to work and manipulate them independently.

Related books

The Diggingest Dog by Al Perkins
The Poky Little Puppy by Janette Lowrey
Harry the Dirty Dog by Gene Zion

—Helen Buemi, Binghamton, NY

Wonderful Web   5+

The children will learn number recognition while enjoying this fun-filled activity.

Materials needed

Large ball of yarn, any color
Number cards (index cards with 1-10 written in black pen)
Large floor space
Tape
One large fake spider

What to do

1. Using index cards, write one number on each. On back of card, draw that number of dots.
2. Children sit on floor in large circle.
3. Shuffle the number cards and give each child a card.
4. Ask children to look at their card and try to determine the number. If they can't, have them turn the card over and count the dots.
5. Ask who has number 1.
6. Give that child the end string on the ball of yarn. The teacher collects their card.
7. Continue counting. Collect card number 2 from whoever has it. Unravel the ball of yarn, allowing a child to hold onto another section of yarn from the ball.
8. Go on counting. Collect cards, unravel ball of yarn.
9. Ultimately, every child will be holding onto a section of the ball of yarn.
10. Holding onto their yarn, have the children stand up in the circle. Ask them what they've made.
(A wonderful spider web!)
11. Lay web on floor. Secure each intersection of yarn with tape.
12. Hang web from classroom lights or ceiling. Hang a large spider from it. The web will have a terrific 3-dimensional shape.

More to do

Children can make their own paper spiders to hang from web.

Related book

Very Busy Spider by Eric Carle

Related songs

"Eensy, Weensy Spider""One Elephant Went Out to Play"

—Norma Jorgensen, St. Paul, MN

NUMBERS

Baa Baa Sheep

3+

Have fun learning and "acting out" the traditional nursery rhyme with these woolly sheep.

Materials needed

Posterboard or tagboard
Nontoxic white glue
Cotton balls
Black paint
Black crayon or marker or hole punch and black paper
Sponge cut into rectangle
Wooden sticks for puppets

What to do

For white sheep:
1. Cut large sheep patterns (the body is approximately 7" x 11") from posterboard or tagboard—one for each child. Have the children help you with the cutting if possible.
2. Draw eyes with a black crayon or marker, or glue black hole-punches.
3. Spread glue over the body.
4. Have the children cover the body with cotton balls.
5. If you want to make it into a puppet, glue a wooden stick to the back of the sheep.

For black sheep:
1. Make sheep patterns as above.
2. Make eye with black crayon or marker.
3. Put black paint in a shallow dish or pan and have children sponge-paint body black.

More to do

Have children sing and move their sheep or sheep puppets to the rhyme.

Related song

"Baa Baa Black Sheep" from *Singable Songs for the Very Young* by Raffi

—*Bobbi Menzenski, Raleigh, NC*

Peter's Pumpkin

3+

Children will learn the nursery rhyme, "Peter, Peter, Pumpkin Eater," and enjoy an art activity that promotes fine motor skills.

Materials needed

White computer paper
Orange and green construction paper
Green marker
Glue
Old magazines

What to do

1. For each child in the class, cut out a pumpkin shape from orange construction paper and make a "window" in the middle (this could be a shutter-style window with two flaps that open and close).
2. Cut out small stems from green construction paper for children to glue on their pumpkins.
3. Give the children old magazines and instruct them to find a "wife" for Peter. Help them rip or cut out pictures of women.
4. Give each child a pumpkin, stem and piece of white paper with "Peter, Peter, Pumpkin Eater" written at the top and the child's name written at the bottom.
5. Recite the rhyme:

   Peter, Peter, pumpkin eater,
   Had a wife and couldn't keep her.
   He put her in a pumpkin shell
   And there he kept her very well.

6. Put some glue on the back of the pumpkin and let the child position it on the white paper. Do the same with the stem.
7. Have the children fold open the window shutters and glue their pictures of Peter's wife inside.
8. Draw vines around pumpkin and from stem outward.
9. Have the children say the rhyme along with you.

—*Darlene Hammond, Syracuse, NY*

Humpty Dumpty

3+

This activity builds vocabulary and exercises fine motor skills along with eye-hand coordination.

Materials needed

Glue
Scissors
Construction paper
Small child-sized bench

What to do

1. Cut out Humpty Dumpty for each child. Put together one Humpty Dumpty cutout for example.

2. Recite "Humpty Dumpty" verse several times. Let children sit on bench one at a time and pretend to be Humpty Dumpty as class recites verse.

3. Put cutouts and glue bottles on table.

4. Hang or pin example up so children can see how pieces fit together.

5. Ask the children to put Humpty Dumpty together again.

More to do

Bring in one raw egg and a boiled egg in shell for each child. Crack raw egg and explore inside. Allow each child to crack their egg and explore the inside. If they like, they can eat their egg. Talk about how cooked and raw eggs are the same or different.

—Terri Garrou, Morgantown, NC

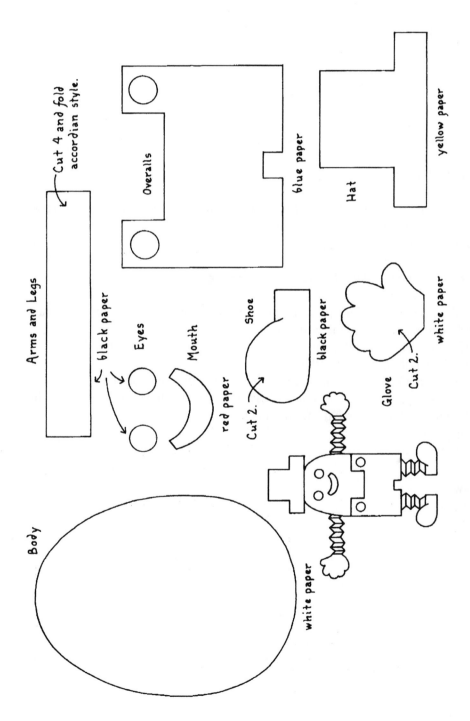

Arms and Legs — Cut 4 and fold accordian style.

Overalls — blue paper

Hat — yellow paper

black paper — Eyes

Mouth — red paper

Shoe — Cut 2. — black paper

Glove — Cut 2. — white paper

Body — white paper

A Story in Sheep's Clothing

3+

This activity uses repetition to familiarize children with two traditional nursery rhymes and the tunes that accompany them.

Materials needed

Sheep in a Shop by Nancy Shaw
While the Shepherd Slept by Matt Novak
The Real Mother Goose published by Checkerboard Press
Glove puppet
Flannel board
Felt figures
Construction paper cut into sheep silhouettes
Glue sticks
Cotton balls

What to do

1. Gather all materials.
2. Practice using glove puppet (finger puppets may be substituted).
3. Cut out sheep silhouettes.
4. Learn the tune and words to both nursery rhymes.
5. Make appropriate felt figures.
6. To begin the activity, recite the entire nursery rhyme "Mary Had A Little Lamb," using a glove puppet. Repeat the rhyme encouraging the children to recite the rhyme with you.
7. Sing the nursery rhyme while using the glove puppet. Sing it a second time and encourage the children to join in.
8. Read aloud the book *While the Shepherd Slept*. Re-read the book encouraging the children to point out the funny details.
9. Recite the nursery rhyme "Baa, Baa, Black Sheep" while placing felt figures on the flannel board at appropriate times. Invite the children to recite the rhyme with you.
10. Take the flannel pieces off the board and hand them out to different children. Ask the children to place them on the flannel board while the whole group sings the song.
11. Read aloud *Sheep in a Shop*. Re-read the book encouraging the children to point out the funny details.
12. Have the children move to tables and chairs. Let each child choose a sheep silhouette. Give each child five cotton balls. Have the children glue the cotton balls to the sheep.
13. Practice "baa-ing" with the sheep.

Related books

Sheep in a Jeep by Nancy Shaw
Sheep in a Ship by Nancy Shaw
The Little Lamb by Judy Dunn

—*Christina Chilcote, New Freedom, PA*

Wee Willie Winkie

Children learn the Wee Willie Winkie nursery rhyme and how to hold a marker.

Materials needed

Large piece of butcher paper (24" x 24")
Masking tape
Colored markers

What to do

1. Write "Wee Willie Winkie...." at the top of the paper.
2. Set out the colored markers.
3. Tape the paper to the table.
4. Recite the "Wee Willie Winkie" nursery rhyme to the children.
5. Have the children choose a marker and help them hold it in their hand. Guide the child's hand as they make large figure 8's and big strokes "going through the town."
6. Recite the nursery rhyme with the children.

More to do

Let the children change markers, and draw houses, trucks, cars and people in the town.

—Darlene Hammond, Syracuse, NY

The Eensy Weensy Spider

3+

The children will learn the song and fingerplay about the eensy weensy spider. They will also produce an art project.

Materials needed

White paper
Stamp pads
Markers

What to do

1. Draw a faucet on each paper and write the words "The Eensy Weensy Spider..." at the top of the page. Write the child's name at the lower corner of the paper.
2. Show the children the faucet and explain that water flows down and out of the spout. Tell them that the spider will be crawling up the spout.
3. Recite "The Eensy Weensy Spider."
4. Do the fingerplay as you recite the song.
5. Have the children join you in the song and fingerplay.
6. Let each child press their fingers into the stamp pad and press them onto the paper.
7. You or the children (depending on age) can draw little legs and eyes on the print to make a spider.
8. Repeat the song and fingerplay.

More to do

Make the fingerprints with different colored ink pads. Show the children that each fingerprint is unique and different.

—Darlene Hammond, Syracuse, NY

Humpty's Broken

3+

By learning the nursery rhyme "Humpty Dumpty" children find out that an egg is fragile and cannot be put together after it is broken.

Materials needed

Colored construction paper
White construction paper
Scissors
Red marker
Black marker
White egg shape
Glue

What to do

1. Write "Humpty Dumpty Sat On A Wall..." at the top of each piece of white paper. Make egg shapes from white construction paper and cut it in half with a zigzag shape as if it has been broken. Write each child's name in the lower corner of the paper.
2. Place the colored paper in front of each child with an egg shape.
3. Recite the "Humpty Dumpty" nursery rhyme.
4. Explain that Humpty Dumpty is an egg and if it is broken, cannot be put back together.
5. Let the child glue the egg pieces to the background paper.
6. Draw a brick wall using the red marker behind the egg.
7. Draw a hat, eyes, nose and frown on Humpty using the black marker.

More to do

Talk about how fragile things can be and sometimes they cannot be fixed. Older children can make Humpty Dumpty's features by themselves using crayons or gluing construction paper cut outs.

—Darlene Hammond, Syracuse, NY

Musical Puppet Play

3+

Children develop finger and arm coordination and focus on the rhythm of the words while singing and moving finger puppets.

Materials needed

Black and white sheep finger puppets, one per child

What to do

1. Children put a black sheep on the pointer finger of one hand and a white sheep on the pointer finger of the other. Ask the children to hide their hands behind their backs and remind them to remember which hand has the black and which the white sheep.
2. Sing the song "Where is Black Sheep, Where is White Sheep?" to the tune of "Where is Thumbkin?"
3. As each sheep is named, the children bring the black and white sheep out from behind their backs.
4. On the words "How are you today, sir? Very well, I thank you" one sheep "bows" to the other sheep in rhythm to the words, always alternating puppets.

More to do

Use different finger puppets like frog, mouse, duck, cow, bear, etc. and sing the appropriate color and animal ("Where is green frog?"). Sing children's names instead of finger puppet characters and have that child stand when his or her name is sung. "Where is Johnny, Where is Stephanie?" (They answer) "Here we are, here we are. I am Johnny, I am Stephanie. Who are you? Who are you?"

—S. Lorna Zemke, Manitowoc, WI

Jack and Jill

3+

What a fun way to learn the rhyme "Jack and Jill"!

Materials needed

Construction paper
Exacto knife (for teacher!)
Glue
Crayons
Craft sticks

What to do

1. Draw a hill, and cut a 5" vertical slit in the center of the hill. Repeat for each child.
2. The children use crayons to add tufts of grass or flowers to the hills.
3. Draw a well at the top of each hill.
4. Children draw faces and clothing on Jack and Jill.
5. Attach Jack and Jills to craft sticks.
6. Move Jack and Jill up and down the hill as you recite the rhyme.

More to do

Have children imagine other things that Jack and Jill could fetch at the top of the hill, e.g. gravel, flowers, fruit, leaves, etc.

—Barbara Corbin, Cincinnati, OH

Hickory Dickory Dock Clock

3+

Besides learning the rhyme, the children will also learn about time.

Materials needed

Construction paper
Glue
Exacto knife
Mouse stickers
Each child needs:
    4" x 4" square
    9" x 3" rectangle with a horizontal 1" slit cut 2" from each end

4" base with 3 25" side triangles
1" diameter circle
2 75" diameter circle (add clock hands and the numbers 12 & 1 in proper clock placement)
12" x .74" construction paper strips
Cut a horizontal 1" slit, 2" from each end of the 9"x3" rectangle

What to do

1. Have children cut out the shapes and assemble them into a grandfather clock, using the square at the top of the rectangle and the triangle as the base of the clock.
2. Glue the clock face to the square.
3. Slide the 12" strip into the 1" slits, starting with the bottom slit, and coming up from the back.
4. Glue the 1" circle to the 12" strip.
5. Place the mouse sticker on the 1" circle.
6. Pull the strip either up or down as you recite the rhyme.

More to do

Use this activity to reinforce shape recognition.

—Barbara Corbin, Cincinnati, OH

Milkweed Pod Cradles

4+

This activity uses nature to integrate nursery rhymes into the curriculum.

Materials needed

Milkweed pods dried
Tree branch
Container
Yarn
Plastic needle
Paper, material or leaf
Crayons
Scissors
Glue

What to do

1. Give each child paper and crayons.
2. Ask the children to draw and color a baby to fit in milkweed pod. Cut out the babies when they are done. Give each child a small rectangle of material or a leaf to use as a blanket for baby.
3. Thread needle with yarn and gently push needle through pod at one end. Do same at other end. Knot end near pods. Grasp the two pieces of yarn and tie together at top.
4. Place tree branch in container or vase and hang cradles from branches.

More to do

Before the activity go on nature walk to find pods. If pods are not available use orange juice containers or frozen juice containers cut in half for cradles.

—Carol A. Patnaude/Cathy Costantino, Warwick, RI

Nursery Rhyme Play

The children have fun putting on a play, wearing costumes and learning their lines.

Materials needed

Large cardboard boxes made into background scenery
Paint
Sponge
Paintbrushes
Props

What to do

1. Have the children help you make the scenery for the play.
2. Use blue paint to paint the sky area and green to paint the grass on the bottom of the scenery. The children can add flowers, trees, birds and the sun for finishing touches.
3. Read the play to the children and assign roles.
4. Practice the play until you are ready for your performance.
5. Invite other classes or parents to attend your play!

Characters:
  Narrator
  Kittens
  Mother Cat
  Miss Muffet
  Spider
  Simple Simon
  Pieman
  Mary
  Lamb
  Pick Up Sticks (can be divided among whole class)

Narrator:
Please join us on a trip to Nursery Rhyme Land. Along the way we will meet many of our nursery rhyme friends. Look, here are the three little kittens.

Kittens:
We're three little kittens who have lost our mittens. So now we have to cry *(Boo Hoo Hoo!)*
(Mother Cat Enters)
Mother dear, see here, see here
Our mittens we have lost.

Mother Cat (quite upset):
WHAT!! Lost your mittens? (Shaking Finger) You naughty kittens! Then you shall have no pie.

Kittens:
Boo Hoo Hoo! Boo Hoo Hoo! Then we shall have no pie!
(Look around, then reach into pockets and pull out mittens)
Mother dear, see here, see here,
Our mittens we have found!

Mother Cat:
Found your mittens! You good little kittens! Now you shall have your pie.

351

Kittens:
Yum, yum, oh what fun!
Now we'll wave goodbye! *(wave and walk off stage)*

Narrator:
Now, who might we have here?

(Miss Muffet enters and sits on a stool.)
Miss Muffett:
I'm little Miss Muffet
Who sat on a tuffet,
Eating my curds and whey.

(Spider enters)
Spider:
Along came me, a spider
And frightened Miss Muffet away
(Spider raises arms, Miss Muffet screams and runs off stage.
Spider laughs a mischievous laugh.)

Narrator:
Poor Miss Muffet had quite a scare!
But let's forget that and go to the fair.
(Enter Simple Simon and Pieman)

Simple Simon:
I'm Simple Simon and I met a pieman
Going to the fair
Please, Mr. Pieman let me taste your wares.

Pieman:
I, the Pieman, said to Simple Simon,
Show me your first penny.

Simple Simon:
(Pulls his pockets out to reveal nothing and sticks his lip out in a sad way)
Indeed, I have not any.
(Both leave stage.)
Narrator:
Poor Simple Simon had no money, but
Let's see a lamb that's funny.

(Enter Mary and her lamb.)
Mary:
I'm Mary who had a little lamb
It's fleece was white as snow.
And everywhere that I went,
The lamb was sure to go.

Lamb:
I followed her to school one day
Which was against the rules.
But, it made the children laugh and play

To see a lamb at school.

Narrator:
Now, let's all join together and play pick-up sticks.
I bet you've never heard it quite like this.
(Two children at a time.)
1, 2, buckle my shoe.
3, 4, shut the door.
4, 6, pick up sticks.
7, 8, lay them straight.
9, 10, a big, fat hen.
11, 12, dig and delve.
13, 14, maids a-courting.
15, 16, maids in the kitchen.
17, 18, maids a-waiting.
19, 20, my plate is empty.

Everyone:
We thank you all for joining us
Joining us, joining us.
We thank you all for joining us
On our trip to Nursery Rhyme Land.

Costume Notes
Cat and Kittens: Attach paper ears to a plastic headband. Make a tail from yarn.
Miss Muffet: Frilly dress.
Spider: Wear a black sweat suit.
Mary: Frilly dress. Carry a cane for the staff.
Lamb: Attach paper ears covered with cotton balls to a plastic headband. Make a tail from felt covered with cotton balls that can be tied around the waist.

—Joyce Montag, Slippery Rock, PA

NURSERY RHYMES ▼

Rocket Ships

3+

This creative activity is one your children will love.

Materials needed

Toilet paper tubes
Cone cups (from water coolers)
Tissue paper
Glue
Paints
Paintbrushes
String
Newspaper

What to do

1. Cover the tables with newspaper.
2. Have each child paint a tube and cup in any or all paint colors.
3. Have them put glue around the edge of the tube and attach the cup.
4. Choose a few colors of tissue paper and stuff it inside tube, leaving some protruding, as fire.
5. Tie a string to each tube.
6. String across room.

—Audrey Kanoff, Bethlehem, PA

Constellations

3+

Children will create their own constellation.

Materials needed

White, gold, or silver crayons
Black paper
Self sticking stars
Crayons
Rulers

What to do

1. Give each child two stars to put on their paper.
2. Have children draw a line between the two stars with a crayon. (They can use a ruler if they want.)
3. Give one additional star to each child to place on the paper and make another connecting line.
4. Continue to give stars until each child says her constellation is finished.

More to do

Have children work in pairs.

—L. Willa Downes, Fairfax, VA

Adventures in Space

Children learn about outer space and its exploration.

Materials needed

Cardboard boxes of various sizes (long, square, large)
2 Pegboard/peg sets
2 Plastic container lids
2 Paper brads
Paint
Scissors
Construction paper
Easel
Shallow box

What to do

1. Cut long boxes into rocket shapes.
2. Cut square boxes into back pack shapes.
3. Tape pegboard onto section of a box to make a control panel.
4. Push brass brad through plastic lid onto another section of control panel for steering wheel.
5. Draw buttons and control panel designs around peg boards and steering wheels (see illustration).
6. Cut large planets and stars out of construction paper.
7. Let children paint boxes with large brushes the day before.
8. Allow children to role play "space exploration" with the boxes and control panel.
9. Have planet-shaped paper to paint on the easel.
10. From construction paper, cut out a star. Put the paper star in shallow box, and pour on small amounts of brightly-colored paints. Put two marbles in the box.
11. Let children tilt the box back and forth to paint patterns on the star with marbles.

More to do

Put the tall rocket ship box in the block area. Allow children to build around the box to form the shape of a rocket ship. Cut rocket shape out of poster board, and glue on buttons, beads, beans, styrofoam, bottle caps, spaghetti, cotton or glitter.

Related music

"Adventures in Space" from *On The Move With Greg and Steve* by Steve Millang and Greg Scelsa

—*Terri Garrou, Morganton, NC*

Control Panel Box

355

Fluorescent Constellations

3+

Through this learning experience, children will understand that stars form patterns in the sky and that they can be named.

Materials needed

Unsharpened pencils with erasers
Razor knife (for teacher!)
Black paper
Fluorescent paints
Black light
Tape
Child's book on constellations

What to do

1.   Use a razor knife to cut the eraser tips of the pencil to look like stars (they can be twinkling, not perfectly formed).
2.   Set up area that can be made entirely dark (block out windows, set up walls, etc.)
3.   For the activity, show the children some pictures of constellations, what their names are and how they were named.
4.   Give each child a piece of black paper and pencil.
5.   Let each child use the pencil as a stamp in the fluorescent paint and make a pattern on their paper and name it.
6.   After papers have dried, tape them onto ceiling or upper wall in dark area and turn on the black light. View the constellations and have each child tell the rest of the children about theirs.

More to do

The teacher can stamp out some of the existing constellations and use a thin paintbrush to connect the stars to form the constellation figure.

—Dixie Havlak, Olympia, WA

The Twilight Zone

3+

This activity will help children develop an appreciation for the world that surrounds our planet.

Materials needed

Large box (refrigerator, stove, etc.)
Paint
Paintbrushes
White butcher paper (optional)
Strong tape (duct tape)
Construction Paper
Scissors
Glue

What to do

1. Form the box to the shape of a rocket ship (i.e., with point at the top) Wrap with white butcher paper if you have it available.
2. Paint the rocket ship with tempera. Paint red and yellow at the bottom to look like fire (red and yellow make orange). Glue on yellow construction paper stars. Paint "USA" in red and blue.
3. Let paint dry.
4. Play in the rocketship with a limited number of children.

—Meg Patterson Comes, Memphis, TN

Space Station
4+

In this activity, children will develop their imaginations while learning about our solar system.

Materials needed

Four large strips of cardboard from a big box
Small squares of cardboard or paper for each child (about 8" x 11")
Scissors
Paper
Fluorescent paints and paintbrushes
Black light

What to do

1. Prepare an area that can be used as a space ship. It is especially dramatic if the space ship can be in the dark. Paint space ship controls onto the cardboard pieces, leaving blank squares the size of the smaller cardboard squares for windows. Let this dry, then install this in the spaceship area and arrange a black light so that it shines on the designs.
2. For the activity, have the children imagine that they are going to be astronauts and take a trip through the solar system.
3. Let them each paint a picture in fluorescent paint of what they would see out of their window. Have them outline their drawings so that they look like a window.
4. Install the pictures as windows in the spaces left in the spaceship control panels.
5. Let the children go inside the space ship, blast off, work the controls to land on their favorite planet, then take off and return to earth. Have the children go in pairs or small groups if necessary.

More to do

Make space helmets. Have freeze dried snacks or astronaut (bite-sized) cookies for snack. Learn about the activities and lives of astronauts. Study the solar system, including interesting facts about each planet.

—Dixie Havlak, Olympia, WA

Star Box

4+

This activity creates an awareness of patterns of stars in the sky (constellations).

Materials needed

Black construction paper
Hole punchers
Constellation patterns (such as the Big Dipper)
Cardboard shoe box
Flashlight
White crayon

What to do

1.   Remove one end of the shoe box. Cut black paper about the size of the cardboard you removed from the shoe box. With white crayon, mark a constellation pattern on the black construction paper. Make one or two constellation patterns for each student.
2.   Have children punch holes in black construction paper (following the constellation pattern)—each hole will represent a star.
3.   Tape black paper onto end of the shoe box.
4.   Darken room and shine flashlight into box to create star picture on the wall.
5.   Identify the constellation. Count the stars.

More to do

Make a star and moon collage. Give children pre-cut star and moon shapes. Let them glue these onto black paper. If they want, have them name their own constellation, label it with white crayon. Tell children to ask their parents if they will take them outside on a clear night to view the stars.

Related books

Good Night, Moon by Margaret W. Brown
Where Does the Brown Bear Go? by Nicki Weiss

Related songs

"Twinkle, Twinkle"
"Good Night, Irene" (substitute children's names)
"Wee Willie Winkie"

—*Jean Bickert Gold, Sacramento, CA*

Kitten, Kitten

This poetic activity will help children develop vocabulary and learn to follow a simple story line.

Materials needed

A copy of the poem, "Kitten, Kitten" (see below)
Appropriate flannel board pieces
Felt in grey, light blue, green, tan
Fabric paints in black, white, red, blue, brown
Glue
Scissors
Flannel board
Brown, red or yellow yarn

What to do

1. Cut a cat from grey felt and embellish with black and white fabric paints.
2. Cut a pair of draperies and a ball of yarn from light colored felt.
3. Cut a little boy or girl from felt. Use fabric paints to make smiling faces. Glue on yarn for hair.
4. During circle time, recite the poem "Kitten, Kitten" for the children.
5. Place the story pieces on the flannel board as the poem progresses.
6. Encourage the children to say the poem along with you.
7. Make the flannel board pieces available to the children for play and/or to retell the poem.

"Kitten, Kitten" by Cory McIntyre

Furry and white,
With stripes of misty grey and black.
Soft and cuddly,
Purring as you sit with me when I read.
Explore and examine,
When no one is around.
Getting into things that you shouldn't,
Climbing mom's curtains,
Digging in her favorite plant,
Chasing a ball of yarn.
Deciding all of a sudden...
You need to be somewhere else.
Kitten, kitten,
You make me laugh and giggle
When I watch you run and play.

—*Cory McIntyre, Crystal Lake, IL*

Kritter Kare

3+

Animals are always interesting to children, and in this hands-on activity, they will learn to identify and sort various items used in pet care while learning about five different types of pets.

Materials needed

Many of these items can be borrowed from fellow teachers, friends, or students.
Large items: dog bed, cat furniture/cubby, rodent cage, bird cage, fish bowl (preferably plastic), large box
Small items: select only non-toxic items, for example:
Dog care: large collar, leash, bowls, rubber bone, comb, canned food
Cat care: collar and bell, catnip ball, rubber mouse, brush, canned food
Bird care: feeder, mirrored toy, cuttlebone, unopened box of bird seed
Rodent care: water bottle, salt lick, exercise wheel, box of hamster food
Fish care: aquarium decorations, box of gravel, water filter, fish food

What to do

1. Introduce pet care items for one animal at a time, focusing on one animal each day. Explain or demonstrate how each item is used and allow the children to examine the items. At the end of the first session, have the children help you place the small items into the large storage box. Place this box and the corresponding large item into the learning center.
2. Repeat this process at the next session. At the end of the second session, allow the children to add the new animal's small items to the storage box, combining them with the items from the previous session.
3. Show the children how to sort the pet care items by removing the small items from the storage box one at a time and placing them with the appropriate (corresponding) large item. For example, all of the dog care items would be placed into the dog bed, or all of the bird care items would be placed into the bird cage.
4. Repeat steps 1 and 2 until all of the items have been introduced. Leave the storage box and large items in the learning center. The children will enjoy sorting the items independently.

More to do

If possible, have a class pet or pets which the children can learn to care for over time. Bring one or more live animals into the classroom to visit and demonstrate how the pet care items are used. Sometimes the children like to bring their pets from home, with their parents' help. Be certain to check the school's pet policy and the children's medical records for allergies in advance.

Related books

Nita's Gerbil by Nigel Snell

—*Marji E. Gold-Vukson, West Lafayette, IN*

A Classroom Pet Store

3+

The children will have fun creating and operating a classroom pet store while improving their vocabulary and dramatic play skills.

Materials needed

Stuffed animals (children could bring from home)
Boxes, furniture, climbing toys or other constructions to be used for cages

Toy cash register and money (optional)
Other pet accessories: leashes (yarn), food bowls, pet toys, old pet food boxes

What to do

1. Set up an area in your room to be the Pet Store. Use classroom furniture, boxes or climbing bars to set up cages and counters. Put various stuffed animals in the "cages," set up a cash register and pet food/supply area.
2. Have children take turns being the store keepers and customers.
3. Let the customers with help from the store keepers, decide what pet they want to have and purchase the accessories they need to care for their pet.

More to do

Have children help make signs for the store. Children can draw and color or paint pictures or photocopies of different pets; then cut out and tape around the pet store at the appropriate locations.

Related books

Little Critters These Are My Pets by Mercer Mayer

—Sandra Suffoletto Ryan, Buffalo, NY

Frog Egg Fun

3+

Through this sensory activity, the children learn that frog eggs are surrounded by clear jelly.

Materials needed

Plain gelatin
Small plastic tubs (as from margarine)—one for each child
Aprons
Large clear container of pond water with frog egg clusters

What to do

1. The day before, make enough plain gelatin to provide a shallow layer of gelatin in each tub to be used.
2. Before you put the frog eggs in a jar, fill the jar with pond water and a few plants from the water.
3. Allow children to observe frog egg clusters. Encourage children to describe what they see.
4. Emphasize vocabulary words: gelatin, eggs, cluster.
5. Explain to children that they can watch the eggs with their eyes, but that it is not safe for the eggs to be touched by anyone.
6. In small groups, have children put on their aprons before playing in the gelatin.
7. Give each child a tub of gelatin. Allow the children to explore the gelatin with their hands.
8. Explain to the children that the gelatin they are touching is like the gelatin that surrounds the frog's eggs.
9. When children are finished, have them wash their hands and remove their aprons.

More to do

Allow children to help make the gelatin. Take children on a field trip to observe the egg clusters in their natural habitat.

Related books

Frogs Body by Joanna Cole
Chickens Aren't the Only Ones by Ruth Heller

—Cheryl Collins, Hughson, CA

Frogs

4+

The children can have fun and use fine motor skills to make these green frogs.

Materials needed

Small luncheon-sized paper plate—one per child
Green paint
Large, round, yellow stickers, or 2" circles of yellow construction paper
4" x 6" rectangles of green construction paper—one per child
Black crayons or non-toxic markers
Scissors
Glue or stapler

What to do

1. Fold the paper plate in half so that the upper part is somewhat smaller than the bottom. Paint the entire plate green and let it dry completely.
2. Use the stickers or yellow circles for eyes. Using the crayons or markers, color the top half of each circle black. Glue or staple the circles to the top folded edge of the paper plate so that they extend above the top of the plate.
3. Cut four 1" x 6" strips from the green construction paper and cut fringes on only one end of each strip.
4. For arms and legs, glue or staple one strip at each side and two at the bottom.

More to do

Use green construction paper to make a lily pad for the frog.

Related book

Jump Frog Jump by Robert Kalan

—*Jyoti Joshi, Framingham, MA*

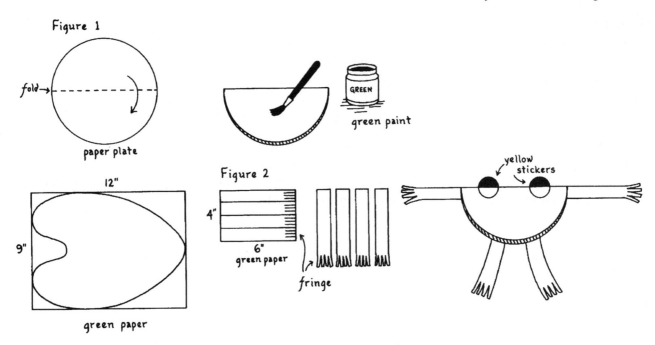

Figure 1

fold→

paper plate

green paint

12"

9"

green paper

Figure 2

4"

6"
green paper

fringe

yellow
stickers

Pet Show and Tell

4+

This activity allows young children to creatively share experiences about their pets.

Materials needed

5" x 7" envelopes—one per child
Black and red felt-tip markers and ball point pens
Blank audiotapes—one per child—plus one extra classroom tape
Tape recorder with fresh batteries
4" x 6" or smaller photograph or drawing of family pet—one per child
Self-sticking photo corners and paste or glue
Paper
Posterboard or computer banner that reads "Pet Show and Tell"

What to do

1. Label the front of each envelope. With the black felt-tip pen print "My name is _____. My pet is a _____." Fill in each child's name and the type of pet in red. If a child does not have a pet, they could answer to "The pet I would most like to have is_____."
2. Use the ball point pens to label a cassette tape in the same way. Then, place the tape and the child's pet photo or drawing into the envelope. Do not seal the envelopes.
3. On your extra tape, record the class singing "How Much is That Doggie in the Window?" Replay it and tell the class they'll each make a special pet tape.
4. Provide a quiet, comfortable area with few distractions. Brush up on your interviewing techniques and prepare a list of pet-related questions which will require detailed responses.
5. Conduct each individual interview by showing a child the envelope you have prepared for him or her and looking at the contents together. Help the child attach the pet picture to the back of the envelope with photo-corners or paste.
6. Establish a comfortable "recording rapport," and using you prepared list of questions, tape the interview.
7. When done, rewind the tape and place it in the child's envelope.
8. Repeat steps 5-7 with each child.
9. Show the children how to operate the tape recorder. Place the envelopes in the listening center under the "Pet Show and Tell" banner. Allow the children to listen independently. Your pet show is ready to enjoy!

More to do

Economize on tapes by grouping students or pets. You can also tape make-believe animal sounds.

Related book

Pet Show! by Ezra Jack Keats

—*Marji E. Gold-Vukson, West Lafayette, IN*

Let's Vote on a Name for Our Classroom Pet

4+

This pet-related activity will help children understand the concept of voting.

Materials needed

Goldfish or beta fish
Fishbowl
Fish food
Containers
Colored beads
Chalkboard and chalk, or experience chart and marker

What to do

1. Display the fish in the fishbowl. Explain to the children that they are going to vote on a name for the fish.
2. Solicit name ideas from the class and write them on the chalkboard or experience chart. Try to limit this to three or four names.
3. Write one of the suggested names on each container.
4. Have the children come up (one by one), select a bead, and put it in the container labelled with the name of their choice.
5. When the voting is finished, have the children count the beads in each container. Write the number of votes for each name on the chalkboard or experience chart and announce the winner.
6. Make a name card for the fish and display it near the fishbowl.

More to do

This method could also be used for pets other that fish. Vote on a snack the same way. Suggest choices appropriate to your group. Make craft paper VOTE buttons to take home on Election Day.

—Judy Contino, Ozone Park, NY

Graphing a Frog's Life Cycle

5+

In this activity, the children will have the opportunity to practice observation, recording, vocabulary and sequencing skills while following the growth of a frog.

Materials needed

Frog eggs in clear container of pond water and plants from pond
Magnifying glass(es)
Informative picture book showing a frog's development
Butcher paper
Paper cutouts representing the various life stages
Vocabulary words printed on large labels (optional)
Large terrarium or box to house mature frogs

What to do

1. Gather eggs, making sure you house them in the same pond water they were taken from.

2. Prepare your science center with books about frogs and amphibians. Display colorful pictures of different kinds of frogs.

3. With the butcher paper, make a graph with sections that allow for daily recordings. Attach it to a wall. Make it low enough so it is clearly visible and easily accessible to the children.

4. Make paper cut-outs for different stages of the frog's metamorphosis.

5. Show the children the picture book about a frog's life cycle and use the appropriate vocabulary to \ describe the various stages.

6. In small groups, allow children to observe the frog eggs. Have a couple of magnifying glasses available for use.

7. Have children choose the cut-out that most closely resembles the frog's development.

8. Each day have a different child take a turn choosing and attaching the appropriate picture to the graph for approximately 2 months or until the adult frogs appear.

9. Set the adult frogs free in an appropriate environment.

More to do

Take children on a field trip and let them observe the eggs, tadpoles, and frogs in their natural habitat. With adult supervision, have children collect worms and insects for food for the adult frogs.

—Cheryl Collins, Hughson, CA

Writing and Singing a New Seed Song

3+

The children will help write the words to a seed-growing song while learning about how a plant grows. This would make an excellent musical extension activity to a unit on plants or gardening.

Materials needed

The Carrot Seed by Ruth Krauss
Chart paper and marker

What to do

1. Read *The Carrot Seed* to the children.
2. Ask the following questions and write the children's responses. Responses listed here are just examples:
   What did the little boy do first? *Response:* He planted a seed.
   Where did he plant the seed? *Response:* In the ground.
   What did he do each day? *Responses:* He watered the seed.   He pulled out the weeds.   He watched it grow.
3. Using the language of their responses as much as possible, create and write down new lyrics for the new seed song (sing to the tune of "Frere Jacques"). Encourage the children to add appropriate motions.
Possible lyrics:

   Plant a seed (dig a hole)
   Plant a seed (dig a hole)
   In the ground (dig a hole)
   In the ground (dig a hole)
   Water it each day (water with a watering can)
   Pull out all the weeds (pull out weeds)
   Watch it grow (shade eyes)
   Watch it grow (shade eyes)

More to do

Bring an autoharp to accompany the song. Have the children take turns; one child can press the C-Major button and another can strum. Add melody bells, C, E and G. Play the song on the bells for the children and accompany their singing. Then allow them to experiment with the bells independently.

Related book

The Farmer's Huge Carrot by Henry O. Kindergarden   —*Kay McAlpine, Lima, OH*

Jack's Beans

3+

Children will observe changes in beans.

Materials needed

Recloseable bag
Water
Tablespoon
Paper
Tape
Paper
Marker
Beans (pinto, navy, lima, green, kidney, soy)

What to do

1. Begin early in the morning.
2. Gather the children and tell them everyone will be observing the beans for several days to note differences, such as which ones swell, which ones sprout and which do neither.
3. Place each type of bean in a recloseable bag with two tablespoons of water.
4. Label the bag.
5. Tape bag to window.
6. Watch beans. The exercise may take up to five days.
7. Record the results and tape them next to each bag.

More to do

Extend the activity by transplanting sprouting beans into a container with soil. Observe the fastest, tallest growing sprouts and any other differences. Sort beans into categories and make a bean collage.

Related book

Jack and the Beanstalk by Paul Galdone

—Angie Becker, San Antonio, TX

The Function of Plant's Roots

3+

Children explore the function of plant roots by play-acting.

Materials needed

Drinking glasses
Straws
Water

What to do

1. If needed, pre-pour the water into the drinking glasses.
2. Lead a group discussion on plant parts, emphasizing roots and their function.
3. Offer each child a glass of water and a straw. Explain that they will play act. The straws are their roots and they are the plants.
4. Encourage the children to grow like plants as they drink the water.

More to do

Show the children a plant with the root system attached and let them handle it. Have a magnifying glass and a plant classification book available.

—Lorene Miller, Fremont, CA

Sunflower

3+

Children identify shapes and colors to learn about science, nature and sunflowers.

Materials needed

Large paper plate, one per child
12" x 18" yellow construction paper
9" x 12" green construction paper
Sunflower seeds
Paper towel or gift wrapping tube, one per child
Stapler
Glue or tape

What to do

1. Show children a sunflower. Discuss how big it is and the shapes and colors of the many parts of the flower.
2. Paint the tube green (see figure 1).
3. Fold yellow construction paper. Cut into 4" x 6" sections, trace child's hand or draw triangle shapes and cut them out. There should be at least eight hand cutouts.
4. Put glue on the paper plate, sprinkle sunflower seeds, and let dry completely (see figure 2).
5. Fold green construction paper, draw leaf shape or trace child's hand and cut out shape.
6. Tape or glue leaves to green tube.
7. Staple petals (from yellow construction paper) around the rim of plate (see figure 3).
8. Staple or tape green stem to the flower (see figure 4).

—Jyoti Joshi, Framingham, MA

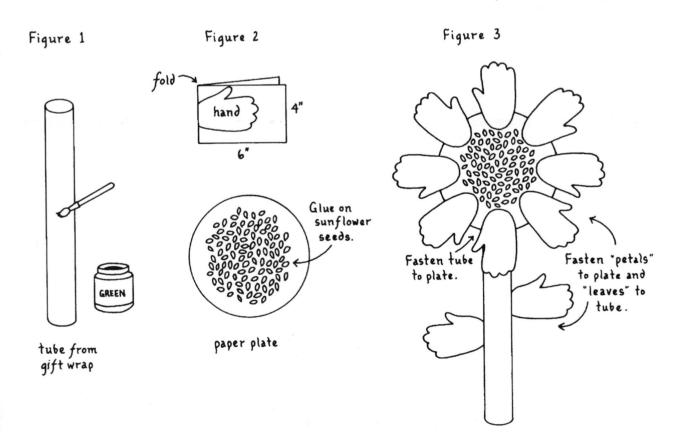

Figure 1

Figure 2

Figure 3

fold

hand

4"

6"

Glue on sunflower seeds.

Fasten tube to plate.

Fasten "petals" to plate and "leaves" to tube.

GREEN

tube from gift wrap

paper plate

Hand Print Tulips

Using lots of fine motor skills, the children will have fun turning painted prints of their hands into fields full of tulips!

Materials needed

Large size manila paper
Pastel color tempera paints (not too thin)
Shallow pans or trays
Old towels or cloths
Green construction paper or non-toxic green markers
Scissors
Glue or glue sticks

What to do

1. Mix the paint and place it in shallow pans or trays.
2. Have the children dip a palm in the paint and print it on the large paper. They may be able to print more than one tulip before dipping again.
3. After wiping their hand on the towel, dip and print again, using a different color of paint.
4. Have the children who are able help you cut stems and leaves out of green paper.
5. Glue the stems and leaves to the flowers, or use the marker to draw them in.

More to do

Try to create different paint-print flowers by using other parts of the hand. For example, print with the bottom of your fist and add petals with thumb prints.

—Jyoti Joshi, Framingham, MA

Sensational Sprouts

Children experience the pleasure of growing sprouts.

Materials needed

1/4 pound of alfalfa sprouts
Baby food jars, one per student
Cheesecloth
Rubber bands
Clean styrofoam egg carton

What to do

1. On the first day, have each child place one of teaspoon alfalfa sprouts in a jar and fill halfway with water, cover with cheesecloth and secure snugly with rubber band.
2. On the second day, drain the water (making sure the cheesecloth is on tightly), rinse the plants with clean water and drain well. Turn upside-down (tip so air can circulate) into egg carton and keep in dark place.
3. On the third, fourth and fifth days, rinse the plants daily and tip them so water can drain and air can circulate. On the last day, spouts are placed in sunlight to turn green.

Note: If the room is warm, sprouts will grow more rapidly. If the room is quite cool, they may require another day or two. They may be stored in refrigerator once they are grown.

More to do

Have a sprout party! Taste the sprouts alone first, to see how good they are. Spread peanut butter on crackers and top with sprouts.

—*Cathy Chenoweth, Columbia, MO*

Water Lily   4+

The water lily is an unusual plant that few children are familiar with. Here is a craft project which allows them to use fine motor skills to create a lovely water lily to complement a study of pond life, water animals or plants. These would make a beautiful and interesting bulletin board display.

Materials needed

Large paper plates, one per child
Small paper plates, one per child
9" x 12" green construction paper, one per child
Yellow crayons, paint or marker
Scissors
Glue or stapler

What to do

1. Prepare the paper plates by drawing the lily petal design on both the large and small plates (see illustration).
2. Have the children help you cut out these petal designs so you have large and small "flower" shapes.
3. Lift the petals of the smaller lily together toward the center with your hand and hold for a short time, until they can stand on their own.
4. Have the children draw or paint some yellow dots in the center of the smaller lily.
5. Glue or staple the smaller lily on top of the flat lily.
6. Draw the shape of a lily pad (like a rounded heart lying on its side) on the green construction paper and have children cut it out (see illustration).
7. Glue or staple the white lily to the green lily pad.

More to do

You could trace around the children's fingers to create the petals on the paper plates. You'll need two hand tracings per plate.

Related book

Jump Frog Jump by Robert Kalan

—*Jyoti Joshi, Framingham, MA*

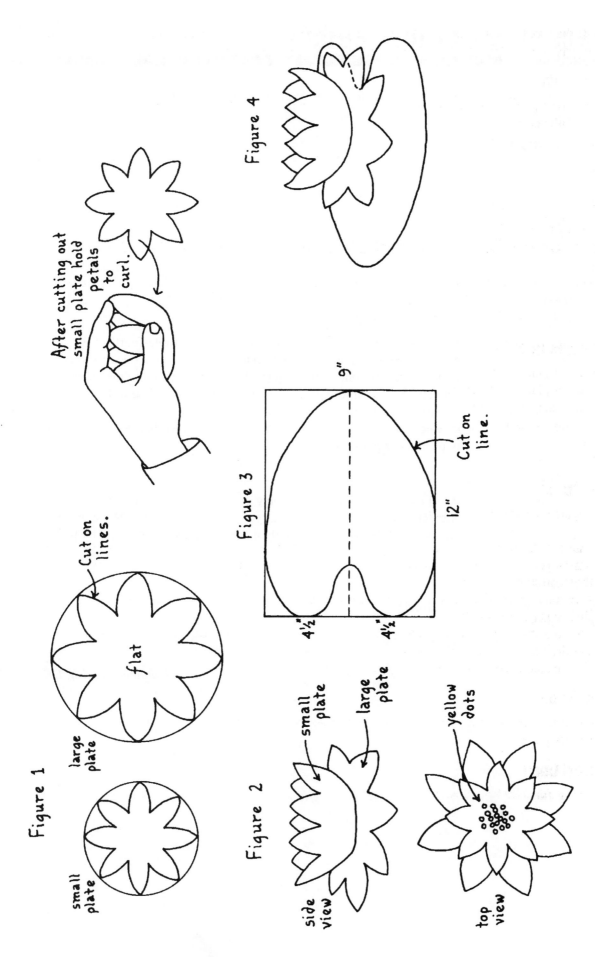

Figure 4

After cutting out small plate hold petals to curl.

Figure 3

9"

Cut on line.

12"

4½" 4½"

Figure 1

Cut on lines.

large plate

flat

small plate

Figure 2

small plate

large plate

side view

yellow dots

top view

Effect of Water on Seeds

4+

Children will use fine motor skills while learning how to plant seeds. They will also learn that seeds need water to grow.

Materials needed

Marigold seeds
Potting soil
Eggshells (two empty halves per child)
Egg cartons
Tablespoons
Water
Labels

What to do

1. Put empty eggshell halves (two per child) into the egg cartons.
2. Tell the children to spoon potting soil into eggshells until they are about three-fourths full.
3. Have children plant three marigold seeds in each eggshell planter and then add one more spoonful of soil.
4. Have children add a spoonful of water to one of their eggshell planters and not to the other.
5. Label eggshell planters with children's names and whether the planter should be watered or kept dry.
6. Keep eggshell planters in a sunny location.
7. Have children continue to water one of their eggshell planters and not the other. Have them compare growths of seedlings in the moist and dry planters.

More to do

Children can observe the effect of sunlight on seeds by keeping one eggshell planter in a dark place and one in a sunny window. Have children transplant seedlings to a larger pot as plants grow. Make decorative containers for the plants. Cut a half-gallon milk container in half and decorate the bottom part by pasting on scraps of various colored tissue paper.

Related books

How a Seed Grows by Helene J. Jordan
The Tiny Seed by Eric Carle
Rain Makes Applesauce by Jullian Scheer

—Jeannette Jundzil, Brighton, MA

Melt Down

2+

Children see the process and results of melting ice.

Materials needed

Clear plastic cups
Permanent markers
Ice cubes of equal sizes
Large sheet of posterboard to graph experiment

What to do

1. Decide on several places in which to time the melting of the ice cubes—on a windowsill, in a corner, in the sun, in the refrigerator or on the sidewalk. Write the place down on the posterboard, and write the place on the cup with marker. Place all the cups in their appropriate places simultaneously.
2. Allow the children to check on the ice cubes periodically. Keep track of when an ice cube has melted, and record the time on the poster.
3. Talk about the differences in temperature in the various places and how it affects the ice.

—Jacqueline Smallwood, Royersford, PA

Underwater Exploration

3+

Children will get a feeling for what life is like for a fish in the underwater world.

Materials needed

Small fish tank
Gravel or small beach pebbles
Large rocks of various shapes and sizes
Sunken ship (preferably split in 1/2, available at a pet shop)
Plastic sea creatures
Plastic green plants
Water

What to do

1. Fill tank 2/3 of the way up with water. Arrange a layer of gravel or stones on bottom of container.
2. Anchor plastic plants in the gravel for the sea creatures to "hide" in. Place sunken ship, large rocks and all sea creatures around the container. Use your imagination to create an interesting undersea world.
3. Let one or two children at a time put on a plastic smock, roll up their sleeves and let their imagination begin. The children make the sea creatures come to life. They can hide the creatures in the ship, behind rocks or in the plants. Children love to play in the water.

More to do

Set up a real fish tank to keep in the class all year long.

SCIENCE

Related rhyme

"Five Little Fishes Song"

Five little fishes swimming in a pool
The first one said "This pool is cool"
The second one said "This pool is deep"
The third one said "I like to sleep"
The fourth one said "Let's swim and dip"
The fifth one said "I see a ship"
The fisherman's line went splish, splash, splish
And away the five little fishes dashed.

—*Susan Batchelder, Englewood, NJ*

Monthly Guessing Jar   3+

This activity develops math skills through estimating, graphing and counting.

Materials needed

Jar or container
Objects to put in the jar (erasers, candy, cotton balls, etc.)
Bar graph with each child's name printed on it

What to do

1. Fill jar with objects and display on your desk.
2. Hang graph on the blackboard.
3. Discuss estimating and graphing with the children.
4. Let children fill in bar graph using crayon or marker during free time to estimate how many items are in the jar.
5. When all children have had a chance to estimate, empty jar and count objects with the children.
6. Divide the counted objects among the children and let them keep them.
7. Those who came closest can get an extra prize from the jar.

More to do

Estimate other objects in the classroom.

—*Joyce Montag, Slippery Rock, PA*

Magnet Painting   3+

Children experiment with magnetic force and create a painting.

Materials needed

White paper plates
Tempera paint (should be thin when mixed)
Paper clips or other small steel objects
Magnets

374

What to do

1. Mix desired colors of tempera paint to a thin consistency.
2. Give each child a paper plate.
3. Place a teaspoon of tempera paint on each paper plate. Place the paper clip in the paint.
4. Give each child a magnet. Instruct them to hold the paper plate up slightly while placing the magnet under the plate. Use the magnet to move the paper clip through the paint and around the plate to create a unique design.

More to do

Mixing primary colors can be used to introduce the concept of primary and secondary colors. You may also have the children select objects they think will be attracted to a magnet, allow them to test these, and use the appropriate objects for painting.

Related book

Mickey's Magnet by Franklyn M. Branley and Eleanor K. Vaughn

—Lyndall Warren, Milledgeville, GA

Hand Magnet Scavenger Hunt   3+

Children will explore and discover what kinds of materials are attracted by a magnet and what kinds are not.

Materials needed

Craft sticks
Magnetic tape
Magic markers

What to do

1. As an introduction, display several different types of magnets and materials for the children to experiment with. Have a brief discussion about magnets and what they do.
2. Tell the children that today they will create their own magnets to use on a magnetic scavenger hunt.
3. Have each child take a craft stick and decorate it using magic markers.
4. Give each child a piece of magnetic tape to adhere to the back of the decorated craft stick.
5. Take children to the room where they will conduct their magnetic scavenger hunt. Talk about where in the room children can search for items that may or may not be attracted by their hand magnets.
6. Ask each child to predict an object that she thinks might be attracted by the magnet. Make a list of the children's predictions.
7. Conduct the scavenger hunt.
8. As a group, go over the prediction list. Ask questions like, "Which of these items were attracted by the magnet?" "What do they have in common?" "What other things did you find on the hunt that were attracted by the magnet?"
9. Make a class list of all items found on the scavenger hunt that were attracted by the magnet.

More to do

Have the children use their hand magnets to conduct a scavenger hunt at home and report their findings to the class. Keep a picture journal of items that were attracted by the hand magnet.

Related book

Mickey's Magnet by Franklin Branley

—Gina Duddy, Arlington, VA

Guessing Tools and Machines   3+

The children will be able to discriminate and guess sounds of machines and tools.

Materials needed

Tape recorder
Cassette tape
Pictures of machines and tools

What to do

1. Look for pictures of machines and tools. Give examples.
2. Record sounds of the machines and tools that have been selected.
3. Put your pictures in the order that they appear on tape.
4. Play tape.
5. Have children guess sound.
6. Show picture after the guesses for the sound.

More to do

Have each child hold a picture and have them stand up or hold the picture when they heard their sound. Have them tell you what the tool is used for (what can we make or do with this tool, etc.). Graph tools that may be used INDOORS and tools that may be used OUTDOORS. (Same for machines.) Graph tools that are QUIET and tools that are LOUD. (Same for machines.) Have a woodworking center in your room. Set up a Fix-It Shop in dramatic play.

Related song

"Johnny Pounds With One Hammer"

—*Sonia Perez, San Antonio, TX*

Ice Castles   3+

The children will observe and experiment with the scientific principles of freezing and melting.

Materials needed

One plastic container for each child (the more different sizes and shapes of containers, the more interesting the castle will look)
Water
Food coloring

What to do

1. Put the water in a pitcher. Label the containers with each child's name.
Have each child pour water into his container (leaving room at the top for the water to expand).
2. Have each child put one or two drops of food coloring into the water.
3. Put the containers outside overnight to freeze (use a freezer if the weather isn't cold enough).
4. The next day pop the frozen creations out of their containers. Place them outside on a flat surface next to one another to form your "ice castle."
5. Watch them throughout the day, and see what happens.

More to do

Place parts of the ice castle in different areas (i.e., in the sun, in the refrigerator, inside the room), and watch what occurs. Write an experience chart with the class on the activity. Freeze fruit juice into popsicles. Play Freeze Tag—have children walk, run, hop, or dance stop when you tell them to freeze.

Related books

The Snowy Day by Jack Ezra Keats
Katy and the Big Snow by Virginia Burton
White Snow, Bright Snow by Alvin Tresselt

—Suzanne Sanders, Cherry Hill, NJ

An Inclined Plane

4+

The children will experiment with different objects to see which will roll down an inclined plane and which will not.

Materials needed

Cardboard tube from inside a paper towel roll
Styrofoam cup
Tape
Small box
A variety of small objects to put through tube (e.g., ping pong ball, paper clip, crayon, thimble, button, pebble, cotton ball)
Two small containers labelled "yes" and "no"

What to do

1. Make an inclined plane with the children. Turn the styrofoam cup upside down on a flat surface and tape one end of the tube to the bottom of the cup (this will be the high end of the inclined plane). Place the small box at the other end of the roll to catch the objects.
2. Give children various objects to put in the tube. Let them discover what kinds of items will roll down and what kinds will not. Ask questions such as, "Do you think this one will roll? Why or why not?"
3. Have children put the object in the "yes" container if it rolls down or in the "no" container if it does not.

More to do

Use a larger tube and larger objects. Make your inclined plane higher or lower. Compare two different planes that are inclined at different degrees and discuss which one allows objects to roll faster.

—Mimi Pearson, Trenton, NJ

Ramp Races

4+

This activity can increase small motor skills and allows children to measure distances by age appropriate means.

Materials needed

Wood plank for ramp
Variety of toy vehicles with wheels
Paper and markers
Blocks

What to do

1. Clear an area for the vehicles to move.
2. Create a record sheet that compares distances of various vehicles and/or of various ramps.
3. Set up a ramp with one end of the plank elevated and the other end on the floor.
4. Children let vehicles go down the ramp.
5. Have them put a block or other marker at the place where the vehicle stopped.
6. They can measure the distance conventionally, or they can decide which of two vehicles went the farthest.
7. This data can be recorded as suitable for the age.

More to do

Comparisons can be made between vehicle sizes. Additional weight can be added to vehicles and compared to runs without the additional weight. Ramp height can be varied and distances compared.

—Lona Parker, Huntsville, AL

Water Table Science

4+

What to do

Children discover what things sink or float and discuss reasons why.

Materials needed

Water table
Paper clips, pennies, ping pong balls, balloons
Styrofoam trays
Baby food jars
Sand
Smocks

What to do

1. Fill the water table about halfway with water. Have smocks available for children to wear.
2. Discuss the various objects gathered and predict which will float and which will not.
3. Give each child a penny to place in the water and observe what happens.
4. Do the same with a small amount of sand and a styrofoam tray. What happens?
5. Now place a paper clip and some sand on the tray. What happens? Why do you think they float?

6. Does a balloon float? Can you sink it? Blow up a balloon for the class to use. Does it float now? Can you sink it now? Why not? Can a ping pong ball float? Can you sink it? Why not? Explain that people can float because they have air in their lungs.

7. Try to float a baby food jar with the cap on. Put some sand in the jar and try again. Take the cap off and see what happens. What changed?

Related books

Water by C.S. Vendrell and J.M. Parramon
Last One in Is a Rotten Egg by Leonard Kessler

—Frances E. Wolff, Setauket, NY

Waterfall Science   4+

Children will see how gravity effects the flow of water.

Materials needed

Half-pint empty milk cartons
Straws (flexible straws work best)
Water in a pitcher
Hole punch
Stairs

What to do

1. Open up each milk carton and punch a hole on one side, about 1" from the bottom. Insert a straw through the hole. Arrange the milk cartons on the stairs so that the end of the straw from the higher milk carton is inside the carton below it.
2. Introduce the concept of gravity and discuss it in a brief and simple way.
3. Have one child pour water into the top carton.
4. Point out how the water flows through the straws down into next carton, and then into the ones below it.

More to do

Take field trips to see fountains, waterfalls, locks, flowing streams or rivers. Make a dam out of sand in the water table.

—Nicki Robinson, St. Augustine, FL

Let's Make Predictions

4+

Children estimate length, weight and volume and extend their vocabulary to include feet, yards, inches, pounds and cups.

Materials needed

Chart paper, large construction paper or posterboard
Markers
Yarn
Apple
Orange
Test tube, small beaker or any other appropriate containers
Small chips for voting
Balance scale
Clear plastic measuring cups

What to do

1. On the first day, make the following chart (see illustration) which compares the length of drawings. Use yarn and have children vote by placing one chip in the envelope of their choice. Use identical lengths of yarn to measure the drawings before counting votes.

2. On the second day, have a real apple and orange for the children to see but not hold. Have children guess which is heavier, and weigh with a balance scale. Count the votes.

3. One the third day, show a pair of containers (perhaps a test tube and beaker), fill with water and have children vote on which holds more water. Pour water from each container into equal-sized clear plastic cups to measure. Count the votes.

More to do

Have children measure each other and objects in the room with lengths of yarn. Use the balance scale to compare weights of things like small plastic eggs, blocks, blocks or corn.

—*Cary Peterson, Pittsburgh, PA*

Straw, Sticks and Bricks

Through this activity, the children will develop their "science" language by seeing, feeling, manipulating and describing straw, sticks and bricks.

Materials needed

The story of "The Three Little Pigs"
Small plastic bag for each child
Small, slender sticks
Straw
2 bricks

What to do

1. Gather materials. Place a small amount of straw and a few sticks in plastic bags for each child.
2. Let children sit in a circle on the rug or carpet.
3. Tell the children that today they will find out how to be a good scientist.
4. Pass out the bags (one for each child).
5. Ask children to take out the straw. Direct children to look at it, feel it, try to break it and to blow on it. Encourage children to talk about the characteristics of the straw.
6. Repeat this procedure with the sticks.
7. Repeat this procedure with the bricks. The teacher should pass the bricks around the circle.
8. Now tell the children the story of "The Three Little Pigs" and that at the end you want them to tell you which of the three pigs was a good scientist and why. Of course it will be the third little pig and children will be excited to look at this story with a new twist. Have a wonderful discussion about the third little pig being a good scientist by knowing which material would be strongest to use for his house and by doing his best in building his house. Close the lesson by singing "Who's afraid of the big, bad wolf?"

More to do

This activity could be extended by giving children three types of paper: a piece of bathroom tissue, a piece of aluminum foil, and piece of stiff cardboard. Let children look at, feel, manipulate and describe each. Then ask: "Which one would be best to use to wrap up a piece of an orange or a piece of ice?" "Why do you think so?" (Teacher and/or children should try it.) "Which one would be best to use to carry a cup of water on?" "Why do you think so?" (Teacher and/or children should try it.)

Related song

"Who's Afraid of the Big, Bad Wolf?"

—*Rhonda Vansant, Marietta, GA*

SCIENCE

Carbon Paper Transfer

4+

By using a method of transferring a design from the surface of an object to another surface, the children will explore textures, increase their awareness of cause and effect, and learn that something does not have to be visible to the eye to cause change.

Materials needed

Carbon paper
Typing paper
Iron
Items to use for transfer (leaves, string, cut out letters of child's name, etc.)

What to do

1. Gather materials. Have carbon and typing paper within easy reach.
2. Set iron at low heat and move table close to a wall outlet so there is not a long cord on the floor.
3. Place typing paper on table.
4. Have one child at a time place items for transfer on the paper.
5. Cover items with carbon paper, carbon-side down.
6. The teacher then presses the iron on top of carbon paper.
7. Lift off iron and carefully remove the carbon paper.
8. All the typing paper will be black except where you placed your items.

—Patricia Kepner, Norwalk, CA

Things That Float

4+

This activity teaches children about some objects that float on water.

Materials needed

Clear containers filled with water
Cooking oil
Porous rocks
Non-porous rocks
Cork
Styrofoam squares (1" x 1")
Wood pieces
Plastic items
Marbles
Soap
Metal nuts and bolts
Chart for recording the students' responses

What to do

1. Design and make a chart for recording results of floating test.
2. Give the children clear glass or plastic containers filled with water and several objects.
3. Explain that some of the objects will float and others will not float.
4. The students will first guess if an object will float or not. Record the predictions on your chart.

5. After each child has made their prediction, have them place the objects, one at a time, in the container to determine the results.

6. Record the results on your chart and compare to the predictions.

—Sue Matlock Gilliland, The Colony, TX

Magnet Testing

This activity allows the children to make guesses about and test a magnet's strength. They will also compare the relative strength of different magnets.

Materials needed

Magnets of various sizes and types (bar, horseshoe, ring, rod, cylinder, etc.)
Large paper clips
Small paper clips
Chart for recording estimated and actual strengths of each magnet

What to do

1. Unbend one of the large paper clips and place it against the side of one of the magnets.

2. Have the children guess how many paper clips the magnet can hold. Draw a picture of the magnet on the chart and record the guess next to it.

3. One at a time, hang small paper clips on the large one until the large paper clip falls off. The strength of the magnet can be measured by the number of paper clips held before they fall off. Record the actual number on the chart and compare it to your guess.

4. Repeat the process with each magnet.

5. Answer the following questions:

Is one type of magnet consistently stronger than the others?

Is the strength of a magnet related to its size?

Are magnets strongest at their ends?

More to do

Make available a basket with different items which the children can sort into two groups—those which are attracted to the magnet and those which are not. Experiment with the strength and pulling power of magnets using assorted materials.

Related books

Adventures in Physical Science by Margy Kuntz
Science With Magnets by Helen Edom
The Science Book of Magnets by Neil Ardley

—Carolyn Jackson, Portland, OR

Magnet, Yes or No?   5+

This activity will lead children to draw conclusions about the kinds of objects that a magnet will attract.

Materials needed

Large horseshoe or bar magnet
Items to be tested with the magnet (e.g., bottle cap, rubber band, leaf, feather, paper clip, ring or earring, coin, piece of yarn, nail file, little metal car, block, sand, slice of bread)

What to do

1. Display all items, including the magnets, on a table.
2. Ask the children what they already know about magnets. Listen for any misconceptions they might have, but don't correct them.
3. Ask the children to predict what items can be picked up by the magnet.
4. Allow them to experiment—either individually or as a group—with the magnet and the items on the table.
5. As the children experiment, sort the items into two piles—those that attract the magnet and those that do not.
6. Lead a discussion afterwards about what the objects that attracted the magnet have in common. Reinforce the idea that metal objects attract the magnet.

More to do

Divide a bulletin board in half and show things a magnet will attract and things it will not attract. Label the bulletin board with a picture of a magnet. Mark each half with a plus sign (for will attract) and a minus sign (for will not attract). Invite the children to bring objects to test with the magnet. Items can be taped, strung, glued, tacked or stapled to the appropriate side of the bulletin board.

Related books

Amazing Magnets by David Adler

—Diane Skoien, Lake Forest, IL

Transparencies   5+

Children will discover the meaning of transparent through experiments with transparencies and an overhead projector.

Materials needed

Overhead projector
Clear transparencies
Transparency markers in assorted colors
White paper

What to do

1. Set up a table with markers and clear transparencies ready to use. Put a sheet of white paper under each transparency so the children can see their drawings.
2. Turn on overhead and close shades, turn down lights. Discuss how the overhead works.

3. Have children draw pictures and designs on clear transparencies. Tell the children the markers they are using cannot go in their mouths because they are toxic.

4. Children take turns displaying the pictures on the overhead projector.

5. They see their picture magnified and displayed on wall and ceiling.

6. They see how the light shining through the color, along with magnification allows their picture to be displayed on the wall.

7. The idea of "transparent" is fascinating and soon the children will begin to overlap their pictures and put opaque items on the projector to make silhouettes. They may use their hands for shadows.

More to do

Transparencies can be used as a catalyst for story telling. They can be presented as a "slide show" or "transparency show" for other classes or parents—a musical background could accompany this. For younger children, pastel crayons or colored glue could be used on the transparencies instead of markers.

—Gail Garfield, St.Louis, MO

What's That Green Stuff?   5+

Through this activity, the children will improve their skills of observation and recording by describing what they see on a daily basis.

Materials needed

Various kinds of bread (two or three kinds)
Small locking plastic bags
Paper to record class observations
Classroom magnifying glass or microscope

What to do

1. Place each piece of bread in it's own plastic bag. Seal the bag.

2. Have the children describe their observations of each piece of bread. Stress that it's important to look in detail and describe only what you actually see.

3. Place the sealed bags in a warm, dark spot.

4. Each day, observe the bread in their bags and have the class dictate descriptions of what they see.

5. The children can get a closer look by using a microscope.

More to do

You can take one piece of bread and break it into small pieces. The children can put these pieces into their own bags. Place the bags in different spots (one cold, one warm, one light, one dark, etc.). See what happens to each bag in each location.

—Jill Ellavsky, Plymouth, MN

Art Appreciation

2+

In this activity, the children will create a year long gift for their parents.

Materials needed

Twelve pieces of paper (we used 8 1/2" x 14") for each child
Twelve pieces of artwork from each child
Folders
Rubber cement
Pencil
Ruler
Scissors
Hole punch
Yarn

What to do

1. Collect twelve pieces of artwork from each child over several months.
2. Make a twelve month calendar and copy one set for each child.
3. Place artwork and calendar in a separate folder for each child.
4. Glue artwork for each month to top of calendar page. (We cut artwork to 7 1/2" x 8 1/2".)
5. After all twelve months are assembled, punch two holes in top of calendar and tie yarn through.

More to do

Decorative covers can be designed by each child to finish off the art calendar project.

—Kay Marshall, Rockford, IL

Yummy Chicken Soup

3+

This seasonal activity gives the children a chance to taste rhyming words as well as hear them!

Materials needed

Chicken Soup with Rice by Maurice Sendak
Saucepan with hot plate or crock pot
One large can of chicken soup with rice
Hot tap water
Small serving cup—one per child
Spoons—one per child
Large wooden spoon
Soup ladle

What to do

1. Read the appropriate season's poem from *Chicken Soup with Rice* at morning group time.
2. Discuss the current season.
3. Re-read and emphasize the poem.
4. Have children help make chicken soup with rice as follows:
   Open can and pour in saucepan or crock pot.

Add full can of hot water if needed.
Stir soup, put lid on saucepan or crock pot, and simmer.
Either heat on saucepan on hot plate to simmering, or heat on High in crock pot for about three hours.

5. Go about the other business of the morning, but occasionally comment on how good the soup begins to smell. Talk about it. Repeat the poem.
6. Stir and ladle up samples when group is ready (works fine as a snack or pre-lunch appetizer).
7. Serve the soup and before eating read the poem of the season again.

More to do

Children can make seasonal or soup related pictures. You could teach the children about rice—how it grows, where it grows, or what it looks like when it's growing. Have the children bring in seasonal vegetables and make a soup with them.

—Janet Munson, Ferndale, MI

Matching Seasonal Items   3+

The children develop eye-hand coordination while playing this seasonal matching game.

Materials needed

Wallpaper sample books
Scissors
Pattern of a mitten (winter)
Pattern of a flower (spring)
Pattern of a tree (summer)
Pattern of a leaf (fall)

What to do

1. For each pattern, cut ten matching pairs from different wallpapers.
2. Have the child pick which season she wants to match and spread all the pieces of that season on the table.
3. The child then makes matching pairs.

More to do

Put two or more of the object groups on the table at the same time.

Related books

The Snowy Day by Ezra Jack Keats
The Very Hungry Caterpillar by Eric Carle
Blue Bugs Vegetable Garden Virginia Poulet
Fall Is Here! by Elaine Good

—Sandra Scott, Vancouver, WA

Four Seasonal Trees

3+

In this project, which could be done over several days, the children will experience the difference between the seasons while sharpening their motor skills.

Materials needed

Construction paper in a variety of seasonal colors
Cotton balls
Glue
Green paint
Red ink pad or small squares of pink tissue paper

What to do

1. Draw a tree trunk with branches on four separate sheets of paper for each child. Allow the children to do this if possible. You could color code the paper colors according to the seasons, for example, blue for winter, pastel pink or green for spring, bright yellow or red for summer, and brown or orange for fall.
2. Create trees for each season from the trunks.
   Winter tree—glue cotton balls onto branches to form the top of the tree.
   Spring tree—use fingerprints and the ink pad to form little buds on the top of the tree or scrunch up small pink tissue paper squares and paste them on the branches for buds
   Summer tree—paint bushy green leaves on the branches.
   Fall tree—glue a variety of seasonally colored leaves to the branches.
3. Collect each child's pictures into a Seasonal Tree Book and staple or punch holes and tie them together.

More to do

Take pictures of the trees outside during the various seasons to post in the classroom, or look for pictures of trees in magazines that can be cut out and posted.

Related books

Four Stories for Four Seasons by Tomie De Paola

Related song

"Raindrops and Gumdrops"

—*Sandra Scott, Vancouver, WA*

Monthly Calendar

3+

This activity gives children an active role in reading the calendar.

Materials needed

Drawing paper
Markers or crayons
Scissors

What to do

1. Children love calendar activities.

Idea #1: Each child draws a picture (thematic or not) or writes their name in each day's square. The teacher covers the squares with colored paper and numbers them, one to be removed every day.

Idea #2: A scene is drawn by the teacher and then covered with individual squares as would appear for each day of the month. Squares are removed every day until the whole picture can be seen.

Idea 3#: Trace the numbers and each day one child follows the number tracing. Circle the days. Put an X on the day's number. Write in the correct number.

Idea #4: Hide stickers under daily squares.

Idea #5: Create a picture, such as a flower, that will be complete at the end of the month. Each day one child adds another part to the picture, such as petals to a flower.

More to do

Use holiday themes, such as Thanksgiving: remove feathers; Valentines: find correct heart and remove.

—Elusa Cameron, Washington, DC

1.

				♀	☀	Allison
Greg		6	7	8	9	10
11	12	13	14	15	16	17
18	19	20	21	22	23	24
25	26	27	28	29	30	

Each child draws a picture in the day's square. Teacher covers with colored paper and numbers.

2.

				21	22	23
24	25	26	27	28	29	30

Scene is drawn by teacher and then covered with individual squares as in #1.

3.

	1	2	3	4	5	6
⑦	8	9	10	11	12	13
✗	15	16	17	18	19	20
21						

Trace days of 1st week.

Circle days of 2nd week.

X days of 3rd week.

Write in days of rest of month.

5. Create a picture by adding a numbered part each day.

Holiday themes:

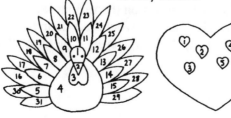

Add or remove feathers.   Add or remove hearts.

The Months of the Year Go Round 4+

In this activity, children learn that the months of the year are a continuous cycle. They will also learn the names of the months and major holidays.

Materials needed

Marker
A long strip of posterboard
Stickers representative of each month
Tape or stapler
String

What to do

1. Talk to the children about what happens in each month starting with January (i.e. the weather, special holidays, etc.). Go through each calendar month.
2. Write the name of each month on the strip as it is discussed and let the
children attach appropriate stickers for each month (e.g., a turkey on November).
3. Review the months with the children each week.
4. Fix the two ends of the calendar strip to each other with tape or staples to make the year go round. Hang with string above your calendar area.

More to do

Have old calendars which the children can flip through in the language center.

—Libby Wojasinski, Pasadena, TX

Four Seasons Game 4+

This activity will increase the children's awareness of the differences in the four seasons of the year.

Materials needed

Paper plate for each child
Small place marker such as a pebble

What to do

1. Divide plates into fourths and draw a simple picture in each section denoting a season, for example, snowflakes, flowers, sun, colored leaves.
2. Review the names of the seasons using pictures.
3. Pass out the plates and markers to the children.
4. Have the children practice positioning the markers on the various seasons.
5. Tell the children you will give them a clue and you would like them to place a marker on the corresponding season. Some examples include, "bare feet," "raking leaves," "picnics," "long, dark nights," "skiing," "Easter bunny," "squirrels and nuts," etc.

More to do

You can write the name of each season on the plate. You could have patterns of the seasonal symbols and have the children trace, cut and glue them onto their paper plates. Have the children make up their own clues and take turns being the "teacher."

Related books

A Book of Seasons by Alice and Martin Provensen
The Year at Maple Hill Farm by Alice and Martin Provensen
Seasons by David Bennett
Caps, Hats, Socks and Mittens by Louise Borden

—*Beckett Jordan, Orrington, ME*

Days of the Week

4+

This train game is a fun way to learn the days of the week and how to sequence.

Materials needed

6" x 12" rectangles of cardboard, posterboard or tagboard
Pictures of a train—drawn or cut out

What to do

1. Make a train, using a 6" x 12" rectangle of tagboard for each car. Under each picture or photo print the following in this order:

   Engine—Sunday, off we go!
   Coal car—Monday, moves real slow.
   Log car—Tuesday, speeds up a little.
   Freight car—Wednesday is in the middle.
   Circus car—Thursday is fifth in line.
   Passenger car—Friday is right on time!
   Caboose—Saturday is lots of fun, now all the week is done!

2. Put the pictures of the train up on a chalkboard or bulletin board.
3. Teach the children the following song (to the tune of "Alouette"):

   Sunday, Monday,
   Tuesday-Wednesday-Thursday,
   Friday, Saturday,
   And let's begin again.
   Sunday, Monday,
   Tuesday-Wednesday-Thursday,
   Friday, Saturday,
   And that will be the end!

4. Point to the correct train parts and sing again.
5. Point to the cars and read the poem about the days. Have the children repeat the phrases.
6. Randomly distribute the train cars to seven children. Have them put the cars in the correct order. Repeat the process until each child has had a chance to participate.

More to do

Give each child a miniature version of the train and have them put the cars in sequential order.

Related books

The Little Engine That Could by Watty Piper
Tootle by Gertrude Crampton

—*Barbara Saul, Eureka, CA*

Seasons in the North and South   5+

After participating in this activity, children will be able to identify signs of season change in the Southern part of the country and to contrast Northern and Southern changes.

Materials needed

Seasonal pictures
Paper
Paint
Crayons

What to do

1. Collect pictures of seasons in the North (e.g. autumn leaves, snow scenes, wheat harvesting, apple picking, etc.). Collect pictures of seasons in the South (e.g. pine and palm trees, orange blossoms, rain or sand storms, etc.).
2. Discuss the changing seasons in your area. In the North this would be snowy winters, new growth in spring, warm fruitful summers and the fall of leaves in autumn. In the South this would consist of mild winters with little changes in palm and pine trees, leaves falling off trees in the spring and then quickly replaced, a warm summer with lots of rain in the Southeast and dry weather in the Southwest and beautiful fall weather noted by slow changing leaf color.
3. After discussing season and area differences, ask the students to name the advantages of each area.
4. Take a walk outside and look at the trees, flowers and other plants to appreciate the weather. Talk about whether each is unique to your area of the country.
5. Ask the children to make a little book by drawing pictures of the seasons in the North and the South on opposing pages.

More to do

Make an alphabet to place in your room based on items found in your particular state. For example, in Alaska the letter "K" would be represented by a kayak and "M" would be a mukluk; In Florida you might choose an alligator to represent the letter "A" and an orange to represent the letter "O."

Related book

Alaska ABC Book by Charlene Kreeger

—*Lucy Fuchs, Brandon, FL*

Big Book of Months

This activity creates a pictorial record of class activities and helps develop memory and fine motor skills.

Materials needed

Colored posterboard
Large sheet of lined paper
Markers
Construction paper
Scissors
Glue
Laminator or clear contact paper (optional)
Metal binder rings

What to do

1. At the beginning of each month, have the children sit together in a group. Hang up a sheet of paper for all the children to see (e.g., on the blackboard).
2. Conduct a brief group discussion of what the class did during the previous month.
3. As children recall the activities, teacher lists them on paper (using complete sentences).
4. When the list is complete, read it back to the class.
5. Have each of the children choose one activity to illustrate and then draw and cut out their pictures.
6. Glue the illustrations around the edges of the posterboard near the appropriate activity.
7. The teacher glues the paper to poster board.
8. Laminate the page or cover with clear contact.
9. Using metal binder rings, assemble the pages into a continuing Big Book of Months.

More to do

Make a copy of what was written on the large page on regular sized paper. Run off a copy for each child to illustrate, take home and keep.

—*Beth Zwick, Ft. Myers, FL*

I Dress Up—I'm Still Me!

3+

Children learn that they will always be the same person, even if they are dressed in costumes. The children will also have the opportunity to discuss their feelings about dressing up and seeing people dressed in costumes and to explore their feelings further through dramatic play.

Materials needed

Accessories such as hat, glasses, scarf, wig
Half-mask
Full mask
Clown make-up
Paper plates
Construction paper
Yarn
Buttons
Pipe cleaners
Glue
Markers
Scissors
Craft sticks
Puppets and dolls

What to do

1. Ask children how they feel when they see people dressed in masks and costumes. Why do you suppose some people are afraid of these things? Encourage children to talk freely about their feelings.
2. Ask the children to close their eyes. Each time they do, try on a different accessory or mask, progressing from those that don't cover your face at all (hats, wigs, scarves) to those that do. Each time you try on a different accessory, have the children open their eyes and ask them, "Is it still me?" Talk with children about people wearing costumes—is it still the same person under the costume?
3. With clown makeup, masks, hats, wigs, scarves and other dress-up materials, encourage children to create their own costumes. Those who are timid about dressing up themselves may want to try dressing up the teacher instead! Allow children time for dramatic play in the costumes they have created.

More to do

Make masks out of paper plates and other materials listed above. Children may create characters with their masks listed above. Children may create characters with their masks and use them for dramatic play. Provide puppets and dolls for the children to dress up and decorate. Make a list of how children will dress up on Halloween. Write the list on chart paper and encourage the children to draw a picture of their costume next to their name. Post the list at the children's eye level.

Related books

Wobble the Witch Cat by Mary Calhoun
There's a Nightmare in My Closet by Mercer Mayer
Where the Wild Things Are by Maurice Sendak

—Marianne Modica, Madison, NJ

We Are Changing/We Are Growing

This activity will teach children that as we grow, we get bigger and learn many new things.

Materials needed

Tape measure
Ribbon
Sticky tack
Paper
Markers
Pictures of one person as an infant, toddler, and young child

What to do

1. Show children pictures of the child, beginning with the youngest stage and progressing to the oldest. Discuss how the baby changed as he or she grew. Ask what things a toddler can do that a baby can't. Encourage children to talk about things they can do now that they couldn't do when they were younger and things they are looking forward to doing when they get older. List their responses on a language experience chart paper, under the headings "Now" and "When I Get Bigger."
2. Measure each child with a tape measure and chart measurement with ribbon reaching from child's height on wall to the floor.
3. Write (or have children write) their names on small pieces of paper and attach to top of ribbons.
4. Ask children to draw pictures of themselves and tape pictures above names.
5. Repeat measuring activity at a future time and compare measurements for each child. Children will be able to see for themselves how much they've grown.

More to do

Create a "time line" on mural paper. Tell children to draw pictures of what they looked like as a baby, what they look like now, and What they will look like when they get bigger. Observe other living things that change and grow, such as pets, trees, plants, etc. Use pictures of them at different stages to create a collage or chart.

Related books

When I Get Bigger by Mercer Mayer
The Giving Tree by Shel Silverstein
The Very Hungry Caterpillar by Eric Carle
My Grandpa Retired Today by Elaine Knox-Wagner

—Marianne Modica, Madison, NJ

SELF ESTEEM

A Very Special Person

3+

Children learn to ease the separation from a parent and to build or reinforce self-esteem.

Materials needed

Small facial mirror
Box large enough to hold the mirror
Paper plate, one per child
Crayons or markers
Yarns of various colors, cut in pieces
Popsicle sticks, one per child
Buttons, two per child
Glue

What to do

1. Place the mirror inside the box and replace the cover.
2. Tell the children that there is a very special person hiding in the box. Give covered box to each child to hold.
3. Instruct the children not to look into the box. They may shake it gently and listen to it but they may not open it.
4. Have each child pass it to the next. Meanwhile, encourage their thinking by asking questions. Who do you think is a very special person? Could that person really fit into this box? When you shake the box, do you hear the sound of a person?
5. After each child has held the box, pass it around again. Tell them they may peek into the box but may not reveal who they saw. Can they keep a secret?
6. Give each child a paper plate to decorate. Using yarn for hair, buttons for eyes and crayons or markers, each child can make a special person. Glue a popsicle stick at the bottom.
7. Write each child's name on the back of the paper plate. Have the children hold the decorated face in front of theirs and one by one say the name of that very special person aloud.

—*Jyoti Joshi, Framingham, MA*

My Special Hand Print

3+

This special activity encourages parents to appreciate the positive and unique qualities of their child and to share that information with their child.

Materials needed

Different colored construction paper
Markers
Fine-tipped markers for open house

What to do

1. This is a good activity to do the day before a school open house. It takes place in two stages. First, the children will make a hand print for display in the classroom. Later, the parents will complete the activity at a school open house.

2. Each child selects the color of construction paper they want. A teacher or helper traces the child's hand on the paper.

3. The child prints their name below the hand print and hangs the hand print on the classroom wall.

4. At the Open House, parents listen to a brief introduction and orientation given by the teacher. Parents are reminded how special and important each of their children are, and the teacher explains some of the activities that they are doing in the classroom to encourage self-esteem.

5. The teacher asks the parents to participate in one of these special activities. She asks the parents to find the hand print of their child hanging on the classroom wall and write a special quality about their child in each digit of their hand print. The teacher wanders among the parents and chats with them while they are completing this activity.

6. Parents are asked to take the hand print home, sit down and share the information with their child, and then, hang the hand print on the refrigerator or wall.

7. You (the teacher) will see the effects of this activity on the children's smiling faces the next morning.

More to do

Parents may want to put this special keepsake in their child's bedroom or in their special baby book. Both parents and the teacher benefit from sharing the positive qualities of the children at the beginning of the school year. This self-esteem building and positive communication activity sets the stage for a myriad of related classroom activities with parents and children throughout the year.

Related poems

"Me" by Walter de la Mare
"Just Me" by Margaret Hillert

—Mary Lou Kinney, Boise, ID

Feeling Sentences Game   3+

Children will learn to understand their feelings.

Materials needed

Sentence strips or language experience paper
Markers
Pictures or symbols of feelings

What to do

1. The teacher writes Feeling Sentences such as:
   I feel good when...
   I feel sad when...
   I feel scared when...
   I feel worried when...
   I feel angry when...
   I feel silly when..., etc.
Write them on sentence strips or language experience paper. You may draw with markers or paste a picture which is symbolic of the feeling next to or in place of the feeling word in each Feeling Sentence. This is particularly important when working with young children.

2. This activity can be used with small and large groups of children. Tell the group that they are going to play a Feeling Sentence Game. Tell them that you started to write some sentences about feelings, and you need their help to finish them.

3. Read the sentences to the children one at a time and ask several children to complete the sentence. Record their answers on the sentence strips or language experience paper.

4. After you have finished reading all the sentences, display them on a bulletin board about feelings or hang them in the classroom.

More to do

Use the sentences to tell a story about the feeling and look for ways to problem solve with the children. Use the sentences to validate a child's feelings and develop empathy by asking if others have ever felt the same way or had the same thing happen to them.

Related song

The old standby "When You're Happy and You Know It" is useful to talk about feelings and reaction. You can substitute or add your own lines:

> *"When you're sad and you now it, wear a frown"*
> *"When you're tired and you know it, give a yawn"*
> *"When you're silly and you know it, giggle, giggle"*

Related books

How Do You Feel by JoAnne Nelson
I Was So Mad by Mercer Mayer
The Grouchy Ladybug by Eric Carle
The Temper Tantrum Book by Edna Mitchell Preston

—Vicki Britt Zaitz, Glenn Dale, MD

Tape Recorder Talk   3+

Children will identify and talk about what they like about themselves and others as a way of giving and receiving positive messages.

Materials needed

A tape recorder or microphone
Group of children

What to do

1. Tell the children that today they are going to be reporters like the people they see on the news. They will talk into the tape recorder or microphone and report about something they like about themselves or something they like about someone else in the group.

2. Take turns allowing each child to stand and face the group as her turn comes up. If you are using a microphone you can clap after each person has talked or if using a tape recorder, play back the tape and allow the children to listen to their own voice on the tape.

3. If a child has difficulty thinking of something you might ask the group to say several things they like about that child and allow the child to choose one to then report about on the tape recorder or microphone.

More to do

Allow children to listen to the tape in the music or listening center for several days after making the tape. Put the tape recorder or microphone in the dramatic play area for several days.

Related books

I Know What I Like by Nora Simon
Leo the Late Bloomer by Robert Kraus
I'm Terrific by Marjorie Winman Sharmat

—Vicki Britt Zaitz, Glenn Dale, MD

Search and Identify

3+

This activity will enable children to develop respect for those who are differently-abled by realizing that people who can't see can do many other things.

Materials needed

Blindfold
Pillowcase filled with many different objects, i.e., hard block, cotton ball, brillo pad, furry animal, etc.
A Cane in Her Hand by Ada Litchfield

What to do

1. Blindfold one child. Ask another child to lead him around.
2. Have each child write his name while blindfolded.
3. Each child may smell things.
4. Sing a song while blindfolded.
5. Have each child close his eyes and reach into the pillowcase of objects. Have them describe what they feel.
6. Have each child describe objects in the pillow case while his eyes are open.
7. Discuss what it felt like being unable to see.
8. With the children, create a list of things they think blind people can and cannot do.
9. Read *A Cane in Her Hand* by Ada Litchfield.
10. Discuss how the little girl felt in the story.

More to do

Look at and feel a book written in braille. Explore other disabilities.

Related books

A Button in Her Ear by Ada Litchfield
Grandma's Wheelchair by Lorraine Henriod
I'm Deaf and It's Okay by Evelyn Mueller
My Mom Can't Read by Muriel Stanek
Our Teacher's in a Wheelchair by Mary E. Powers

Related song

"I Am Freedom's Child"

—Linda Wishney, Chicago, IL

"Me" Balloon

3+

Children will develop a deeper understanding of self and a good self-esteem.

Materials needed

Large pieces of colored paper (size depends on space where you will hang the balloons)
String or ribbon, cut into three feet lengths (one for each child)
Hand prints of each child
Markers

What to do

1. Cut out balloon shapes from large colored paper. Have pictures of children ready.
2. Discuss with children what "favorite" means.
3. Put child's name on the balloon in a decorative way. (You could let them choose the color they want for their balloon.)
4. Ask the child about her favorite things such as: Who lives at your house? What's your favorite color? Who is your special friend? What is your favorite thing to do at school? What is your favorite thing to do at home? What is your favorite food? What is your favorite T.V. show? What is your pet's name?
5. Write their answers on their balloons and say what you are writing as you write it.
6. Attach the balloons to the wall.
7. Tie ribbon or string to the bottom of the balloon.
8. Place handprints 2 or 3 feet from the bottom of the balloons and attach the ribbon or string to the hand prints.

More to do

The children could share with the class what their favorites are. They could bring their pets. They could have a discussion of families and make a graph of how many family members. They could graph favorite foods.

Related book

The Me Book by John Johnson

Related song

"I Am Special" (Look all the world over there's no one like me.)

—*Kathy Goatley, Hickory, KY*

I Know You! I Know You!

4+

Children will develop short-term memory skills, recognize members of the class and learn each other's names.

Materials needed

Photo of each child in the class
Posterboard
Scissors
Contact paper

What to do

1. Photocopy two copies of each child's photo.
2. Glue the photos on squares of posterboard for sturdiness. Cover with contact paper for durability.
3. Lay all cards face down in front of two or three children.
4. Instruct the children to turn over two cards they think match.
5. If a match results, remove the cards from the play area and allow that child to go again.
6. If no match results, all children attempt to remember which cards were turned over and where they are now located.
7. Return the unmatched cards to a face-down position.
8. The next child takes a turn.
9. The game continues until all cards are paired.

More to do

Lay all cards face-up. Have the children study the cards closely and close their eyes. Remove one or more cards. Ask the children to identify who is missing.

—Dennie Byrne, Fairfax, VA

Color Yourself

4+

Children will begin to identify their individual physical characteristics and to identify that each individual is unique through this learning activity.

Materials needed

Crayons in 5 skin tones
5 eye colors
5 lip colors
5 hair colors
4 crayon boxes
8 1/2" x 11" pictures of Asian, Hispanic, Native American, African and Caucasian faces
(Specific number and variation depends on your ethnic diversity)
Paper for drawing
Tabletop
Mirrors

What to do

1. Label crayon boxes with a picture of the body part to be colored (i.e., eyes, lips, hair and skin). Place appropriate crayon colors in each box.
2. Explain to the class how everyone is a unique combination of colors and features.
3. Show them the different face pictures and let them look in the mirrors. Let the children pick out the face that is closest to theirs.
4. Pass out the paper for drawing.
5. Let the children look in the mirrors again to select a skin color and then have them color their face.
6. Repeat process for lips, eyes and hair.
7. Have each person in group share their face and say what is special about them.

More to do

Get more specific by examining the shapes of peoples eyes, their noses, chins, mouths, etc. Measure how long everyone's left arm is, their right arm, big toe, or how big their thumbnail is.

—Dixie Havlak, Olympia, WA

Faces of the World

4+

Children develop an awareness of the variety of people's skin tones.

Materials needed

Variety of colors of paper depicting skin tones (check notepads, grocery sacks, wrapping papers, stationery, construction paper and paper from printers)
Glue sticks
Brightly colored background paper
Markers or crayons

What to do

1. Pre-cut the skin tone papers into various circles and ovals (about 3-4" in diameter) to be used as starter shapes to create faces. Cut enough so each child can have several.
2. Place the background papers, glue sticks, markers or crayons and pre-cut "face" shapes on the art table.
3. The children glue the ovals on their paper in order to create faces.
4. Then use markers or crayons to add eyes, mouths, hair, noses and ears.
5. Keep your suggestions to a minimum to allow the children's creativity to come through.

More to do

You may want to have pictures of people, especially children, of various cultures and races at or near the art table to spark conversation and interest.

Related songs

"The World Is a Rainbow" by Greg and Steve
"Like Me and You" by Raffi

Related book

Brown Bear, Brown Bear, What Do You See? by Bill Martin Jr.

—Cherie Schmiedicke, Madison, WI

Feet Painting

Children will experience art through the sense of touch.

Materials needed

Paper roll
Newspaper
Different colored paints
Flat pans such as styrofoam meat trays
Wet sponge
Dry towel, soapy water

What to do

1. Spread a long roll of paper on top of newspaper on the floor.
2. Pour paints into flat pans.
3. Have the children dip their toes and feet in the paint.
4. Have them paint on the paper with their feet.
5. After the activity is finished, have soapy water ready in a shallow tub the children can stand in. Wash their feet thoroughly and dry with the towel.

—*Tina Fisher, Fairfield, CT*

Stewed Pears

As the children help make stewed pears, they will have the opportunity to use all of their senses, and notice what each part of the body can sense.

Materials needed

Electric skillet
Pears, approximately one for every two children
Plastic knives
Small cutting boards (optional)
One tablespoon butter or margarine
¼ cup honey or sugar
Cinnamon (just a small amount is needed, depending on how many pears you use)
Water, as needed

What to do

1. Wash hands thoroughly before beginning food preparation.
2. Have children help you wash pears, then cut them in quarters and core.
3. Using plastic knives and small cutting boards, children cut their own pear quarters into small pieces. Have each child taste a piece of raw pear. Talk about the taste, texture (firmness), color and smell.
4. Turn on skillet. Be sure that you stay near the skillet at all times when it is hot, and that the children are very careful around it. When skillet is hot, add butter or margarine. Listen to the sound that the butter makes as it sizzles in the skillet. Add the pieces of pears.
5. Allow the pears to simmer until a fork easily pierces the fruit. Stir frequently and add water as needed. Cooking will take about 15 minutes. Notice the sounds, smells and the changes in the pears as they cook.

6. Add cinnamon and honey or sugar. Stir well. Notice the new smells and colors.

7. Let the mixture cool before eating. Let children taste the pears. Do they taste the same as before they were cooked? What's different?

More to do

Sing this song to reinforce the relationship between senses and body parts.
(To tune of "The Farmer in the Dell.")

> *I see with my eyes*
> *I see with my eyes*
> *Heigh ho the dairy-o*
> *I see with my eyes.*
> *I hear with my ears,...etc.*
> *I smell with my nose...etc.*
> *I touch with my fingers...etc.*
> *I taste with my tongue...etc.*

—*Phyllis Esch, Pittsburgh, PA*

Food Roulette

3+

Children learn about the five senses.

Materials needed

Posterboard
Scissors
Glue
Pictures that go with each sense, such as:
  Smelling—flowers, herbs, spices, perfume or lemon.
  Hearing—dogs barking, people singing, bells ringing or a girl whistling.
  Seeing—sky, planes or ourselves in a mirror.
  Tasting—ice cream, milk, cookies or cereal.
  Feeling—gloves, bunny rabbit, sand paper or sand.

What to do

1. Cut out the pictures.
2. Put the pictures of the five senses on a table or floor in random order.
3. Explain to the children they are to sort the pictures according to how they sense the object represented.
4. Have them glue the pictures onto separate pieces of posterboard according to the sense employed.

More to do

Find pictures depicting seasonal or holiday objects and discuss how the five senses are used in each picture.

—*Annette Olivencia, San Jose, CA*

Texture Finger Painting

The children get to see how materials can change and experience the sense of touch. The glue is wet and drippy when they first use it, but as it dries it becomes hard and smooth. This is a wonderful tactile experience.

Materials needed

White glue in squeeze bottle
Finger paint (can be homemade using soap flakes and water)
Paper

What to do

1. Prepare finger paint by slowly adding water to soap flakes until a desirable consistency is reached. Add food coloring or a little tempera paint to color the paint.
2. On the first day, have glue bottles ready for children to use.
3. Have the children squeeze glue onto the paper. Encourage them to keep the glue bottle moving to avoid creating large puddles, because these take a long time to dry.
4. When they are satisfied with their designs, set the pictures aside to dry until the next day. Ask them questions. "What do you think will happen to the glue?" "How will it feel later?" "How will it feel tomorrow?" Encourage the children to observe the changes in their pictures during the day.
5. The next day, have their dried glue designs and finger paint ready.
6. Lay the children's designs out. Let them feel how hard and bumpy they are. Encourage them to use descriptive words to describe how it feels.
7. Provide finger paint to rub over the dried glue designs. Ask the children how it feels and how it looks.

More to do

It is fun to experiment with different types of music to "set the mood" while painting. Have children close their eyes or pull a hat over their eyes and finger paint over the glue design.

—*Heidi Benson, Batavia, IL*

Sensory Bear

Children learn about their senses.

Materials needed

Flannel pieces colored and cut out to match the pieces necessary to tell the story (see below):
Florence the Bear
Flowers
Lollipop
Bee
Two small bells to put on Florence's toes

What to do

1. Cut out the flannel into the shapes necessary to tell the story.
2. Rewrite the story on a card to have available when telling it.
3. Gather group to the area where the flannel board is kept.
4. Begin to tell the children the story.

5. While reading the story, place the appropriate pieces on the flannel board.

Hi, my name is Florence. I love to smell beautiful flowers and taste lollipops more than anything else in the world. One day I was doing just that, smelling flowers and tasting my lollipop, when all of a sudden I saw a bee buzzing around my head. I did not like him near me, and I was afraid he would touch me and I might get hurt. So I ran away from the bee as fast as I could. But the bee could hear the bells on my toes, and he liked to look at the shiny bells. So when running didn't work, I stopped and stood really still. Well, the bee flew around a little and then landed on my toe bells. I was so scared, but I stood still and was brave. After awhile the bee decided he did not like to touch the hard bells. He flew away, and then I could smell my flowers and taste my lollipop again.

More to do

A bear puppet can also be used with the items sewn onto the bear.

—Melissa Browning, West Allis, WI

Feely Boxes

3+

Children develop the ability to identify objects using their sense of touch.

Materials needed

6 empty facial tissue pop-up boxes
Glue gun
6 items with different textures to touch (pine cone, carpet piece, stone, etc.)
Large cafeteria tray or piece of heavy cardboard

What to do

1. Glue the tissue boxes to the tray.
2. Glue one item to the bottom of each box.
3. Show the children the tray and the boxes.
4. Tell them there is something in each box.
5. Ask them if they can guess what is in the boxes without looking.
6. Ask them to think of other ways to find out what the items are.
7. Allow the children to explore the objects by putting their hands in and feeling the items.

More to do

Have the children choose the items to put into the boxes for another set of feely boxes. Put items in the boxes that use the sense of smell (cinnamon, onion, socks).

Related books

The Five Senses: Touch by Maria Rius
The Five Senses: Sight by Maria Rius
The Five Senses: Smell by Maria Rius

—Anne Schweiss, St. Louis, MO

Simon Says in Sign [Language]

3+

This is a new twist to an old favorite, Simon Says. The children will sharpen their listening skills and practice following directions while exercising their large muscles. They will also become aware of sign language and how it allows some people with special needs to communicate.

Materials needed

Teacher will need to be familiar with the signs used in the game—see illustrations

What to do

1. If the children are not yet familiar with Simon Says, explain how it is played.
2. Demonstrate the signs and have children try to guess what they are. For example, begin with the sign for "stand." Explain that your open palm is the imaginary floor, and the two fingers are a person. Ask them, "What is this 'person' doing?" For the "sit" sign, explain that one hand is a chair, and the "person's" legs are dangling over the side. When using the "fall" sign, you may want to consider a gentle squatting motion.
3. Demonstrate the name sign for "Simon" and the sign for "says."
4. Play Simon Says in the usual manner, using the signs and spoken words simultaneously. When the children are comfortable with the game, try playing without speaking the words you sign.

More to do

Introduce the signs "boys" and "girls." Instruct the children to follow only their designated instructions. For example, "Simon Says Girls Stand!" Add a number designation after the "jump" sign. Example, "Simon Says Jump Three (times)!"

Related books

The Joy of Signing by Lottie Riekehof
My First Book of Sign by Pamela J. Baker
I Can Sign My ABC's by Susan Gibbons Chaplin

—*Martha Mowry, Forestdale, MA*

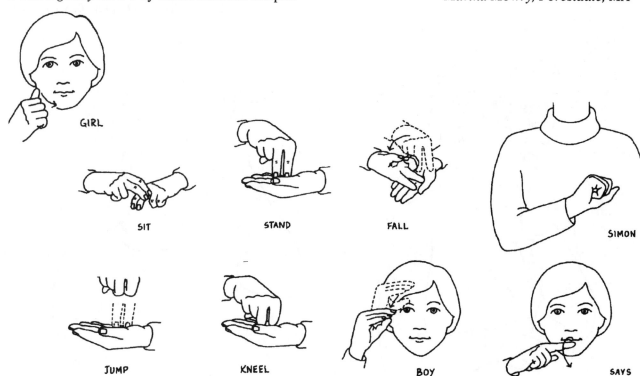

GIRL

SIT   STAND   FALL   SIMON

JUMP   KNEEL   BOY   SAYS

Family Signs

3+

Children will become familiar with sign language by learning to associate family words (mother, father, sister, brother) with their correct signs.

Materials needed

Pictures from magazines of people who could be mothers, fathers, sisters, and brothers

What to do

1. Mount photos on construction paper.
2. Demonstrate the sign for mother.
3. Help children say the word and practice the sign for mother.
4. Have children say and sign mother without your help.
5. Demonstrate the sign for father.
6. Help children say the word and practice the sign for father.
7. Have children say and sign father without your help.
8. Make the sign for mother or father and ask children to say the correct word.
9. Make the sign for mother or father and ask children to point to the correct magazine photo.
10. Repeat these steps for brother and sister.

More to do

Teach children the signs for "my" and "is." Ask children to sign "My mother is" and say their mother's name. Repeat for father, sister, and brother. Have children show photos or drawings of their own family members and tell in sign if the person is their mother, father, sister or brother.

Related books

Signs for Me: Basic Sign Language for Children by Ben G. Bahan and Joe Dannis.

—Nancy Dentler, Bay City, TX

sister

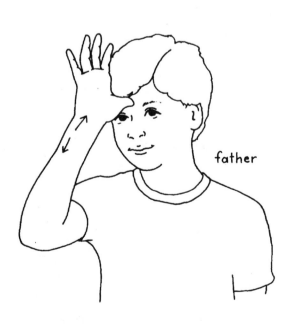

father

SENSES

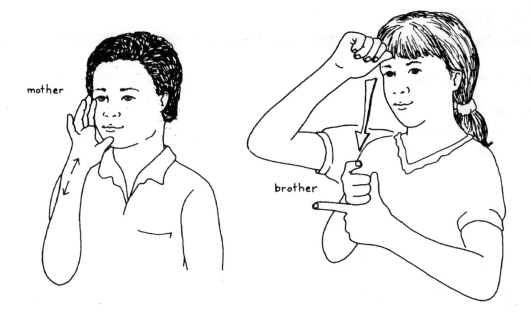

mother

brother

Sign and Do

3+

Children will learn signs for actions and another way of communicating.

Materials needed

Sign language book with many action signs or person with knowledge of sign language who can teach action signs

What to do

1. Show the children the signs, say the word and ask them to copy you.
2. When they have learned to sign all the words, have them stand up.
3. Explain that when you sign "walk," they should just walk four steps forward and then walk back to their mark. Have them try it. When you sign "run," they should run in place, staying on their mark. Demonstrate. Have them try it. Explain that when they jump and hop that they may move a little. Remind them that they need to watch you to know what to do next.
4. Sign the actions one at a time, signing "stop" after "hop," "jump," and "run," and "stand" after "sit". You can play where no one loses and just have a great time. Then have someone else be the leader while you join the game. Depending on the number of children and time alloted, each child could take a turn being leader.
5. If you prefer to play a competitive game, don't put a child out for not remembering a sign, but instead have one or two children sit each time you sign "stop" to encourage them to pay attention; the last one still in the game after everyone is sitting can be the leader.

More to do

This activity could be done outdoors as well as indoors. It may be more difficult to keep their attention, though. You could play it like "Red light, green light" where they start far away (not too far to see) and the object is to reach you by performing the action. If they fail to stop when you sign "stop," they start back at the beginning.

—Joyce Dowling, Clinton, MD

Mr. Senses

3+

To better understand what our five senses are and how we use them

Materials needed

Eight or nine inch paper plates
Crayon or markers

What to do

1. Give each child a paper plate. These are faces.
2. After discussing each sense, have the children add which sense you have been talking about—eyes, nose, mouth and ears.
3. Let the children trace their hands, then cut them out, they can be used for hair. The children can better relate to a "person" in understanding the five senses.

More to do

Introduce each sense by showing the children what each sense does. For example: "Touch" show different textures of materials.

Related book

The Five Senses by Maira Rius

Related song

"Naming the Parts of the Body" (sung to "Twinkle, Twinkle Little Star")

> *If a bird you want to hear,*
> *You have to listen with your _____. (ear)*
> *If you want to dig in sand,*
> *Hold the shovel with your _____. (hand)*
> *To see an airplane as it flies,*
> *You must open up your _____. (eyes)*
> *To smell a violet or a rose,*
> *You sniff the fragrance through your _____. (nose)*
> *East and West and North and South,*
> *To eat or talk you use your _____.(mouth)*

—Rebecca Yahm, Otis ANGB, MA

Smell Bags

3+

Children distinguish between odors.

Materials needed

Large pieces of lightweight fabric
Scissors
Odorous materials—mint, basil, oregano, or rosemary; flower petals; dried lemon or orange peel; pieces of cinnamon bark, cloves, anise; eucalyptus leaves, bay leaves or pine needles.
20" pieces of yarn

What to do

1. Cut fabric into 5" diameter circles.
2. Encourage children to smell, share and talk about the various items.
3. Have children choose a fabric circle, if a variety of fabric pieces were used to make circles.
4. Children choose items that they like the smell of, place them on their cloth circles, then gather them up with the cloth circle to see if they like the way they smell together. Encourage children to try many items in different combinations.
5. When children have the items that they want for their smell bag, they place them in the center of their circle and gather up the edges of the cloth to make a pouch.
6. Help the children wrap yarn around their pouches and tie the yarn securely.
7. The long ends of the yarn are then tied together so that the smell bag can be worn around the child's neck like a pendant.
8. Encourage children to smell each other's bags and talk about their smells.

More to do

Use in connection with other sensory activities. Make smell jars to identify contents, identifying cubes of look-alike foods by smell (raw pieces of potato, turnip, radish, apple, pear).

Related books

My Five Senses by Aliki
Smelling by Henry Pluckrose

—Judith Dighe, Rockville, MD

Feel Box   3+

Children will practice identifying objects using only their sense of touch.

Materials needed

Cardboard box
Glue
Scissors
Felt square the size of box top
Small objects from around the classroom (block, comb, pencil, spoon, cup, string, doll shoe, etc.)

What to do

1. Cut out a circle in the top of the box. Children should be able to pass their hands easily through the opening.
2. Trace a circle the same size onto the felt square but do not cut it out. Instead, cut two slits across the circle in the form of a cross. Glue the felt piece over the box cover so the two circles line up.
3. Place one or more small objects in the feel box.
4. Have each child reach in, feel an object and try to identify it without looking. After the child has made a guess, allow her to pull out the object and examine it.

More to do

Put several blocks of different sizes into the box and ask children to find the largest, smallest, etc. Put objects of different textures into the box and ask children to find something smooth, something rough, etc.

—Manisha Segal, Burtonsville, MD

Scent Matching

3+

Children will use their olfactory sense to match different scents.

Materials needed

Twelve tongue depressors
Six scented votive candles (different scents)
Six small cans
Electric skillet

What to do

1. Make six pairs of scent sticks in advance: (a) place six small empty cans in one inch of water in an electric skillet; (b) heat water to 300 degrees; (c) place one scented votive candle in each can; (d) when candles are melted, dip two tongue depressors in each. (Note: wax should cover the bottom 1 1/2" of stick—don't let wax get too thick or it will peel off.)
2. Place the scent sticks on the table before a small group of children.
3. Have one child close both eyes and smell one stick. Tell the child to smell the other sticks until he can find the one with the same scent.
4. Continue until all the children have had a turn.

More to do

For preschoolers, mark the pairs with shapes or colors to make the game self-correcting. Let older children make their own scent sticks under careful adult supervision. Incorporate science concepts by discussing the words "solid," "liquid," "melting," etc.

—*Donna Rehder, Sonora, CA*

Texture Corner/Divider

3+

Children will experience and match a number of materials that vary in color, texture and shape in a special quiet place.

Materials needed

Large appliance box
Scraps of different materials such as flannel, felt, lace, upholstery, plastic, velvet, satin, silk, fake fur, stretchy knits, corduroy and mesh (two identical pieces of each)
Rubber cement or glue
Scissors
Contact paper

What to do

1. Cut the box so that it is three feet high and open at the top and on one side.
2. Cut out enough pieces of material to cover the entire inside of the box. Pieces can vary in size and shape, but make sure you have two of each that are exactly the same.
3. Plan how you will arrange the pieces on the inside of the box, making sure that you have enough to cover all three sides. Then use glue or rubber cement to attach the scraps of material.
4. Decorate the outside of the box with contact paper.

5. Show children the box and let them climb inside, one by one. Explain that this box will be available to them when they want a little quiet time. Point out the different kinds of materials inside and encourage the children to touch them. Tell the children that every piece of material has a match somewhere inside the box and that it's fun to try to find them.

More to do

Make this box a special reading corner by putting a few books inside or a music corner by putting in a cassette player and tapes. Tell the children that they may go there whenever they don't feel like playing and just want to be by themselves.

Related books

Things I Like to Do by Beth Clure and Helen Rumsey

—Janice Parks, Stockdale, TX

I Can Do

3+

This activity introduces children to the five senses using the "I Can Do" method and promotes self-esteem and developmental growth.

Materials needed

Flash cards depicting the five senses
Music

What to do

1. Learn the following song (to the tune of "Watch Your Eyes"):
"I Can Do"

I can smell, I can smell with my nose.
I can see. I can see with my eyes.
I can hear with my ears and speak with my lips. I can touch with my hands.
I can do.
I can see, smell, hear, speak and touch. I can do.
I can see, smell, hear, speak and touch. I can do.
I can do. I can do all of these just for you.
Look at me. Look at me. I can do.

2. Prepare all materials. Make flash cards of the five senses.
3. Have all children sit in a circle in the room.
4. Reveal the flash cards to the children. Explain each sense as you hold up a card and talk about the part of the body that uses that sense.
5. Hold up the cards and see if the children can now identify the senses named on the card.
6. Introduce the song to the children. Sing it once and then ask the children to join in and point to the part of their body that is mentioned as you sing.

More to do

You can also use this type of activity to introduce the other body parts to the children such as the arms, legs, feet, etc.

—Gail N. Sherfield, Rockmart, GA

Roll Over

3+

This activity teaches the children to make playdough and uses the sense of feeling.

Materials needed

Flour
Oil
Water
Salt
Cream of tarter
Food coloring or tempera paint
Saucepan and hot plate or electic frying pan
Old hair rollers

What to do

1. Gather all ingredients for playdough.
2. Mix ingredients in sauce pan and cook over medium heat.
    1 cup flour
    1 tablespoon oil
    1 cup water
    1/2 cup salt
    2 tsp cream of tartar
3. Stir constantly until mixture forms a ball.
4. Take out of pan and knead until smooth. Add food coloring if desired.
5. Hand out some playdough to children and ask them to flatten it out.
6. Show the children how to roll the hair curler over the dough to make a textured effect.
7. Ask them to do the same and then feel the different patterns they make.

More to do

Let the playdough dry.

—Darlene Hammond, Syracuse, NY

Scent-Sational

3+

The children will use their sense of smell to describe and appreciate different scents.

Materials needed

A variety of spices (ginger, cinnamon, nutmeg, oregano)
Extracts (vanilla, lemon, mint, orange)

What to do

1. Discuss how we use our noses to smell. Our nose tells us whether we think a smell is pleasant or not.
2. Give each child an opportunity to smell the different scents.
3. Let each child try to identify the smell and decide whether or not they like it.

More to do

Add scents to water in a plastic tub, then practice measuring and pouring with empty spice bottles. Make a great smelling cooking project like soup or cinnamon toast!

Related books

What Your Nose Knows by Jane Belk Moncure
The Nose Book by Al Perkins
Smell by Maria Rius, J.M. Parramon and J.J. Puig

—Sandra Acuna, San Antonio, TX

Veggie Shuffle

3+

Children will identify vegetables by smell.

Materials needed

Six-ounce paper cups
Foil
Rubber bands
Toothpick or other sharp, pointed object
Tray
Vegetables that have strong aroma—green pepper, onion, tomato, radish or turnip

What to do

1. Cut a small portion from each vegetable and place each one in a paper cup. Place the remainders on the tray, spaced sufficiently so smells do not mingle.
2. Cut circle of foil to fit paper cup, attach foil to cup with rubber band. Make several holes with a toothpick so aroma can be smelled.
3. Place cups on table or area being used, across from tray of vegetables.
4. Tell children to chose a cup and smell it.
5. As each child smells, ask if she can identify the vegetable by name.
6. Ask each child to take the cup to the tray and place in front of vegetable she thinks it matches.

More to do

Children can name colors of vegetables or identify those with seeds and those without. Mix fruits with vegetables and have children sort into categories.

Related book

The Carrot Seed by Ruth Krauss

—Angie Becker, San Antonio, TX

Touch 'n Such

3+

Children use the sense of touch to identify objects.

Materials needed

Feely Bag (large grocery bag)
Several items with different textures, shapes and weight (it is usually good to have one item per child to "guess" what is in the bag)
Blindfold

What to do

1. Gather items from the classroom that the children are familiar with—cotton balls, rocks, seashells, styrofoam cup, pencils, little cars, stuffed toys, paper clips, spoons, rubber bands, balloons or anything that will fit inside the bag!
2. Explain to the children that they are going to play a guessing game using one of the five senses, and everyone gets to have a turn.
3. Tell the children you have a special bag full of things, and they are to guess what is inside the bag by reaching in and pulling out one item. They must keep their eyes closed or blindfolded until they guess.
4. The teacher might want to be sure and tell the other children to be very quiet and to not tell what it is, so it can be a surprise!
5. If the child is having difficulty guessing, ask questions. Is it smooth, rough, hard, soft, etc? If the child still has trouble, ask additional questions. Do you think you could play with it? Do you think you could eat with it? You want the child to succeed. Continue to ask guiding questions until the child guesses correctly.
6. If you have a large number of children, play with half the class at a time, so they don't become restless.

More to do

Let the children make their own Feely Bag. Have the children decorate a brown lunch bag with crayons, markers, or paint.

Related books

The Velveteen Rabbit by Margery Williams
The Snowy Day by Ezra Jack Keats
Geraldine's Big Snow by Holly Keller

Related songs

"Senses" (from the musical "Down by the Creekbank")
"Head, Shoulders, Knees, Toes"

—*Sheryl A. Smith, Johnson City, TN*

Mud Finger Paint

4+

Children explore the sense of touch and have fun with farm animal art.

Materials needed

Pale pink construction paper
Marking pens or crayons
Mud or dirt (Potting soil does not work well for this project. It needs to be real earth dirt.)

What to do

1. Using pale pink construction paper, cut out a large profile of a pig's body (do not cut out the legs or tail).
2. Wet the dirt so it is a nice consistency for finger painting.
3. Have the children draw on one eye, one triangle ear, one snout nostril (this is only one side of his face) and a mouth.
4. Have child glue pig body onto a bigger sheet of paper and draw four legs and a curly tail.
5. Have the children finger paint mud on the pig.

More to do

Children can mud finger paint on a big sheet of slick paper or the table just for fun.

Related book

Small Pig by Arnold Lobel

—Joyce Nelson, Lafayette, CA

Foot Feelings

4+

This activity will help children develop fine motor skills and produce a picture through the sense of touch.

Materials needed

Buckets
Small objects such as marbles, toys, spools, plastic fruit, sand and blocks of wood
White drawing paper
Water color paints
Paintbrushes
Water/cups

What to do

1. Prepare buckets by putting objects inside them.
2. Give each child a piece of drawing paper, some paints, a brush, a cup of water and a bucket that contains an object. Make sure that the children do not see what is in their buckets.
3. Tell the children to stick one foot into their buckets and feel the object inside. Remind them again not to peek.
4. Have the children paint a picture of what they think the object looks like. Give them hints on color and design to get them going.
5. When they are finished, allow them to look inside their buckets and ask them to share their objects and paintings with the class.

SENSES

More to do

Play different types of music and have the children paint what they feel as they listen to it.

—Laura L. Nettleton, Housatonic, MA

Sign Language

4+

Children learn about sign language and why it is used, handicaps and their causes and develop their fine motor skills.

Materials needed

Earmuffs (several pairs)
Sign language books
Sign matching cards—pairs of cards with a color, shape or object on one and the sign language representation on the other
Posters of handicapped children/adults
Poster of the sign language alphabet
Comb
Wax paper

What to do

1.   Place sign language poster and sign language books in the reading area.
2.   Make sign matching cards with a master check-sheet on which the children can verify their matches.
3.   Place earmuffs in the dramatic area.
4.   Place wax paper and comb in the science area. Fold the wax paper over the teeth of the comb, place your lips over the wax paper and hum. Have children do the same. Ask them how it feels, and then explain about sound and vibrations.
5.   Discuss handicaps during circle time. How do they feel? How are they caused? What do they inhibit?
6.   Sign the first letter of each child's name and "Good Morning" each day. Add signs for colors and animals.
7.   At music time, have some children wear earmuffs while others sing or play music. Discuss what it would be like not to hear music.
8.   In the large motor area, have some children stomp, walk or run while the others lie down and feel the movements from the floor.
9.   In the math area, use signs for numbers to work with children.

More to do

Invite a hearing-impaired visitor to your classroom.

Related books

Sesame Street Sign Language by Children's Television Workshop
Handtalk by Remy Charlip
Signs for Me by Ben Bahan and Joe Dannis

—Debi Lemieux, Reedsburg, WI

The Sense of Sight

4+

The students will develop an understanding of the handicapped by recognizing qualities that are the "same" between the handicapped and their non-handicapped peers.

Materials needed

Pin The Tail On the Donkey or modified version of the game
Blindfold

What to do

1. Hang the game on the wall before the children arrive.
2. Ask the children what their eyes do. What does it mean to be blind? Allow questions and encourage discussion. Mention that blind people use seeing eye dogs and canes so they can be active. Stress qualities that are the same about seeing and non-seeing people.
3. Explain that the children are about to play a game which will help them understand what it feels like to be blind. Although blind people may not be able to see, they can still walk, feel, hear and smell.
4. Begin "Pin the Tail on the Donkey" activity by explaining the rules to the children. (Do not force a hesitant child to wear the blindfold—simply allow them to cover their eyes with their hands or to close their eyes.)

More to do

Play the game "Who Am I." Have one child sit in a chair with a blindfold on or their eyes covered. A second child stands behind the first and gives clues to their identity without saying their name. Have the seated child use their sense of hearing to guess who it is.

—*Margaret Dubaj, Niles, OH*

ABC Braille

5+

Children will learn about and experience braille symbols.

Materials needed

Objects with a pointed end, such as knitting needles or pencils
Construction paper
Newspapers
Crayons or markers

What to do

1. Mark in dots the inverse outline of one or more letters on the upper-half of each child's paper.
2. Give children a brief explanation of braille and how it is "read" by people who are visually impaired. If possible, pass around something printed in braille for children to see and feel.
3. Have the children poke the dots on their papers, using an object with a pointed end. This will give the other side of the paper a raised effect, like braille.
4. Have the children turn their papers over and feel the outline of the letters with their fingers. Then have them write the letters on the lower-half of the paper with crayons.

More to do

Give each child a different letter. After all the children have poked the dots through and turned their papers over, have them exchange papers and use their fingers to identify the new letters. Create simple pictures in braille and see if children can identify them (e.g., outline of a house, sun, tree, car, person).

—*Dana Musch, St. Paul, MN*

Shapes Spectacular

2+

Children will learn to recognize and identify geometric shapes by playing these three different shape games.

Materials needed

Construction paper shapes: circles, squares, triangles, rectangles, etc.
Flannel board
Felt shapes as above
Tape
Boxes for shape storage—one for each shape—labeled with a cutout shape

What to do

Game #1
1.   Give each child a felt shape. Talk about each of the shapes.
2.   Place a square shape on the flannel board while singing "Square-O" (see below). Have the children clap with you for each letter as you spell the shape name.
3.   Have the children with squares come and place their shape on the board. Make sure all the children have a turn.
4.   Repeat the game using different shapes and substituting the new shape names in the song—"Circle-O," "Oval-O," or "Triangle-O," for example.
"Square-O" (to the tune of "Bingo")

> *There was a teacher who had a shape*
> *And square was it's name-o*
> *S-Q-U-A-R-E*
> *S-Q-U-A-R-E*
> *S-Q-U-A-R-E*
> *And square was it's name-o!*

Game #2
1.   Before the children arrive, hide cut-out shapes around the room, some in obvious places and others more hidden.
2.   Sing the "Children Children" song (see below) and have the children hunt for the shapes around the room. Try to make sure each child finds at least one.
3.   Have them bring their shapes back to the circle and place them in boxes labeled with the correct shape.
"Children, Children" (to the tune of "Doggie, Doggie Where's My Bone?")

> *Children, children*
> *Where are my shapes?*
> *Somebody took them from their place.*
> *Guess who? Who could it be?*
> *Please won't you bring them back to me!*

Game#3

1. Play this game after the children are familiar with the various shapes they will be hunting for.
2. Say the following verse and have the children look around the room to find objects which are shaped like a circle. The second verse can be changed to focus on different shapes.

We're going on a shape hunt,
A shape hunt, a shape hunt.
We're going on a shape hunt,
So let's all find this shape.
We're looking for a circle,
A circle, a circle.
We're looking for a circle,
That goes around like this. (draw a big circle in the air)

Related books

My First Look at Shapes by Stephen Oliver
Spot Looks at Shapes by Eric Hill

—Jane Jergensen, Glenpool, OK

Round and Round   2+

Children learn about circles and develop their fine motor skills.

Materials needed

Scissors
Corrugated cardboard
Plain flannel pillowcase
Tape
Sponges or foam rubber packing

What to do

1. Cut cardboard to approximately 15" x 18".
2. Slip cardboard into the flannel pillowcase. Tape the underside so the front is taut.
3. Cut four circles and two oblong shapes from the sponges.
4. Lay board flat on the floor or lean it against a wall.
5. Put the cutouts beside the board.
6. Encourage the children to pick them up and place them on the board.
7. Show how the circles look like wheels when they are placed below the oblong shapes.
8. Say "round" when the circles are being placed.

More to do

Pretend shapes are a train. Ask the children how a train sounds. Serve round pretzels for snack and talk about their shape.

Related books

Round and Round by Tana Hoban
Freight Train by Donald Crews
Truck by Donald Crews

—Peggy Eddy, Johnson City, TN

Shape Awareness

2+

This activity teaches children to recognize basic shapes, builds vocabulary and exercises fine motor skills.

Materials needed

Playdough ingredients (see recipe below)
Shape cookie cutters
Rolling pins or wooden cylinder blocks
Craft sticks
Scissors

What to do

1. Have enough cookie cutters, rollers, craft sticks and scissors so each child will have something to work with. Hang or pin shapes around work area so children can see the shapes they are trying to make.
2. Make playdough. Mix together:

2 cups flour
2 cups water
1 cup salt
2 tbsp. oil
4 tsp. cream of tartar

Cook on medium heat stirring constantly until mixture pulls from sides of pan. Cool on wax paper. Separate dough into four or five balls. Make a hole in each ball. Place 4-6 drops food coloring in each ball and close hole. (Recipe can be doubled or tripled to accomodate your classroom needs.)
3. Give each child a ball of dough. Explain there are color drops inside. Show children how to gently knead the color into the dough. Tell children not to squeeze dough or color will squirt out all over their hands.
4. Demonstrate how to roll the dough flat and press cookie cutter on dough to make shape.
5. Use scissors with dough to cut shapes. Playdough is a good medium to use when learning to cut. Use craft sticks to make shapes in dough.

More to do

Put dough shapes together to make design or picture. Let children experiment with mixing colors using small pieces of dough. Combine yellow dough with blue dough to make green dough. Combine yellow dough with red dough to make orange dough.

Related songs

"Getting to Know Myself" by Hap Palmer
"Movin'" by Hap Palmer

—Terri Garrou, Morgantown, NC

Magnetic Shape Pick-Up

Children will improve their knowledge of shapes—circles, squares, rectangles, triangles, diamonds, ovals, etc.

Materials needed

Magnetic shapes
Magnetic wands
Meat trays

What to do

1. Ahead of time, purchase a large magnetic canvas and cut it into shapes.
2. Give each child a meat tray with shapes on it and a magnetic wand.
3. Talk about the different shapes and what they are called.
4. Show the children how they can pick up the shapes using the magnetic wand.
5. Tell them that you are going to name a shape and that they should pick up that shape with their magnetic wands.
6. Vary the task by asking them to pick up a certain number of shapes or to pick up all of one shape and count how many they have.

More to do

Purchase the magnetic canvas in different colors. Then have the children find a shape of a specific color (e.g., a red circle, a blue square). Cut big and little shapes out of the canvas and work on sizes.

—Rebecca Mattis, Ellicott City, MD

Passing the Shape

Here is a combination of a familiar song and game with a new shape! The children will learn to recognize shapes as they sing and play.

Materials needed

Small shapes made from cardboard or posterboard, laminated or covered with clear contact paper for durability, or ready-made plastic shapes: circle, square, triangle, rectangle

What to do

1. Join the children sitting in a circle on the floor. Keep the shapes hidden in your lap. Teach the children the following song, sung to the tune of "Row, Row, Row Your Boat."

    Pass, pass, pass the shape,
    Is the game we play.
    When this little song is through,
    The shape's name we will say.

2. Explain that once the children take the shape, they must pass it to the next person.
3. Begin the song, and at the same time, hold up one shape and give it to the child next to you. This child passes it to the next and so on around the circle, until the song is sung.

4. The child holding the shape when the song stops says the name of the shape and then places it in the center of the circle.

5. Repeat steps three and four with a new shape. Vary the tempo of the song and the direction in which you pass the shape so that different children get to name the shape.

6. Once all shapes are in the center of the circle, choose a child to pick a shape and begin passing it for each verse of the song. Play the game until all the children have had a chance to name a shape.

More to do

Once children have mastered basic shapes, add others, such as diamonds, ovals, hearts or stars. Depending on the ages of the children, provide either pre-cut construction paper shapes or cardboard shapes to trace on construction paper and cut out. The children use these shapes to form a picture or design on drawing paper, gluing each shape in place.

—Carol G. Taylor, Pineville, LA

Triangle Angel

3+

The children will learn about triangles while enjoying this lovely activity.

Materials needed

White construction paper
Aquarium filter floss
White yarn or gold thread
4" gold braid per child
Glitter
Glue
Scissors
Crayons

What to do

1. Cut out triangles and circles. Each child will need two triangles with 4,75" sides and a 2.75" bottom, one triangle with 7.5" sides and a 6" bottom and 6"-8" lengths of yarn or thread. Help those children who need it.

2. Assemble into angels by gluing top points of small triangles in back of large triangle so they overlap.

3. Glue circle on front of large triangle for head.

4. Use crayons to add facial features.

5. Glue small amount of filter floss on head for angel hair.

6. Glue gold braid around head to form halo.

7. Glue glitter on body and wings.

8. Attach yarn or gold thread to use as a hanger.

More to do

Use for holiday bulletin board or as Christmas tree decoration.

Related books

The Littlest Angel by Charles Tazewell

—Barbara Corbin, Cincinnati, OH

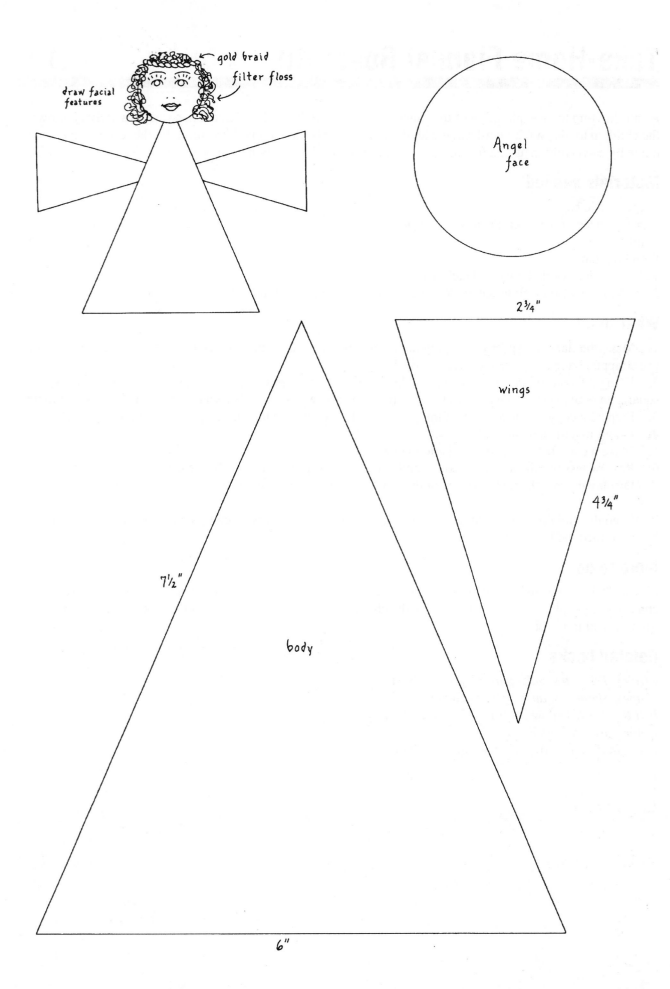

draw facial features

gold braid
filter floss

Angel face

2¾"

wings

4¾"

7½"

body

6"

Take-Home Flannel Board Kit

3+

As a follow-up to an exploration of the concepts of shape, color and placement in space, this activity allows the children to play a felt board game with their parents. The take-home kit is made by the teacher and taken home by each child in turn; a fun and easy way to involve the family in school activities.

Materials needed

Large plastic bag
8" x 10" piece of heavy cardboard
Stapler
Strapping tape
12" x 12" piece of dark blue or black flannel or felt
2" x 2" pieces of flannel: green, yellow, purple, orange, white, red, blue, brown and pink

What to do

1. Make the flannel board by wrapping the cardboard with dark blue or black flannel. Staple the edges, and use strapping tape to secure the edges on the back.
2. Using the colorful pieces of flannel, make the following shapes: a green tree, a yellow square, a purple square, an orange circle, a white circle, a red triangle, a blue triangle, a brown rectangle and a pink rectangle.
3. Prepare a copy of a letter to the family to be enclosed with the take-home kit (see sample letter below).
4. Put all materials in large plastic bag.
5. Make a class list and post it on bulletin board.
6. Review lessons about shapes, colors and placement in space with the children in class.
7. Display the take-home kit to the children and demonstrate how they can use it at home with their families.
8. Send the kit home with a different child each day and check off each child's name on the list when they have returned the kit to school.

More to do

Play a Chair Game. Ask a child to put a particular color and shape in a specific place in proximity to the chair. For example, put the green circle on the chair; put the orange rectangle under the chair; put the purple triangle next to the chair.

Related books

Circles, Triangles and Squares by Tana Hoban
Shapes, Shapes, Shapes by Tana Hoban
Is It Red? Is It Yellow? Is It Blue? by Tana Hoban
Color Farm by Lois Ehlert
Bears in the Night by Stan and Jan Berenstain

Sample Letter to Families

Dear Families,

Here is a flannel board game for you to play with your child. This game focuses on the concepts of color, shape and placement in space (on, over, under, near, etc.). When you read the poem to your child, please watch as your child finds the appropriate colored shape and puts it in the appropriate place on the flannel board. After each stanza, have your child remove the previous shape to make room for the next shape. The green tree should be the only shape that remains on the board. Otherwise, there will be too many shapes on the board, making it confusing for your child.

I hope that you have fun using this game together tonight. Please make sure that your child carefully places all of the shapes and the flannel board back into the plastic bag. Please return the kit to school tomorrow so that another child may borrow it. Thank you.

Sincerely yours,

Look here, look here,
What do you see?
I see a brown rectangle,
Next to the tree.
Look here, look here,
What do you see?
I see a yellow square,
Under the tree.

Look here, look here,
What do you see?
I see a white circle,
In front of the tree.
Look here, look here,
What do you see?
I see a purple square,
Above the tree.

Look here, look here,
What do you see?
I see a blue triangle,
At the top of the tree.
Look here, look here,
What do you see?
I see a red triangle,
Behind the tree.

Look here, look here,
What do you see?
I see an orange circle,
Beside the tree.
Look here, look here,
What do you see?
I see a pink rectangle,
At the bottom of the tree.

—Marjorie Debowy, Moriches, NY

Shape Pets

3+

The children practice identifying various shapes by name and use them to construct a shape pet.

Materials needed

Construction paper—15-20 sheets
1/4 yard felt
Scissors
Flannel board
Laminate material
Glue
Markers

What to do

1. Cut a circle, rectangle, square, triangle, half-circle, diamond and oval from felt.
2. Construct sample shape pets and mount to construction paper. Use markers to add features. Laminate the finished product.
3. Using flannel board and felt shapes, introduce the name of each shape. Have the children repeat the shape names. Ask the children if everything has a shape?
4. Show the class the pet pictures you have made. Ask the children to name the pets.
5. Show the pictures again one at a time. Ask the children identify and point to shapes that were used to create the pet picture.

More to do

Before laminating pictures, attach an envelope to the back of shape pets picture. Place shape pieces made from felt, laminated construction paper or posterboard in the envelope that match the shapes used to make the picture. Have the children match the shapes in the envelope to the shapes in the picture. Provide construction paper shapes or stencils, markers and scissors for children to make their own shape pets.

Related books

Have You Seen My Cat? by Eric Carle
Where's Spot by Eric Hill

—*Marzee Woodward, Murfreesboro, TN*

Triangle Size Seriation

3+

This learning activity teaches the math terms large, medium and small and promotes reading readiness by teaching the children to work from left to right.

Materials needed

Two colors of construction paper
A large, medium and small triangle shape
Scissors
Crayons
Glue

What to do

1. Trace three triangles onto contruction paper from smallest to largest. Cut out the same sized triangles from a different color of construction paper.
2. Pass out the papers with the traced triangles to the children.
3. Have the children start at the left side and trace the "large" triangle with their pointer finger. Next have them trace the medium and small triangle.
4. Pass out the crayons and have the children trace each triangle with a crayon.
5. Pass out the large sized triangle cutout and have the children match it to the one on their paper. Have them glue it in place. Do the same for the medium and small triangles.

More to do

Trace the second set of triangles and have the children cut these out themselves. Have the children arrange the triangles by size. Repeat this activity throughout the year.

—Laura G. Symonds, Belmont, CA

Sing a Song of Shapes

4+

Through this activity, children will review shape names while singing a song.

Materials needed

Posterboard or tagboard shapes (laminated construction paper shapes work well too)

What to do

1. Make at least one shape for each child. Use different sizes, colors and different kinds of triangles or rectangles as you can.
2. Have children seated in circle. Hand out shapes.
3. Talk about what children notice: colors, names of shapes, sizes, etc.
4. Sing the following to the tune of "Where is Thumbkin?"
    Where are the circles?
    Where are the circles?
The children who are holding circles stand and respond:
    Here we are!
    Here we are!
Teacher:
    How are you today circles?
Children:
    Very well, we thank you.
Teacher:
    Sit back down.
    Sit back down.
5. Continue going through all the shapes. Last verse: "Where are all the shapes?" All children stand and sing.

More to do

Once children are comfortable with recognizing and naming the shapes, make the questions more of a challenge by calling for specific colors as well: "Where is the yellow square?" When the song is finished, sort by shape. When children can handle the challenge, sort by size/color/shape.

Related book

Shapes and Things by Tana Hoban

—Ruth Cohenson, Pleasantville, NJ

There Was a Little Mouse

4+

The children will enjoy helping the little mouse match his keys to the appropriate doors in this unusual shape identification game.

Materials needed

1 large piece of posterboard or oak tag, white or colored
1 sheet colored construction paper
1 sheet white construction paper
Clear contact paper
Felt marker
Velcro tape

What to do

1. Draw a large house on the piece of posterboard. Make two rows of rectangluar shaped doors on the house, four upstairs and four downstairs. Draw one shape on each door. For example, circle, diamond, heart, triangle, square, rectangle, bell or star.

2. Use the colored construction paper to make eight keys. On each key, draw one of the eight shapes indicated on the house. Laminate or cover the keys with clear contact paper for durability. Put a piece of velcro on the back of each key and on the front of each door.

3. Draw, cut out, color and laminate a mouse and cape using the white construction paper. Put a piece of velcro on the back of the cape and on the front of mouse.

4. Using the props that you have already made, tell this story:

There was a little mouse who lived in a house.
There were lots of doors. I think maybe seven or more.
Each door had a key because that is how the mouse thought it should be.
Each key had a shape and he kept them under his cape.
He loved to play a matching game. Can you do the same?

5. Place all the keys in front of the children and help them name the shape on each key. Then remove the keys and hide one under the mouse's cape. Call on one child to come find the key and match it to the door which has the same shape. Continue until all the shapes are matched. If you need to do more to include every child, call on them to remove a certain shape key.

6. After the children have become accustomed to playing the game, you can allow them to play it independently or in small groups.

—*Marzee Woodward, Murfreesboro, TN*

House Sounds

3+

Children identify different sounds and match them with picture cards to develop auditory memory and sequencing skills.

Materials needed

Tape recorder
Blank cassette tape
6 index cards
Colored pencils
Sand paper
Glue
Scissors
Magnets
Flannel board or magnetic board

What to do

1.   Record common house sounds such as running water, dishes being put away, a door closing, a doorbell or telephone ringing, a garbage disposal, popcorn popping, a car engine starting, hammering or sawing.
2.   Using index cards and colored pencils, draw a simple picture to match each sound heard on the tape.
3.   If you will use this as a flannel board activity, cut the sand paper into 1" x 3" pieces and attach to the back of the cards. Cut 3" pieces of magnetic tape if you are going to use the activity along with a magnetic board.
4.   This works best if done at circle time. Tell the children that they need to listen very carefully, and play the tape.
5.   After each sound is played, stop the tape and let the children talk about what they heard. "Where else can that sound be heard?"
6.   After the sequence of sounds is heard, rewind the tape and play the sounds three at a time. Stop the tape and have the children place the picture cards on the flannel board in the order they think they were heard.
7.   Replay the tape to see if the order of the picture cards matches the order of the sounds heard.

More to do

Encourage the children to go around the room and find things that make a distinct sound. Each week have a couple of children make another tape of sounds. Then they can share the finished tape with their classmates.

—Cory McIntyre, Crystal Lake, IL

Hello Game

Children will learn to recognize voices or other sounds.

Materials needed

Chair
Blindfold

What to do

1. Seat the children in a large semi-circle.
2. Place the chair inside the semi-circle, facing away from the group.
3. Explain to the group that you will have one person sit in the chair and wear the blindfold.
4. Explain that while the child is wearing the blindfold, you will point to another child who will walk up, stand behind the child wearing the blindfold and say "Hello."
5. The blindfolded child then gets three chances to guess who is saying "Hello."
6. Choose other children to sit blindfolded in the chair.
7. Encourage the children to change their voices and try to disguise themselves.

More to do

Children or teachers could make a tape of noises in the classroom and then ask others to guess what they are.

—Melissa Browning, West Allis, WI

Sound Lotto

Children learn to identify different sounds and match them with a photo.

Materials needed

Camera
Tape recorder
Posterboard
Blank tape
Clear contact paper or laminating machine

What to do

1. Talk about listening and sounds as part of a unit on the five senses.
2. Take a walk around class or school or outside, listening for different sounds.
3. Tape familiar sounds like water running, a musical instrument playing, voices talking or singing, music, and so on.
4. Take a photograph of everything recorded.
5. Develop the film and get a two sets of prints.
6. Make a lotto board using photos.
7. Glue the extra photos on cards and cover everything with clear contact paper (or laminate).
8. Place lotto board and tape recorder in listening area.
9. Children listen to sounds and match picture on cards to picture on lotto board.

More to do

Children can tape a sound at home (with parents' help) and bring it in to share with the class. At nap time, listen to tapes of nature or water sounds.

—Audrey Kanoff, Bethlehem, PA

Now Hear This!

3+

Children have fun while using their visual and auditory skills.

Materials needed

Paper of various sizes
Tape, stapler or glue
Crayons, markers, collage materials (optional)

What to do

1. Make a megaphone by rolling a piece of paper into a funnel shape and taping the edge down.
2. Leave it on the table with paper and tape. Have the children make their own, following your example.

More to do

Suggest making animal sounds, giant sounds, vehicle sounds. Experiment with making the opening wider or narrower. Which way can you hear better? Which way makes a louder sound?

Related books

Polar Bear, Polar Bear, What Do You Hear? by Bill Martin, Jr.
David's Father by Bob Munsch

—Wendy Soderlund, Farmington, MO

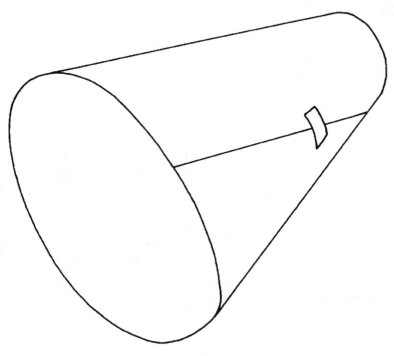

Wood Xylophone

Children explore sounds made by different size logs.

Materials needed

Wood xylophone components:
6-8 small logs with bark intact, each approximately 16" long. Each log must have a different circumference
2 pieces of foam approximately 28" long, 4" wide and 3" high
2 wooden drumsticks, mallets or dowels

What to do

1. Assemble the components on a table.
2. Demonstrate how to place the two pieces of foam parallel to each other with about 10" between them.
3. Demonstrate how to place the logs so a piece of foam supports each end. Logs should not be touching.
4. Demonstrate how to hit logs with the drumstick or mallet to create a sound.
5. Encourage children to experiment with the wood xylophone. What will happen if they rearrange the logs? What if they change the way they hit the logs?

More to do

Have a metal xylophone available. What do the children notice? How are they the same? How are they different? Fill glass bottles with different amounts of colored water and create a water xylophone. Compare and contrast it to the wood xylophone.

Related books

I See a Song by Eric Carle and Thomas Y. Crowell
Listen to That by H. Klurfmeyer
Max the Music Maker by Miriam Stretcher and Alice Kendall

—*Jan Clark, Livonia, MI*

Spring Mud Painting

3+

Playing in mud is fun! This activity brings the fun and creative experience indoors.

Materials needed

Pre-sifted dirt or potting soil
Water
Empty ice cream pails or large containers for mixing mud
Large spoons for mixing, measuring cups and spoons
Newspaper
Finger paint paper or freezer paper
Aprons or paint smocks

What to do

1.   Cover the work surface and have children put on paint smocks or aprons. Divide them into small groups. Supply each group with a spoon, pail with dirt, and measuring cup with water. Give each child a sheet of paper.
2.   Have each group work together to mix their own mud, and have the children finger paint with it. Let their mud art dry completely and display.
3.   Allow time for the children to share their feelings and observations about the mud paintings. Everyone who participated can help clean up.

More to do

Do the entire activity outdoors, and allow the children to play more extensively with the mud. Measure the amounts of dirt and water used and write out a mud "recipe." Use utensils instead of fingers to make a painting. This may be helpful for those who do not wish to put their hands in the mud.

Related song

"Mud, Mud, Mud Is Fun" (to the tune of "Row, Row, Row Your Boat")

> *Mud, mud, mud is fun*
> *Watch us stir it up*
> *Round and round and round and round*
> *Mud is fun to make.*
> *Mud, mud, mud is fun*
> *Listen to it squish*
> *Through our fingers, round our toes*
> *Squish is how it goes.*

Related books

The Mud Pony by Caron Lee Cohen
Mud Puddle by Robert N. Munsch

—*Mary Rozum Anderson, Vermillion, SD*

Lilacs

After experiencing real lilacs, the children will have the opportunity to create some of their own. This is a good craft activity to complement a unit on spring.

Materials needed

A vase of lilacs
Purple tissue paper cut in 2" squares
Glue
9" x 12" white or manila paper
Green markers, or green stems and leaves cut from construction paper

What to do

1.   Bring some lavender lilacs into the classroom. Show the children the flowers and discuss their name, color and shape. Discuss how bunches of them cling to the same branch. Notice the fragrance. Talk about the season in which they bloom.
2.   Use the green marker to draw the stems on the white paper, or give each of the children a certain number of precut green stems to glue onto their papers.
3.   Have the children crush the tissue paper squares and glue them to the paper to resemble bunches of lilacs.
4.   Add construction paper leaves, or draw them on with markers.

More to do

Using finger paints, make thumb prints for the lilac petals instead of tissue paper. Forsythias can be made by using yellow tissue paper.

—Jyoti Joshi, Framingham, MA

Meet the Spring

The children will explore the changes that take place in nature during the spring and practice choosing words that describe both these changes and their feelings about them.

Materials needed

Polaroid or other camera
Posterboard or construction paper
Yarn or string
Paper and crayons
Clear contact paper (optional)

What to do

1.   Take photos of nature (e.g., trees, bushes, grass, nesting sights, sprouting bulbs, tips of evergreens, mud puddles) around your school building. Take one photo for each child in your class.
2.   Mount each photo on construction paper or poster board and cover with clear contact paper if you plan to reuse it.
3.   Make each child in the class a photo necklace by punching a hole in the top of a the mounted picture and threading through some string or yarn.

4. Tell the children that just as we have photos of ourselves to see how we grow and change, we now have some photos of nature's family around us. Ask each child to describe what he sees in their picture. Add names to what the children describe (e.g., magnolia, tulip, maple leaf).

5. Take the children outside. Tell them that they should look for the "nature friends" in their pictures and that when they find one they should take time to "meet" it (i.e., take a moment to see, hear and touch with care).

6. Encourage each child or team of children to find the nature object that matches the one in the picture on their necklaces. As the children discover the objects, ask them to describe what they see and feel.

7. In the classroom, collect the photos (make sure each child's name is on the back) and have the children draw pictures of their nature friends.

8. A week later, return the photo necklaces to the children and have them go back outside and find their nature friends. Ask them to look closely and describe what has changed and what has stayed the same.

—Victoria Orlando, Somerville, NJ

Spring Cleaning

3+

The children will participate in the "spring cleaning" of their classroom.

Materials needed

Housekeeping area

Cleaning supplies: rags, washcloths, old towels, spray bottles, empty bottles, water, brooms, mops, feather duster

What to do

1. Set up your dramatic play center as a housekeeping area with a stove, a sink, a refrigerator, table and chairs.

2. Put out the cleaning supplies listed above.

3. Begin to clean in the housekeeping area. Encourage the children to join you and allow them to clean windows, sweep and mop floors, wipe and dust shelves, etc. This could expand to cleaning the entire room.

4. Your room is suddenly spic and span!

More to do

Children could also clean up for visitors, an important holiday, or a special occasion. Clean up outdoors—rake, sweep and pick up trash to help take care of the environment.

Related song

"This Is the Way We Clean" (sung to "Here We Go Round the Mulberry Bush")

> *This is the way we clean our room,*
> *Clean our room, clean our room,*
> *This is the way we clean our room,*
> *Until it's spic and span!*
> *This is the way we sweep our floors, etc.*

—Renee Zuniga, San Antonio, TX

Flower Colors Match Up

Using picture cards, children develop their cognitive color skills.

Materials needed

Nursery catalogues
Posterboard
Markers
Ruler
Clear contact paper
Scissors
White glue
Recloseable bag

What to do

1. Cut out 3" squares of different pictures of flowers.
2. Cut posterboard into 3" squares.
3. Glue flower pictures to posterboard squares and let dry.
4. Cut more posterboard into 2-1/2" x 5" pieces.
5. Print "RED" with a red marker on one card, "BLUE" with blue on a second, "YELLOW" in dark yellow on a third, and so on.
6. Cover front and back of all pieces with clear contact paper. Use a recloseable bag to store the game.
7. Invite the children to compare the different colored flower cards to one another.
8. Encourage them to match all the blue flower cards to the "BLUE" card, yellow flower cards to the "YELLOW" card, etc.

More to do

This is a good manipulative table top game to set out during a week on spring, gardens or flowers. Encourage children to draw or paint a picture of what their garden might look like.

Related books

Little Blue and Little Yellow by Leo Lionni

—Cory McIntyre, Crystal Lake, IL

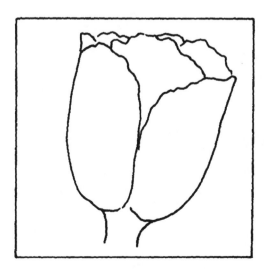

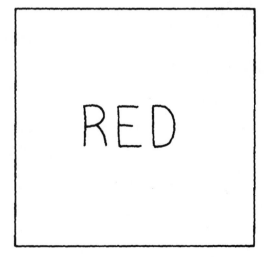

Spring Is Here!

Through creative movement, the children will explore what happens during the spring.

Materials needed

Tambourine
Ribbons: pink, black, grey, blue and yellow (at least one ribbon for each child)

What to do

1. Talk to children about what happens to flowers in the spring. Discuss what flowers and other plants need in order to grow.
2. Assign each child a dramatic role (i.e., flower, sun, thunder, lightning, or rain) and give him or her an appropriate ribbon: pink for flowers, black for thunder, grey for lightening, blue for rain, and yellow for sun.
3. Tell a story about a flower seed and how it began to grow. Use the tambourine to make the sounds of thunder and rain, and encourage the children to move around freely and dramatically as they act out their roles.

More to do

Go for a nature walk. Have children narrate their own stories about an animal or plant and how it is affected by the spring.

Related book

The Carrot Seed by Ruth Krauss

—*Debbie Bubelis, Richmond Hill, Ontario, Canada*

Pick an Apple—To Learn Your Name 2+

This activity teaches children to recognize their names.

Materials needed

Green, brown and red posterboard
Small box, basket, pail or crate
Contact paper or laminating film
Masking tape

What to do

1. Cut out a green tree-top and brown trunk from the posterboard. Cut a red apple for each child. Make sure the tree top is big enough to place an apple for each child. Laminate the tree and apples.
2. Write a child's name on each apple.
3. Place the tree on a wall or door low enough for children to reach.
4. Put apples on the tree with masking tape rolled sticky side out.
5. Call a child's name and let the child pick his name apple and put it in the container.

More to do

This could be used for surnames, numbers, letters of the alphabet, etc.

—Sheila Wood, Arlington, TX

Teddy Bear Picnic 2+

The children will develop social interaction skills as they participate in a group picnic activity.

Materials needed

Large blanket
Teddy bears from home
Teddy Bears Picnic by Renate Kozikowski

What to do

1. Read *The Teddy Bear's Picnic*. Discuss what people do and take on a picnic.
2. Find a shady spot outside.
3. Encourage the children to sit on the blanket with their teddy bears to have a snack.

More to do

Make teddy bear sandwiches with butter and honey. Make and decorate a sun visor to wear on the picnic.

—Sandra Acuna, San Antonio, TX

Photo/Name Match-Up Game

3+

The memory strengthening activity, teaches the children name/letter recognition, language development and how to take turns.

Materials needed

A snapshot of each child
Cardboard
Clear contact paper or laminating materials
Markers

What to do

1.   Make a card with each child's picture backed by cardboard of the same size. The cardboard may be decorated with construction paper or left plain as long as all of the backs look the same.
2.   Make a deck of cards using the name of each child corresponding with the photo cards. (Perhaps some children could write their own names.) The backs of these cards should also remain plain or be decorated the same way.
3.   Laminate both sets of cards.
4.   Before playing this game, make sure the children have had some exposure to their written names.
5.   Invite a group of 2-6 children to play the Photo/Name Match-up Game.
6.   Place all of the photo cards face down in rows and columns on the table.
7.   Place the name cards in a deck, face down where everyone can reach them.
8.   Each player, in turn, picks a name card from the deck (they may need help from the others to read the name) and then turns over a photo card, trying to match the name card. The first few tries will be difficult, but as the game goes on, the children will use their memories to match names to photos.
9.   Try not to emphasize who "wins" the game, rather give praise to each child for any match made or even for reading the names or naming the photos!!

More to do

This game can also be played with the photos facing up to make it easier for beginners or younger children. Switch the photo cards to the deck and the name cards to table. You may also want to add last names to the deck for advanced children.

—*Elaine Bonanno, Lynn, MA*

The Name Game

3+

Watch out! The children will want to do this activity over and over.

Materials needed

None needed

What to do

1.   Explain to the children that they should be proud of their names, and that you are going to give them many opportunities to celebrate their names.
2.   Have each child cheer their name.
3.   Have each child say their name while they are giggling.

4. Have each child wiggle and say their name.
5. Have each child growl their name.
6. Have each child howl their name.
7. Have each child say their name very slowly and stretch it out.
8. Have each child chant their name five times.
9. Have each child pant their name.
10. Have each child sing their name.
11. Have each child clap their name.
12. Have each child snap their name.
13. Last, have each child yell out their name.

More to do

Children can do all these things together or one at a time. Each child may come up to the front and sing their name. Then the rest of the children will echo the way she sang it. They may dance out their name also.

—Linda Wishney, Chicago, IL

Class Quilt   3+

Children will take part in making a class quilt.

Materials needed

Cotton squares (approximately 12" x 12")
Tempera paint in bright colors
Paintbrushes
Needles and thread

What to do

1. Cut out the squares, making one for each child in the class.
2. Put out the paint and give each child a square.
3. Tell the children to paint their squares however they like, then hang them to dry.
4. Sew the squares together using large X stitches and hang the quilt on the wall or bulletin board for all to enjoy.

More to do

Bring in a real quilt for children to examine. Have someone demonstrate how a real quilt is made.

Related book

The Quilt Story by Tomie De Paola

—Rachel Stickfort, Newark, DE

Unpack Your Bag 3+

This activity is designed to make a new member of the class feel welcome in the classroom and to help the other children learn more about the new child.

Materials needed

One small canvas bag or suitcase
Objects such as child's favorite book, toy or game; photographs, maps, etc.

What to do

1. Label bag, "All About Me".
2. Prepare a list of objects suggested by child or parent to be put in the bag. Some ideas:
   Favorite book
   Favorite toy or game
   Photographs
   Maps
3. As you remove each item, the teacher or child can describe the item and tell about its importance.

More to do

The activity could be carried out by all children in the classroom as a "Special Person of the Week" activity.

—*Karen W. Ponder, Raleigh, NC*

My Name 3+

Children will learn to recognize their own name when it is printed. Over time they will also recognize individual letters in their name.

Materials needed

Construction paper, two different colors
Glue or paste
Paper plate to put glue or paste on
Utensils to spread glue or paste with, e.g., brushes, plastic knives or spoons, wooden ice cream spoons
Scrap paper
Marker
Wipes for clean up, optional

What to do

1. Trace and cut out letters to spell out each child's name (using upper case for first letter only). Use all one color for letters. (Tip: To keep each child's letters separate I put them in small plastic bags and mark them.)
2. Write child's name on the scrap paper with marker exactly the way it will look (first letter uppercase, others lowercase).
3. With the cut out letters for his name on the table, help each child find the first letter of his name by matching it to what you wrote.
4. Apply glue or paste and stick letter to piece of construction paper (different color than letters).
5. Repeat steps 2 and 3 for each letter of child's name.
6. Allow child to clean up sticky hands if necessary.

7. Display (at day care, school or home) child's name picture and help him to identify it.

More to do

Cut construction paper that the name is glued to in shapes. Examples: school bus, car, pumpkin, caterpillar, etc. Attach a photo of child to his name picture. Use another name (Mom, Dad, etc.) or word (happy, sad, stop, ho!ho!ho!). Decorate with ribbon, lace, glitter, buttons, macaroni shapes, etc. They can be given as gift for Valentines Day, Mother's Day, Christmas, etc.Use a variety of mediums such as crayons, paint, chalk, markers, stickers, etc. to decorate and personalize either the letters or background paper. Use felt or dough instead of construction paper to form the letters.

Related books

Use any book and insert names of children in the class in place of names in the story.

Related songs

Name clapping: Clap child's name out in syllables. Use rhythm sticks, xylophone, etc.
"Head, Shoulders, Knee and Toes"
"Everything Grows" by Raffi

—Susan Rinas, Parma, OH

Circle Time Interviews

4+

Children learn basic safety information (address and telephone number), increase their self-esteem and recognize their names in print.

Materials needed

Individual posterboard cards
Felt pen

What to do

1. Print each child's name on one side of a card, and their address and telephone number on the other.
2. Have the children pretend one of the children is going to be interviewed on television. You will ask him questions and the child will give the answers.
3. Choose a child to come in front of the group and begin the "show" with a standard introduction, such as "Today we have a special person here. Your name sir/miss is?" (It helps to make sure you choose someone you know likes to talk in front of a group the first few times you use this activity.)
4. Begin with "Where do you live?" (whisper answer from back of the card if the child is not sure of address). "Who lives in your house with you?" "Do you have any pets?" "Do you have a favorite toy?" If a friend wants to call you on the phone to come and play, what number would he/she call? (Child may want you to whisper numbers or read the numbers from the card at first).
5. Thank the child for the interview. Choose one child each day to be interviewed as a part of your regular circle time routine.

More to do

Make a house out of shapes or let children draw a picture of their house. Then have them tell you where they live and you write it at the bottom of the picture. After the class is comfortable with the interview process, ask them to look at the name on the card to see whose turn it is. When the theme of the interview questions is routine, have another child be the interviewer.

Related book

In A People House by Dr. Seuss

—Frances E. Wolff, Setauket, NY

Our Big Class Family

4+

This bulletin board display is a wonderful way to start your year, or to follow-up a study of families or your community. Let the children help as much as possible.

Materials needed

Bulletin board, background paper and border
Colored construction paper
Recent photograph of each child (ask the parents for help with this)
Scissors
Markers and crayons

What to do

1. Cover your bulletin board with light background paper and an appropriate border. Make a red cut-out figure of the school and post it in the center. Make an opening door by cutting around 3 sides of the door, but leave the fourth side attached to act as a hinge. Put your picture behind the door. If your class has more than one teacher or assistants, put their pictures behind other doors or windows (hinge as for doors).
2. Make a construction paper house for each child. Cut two houses at a time by folding the paper in half. Write each child's name, address, and telephone number on her house. Have the children cut out and decorate the houses with crayons as abilities allow. Make a hinged door and two windows in each house and post the child's picture behind one.
3. Draw streets leading from the school, and arrange the houses along them.
4. Make cut-outs of different family members, (mother, father, sister, brother, baby, cat, dog) which the children can color, or ask the children to draw and make cutouts of family members. Write the correct names on the cutouts and put them in the yards of the houses.
5. Add construction paper cutouts of trees, flowers, cars, trucks, a school bus and stop signs. Draw in swing sets, tricycles, etc. Utilize the children's help and ideas for adding details.

More to do

The children will probably become interested in maps. Help them create a map of the playground—with a treasure! Create a graph that shows how many of the children's families live in houses, apartments, town houses and mobile homes.

Related song

"The Finger Family" (to the tune of "Where Is Thumbkin?")

Mommy, pointer
Sister, pinkie
Daddy, tall man
Baby, thumbkin
Brother, ringman

—*Patricia Cawthorne, Lynchburg, VA*

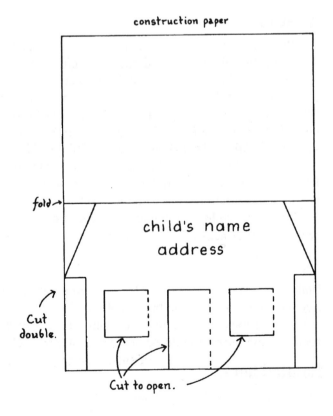

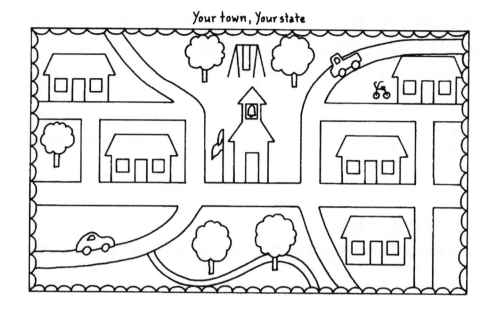

Your town, Your state

Paper Doll Examples

Daddy

Mom

Billy

Me

Sue

Puff

Spot

Children may draw their family members.

Name License Plates

4+

This activity uses fine motor control and teaches the children to spell their names.

Materials needed

License plate outlines (works best on 8 1/2 x 14 " paper)
3 x 5 cards
Glue
Crayons

What to do

1. Write an upper case letter of the alphabet on each of the 3 x 5 cards. Make sure you have enough letters to spell out the names of each child in your class. Outline the letters thickly with glue and let them dry thoroughly.

2. Have each child find the letters of their name on the 3 x 5 cards. Ask them to line these up to spell their name.

3. Have the child lay the license plate outline sheet over the letters.

4. Using the side of the crayon, have the child rub over the letters to "print" the letters of their name on the license plate.

More to do

Walk through a parking lot and look for different state license plates and identify the letters and numbers.

—Rachel Stickfort, Newark, DE

Kangaroo Buddies

4+

Children learn the importance of cooperation and improve their jumping.

Materials needed

Kangaroo feet, two pairs for each team (see attached pattern)
Tape
Chalk or flags to mark starting line
Whistle

What to do

1. Cut out and laminate kangaroo feet. Mark off a starting line.

2. Gather all the children together in one large standing circle.

3. Discuss any previous knowledge of kangaroos: what they look like, where they live and how they move.

4. Have the children choose a "kangaroo buddy." Explain to them that the activity they are about to enjoy involves helping each other. They won't be able to complete the activity unless they help each other.

5. Have the children move to one end of the playground or room.

6. Give each team two pairs of kangaroo feet. Let them examine and discuss different ways they can be used.

7. Explain the rules of the activity. The teams must decide which of them will be the kangaroo first and which one will be the buddy. Explain to them that they will switch jobs, so everyone will get a chance to be a kangaroo.

8. Have the kangaroos stand on the starting line. Have the buddies place two of the kangaroo feet in front of their partner. The kangaroo then jumps onto the feet. The buddy then places the second pair of feet in front of her partner. They are to continue this pattern until the teacher blows the whistle, and the team switches jobs.

9. If the children wish, they may try to complete the activity without a buddy. This will reinforce the necessity of cooperation.

More to do

Ask the children to count the number of times they jumped before the whistle was blown. Ask the children who tried it both ways if it was easier with or without a buddy.

Related books

My Grandma Lived in Gooligulch by Graeme Base *Animal Jumpers* by Kenneth Lilly
Is Your Mama a Llama? by Deborah Gauarino

—Angelica Lewis, Wichita, KS

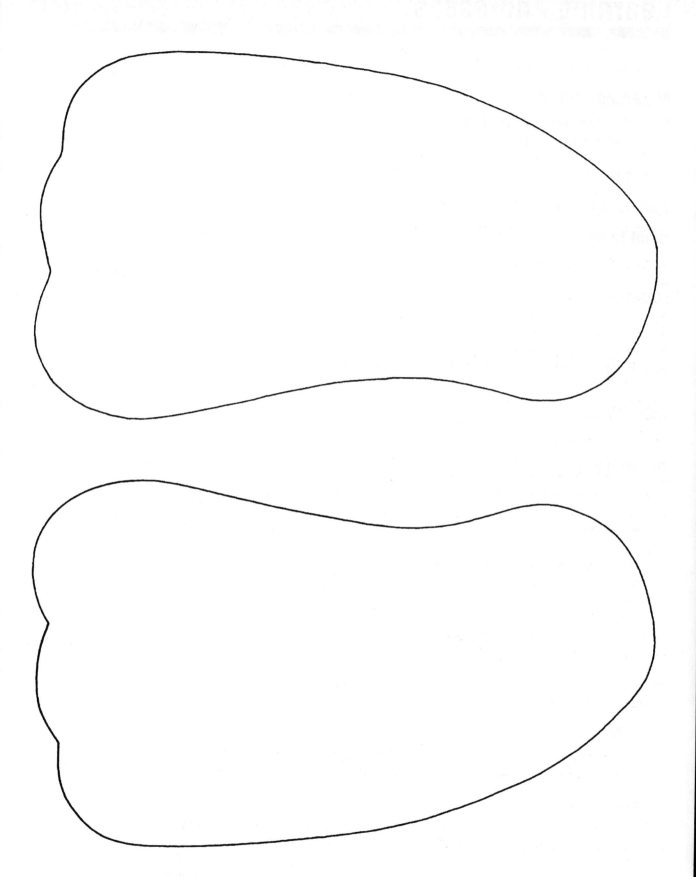

Learning Addresses

4+

The children will learn to memorize home address and to understand the function of a post office.

Materials needed

12" x 18" white paper (one per child)
6" x 4" (approximately) paper (one per child)
Markers
Writing paper
Letter-sized envelopes
The Post Office Book

What to do

1. Write each child's address on large white paper "envelope." Display these envelopes.
2. Read *The Post Office Book*. Talk with the children about the book. Arrange for a tour of a local post office.
3. Have children "write" letters to a family member. Address envelopes and insert letters.
4. Tour post office. Let each child buy a stamp to mail letter.
5. Use 6" x 4" paper to make "stamps" for the large envelopes on display in classroom. Children can design their stamp after having opportunities to see a variety of stamps. Children take these home as they learn their address.

More to do

Start a stamp collection at school. Each child can bring in a stamp from home.

Related book

The Post Office Book by Gail Gibbons

—Brenda McAbee Grant, Farmville, VA

Watermelon

3+

Watermelon is often a favorite summer food. This activity allows the children a sensory experience of watermelon before they make their own—with real seeds!

Materials needed

Fresh watermelon
Large paper plates—one per child
Red and green paint, markers or crayons
Paintbrushes
Glue

What to do

1. Cut watermelon in half and talk with the children about the colors, shape, smell, etc. Serve the watermelon for snack. How does it taste? Ask if anyone has ever seen a watermelon vine?
2. As children eat their pieces of watermelon, have them save the seeds to dry.
3. Color or paint the outside border of the plate green to make the rind and the inside red to make the fruit. Let dry completely.
4. Fold the paper plate in half.
5. Glue the saved watermelon seeds onto the red portion of the plate.
6. Have children count the number of seeds on their watermelons.

—Jyoti Joshi, Framingham, MA

Pack Your Bags

3+

The children will use dramatic play to explore the materials needed for a camping trip.

Materials needed

Large cardboard box or large backpack
Flashlights
Sleeping bags
Coats, hats, mittens
Pots and pans
Any gear pertaining to camping

What to do

1. Assemble the materials on the floor during circle time.
2. Teach the children the "We Love Camping" song (to the tune of "London Bridges"):

We will pack our sleeping bags,
sleeping bags,
sleeping bags.
We will pack our sleeping bags.
We love camping!
We will pack our warmest clothes,
warmest clothes,
warmest clothes.
We will pack our warmest clothes.
We love camping!

3. As you sing the camping song, have one child pack the item named in the verse.
4. Continue to add verses and pack your gear until all of the children have had a turn.

More to do

Set up a real tent in your classroom and let the children unpack the items for play. Build a pretend campfire out of paper rolled to look like logs. Make flames out of crepe or tissue paper and make a fire ring with rocks. Sit around the campfire and sing songs or eat a snack.

—Donna Rehder, Sonora, CA

Let's Go Camping

In this activity, children learn camping safety and how to care for the environment through dramatic and co-operative play.

Materials needed

Ten rocks for campfire, 5" to 6" in diameter
Camping gear: for example, lantern and stove (without fuel), pots, dishes, utensils, small tent, two sleeping bags, fishing poles with paper clips for hooks, small portable barbecue, pieces of firewood to put in campfire, skewers, flashlights, dress-up clothes, clothes line
Paper fish with magnetic strip attached (available at most hardware or craft stores—cut to desired length)
Blue blanket or tumbling mat to simulate water
Marshmallows

What to do

1. Decide where to set up your camping center, inside or outside. This will determine some of the following steps.
2. Make your camping center as realistic as possible. Use real stones and wood to make the campfire.
You may be able to light it if it is set up outdoors. Take proper safety precautions, check with your local fire department and get necessary permits.
3. If you have a portable climbing structure, set it up for the children to stand on and fish from. Put a blue mat or blanket under the structure and pretend it is water. Throw the paper fish into the "water" so children can catch them with their fishing poles.
4. At some point, plan to light the barbecue or campfire (outside) and let children toast marshmallows.
5. Model the proper use of all equipment and discuss safety tips.
6. Practice ways to keep the environment safe and clean: pick up trash, stay on marked trails and avoid walking on plant life.

More to do

Let children make their own fish. Invite a professional, perhaps a forest ranger to speak to the children concerning camping safety. Find someone who plays guitar and sing songs around the campfire.

Related books

Life in the Forest by Eileen Curran (Cassette tape also available)
Just Me and My Dad by Mercer Mayer

—Cheryl Collins, Hughson, CA

Making a Classroom Campfire

Children can help to make a campfire for indoor dramatic play.

Materials needed

Newspaper
Brown paint
Tape
White construction paper
Red, yellow, and orange paint or crayons

What to do

1. Roll sections of newspaper to look like logs and tape to hold.
2. Cut out flame shapes from white construction paper.
3. Have children paint the logs brown and the flames red, yellow and orange.
4. After paint dries, make a pretend campfire with the logs, and tape the flames between the logs.
5. Use the campfire for dramatic play along with other classroom camping activities.

More to do

Have children help roll the logs and cut out the flames. Hide the logs around the room and have the children try to "find logs for the fire." Eat pretzel logs for a snack.

Related book

Just Me and My Dad by Mercer Mayer

—*Sandra Suffoletto Ryan, Buffalo, NY*

Under the Sea

The children will discover what lives under the water.

Materials needed

Blue and green crayons
Cheese grater
Wax paper
Iron
Sea animal shapes
Towel

What to do

1. Cut out shapes of sea animals (fish, octopus, sea horse, crab, star fish, etc.). Peel paper off crayons. Heat iron away from children. Have two pieces of wax paper for each child. Place grater on top of one piece of wax paper.
2. Let the children rub the crayons on the grater.
3. Let the children add animal shapes to their picture.
4. Place another piece of wax paper on top of picture.
5. Put picture on top of towel.

6. The teacher can iron the wax paper together. Press lightly and the children can see steam and feel heat coming off of iron. Watch how the iron melts the crayons and it makes it seem like ocean water.
7. Hang in window when finished.

More to do

If you are near a beach, visit or have someone bring in a bucket of ocean water to examine what's in it.

Related books

Swimmy by Leo Lionni

—Kim Damarjian, Old Saybrook, CT

Beach Wreaths 3+

Children will enhance fine motor skills and become more appreciative of their environment as they make wreaths of ocean treasures.

Materials needed

Heavy white paper (watercolor paper works well) or tagboard
Yellow watercolor paint or yellow crayon
Glue
Hole puncher
Yellow yarn
Objects from the beach (sand, small shells, pebbles, dried seaweed, etc.)
Whole dried bay leaves

What to do

1. Cut wreath shapes out of paper and punch a hole at the top of each.
2. Have the children paint or color the wreath shape. Let dry.
3. Dribble glue all over the wreath, then sprinkle on the sand and let dry.
4. Glue on shells, pebbles, seaweed, bay leaves, etc.
5. When dry, tie yarn in a loop through hole at top of wreath for hanging.

More to do

Take a field trip to the beach to gather the materials. Provide extra materials in baskets for sorting or to add to an indoor sandbox. Make other seasonal wreaths. For fall, use pressed leaves, dried flowers, seeds and nuts, berries. For winter, use cones from different evergreens (especially little hemlock cones), nuts like almonds, whole cinnamon, nutmeg, star anise, gold stars, red ribbon. For spring, make heart-shaped wreaths and use paper dollies and dried flowers tied with pink ribbon.

Related books

At the Beach by Anne and Harlow Rockwell
The Beachcomber's Book by Bernice Kohn

—Linda Atamian, Charlestown, RI

Beach Party

You can play a day at the beach even if it's rainy outside!

Materials needed

Towels
Swimsuits
Sunglasses
Fruit
Sand
Shells
Small wading pool

What to do

1.   Have each child bring their own towel, swimsuit and sunglasses to school. (Bring extras for children who have none or who forget.)
2.   The children can help you cut up fruit to make a fruit salad.
3.   Make separate areas for each of the following: sand with shells, pool with water, towels and picnic.
4.   After changing into their swimsuits, the children spread out their towels. They may or may not choose to wear their sunglasses.
5.   Each child can choose between various activities that are available at the beach—looking for shells in the sand, taking a swim, resting on their towels or having a refreshing snack.

More to do

Have the children use their imaginations to each draw a picture of all the things they saw on their trip to the beach.

Related book

A Day at the Beach by Mircea Vasiliu

—*Sandra Scott, Vancouver, WA*

Sea Collage

3+

The children will create a work of art from objects associated with the sea.

Materials needed

Small pieces of heavy white cardboard about 6" x 8" (scraps of mat board from a picture framing business are ideal)
Damp sponges
Powdered blue and green tempera paint
White glue
Sand
Small sea shells, smooth stones, dried seaweed, bits of driftwood
Masking tape
One-inch lengths of fine wire

SUMMER

What to do

1.   Give children damp sponges and have them dip the sponges first in blue and then in green tempera powder.
2.   Have children apply the paint to the cardboard in a swirling motion to create a blue-green sea wave effect. Show children how to dribble white glue onto the picture and add shells, seaweed, and other decorations to create a design.
3.   Have children sprinkle sand over the picture (it will adhere to the extra glue and add texture to the design).
4.   Let the picture lie flat until the glue dries.
5.   Tap the picture to remove excess sand.
6.   Tape a wire loop on the back of each piece of cardboard for hanging.

More to do

Talk about the pictures and the sea objects used. Describe the various textures with words like scratchy, smooth, dry and brittle. Talk about the sea and sea life. Read books about the sea.

—*Mary Jo Shannon, Roanoke, VA*

Class Seaside Collage   3+

The children will work together to create a seaside collage which can become a record of their study of sea life.

Materials needed

Glue
Cups for glue
Glue brushes
Blue paint
Beach treasures—sand, shells, seaweed, beach glass, driftwood, etc.
Large piece of posterboard

What to do

1.   If possible, take a trip to a beach and collect the materials needed for the collage. Or, have the children bring beach treasures from home.
2.   Pour a few drops of blue tempera into the glue and mix. Continue to add the paint until the glue is the color of the ocean.
3.   Discuss with the children things that are found in the ocean and at the beach, using pictures and books.
4.   Have the children take turns "painting" the glue onto the posterboard. This will serve as the ocean background.
5.   Encourage the children to create an ocean scene by gluing sea shells and other items to the posterboard. Use a lot of glue to hold the shells in place.
6.   When the children have finished, them sprinkle sand lightly over the entire picture.
7.   Allow ample drying time, preferably overnight.
8.   Display the collage on a bulletin board or in another appropriate place.

More to do

This picture can be the beginning of a unit on sea life. Add pictures or cut-outs of different sea creatures as they are introduced.

Related books

Beside the Bay by Sheila White Samton
The Little Island by Golden MacDonald and Leonard Weisgard

—Jacqueline Schweitzer, Effort, PA

Camping Week

4+

In this activity, children will engage in extended dramatic play, language development and socialization skills.

Materials needed

Sleeping bag for each child
Small camping tent
Camping equipment
Lincoln logs (to make pretend fire)
Colored tissue paper (to make pretend fire)

What to do

1. Notify parents of your activity. Ask them to provide a sleeping bag or bed roll for their children. This will be kept at school for one week. Ask them also to provide any camping gear such as mess kits, canteens, flashlights, backpacks, etc.
2. Set up the play area with the available equipment.
3. Talk about what is needed when we go camping and demonstrate the camping equipment. Talk about the children's own camping experiences.
4. Act out things families do when they are camping (setting up tent, fishing, cooking, roasting marshmallows).
5. Compare camping out to being in one's own home.
6. Read the children a story while they snuggle in their sleeping bags or bed rolls.
7. Allow the children to use the camping equipment during free play time.

More to do

Lay a trail throughout the building or playground for the children to follow. At the end, have a special treat or game. Make hot dogs and beans or campfire stew for snack time.

Related book

The Berenstain Bears Go to Camp by Jan Berenstein

Related songs

"Whole World In His Hands"
"Michael Row the Boat Ashore"
"Three Jolly Fisherman"
"Kumbaya"

—Rayne P. Reese, Glendale, MO

A Day at the Beach

4+

Young children will use their five senses to explore the environment during "a day at the beach."

Materials needed

Be creative as you set the scene for your day at the beach. Examples of materials that you might select include:
Sea shells
Driftwood
Sound effects records or tapes of sea gulls, waves breaking, etc.
Dried sheets of seaweed (available in Asian markets)
Large, multi-colored beach blankets and towels
Beach balls
Swimming tubes
Inflated rafts
Travel posters depicting beach, seaside, and ocean scenes
Beach umbrella
Sand table (filled with sand, pails, shovels...)
Water table (with salt water, perhaps)
"Summery" picnic plates and napkins for snack time
Child-provided bathing suits, sun glasses, sun visors, hats...
Blind fold

What to do

1. Send a note home inviting the children to a beach party. Ask the parents to have their children wear their bathing suits under their regular clothes. They may also want to bring sunglasses, hats or visors.
2. Gather the following items (or appropriate substitutions), but keep them hidden from the group: sea shells, driftwood (touch), sound effects record or tape (hearing), salty water (taste), dried seaweed (smell, taste), blindfold.
3. Use the materials you have gathered to transform your classroom into beach front property!
4. Review the five senses with your children. Encourage the children to be especially aware of their five senses as they explore the classroom "beach".
5. Blindfold a child volunteer. Allow the child to examine and identify one of the items listed above and to explain which sense was mainly used in identifying it. Continue with additional volunteers until all of the items have been identified.
6. Ask the group to explore the room with their eyes. Have the children describe what they see and to guess how some of those things might smell, feel, sound, or (at your discretion) taste. Test out their hypotheses.

More to do

Set up a variety of beach-related learning centers. Children will love to make sand castles at the sand table and waves at the water table. "Beach Ball Bounce" and "Swimming Tube Toss" would be wonderful gross-motor experiences, if you have access to a gym or other large area. Fill cake pans with wet sand and have each child make a firm hand print or footprint in the sand. Use the print as a mold and fill it with plaster of Paris. At the end of the day, each child will have a souvenir to take home from the "beach"!

Related books

Let's Take a Walk on the Beach by Karen O'Connor
The Seaside by Maria and Parramon Rius
At the Beach by Anne Rockwell
A Day at the Beach by Mircea Vasiliu

—*Marji E. Gold-Vukson, West Lafayette, IN*

Beach Scene

The children will experience the feel and texture of sand and learn to identify some animals that live in the water.

Materials needed

12" x 18" light blue construction paper—one sheet per child
Sand
Glue
Brown paint
Paintbrushes
Crayons or markers
Small shells
Blue cellophane paper
Cotton balls

What to do

1. Divide the sheet of paper into thirds with three horizontal lines.
2. Set out the paint and paintbrushes.
3. Have the child paint the bottom third of paper with brown paint.
4. While the paint is still wet, have them pour sand on the paper. This can be done inside or at the sand box. The sand will stick to the wet paint.
5. When the bottom section is dry, draw fish and other sea life on the middle section of the paper. You could use stickers or precut shapes, as well.
6. Cover the middle third with blue cellophane paper.
7. Paste the cotton balls onto the top section of the paper and pull them into cloud shapes.
8. Paste small shells on the sandy beach.

More to do

Use the sand to build a castle. Take a field trip to a beach or sandy area.

Related book

A Day at the Beach by Mircea Vasiliu

—*Carol Nelson, Rockford, IL*

The Luau Play

The children will have fun putting on a play, perhaps as the culmination to a unit on Hawaii or the beach. Ask for the parents help with costumes and refreshments and send them invitations to this special performance.

Materials needed

Large piece of cardboard
Paint/paintbrushes
Sponges
Glue
Shells
Appropriate costumes

What to do

1. Read the play to the children and assign roles.
2. Let the children help you make the scenery. Paint the top of the cardboard blue for the sky and the bottom, brown for the sand. The children can add items like shells, fish, or palm trees to the scenery.
3. Find appropriate costumes as needed.
4. Practice the play.
5. Have the children make invitations to send home inviting their parents to the play.

Characters:

> *Hula Dancers*
> *Hawaiian Boys*
> *Beach Kids*
> *Starfish*
> *Crab*
> *Seahorse*
> *Clam*
> *Seagull*
> *Conch Shell*

(Beach kids enter dressed in summer clothes, sandals and sun hats.)
Beach Kids:
(To the tune of "London Bridges")

> *We are going to the beach*
> *To the beach, to the beach.*
> *We are going to the beach*
> *In our bathing suits.*
> *We will find rocks and shells*
> *Rocks and shells, rocks and shells.*
> *We will find rocks and shells*
> *To gather by the sea.*

One Beach Kid:(points across stage)
Look, everyone! Let's see what's over there.

(Starfish, crab, seahorse, clam, conch shell and seagull enter one at a time and say the appropriate line.)
Starfish:
I'm a starfish. I have five legs. 1-2-3-4-5 (count and hold fingers up).
Crab:
I'm a crab. Be careful or I might snap your toes.
Seahorse:
I'm a seahorse. My head looks like a horse, but I have a curly tail and live in the sea.
Clam:
I'm a clam. People who like seafood like me a lot.
Conch Shell:
I'm a conch shell. If you put your ear close to me you can pretend you hear the sea.
Seagull:
I'm a seagull. I like to eat anything I find, especially food at a luau.
One Beach Kid
That's where we're going now. Come and join us.

(The Beach Kids and sea creatures skip to the other side of the stage while singing the following song to the tune of "Mary Had a Little Lamb.")

> *We're going to a luau now*
> *Luau now, luau now.*
> *We're going to a luau now*
> *With food and hula dancers.*

(The Beach Kids and characters sit down and the Hula Dancers and Hawaiian Boys come out.)
One Hula Dancer:
Aloha! In Hawaii the hula dancer tells a story using hands, not words. We would like to perform a hula dance to Twinkle, Twinkle, Little Star.
(Hula Dancers and Hawaiian Boys pantomime song while humming the tune.)

> *Twinkle, twinkle (both hands high in the air, open and close fists)*
> *little (hands in front of the chest with fingers pinched together)*
> *star (hands high in air, open fists and stretch fingers)*
> *How I (cross open hands over chest)*
> *wonder (raise shoulders and place palms of hands up as if saying "I don't know)*
> *what you are (bring hands together in front of chest; raise both above head and open them in circle ending at waist.)*
> *Up above the world (slowly raise hands in a circle above head)*
> *so high (keep hands raised in circle and get on tiptoes)*
> *Like a diamond (fingers make diamond shape at chest level)*
> *in the sky (carry diamond shape up high over head)*

(Then repeat first six lines)
(The children exit the stage all singing to the tune of "Mary Had A Little Lamb")

> *Now we'll head home with sunburned cheeks*
> *sunburned cheeks, sunburned cheeks.*
> *Now we'll head home with sunburned cheeks*
> *And treasures from our visit.*

Mahalo everyone!!! *(that means thank you in Hawaiian)*

More to do

Have a "luau feast" with special foods, for example, pineapple, melons, etc. and invite your audience (parents) to join in.

—*Joyce Montag, Slippery Rock, PA*

How Do I Get There?

2+

Children practice identifying and discussing various modes of transportation by guessing the identity of toy vehicles in a grab bag.

Materials needed

Puppet
Large bag
Various toy vehicles, such as helicopter, train, airplane, car, truck, motorcycle, boat, rocketship or horse

What to do

1.   Put all the toys in the bag.
2.   Introduce the puppet: "My friend has a problem. He needs to go to ____. How can he get there?" Let children name different ways the puppet can travel. Ask if they will be good ways to travel. Why or why not?
3.   Show the bag. Explain that inside the bag are ways that we can travel, and that the word we use is transportation. This is how we get from one place to another.
4.   Describe a mode of transportation that you have in the bag. Have the children make guesses. When it is correctly named, remove the toy from the bag. Continue until all toys are named.

More to do

Sort the toys as to whether they are ways to travel by air, land or water. Play the song "Sammy" by Hap Palmer on the *Getting to Know Myself* album. Show pictures of each animal/insect in song. How does it move? Have the children move according to the song.

Related song

"This is the Way We Row a Boat" sung to the tune of "Here We Go 'Round the Mulberry Bush"

This is the way we row a boat,
Row a boat, row a boat.
This is the way we row a boat,
Early in the morning.
This is the way we fly a plane...
Drive a car...
Ride a horse...

—*Marzee Woodward, Murfreesboro, TN*

Tire Prints

2+

Children develop fine motor skills using spools to print on paper.

Materials needed

White paper
Tempera paint (black)
Empty spools
Sponges

What to do

1.   Pour mixed paint onto sponges and let it soak in.
2.   Children choose one spool at a time and lightly press onto sponge.

3. Press spool onto paper to make tire prints.

Related books

Boat Book by Gail Gibbons
The Little Red Engine that Could
Teddy Bear's Take the Train by Susanna Gretz and Alison Sage
The Biggest Truck by David Lyon

—Leann Jarzen, Starkville, MS

Constructing a Car   3+

The children can use their imaginations while constructing a car from various art supplies.

Materials needed

Small box, one per child
Paints of various colors
Paintbrushes
Glue
Markers
Assortment of small construction paper shapes

What to do

1. Have the children bring small boxes from home.
2. Cut out small construction paper shapes that are proportional to the size of the boxes.
3. Talk to children about how people usually move from one place to another. Show a finished car model and discuss how you made it.
4. Have children paint the boxes and let them dry.
5. Have the children glue on shapes for wheels, doors, and windows.
6. After the glue dries, use markers to draw in other features.

More to do

Use large butcher paper and markers to create a town. Children can help draw roads, buildings, etc. Use constructed vehicles to move around the neighborhood. Let children display finished products and tell others in group about their vehicles.

Related books

Away We Go illustrated by Irene Friedman
The Great Big Car and Truck Book illustrated by Richard Scarry

Related song

"Wheels on the Bus"

—Marzee Woodward, Murfreesboro, TN

Airplane

The children use their fine motor skills to create these simple airplanes.

Materials needed

Paper towel tube, one per child
4" x 12" posterboard or heavy white construction paper, one per child
Scissors
Glue
Round or rectangular shape stickers
White paint (other colors optional)
Paintbrushes

What to do

1. Have the children paint the paper towel tube white.
2. Fold the cardboard/construction paper lengthwise. Draw a simple wing shape on the folded paper and cut it out (see illustration).
3. Have the children glue the wings to the underside of the paper towel tube.
4. Put stickers on the tube for windows.

More to do

Take the children outside to fly their airplanes.

—*Jyoti Joshi, Framingham, MA*

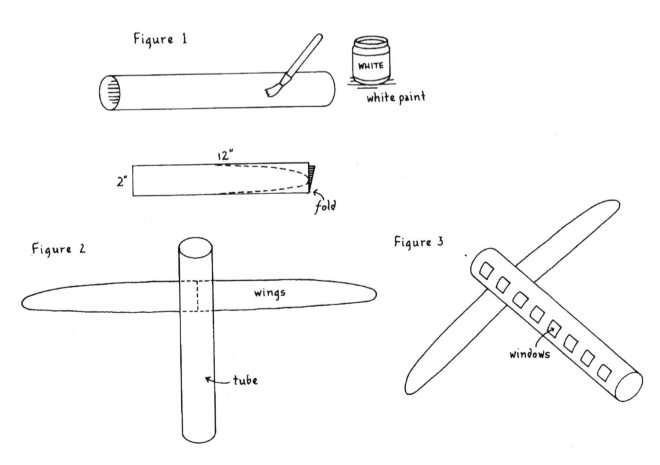

Figure 1

white paint

12"

2"

fold

Figure 2

wings

tube

Figure 3

windows

Tugboats

The children improve their fine motor skills while making these seaworthy tugboats.

Materials needed

1/2 pint milk cartons, one per child, cut in half lengthwise with bottoms stapled together
Black construction paper circles, six per child, to fit on sides of cut carton
Empty toilet paper tubes, one per child, with two 1" slits in bottom directly across from one another
Cotton balls
Red and black tempera paint
Glue

What to do

1.   Have the children paint the sides of the milk carton red and the toilet paper tube black. Add some white glue to the red paint to help it adhere to the milk carton.
2.   Before the paint dries, the children can add black circles to the sides of the boat, three to a side. They will stick without gluing when glue is already in paint.
3.   Push the tube onto the stapled connection in the center of the boat.
4.   Pull and stretch the cotton ball to resemble smoke, and glue it to the top of the tube.

More to do

After the boats dry, attach a string to the front of each and use them in the water table for play.

Related books

Boats by Anne Rockwell
Big City Port by Betsy Maestro and Ellen DelVecchio

—*Sandra Suffoletto Ryan, Buffalo, New York*

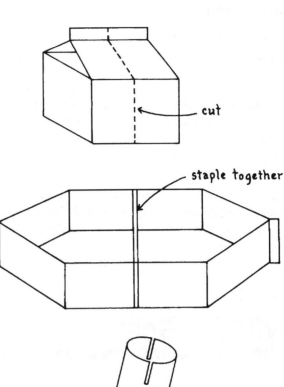

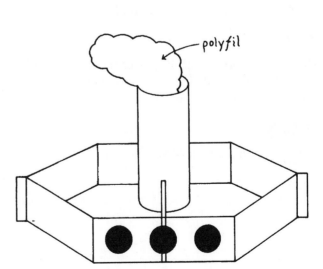

Carpet Boating

3+

Children give their large muscles a workout as they pretend to boat across the water.

Materials needed

Carpet squares and a clean floor

What to do

1. Have the children put the carpet on the floor with the carpet side down (slides better).
2. Have them sit on the carpet piece with their feet extended out in front and their knees bent.
3. Explain how they can pull themselves forward with their feet. Have them work their arms as if they are rowing a boat.
4. Sing "Row, row, row your boat."

More to do

Have children kneel on the carpet and pull themselves forward (scooter style), or have them put their hands on the carpet and run pushing carpet on the floor (wheelbarrow style).

—Katherine Ojala, Ely, MN

Mayflower Boat

3+

Children enjoy making these little boats for water play.

Materials needed

Half a walnut shell, one per child
Toothpicks, one per child
Modeling clay
One-inch paper triangles, one per child

What to do

1. Have the children carefully pierce the triangle with the toothpick.
2. Have them put modeling clay in the shell.
3. Stick the toothpick in the clay.

More to do

Make an ocean to put your Mayflower in.

—Joyce Wildasin, Hanover, PA

Vehicle Collage

Children combine pictures of different modes of transportation to create a collage.

Materials needed

Magazine pictures of vehicles or precut shapes
Glue
Construction paper

What to do

1. Cut out vehicle pictures from magazines ahead of time, or have the children cut them out on their own.
2. Have the children choose which vehicle pictures they want.
3. Let them arrange and glue the pictures onto construction paper to form a collage.

—Leann Jarzen, Starkville, MS

Egg Carton Choo-Choo

3+

Children learn shapes and colors while using fine motor skills.

Materials needed

Bottom half of egg cartons, one per two students
Scissors
Glue
Empty spool, one per child
Toilet paper tube, one per child
Black construction paper
Small paper cup to trace (3-ounce size)
Chalk
Black and red paint

What to do

1. Cut the bottom of an egg carton in half lengthwise and give one half to each child.
2. Have each child glue a toilet paper tube on top of their first egg cup and a spool on top of their last.
3. Have them paint the spool and the adjoining egg cup red. This is the caboose.
4. Have them paint the rest of the egg carton black and let dry.
5. Using the small paper cup, trace ten circles on the black construction paper. Cut these out to be wheels.
6. Glue five wheels on each side of the train.

More to do

Ask the child to draw railway tracks with crayon on big manila paper, and glue the train on the tracks.

—Jyoti Joshi, Framingham, MA

TRANSPORTATION

Paper Plate Car

3+

Children hone their fine motor skills while learning about shapes and colors.

Materials needed

Large paper plates (9" diameter)
Scissors
Glue or stapler
Two cups of paint, one black and another of child's choice
Markers
Ruler
Small paper cup (3-ounce) to use for tracing

What to do

1. Let the child draw a line in the middle of the plate with a ruler and marker, making two half-circles.
2. Cut along the line while talking about half-circles.
3. On one half, trace two small circles for wheels using the small paper cup.
4. Cut out the wheels, paint them black, and let them dry.
5. Paint the other half-circle the child's favorite color and let dry.
6. Staple or glue two wheels to the car.

—*Jyoti Joshi, Framingham, MA*

Road, Sky or Water

3+

Children learn to classify types of transportation according to where they are used.

Materials needed

Pictures or models of boats, airplanes, cars and trucks

What to do

1. Make signs with illustrations for "Road," "Sky" and "Water."
2. Talk to the children about different modes of transportation.
3. Show the children the signs and the pictures or models of boats, airplanes, cars and trucks.
4. Ask the children under which sign each picture or model should go, and place it there.

More to do

Let children play with toy boats in the water table or with cars and trucks in the sand table.

Related books

Mike Mulligan and His Steam Shovel by V. L. Burton
Round Trip by A. Jonas
The Little Sailboat by L. Lenski
Little Airplane by L. Lenski
Cars and Trucks and Things That Go by Richard Scarry

—*Elaine Root, Garland, TX*

Car Painting

Children will enjoy a fun art activity and learn that tires have different kinds of treads.

Materials needed

Several small vehicles with different kinds of tires
Paint
Paper
Trays for paint
Painting smocks

What to do

1. Gather a variety of toy vehicles with different kinds of tires. Include tractors, motorcycles, and trucks as well as cars.
2. Mix up paint so it is a little thick.
3. Put out paint trays and the different vehicles.
4. Put the paper on the table.
5. Have the children place the wheels of the different vehicles in the paint and then roll them across the paper. Talk about the different designs or tracks each vehicle makes.

More to do

Place some cars, trucks and tractors in the block area. Sing transportation type songs during music.

—Janice Parks, Stockdale, TX

Building Bridges

4+

Children brainstorm to develop the concept of a bridge.

Materials needed

Tables and chairs, placed about 3 feet apart
Several toy cars or dolls
Recycled materials including paper towel tubes, milk cartons, cans, butter dishes, meat trays and boxes
Masking tape

What to do

1. Create two play towns with dolls, cars and houses. Place one town on each table and place the tables about 3 feet apart. Use the figures to explain the story as you tell it:

> *"Once upon a time there was a little boy who lived in a town (city, farm, or whatever is most familiar to the children). He was not happy because he had no one to play with. One day he went outside and in the distance he saw a little girl. He got in his car and headed for her house, but he found a great big hole in the way (show the big space between the tables). He tried to jump the space but it was too far.*

2. Ask the children to help the boy by building him a way to get across. Tell them that they will each have a space to build in (children can build from one table to the next or from a chair or bookshelf to the tables).
3. Provide them with a space, recycled materials, and masking tape. If possible, let them choose the materials to use.

TRANSPORTATION

469

4. Circulate, asking the children questions like: What are you making? What is this for? How does this help the boy?

5. Let each child demonstrate his creation. Praise all attempts at originality, even if unsuccessful the first time.

6. Have the children walk around the classroom to see each others' creations.

More to do

Have children draw pictures of bridges. Adapt "Old MacDonald Had a Farm" to "This Is the Way We Build a Bridge" and let children add parts of the bridge instead of animals.

Related books

Richard Scary's Book of Transportation by Richard Scarry
The Three Billy Goats Gruff by Paul Galdone
The Little Engine that Could by Watty Piper

—*Beth W. McKenna, Stoneham, MA*

Transportation Tally   5+

Children learn about road transportation.

Materials needed

9" x 12" paper with simple drawings of vehicles
Crayons
Firm surface such as a slate or a book
Chart paper and marker to record results

What to do

1. Draw simple pictures on separate sheets as children name types of road transportation (car, van, truck, motorcycle).

2. Choose a safe site to observe road transportation.

3. Have the children tally number of times types of transportation is observed.

More to do

Encourage children to bring toy trucks, vans or other vehicles for use in the block area. Encourage the children to build roads and cities with unit blocks.

Related books

The Big Book of Real Trucks by Walter Retan
A Letter to Amy by Ezra Jack Keats

—*Susan Oldham Hill, Lakeland, FL*

Mass Production

Children learn about factories and mass production while developing fine motor skills.

Materials needed

Basic car shape with window and axle-holes cut from a two-by-four (see pattern), one per child
Sandpaper (four pieces of medium-grain)
Two 3'-long 2"x4" boards
Upholstery tacks
Four small "C" clamps
2" clean paintbrush
Tempera paint
Paintbrushes (child size)
Wooden wheels, four per child
Plastic axles, two per child
Hammer (6-ounce)
Children's workbench or rectangular table
Safety goggles (optional)

What to do

1. Cut out and trace the car pattern onto stiff cardboard. Trace the pattern onto the two-by-fours and cut them out. Drill holes for the windows and axles (you might ask an industrial arts teacher or a parent to help you with power tools).
2. Set up your Car Factory.
3. Using upholstery tacks, attach two pieces of sandpaper to each two-by-four and mount these on opposite sides of the work bench (table).
4. Put the unsanded cars in a box at one end of the workbench and an empty box at the other end.
5. Discuss the concept of factory mass production. You could use pictures, small dolls and toy cars.
6. Give the children a list of workers, showing who will be sanders, dusters, painters and wheel attachers. Help them get started.
7. Hang painted cars on a dowel suspended between two milk crates to dry. Have each completed car tested.

More to do

Take a field trip to a lumber yard to purchase the necessary supplies. Make a fruit salad using an assembly line process, making each child responsible for adding a specific fruit to the salad as the dishes go by.

—Julie Israel, Ypsilanti, MI

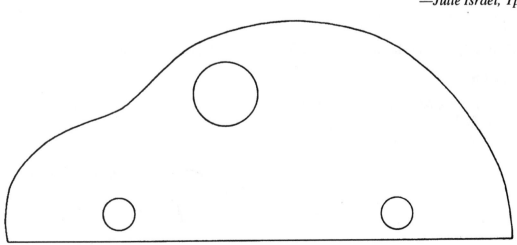

Mr. Weatherbear

2+

This activity teaches children about weather and how to dress properly for the changing seasons.

Materials needed

Corrugated cardboard
Scissors
Brown flannel
Different colored pieces of felt

What to do

1. Cut the shape of a bear from corrugated cardboard and cover the board with brown felt. Make a variety of clothes (jeans, sweatshirt, coat, hat, boots, etc.) from felt pieces.
2. Call on a child each day to check the weather.
3. Ask the child to pick out an outfit for Mr. Weatherbear according to the weather that day.
4. Gently press felt clothes on bear.

More to do

Mr. Weatherbear may also be used to demonstrate community helpers and celebrate different holidays.

—Terri B. Piette, Jarrettsville, MD

Weather Game

3+

Children learn weather words and social game skills, including taking turns.

Materials needed

Game board (see attached)
Dice and game pieces

What to do

1. Laminate game board and set up on table.
2. Have children take turns rolling dice and moving, following the directions of the spaces on which they land.

More to do

Maintain a daily calendar, and have cutouts of different types of weather which can be applied to that day.

Related books

Cloudy with a Chance of Meatballs by Judith Barrett
Skyfire by Frank Asch
Thundercake by Patricia Polacco

—Rachel Stickfort, Newark, DE

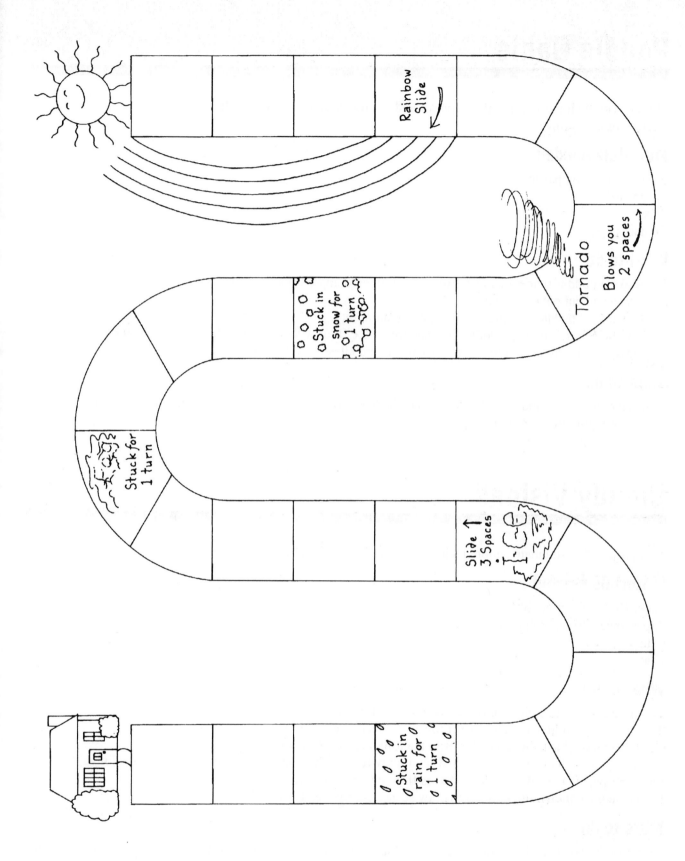

Rainbow Slide

Tornado
Blows you
2 spaces

Stuck in
snow for
1 turn

Stuck for
1 turn

Slide
3 Spaces
ICE

Stuck in
rain for
1 turn

Puddle Game 3+

This activity facilitates gross motor control and reinforces spatial concepts. It can be used as part of a unit on weather or on a rainy day.

Materials needed

Blue construction paper
Cardboard
Scissors
Contact paper

What to do

1. Make a puddle-shaped template from the cardboard approximately 8" x 12" in size.
2. Trace and cut out eight to ten blue "puddles."
3. Cover the "puddles" with contact paper for durability.
4. For the activity, line up puddles in a pattern on the floor with 12" spaces between each puddle.
5. Have the children take turns jumping over the puddles.

More to do

You can combine the individual puddles to make larger ones to jump over. The children can pretend to be animals jumping in and out of the puddles.

—Sheila Ach, Syosset, NY

Cloudy Visions 3+

This project will stimulate children's imaginations and help them improve small motor skills.

Materials needed

Paper (light blue if possible)
Paper towels from a roll (plain white)
Glue
Crayons

What to do

1. Give each child a piece of paper and one sheet of paper towel.
2. Have the children tear their paper towels into small cloud shapes.
3. Help them glue their cloud shapes to the top third of the paper.
4. Tell them to look at the shapes and see if they remind them of other familiar objects. Encourage them to turn their papers to study the cloud shapes from different angles.
5. Have the children use crayons to draw scenes below the clouds.

More to do

On a cloudy day, take the children outside and lay in grass. Ask them to describe what shapes they see in the clouds overhead.

Related books

The Cloud Book by Tomie DePaola
It Looked Like Spilt Milk by Charles Shaw

—Lona Parker, Huntsville, AL

When It Rains, Where Does It Go?

This activity introduces understanding of the absorption capacity of different substances.

Materials needed

Eyedropper
Cup or shallow bowl
Colored water or thin paint
Two 1/2"-3" squares of at least six materials with varying absorption capacities, such as cellophane, styrofoam, cardboard, absorbent cotton, synthetic fabric, paper towels, newspaper
Stapler or tape
Large sheet of paper to which samples can be affixed
Tray or plate
Waterproof marker or pen

What to do

1. Arrange samples of materials to be tested next to tray or plate. Place a cup of colored water and eyedropper near the tray also. (You may want to make a sign for this display with a caption like "How will raindrops be absorbed by....?")
2. This activity can be done as part of unit on weather, seasons or the environment. Appropriate introductory discussions can be held with the class or small groups in advance. Children may be particularly intrigued by this on a rainy day or during a rainy season.
3. Make sure each child can manipulate an eyedropper. Help her practice if needed.
4. Allow each child to choose a material to be tested first. Place that sample in tray. Some children may choose to test two or three samples at once.
5. Have the child squirt "raindrops" on various samples observing the rates at which moisture is absorbed, if at all.
6. The teacher or child attaches the samples to background paper, labeling each sample with the child's name using a non water soluble pen or marker creating a record of the experiment for each child.

More to do

The class can discuss their finding as a group and address questions such as: What familiar surfaces outdoors will or will not absorb rain? What type of clothing would best protect us from rain? What causes flooding in urban areas? Have the children select the most absorbent materials and test to see how many drops can be absorbed before the saturation point is reached.

Related book

Water Everywhere by Henry Pluckrose

—E.L. Nadler, Jerusalem, Israel

Rainbow Mobile

4+

After a study of weather, take a weather walk to collect small fallen branches, so that the children can make this rainbow mobile to take home and share with their families.

Materials needed

9" paper plates, two for each child
Yellow and black paint
Paintbrushes
Branches or hanger, one for each child
String or yarn
Pipe cleaner
Crayons or non-toxic markers
Hole puncher
Scissors
Stapler

What to do

1. Cut one paper plate in half. Put one half aside for later use and cut curves along the flat edge of the other to make the scalloped edge of an umbrella. Paint the umbrella black.
2. Paint the other plate yellow and let dry completely.
3. Using the leftover half plate from the umbrella, color in a rainbow. Have a sample rainbow available so the children can copy the color order in the rainbow if they wish.
4. Cut a fringe around the edge of the yellow plate.
5. Bend the pipe cleaner into the letter "J" and staple it to the umbrella to act as a handle.
6. Punch a hole in the top of each figure, string the yarn through, and tie to the branch or hanger. The figures can be strung to hang at different levels.

More to do

Bring in crystals to hang in the windows and watch the rainbows dance round the room when the sun shines through.

—Jyoti Joshi, Framingham, MA

"I Think The Weather Is..."

The children practice labeling, describing and differentiating different types of weather.

Materials needed

Pictures or symbols of different types of weather
1/2 index cards
Photo of each child
Tape or adhesive
Marker

What to do

1. Draw or cut out simple figures of weather symbols (umbrella/rain; sun/sunny; cloud/cloudy; snow-man/snowy; etc.)
2. Take a photograph of each child or ask for one from home.
3. Laminate materials.
4. Put a background and border on the bulletin board along with the caption "I think the weather is..."
5. Position weather symbols around board leaving enough space for children to place their photographs around the symbols.
6. Make word cards from the index cards writing the names of the weather symbols you have made. Place these on the bulletin board also.
7. To begin the activity, discuss each weather symbol with the children. Let them identify each and describe what they mean.
8. Encourage the children to identify the weather conditions throughout the day and place their picture by the symbol that best describes the weather at that time. (Remember that more than one symbol may be appropriate for the weather description.)

More to do

The teacher could play a game by describing a weather symbol and having the children guess which one she is describing. You could also cut out pictures of clothing that is weather-appropriate and have the children decide which type of clothing is best to wear during certain types of weather.

Related books

The Snowy Day by Ezra Jack Keats
Bear Shadow by Frank Asch
Rainy Day Kitten by Linda Hayward
It Look Like Spilt Milk by Charles G. Shaw

—Marzee Woodward, Murfreesboro, TN

WIND & AIR

Wind Sock

3+

Through this activity, children will observe that the wind blows hard and soft and from different directions.

Materials needed

Paper
Markers
Stapler
Streamers (three 10" strips per child)
Ribbon (10" per child)

What to do

1. Have the children decorate their papers using markers.
2. Roll each paper into a cylinder and staple it.
3. Attach the streamers to the bottom of the cylinder.
4. Attach a ribbon to the top for hanging.
5. On a windy day, hang the wind socks outside where the children can observe them. Perhaps leave them up for several days, so they can see how the wind changes over time. Talk about the direction the wind is blowing and whether it is blowing hard or soft.

More to do

Allow children to take their wind socks home and observe them for a longer period of time.

—Gypsy Lee, Perrysville, OH

Wind-O-Meter

3+

Children will experience the wind by holding up a wind-o-meter.

Materials needed

One strip of wind cloth (Aspen cloth, Rip-stop, taffeta-type cloth) 2" x 45"

What to do

1. Assemble children outside and have them hold the cloth (wind-o-meter) with outstretched arms.
2. Have children observe which way the wind-o-meter is blowing and deduce which way the wind is blowing.
3. Have the children run into the wind to see what happens to the wind-o-meter (it really flies).
4. Have the children run with the wind to see what happens to the wind-o-meter (it may stop flying altogether).
5. Have the children run at right angles to the wind and observe their wind-o-meter.

More to do

Use the wind-o-meter in the gym or classroom where students create all the wind. Fasten several wind-o-meters together and observe and state what happens to a longer wind-o-meter.

—Susan Clark McNamee, Livonia, MI

Making Windsocks

Children will discover the effects of wind while practicing fine motor and color recognition skills in this activity.

Materials needed

White construction paper 12" x 18"
Scissors
Three to four colors of crepe paper rolls
10" brightly colored yarn pieces
Hole puncher
Glue
Margarine tub lids (optional)
Cotton swabs (optional)
Pen or marker

What to do

1. Before activity, cut construction paper lengthwise to make enough 6" x 18" pieces for each child to have one. (This is the "body" of the windsock.) Also cut yarn pieces. For very young children, cut crepe paper strips about 18" long, enough for each child to have six to eight. Make one sample windsock to show the children.
2. Gather all materials and place them near the table where children will be working.
3. Show children the sample windsock, label it and explain that it tells which way the wind is blowing, and that it can be used at airports, weather stations, or at homes as a decoration.
4. Give each child a 6" x 18" piece of construction paper, scissors (if they are cutting their own crepe paper), a margarine lids with glue in it and a cotton swab.
5. Place containers of pre-cut crepe paper strips around on the table, or rolls of crepe if they are to cut their own.
6. Demonstrate spreading some glue along one side of the construction paper, and pressing several strips on it so that they hang down the same side.
7. Roll it up like a cylinder and staple in two places.
8. Punch two holes in the cylinder, and tie yarn piece through the holes.
9. Have children write their name (or help them) and date it if you wish.

More to do

Have children label colors they are gluing on windsock or make a pattern with the color strips. Take the completed windsocks outside to watch them blow in the wind.

—*Carla Scholl, Fairplay, CO*

WIND & AIR

Full of Hot Air

3+

Children will learn about the properties of air.

Materials needed

Balloons
Parachute or large cloth, such as a flat sheet or tarp

What to do

1. Seat children on the floor in a circle around you and blow up a balloon (but don't tie it) to show them that air takes up space.
2. Let go of the filled balloon and have the children watch as it propels itself through the air. This will show that air has power.
3. Blow up the balloon again and release a little bit of air in each child's face to show that air can be felt.
4. Blow up the balloon again and pinch the ends, allowing a bit of air to escape. This will make a funny noise.
5. Have the children hold the ends of the sheet and place several blown-up balloons on top.
6. Tell the children to move the sheet slowly up and down, making a gentle breeze. Then have them move the sheet a little faster to create a stronger wind. Have them observe how the balloons move in the air around and above the moving sheet.

More to do

Sing "Air, Air Everywhere."

Related songs

"Air, Air Everywhere"
"What the Wind Told"

—Dalia Behr, Ozone Park, NY

Cotton Ball Race

3+

Children learn to predict the effects of air movement on an object while considering the location of the air source.

Materials needed

One large cotton ball for each child
Large open space on the floor
Masking tape

What to do

1. Place one long piece of masking tape on the floor to mark a starting line and another piece to mark a finish line.
2. Position two to four children on their hands and knees at the starting line. The rest of the group may act as spectators to cheer the racers on.
3. In front of each child place one cotton ball.
4. Instruct the racers that when the signal is given, they are to begin blowing upon the cotton ball that is in front of them.

5. The first cotton ball to cross the finish line wins.
6. Hands should not be used during the race.
7. Encourage the children to experiment with the angle at which they blow on the cotton ball.

More to do

Discuss with the group the effect that positioning has on the movement of the object. Following the discussion, have the children predict the winners of the next race and check these following the race. Substitute other objects for cotton balls. Ping pong balls may be used with older children, which require much more control.

—Lyndall Warren, Milledgeville, GA

Blowing Game   3+

Children will experience how air affects objects of different weights and shapes.

Materials needed

Cotton ball or ping pong ball
Medium-sized lid from a cardboard box
Scissors or pocket knife

What to do

1. At one end of the lid, cut a hole for the cotton ball or ping pong ball to fall through.
2. Place the lid right side up on the table in front of a child, with the hole at the end farthest from the child's mouth.
3. Have the child try to blow the ball across the lid and into the hole. Allow several tries.
4. Repeat until everyone has had a turn.

More to do

Have the children try to blow a number of different objects (e.g., pebble, piece of paper, small leaf, dime) across the lid and into the hole. Ask them which objects need hard blowing and which need soft blowing to reach the hole.

—Susan Westby, Palm Bay, FL

Bubbles   3+

This simple activity can be one of the best sources of enjoyment and spontaneous learning you can imagine. So mix up the solution and let the bubbles begin!

Materials needed

Bubble mix #1:
  1 gallon water
  1 cup scent-free liquid dishwashing soap
  2 tablespoons glycerin

Bubble mix #2:
1 gallon water
1 cup liquid soap
1/4 cup corn syrup (increases life span of bubble)

Straws

Towels, newspaper, mop & bucket

Other possible makers: assorted sized funnels; cans and paper or styrofoam cups with ends removed; geometric 3-D shaped forms; spools; wire or coat hangers

An understanding janitor

What to do

1. Combine bubble solution ingredients, mix them thoroughly and label solutions. One can mix a solution a week in advance and age it. Generally, this will make a thicker soap film.

2. Blow bubbles. Make dome bubbles, free floating bubbles, big-to-little bubbles, bubbles within bubbles and bubble sculptures.

3. Once the children have had an opportunity to play and explore the bubbles, experiment with the alternative bubble makers. Blow bubbles and observe, predict, measure (use string), and make comparisons. Draw conclusions and record your findings.

More to do

Try making giant bubbles with hula hoops. Use the corn syrup solution. Measure and record bubble sizes. Have the children bring possible bubble makers from home.

Related books

Bubble Bubble by Mercer Mayer
Soap Bubble Magic by Seymour Simon

—Carolyn Jackson, Portland, OR

What Can We Move by Blowing?

3+

Children will experience which objects move and which ones don't when blown upon.

Materials needed

Feather
Tissue
Leaf
Paper
Rock
Magnet
Stick
Spoon
Marker
Poster paper

What to do

1. Ask children which objects they think they can move by blowing on them. Write their answers on poster paper.

2. Have children blow on different objects. Only one child should be blowing at a time.

3. Write down what the children moved and what they didn't move.
4. Have children blow all together at a heavy object that couldn't be moved in previous trial.
5. Write down the children's observations and compare them.

More to do

As a class, look out the window on a windy day. Observe what is and isn't moving and discuss why. Take a walk outside on a windy day. Ask children how it feels to be blown by the wind. Fly a kite.

Related books

Gilberto and the Wind by Marie H. Ets
The Wind Blew by Pat Hutchins
When the Wind Stops by Charlotte Zolotow

—Jeannette Jundzil, Brighton, MA

A Windy Day! 4+

Children will explore the movement of air and its effect on a variety of objects.

Materials needed

Fan
Assortment of small objects that vary in weight and size (e.g., paper, feather, small ball, balloon, crayon, string, ribbon)

What to do

1. If possible, discuss windy days with the class prior to the activity.
2. Set up the fan and place objects on a tray or in a box.
3. Gather the children in a circle on the floor. Explain that air is all around us and that we can feel its movement on a breezy or windy day.
4. Invite the children to recall what the wind does to objects outside (a newspaper in the street, a hat on someone's head, a leaf falling from a tree).
5. Tell the children that you are going to hold out some objects in front of the fan and that they should watch closely to see which objects are moved easily by the "wind" and which are not.
6. Demonstrate with the fan on medium speed.
7. Work on vocabulary related to the activity, such as float, move, fall, blow, gentle, heavy and light.

More to do

Place a small amount of "runny" white paint (the clouds) in the center of blue paper (the sky). Instruct the children to blow gently on the paint as if they were "breezes" (it is best if children do not work across from each other). Have them observe the movement of the paint and the shapes of the clouds they make. This is a fun activity but needs supervision.

Related book

The Wind Blew by Pat Hutchins

—Cathlene Hedden, Livonia, MI

WIND & AIR

Let's Be the Wind

4+

Children use creative movement to learn about wind.

Materials needed

Crepe paper streamers, two to three feet long, one per child
"Who Has Seen the Wind" by Christina Rosetti, or another poem or fingerplay about wind

What to do

1. Allow enough space for children to move while twirling streamers.
2. Assemble children in a sitting group.
3. Read the book aloud to the children, recite a poem or do a fingerplay.
4. Review or discuss what the children know about wind. Ask questions: Can you hear wind? Can you make a sound like wind? Can you feel the wind? How does it feel against your body? Can someone show us how you would walk if the wind were blowing hard? What kind of weather can we have when the wind is blowing?
5. Tell children they will pretend they are the wind.
6. Define your space boundaries and give each child a streamer.
7. Have them wave the streamers around in front of them, to the side, over their head.
8. Encourage the children to move as if they were the wind. Guide them with words: "Blow high in the air, blow low to the ground, twirl around and around. Be a strong wind, be a gentle wind, settle down, down, down to the ground."
9. Ask the children what they liked best about pretending to be the wind.

More to do

Ask children to pretend they are kites flying on a windy day. Make or buy a wind sock to observe wind direction outdoors.

Related book

The Wind Blew by Pat Hutchins

Related song

"The Wind" from *Piggyback Songs*

—*Margery Kranyik, Bridgewater, MA*

To Move or Not to Move

4+

Children compare the effects of air movement on objects of varying weights and learn to use graphs.

Materials needed

Four egg cartons with tops removed
Markers
Four lunch bags or small plastic containers
Variety of small objects of varying weights
Drinking straw for each child

What to do

1. After removing the tops from each egg carton, decorate one row of each carton with a smile and the word yes.
2. Decorate the other side of each carton with a frown and the word no. The cartons will be used as a graph during the activity.
3. Collect a variety of objects which vary in weight—cotton balls, popsicle sticks, crayons, small plastic blocks, small wooden blocks, plastic animals, paper, paper clips, sea shells and rubber bands.
4. Place eight to ten different objects in each lunch bag or plastic container.
5. Color each bag or container so they can be distinguished from one another.
6. Place materials, egg carton graphs and containers of objects in center area of classroom.
7. Have each child choose one plastic container and an egg carton graph.
8. The child should then experiment with the objects in the container to determine which objects can be moved when blown upon and which ones cannot.
9. The child should place the objects on the correct side of the graph, one object per cup in the carton.
10. The children may experiment with all containers of objects.
11. Encourage discussions among the children in the center. Have them compare among themselves which objects seemed to be heavier, which seemed to be lighter, as well as why some objects would move and others would not.

More to do

Have the children make and record predictions. The children can then refer back to the chart to check the predictions as each object is tested. The actual results of the experiment could then be recorded on a wall graph for later reference. A fan may also be used to provide air movement.

—Lyndall Warren, Milledgeville, GA

Air, Rain, Sunshine   4+

Children learn that air takes up space.

Materials needed

Paper napkin
Glass
Deep bowl filled with water

What to do

1. Crumple a paper napkin and push it to the bottom of a glass.
2. Fill a deep bowl with enough water to cover the glass.
3. Turn the glass upside down and push it straight into the water. Don't tip the glass.
4. Now, without tipping it, quickly pull the glass out of the water.
5. Take out the napkin. What happened? The napkin stayed dry!
6. Explain that no water came into the glass because air was already there taking up space.

More to do

Take the children outdoors with soap bubbles on a windy day. Have the children blow bubbles. Where are they going? Where is the wind taking the bubbles? Discuss wind and the direction of the wind. Use straws to blow dabs of paint across paper into unique designs. Like your breath, wind is moving air.

Related books

Gilberto and the Wind by Marie Hall Ets   *—Kristin Fary, Charleston, SC*

Soft-Snowman

2+

The children will develop their vocabulary—soft, sticky, on/off, touch, white—while exploring this sensory activity.

Materials needed

Cottonballs
Clear contact paper
Snowmen shapes and features

What to do

1.   Draw a simple snowman with a large tummy area for each child.
2.   Staple contact paper down to the snowman's tummy. Do not remove the backing, but turn one corner so that it is easy for the children to pull it off.
3.   Help each child pull the folded edge.
4.   Have the children touch the sticky contact tummy.
5.   Have lots of soft cottonballs available to touch.
6.   Show the children that the cotton can go on the tummy. If a child pulls the cottonball off, some cotton will still stick.
7.   Talk about and touch the cotton with the child.

More to do

Sing Snowman songs and fingerplays. Bring in snow from outside. Play with in inside in a sensory table or tub. Children can wear mittens. Melt some now in a glass. Observe the dirt. This reinforces "Don't eat snow." Act out building a snowman. Pretend to be a snowman and "melt." Dance like a snowflake. Pretend to iceskate. Put out cotton batting and cotton balls with the smaller building blocks to build a town in the snow.

Related books

Seasons by Brian Wildsmith
Snow by Roy McKie

Related rhymes

"Chubby Little Snowman"
The Snow Came Down"

—*Linda Ann Hodge, Minnetonka, MN*

Fun With Ice

2+

Children have fun and enjoy cold-weather activities while learning about winter and winter words like cold, ice, frozen, melt and snow.

Materials needed

2 large bags of crushed ice
Empty sand/water table
Child-sized aprons
Water play toys

What to do

1. Pour the crushed ice into the water table.
2. Seat four children at the table wearing aprons to protect clothing from water splashes.
3. Add some water play toys such as scoops, bowls, spoons, measuring cups or tongs.
4. Encourage children to handle the ice. Ask how the ice feels. Is it hot? What happens to the ice after we play with it for a while?

More to do

Make your own ice by filling ice trays or small containers. Add food coloring to the ice that you make.

Related books

The Penguin Who Hated the Cold adapted by Barbara Brenner
A Book of Seasons by Alice and Martin Provensen

—*Susan M. Myhre, Bremerton, WA*

Winter Fun   3+

Children will use different media to create a picture and learn about seasons.

Materials needed

Blue construction paper
Strips of black construction paper about 5 inches long for sled
Cotton balls
Yarn
Scissors
Runners
Crayons
Glue
Paintbrushes
Newspaper

What to do

1. Cover table with newspaper.
2. Put glue in small containers with a paintbrush for each child.
3. Give each child enough cotton balls to cover half of the picture.
4. Explain to the children how much fun it is to sled down a snow-covered hill. Tell them it is much easier to slide on snow than grass.
5. Have the children glue cotton balls on an entire hill (pre-drawn for younger children) on blue construction paper.
6. Have them cut a rectangle out of black construction paper for a sled. For younger children you can have the rectangle cut already.
7. Glue yarn for sled handles.
8. The children can use crayons to draw themselves on the sled.

Related song

"Sledding at Home" (sung to "Mary Had a Little Lamb")

Snow piled up will make a hill, make a hill, make a hill.
Snow piled up will make a hill for sledding in a yard. (pretend to pile snow)
We roll it up in great big balls,...and pound it 'til it's hard. (roll hands and then pound one fist on the other palm)
Though other children call to us...to take our sled outside. (place hands to mouth).
We don't go out but stay right home...and slide and slide and slide. (make sliding motion with hand)

Related books

The Mitten by Alvin Tresselt
The Snowman by Raymond Briggs
The Snowy Day by Ezra Jack Keats

—*Kathleen Shea, West Brookfield, MA*

Snowflakes

3+

This fun art project teaches children that all snowflakes are unique.

Materials needed

Metal juice lids (enough for each child in class)
White tissue paper, bond paper or tissues torn in small pieces
Glue

What to do

1. Save enough metal juice lids for each child to make one or more snowflakes.
2. Cover the flat side of the juice lid with glue.
3. Ask the children to tear or cut small pieces of paper and put them on top of the glue on the lid.
4. Cover this with glue again and let dry overnight.
5. When it is dry, the "snowflake" easily pops off the lid.
6. Hang the snowflakes all over the room or in the windows.

More to do

These turn into miniature stained glass windows if you use colored tissue paper. You can add powdered tempera to the glue and mix the colored glues or add glitter.

—*Barbara Bergstrom, Spokane, WA*

Igloo Art

3+

Children develop small motor coordination while enjoying this unusual art medium.

Materials needed

9 oz. clear plastic punch cups
White flake laundry detergent
Water
6" paper plates

What to do

1. Cut a small square opening in the rim of the plastic cup.
2. Mix water with detergent to make a heavy paste.
3. Turn the cup upside down on the plate so that it looks like a dome with a door.
4. Have the children use their hands to cover the cup with the detergent mixture until it resembles an igloo.

More to do

Compare igloos with other homes.

—Joyce Montag, Slippery Rock, PA

Belly Bingo

3+

Children learn to match color patterns.

Materials needed

Cold-weather animal bingo cards, one for each child
Bingo calling cards to match your bingo cards
Goldfish crackers used as markers

What to do

1. Talk to children about cold weather animals: polar bears, walruses, penguins and seals. Remark that each of these animals eat fish.
2. Tell the children they will be able to feed the animals by playing "Belly Bingo."
3. Let the children decide which cold-weather animal they would like to be.
4. Give each child nine fish crackers.
5. Explain to the children that the fish are to be used as markers and that they are not to eat the crackers. This will be done at the end of the game!
6. Tell the children they will be shown a card. If they have a space on their card that looks like that animal, they may put a fish cracker on that spot. You will continue holding up cards until someone gets "Belly Bingo."
7. Bingo can be accomplished by filling in the squares vertically, horizontally or diagonally. Then the child is to yell "Belly Bingo."

Related books

Penguin Pete by Marcus Pfister

Related fingerplay

"Five Little Polar Bears"

> *Five little polar bears, (Hold up 1 hand) Playing on the shore;*
> *One fell in the water, And then there were four. (Put down 1 finger)*
> *Four little polar bears, Swimming out to sea;*
> *One got lost, And then there were three. (Put down 1 finger)*
> *Three little polar bears said "What shall we do?"*
> *One climbed an iceberg. Then there were two. (Put down 1 finger)*
> *Two little polar bears, Playing in the sun*
> *One went for food, Then there was one. (Put down 1 finger)*
> *One little polar bear, Didn't want to stay;*
> *He said "I'm lonesome," and swam far away. (Put down last finger)*

—Bernadine Shawd, Sioux Falls, SD

Building Snowpeople

3+

The children will learn to make artistic decisions on materials chosen and used to design and complete the making of a playdough snowperson.

Materials needed

White playdough (in bowl mix: 4 cups flour, 1 cup salt, 1 3/4 cup warm water)
Raisins
Twigs, 2 1/2" long
Recycled colored cloth gloves
Aluminum pie tins or packaged meat trays (empty)
8 1/2" x 10 1/2" construction paper
Marking pen
Masking tape
Scissors
Carrots
Plastic sectional serving tray (with approximately six sections, can be purchased in party stores)

What to do

1. Prepare playdough. Cut twigs approx. 2 1/2" long (for snowperson's arms and fingers).
2. Cut glove fingers off, cut fingers in half and save the top pieces (for snowperson's hat).
3. Cut carrots into sticks (approximately 1").
4. Fold paper in half, print "Can you build a snowperson?"
5. Place raisins, carrot sticks, twigs and glove finger tops each in separate sections of the serving tray. Place serving tray and paper sign in the center of the table.
6. Put a pie tin or packaged meat tray in front of each seat (a permanent base for the snowperson). Put a piece of masking tape in the bottom half of the tin or meat tray (used to write on child's name). Place a ball of playdough about the size of an adult's fist on each tray. Save extra playdough in the center of the table.
7. The children take turns doing this activity.
8. The teacher reads the "Can you build a snowman?" sign.
9. Show the children each item on the tray and encourage them to think how to use the materials to build their snowpeople.
10. The children creatively design and build their snowpeople. Make sure that extra playdough is available.

More to do

Children participate in the Snowperson poetic dramatization by Sally Davis.
"Snowperson" by Sally Davis
(Teacher and children recite poem)
_____ the snowman (lwoman) came out to play (insert the name of a child)
In the sind and the sun on a cold winter's day
The hat on his (her) head shook from the cold
And the broom in his (her) hand was frozen to hold
The icicles hung like a wreath round his (her) chin
And he (she) knocked on my door,
"Let me come in!"

Related books

The Snowman by Raymond Briggs
The Snowy Day by Ezra Jack Keats
The First Snowfall by Anne and Harlow Rockwell

—Sally Davis, Newton Centre, MA

Making a Picture Book Sequel

Students draw a picture to illustrate things covered in snow.

Materials needed

Rain by Robert Kalan
Sentence strip for each child
Dark blue or black construction paper for each child
Glue
White crayon for each child or white finger paint
Sponge or brush for each child

What to do

1.   If using paint, mix this ahead of the activity. Cover the work table with plastic and prepare paint smocks.
2.   Make sentence strips with the words "Snow on the _____" for each child.
3.   Read the story *Rain* to the children.
4.   Reread the story and insert the word "snow" for the word "rain." Have the children say this word aloud with you as you read the book.
5.   Ask the children what they could say on the last page instead of "rainbow." ("Winter" or "Blizzard")
6.   Discuss other things that can be covered with snow.
7.   Ask the children to color snow on their piece of construction paper and draw something that the snow is covering.
8.   As the children color or paint, the teacher can circulate and ask each child to talk about their picture. The teacher can fill in the sentence strip "Snow on the _____" for each child.
9.   When pictures are completed, children can glue their sentence strip at the bottom of their picture.
10.   Collect all the pages and assemble them into a book.
11.   Let each child read their page.
12.   The teacher can illustrate the last page to make a contribution to the book.

More to do

Sing "Frosty the Snowman" or read snow poems to the children.

Related books

The Snowman by Raymond Briggs
Weather by Pascale De Bourgoing

—*Kay McAlpine, Lima, OH*

Building a Snowman

Children learn about winter, snow, shapes and size in this activity.

Materials needed

White circles in small, medium and large sizes
Large piece of light blue construction paper
Scraps of yarn, material and buttons
Glue or paste
Copy of the poem "The Snowman"
Chalk or crayons

What to do

1. Trace the different circles on white construction paper. Cut out the circles or if children are old enough, you can have them do this.
2. Set up the art table for two or three children at a time.
3. Discuss the color white, snow, the circle shape and the concept of small, medium and large. Recite "The Snowman" poem.
4. Give each child the materials to make the snowman.
5. Have each child glue the circles together to make a snowman. They can draw on the face or other details. Give the children the scrap materials to decorate the snowman.
6. Have the children glue the poem on their snow scene.

More to do

Have the children tell a story about the snowman for language arts. Write the story down and attach it to the back of the snowman picture. Bring in snow or make fake snow for the water table.

Related books

The Snowman by Raymond Briggs
The Jacket I Wear in the Snow by Shirley Neitzel

—*Victoria Cetrone, Steger, IL*

Snow Fun   4+

Children will observe the various effects different temperatures have on snow and learn new vocabulary to describe the effects.

Materials needed

Three bowls
Snow

What to do

1. Have the children collect snow and place it in two of the bowls.
2. Leave one bowl of snow at room temperature.
3. Place the other bowl of snow in the freezer.
4. After a period of time (when snow at room temperature has melted), gather the children to compare, observe and discuss the differences in the two containers. Vocabulary to use includes: frozen, melted, watery, liquid, hard, wet, solid, etc.
5. Divide the water from the room temperature container and put some into your third bowl. Place this in the freezer, leaving some water in the bowl at room temperature.
6. After sufficient time, compare the two frozen containers. Have the children pay special attention to the differences between the snow and the icy container. Vocabulary to use includes: frozen, solid, ice, snow, bumpy and smooth.

More to do

Have the children make a snowman cookie. Frost sugar cookies with white frosting. Add raisins for eyes, peanut or carrot piece for nose and a piece of red string licorice for the mouth.

Related book

Sadie and the Snowman by Allan Morgan

—*Cathlene M. Hedden, Livonia, MI*

Snowman!

Children will use fine motor and visual discrimination skills to reproduce a snowman on the flannel board.

Materials needed

Flannel board
Felt snowmen (two)

What to do

1. Cut two snowmen out of felt and make felt hats, eyes, carrot noses, mouths and buttons. (You might also make felt scarves, arms or other details.)
2. Build one snowman on the flannel board, naming each piece as you put it in place.
3. When the snowman is finished, talk to the children about each step you took when building it.
4. Ask one child to come up and copy the snowman using the other felt pieces. (You could also invite two children to come up and work together on the second snowman.)
5. When the child is finished, encourage the other children to comment on the snowmen.

More to do

Give the children playdough and have them build snowmen. If possible, give them different colors to use when making body parts and clothing.

Related books

Frosty the Snowman by Carol North
Friendly Snowman by Sharon Gordon

—Leann Jarzen, Starkville, MS

California Snowman

This activity teaches about shapes and the weather.

Materials needed

Sand
Pebbles
Glue
Paper

What to do

1. Draw three circles on each paper in the shape of a snowman.
2. Have the children spread glue in the circles.
3. Pour sand onto the glue areas.
4. Remove the excess sand.
5. Glue on pebbles for eyes and buttons of the snowman.
6. Ask the children to color or draw a beach scene on remaining paper.

More to do

Sculpt a snowman in the sandbox using water and tools.

—Lesli Brown, Carlsbad, CA

Stick Snakes

2+

Children will learn about snakes and enjoy a fun art activity.

Materials needed

Long sticks
Paint
Buttons
Glue

What to do

1. Talk to children about snakes and their habitats. Show them pictures of snakes and point out the different kinds of markings on their skin.
2. Present the children with a pile of interesting sticks that resemble snakes. Tell them to come and pick one stick each to decorate like a snake.
3. Set out paint and buttons and instruct the children to paint their snakes and glue on buttons for eyes.

More to do

Take the children on a walk and let them pick out their own sticks to decorate as snakes. Have the children build make-believe habitats for their snakes. Hide toy snakes outdoors and have children look for them.

—Carol Patnaude/Cathy Costantino, Warwick, RI

The Lion's Whiskers

3+

Children develop the ability to follow two-part directions.

Materials needed

One paper plate
Brown or gold yarn
Black marker
Glue
Scissors
Paper

What to do

1. Cut the yarn into 2" pieces and glue it around perimeter of plate.
2. Draw the face of a lion in the center of the plate, and cut four or five small slits on each side of the nose.
3. Cut strips of paper to fit into the slits on its face. These are the whiskers.
4. Write simple two-part directions on the strips of paper, such as, "Crawl around and growl like a lion," "Turn around three times and sit down," or "Touch your nose and turn around."
5. Explain to the children that each whisker has directions on it. Each child has a turn to pull a whisker from the lion's face. The child gives the whisker to the teacher to read.
6. The child then follows the instruction on the whisker.

Related book

Leo the Late Bloomer by Robert Kraus

—Melissa E. Kohler, St. Louis, MO

Alligator

Children are fascinated by animals such as alligators. With this activity, they will use fine motor skills to create an alligator of their own.

Materials needed

Cardboard egg cartons, one per child
Tape or stapler
Green paint
Glue or glue sticks
Round white stickers (optional)
Black markers (optional)

What to do

1. Separate the bottom and top of an egg carton. Cut one pair of egg cups off the end of the bottom section.
2. Turn the bottom section upside down. The egg cups will be the alligator's teeth.
3. Place the top of the egg carton on top of the inverted bottom, and tape or staple them together at one end, so the alligator's mouth can open and close.
4. Glue the pair of egg cups to the top section above the hinge. These will be his eyes.
5. Paint the alligator's head green and set aside to dry.
6. Stick the two round stickers to the pair of egg cups and draw eyes with the marker.

—*Jyoti Joshi, Framingham, MA*

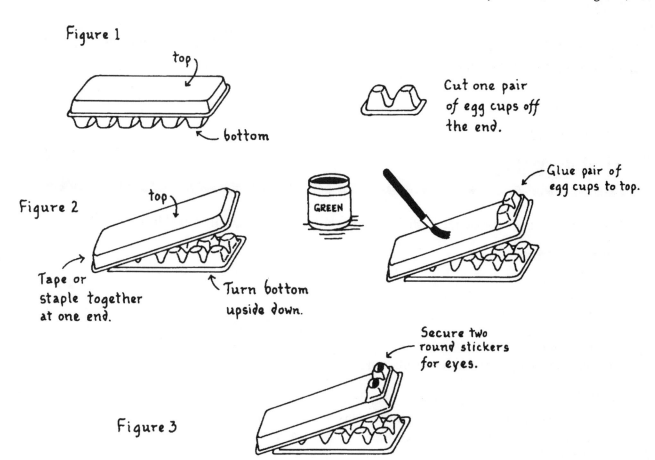

Figure 1
top
bottom
Cut one pair of egg cups off the end.

Figure 2
top
Tape or staple together at one end.
Turn bottom upside down.
GREEN
Glue pair of egg cups to top.

Secure two round stickers for eyes.
Figure 3

Making Authentic Snakes

3+

Children are made aware of the many varieties of snakes. This familiarity can help them avoid or overcome their fear of the reptiles.

Materials needed

Picture book with at least five color pictures of snakes
Uncolored modeling clay of any type that can be hardened
Colored paints
Paintbrushes

What to do

1. Prepare the clay (if necessary) and locate a place in your room for projects to dry.
2. Become familiar with two to five interesting pieces of information about each snake presented, such as habitat, favorite foods, types of eggs, how the snake helps or harms humans, unique physical features, etc.
3. Show pictures of snakes and talk about them.
4. Have children roll out clay into shape and size of their favorite snake. Keep the length to about 5" by controlling the amount of clay given. Help children learn how to roll clay and then to form a head.
5. Bake clay or let dry, depending on type of clay.
6. At next gathering, present pictures again.
7. Have table set up with cups of different colored paints and brushes. Children will paint their snakes to match their favorite species. Let them dry!

More to do

Make habitats for snakes in paper plates with strong rims or in shoe box lids or meat styrofoam or cardboard holders. Habitats could be desert sand, grass and weeds, or sticks and branches representing the forest. Make eggs or baby snakes when making original snakes.

—Dixie Havlak, Olympia, WA

Zoo Animals

3+

Children learn the names and characteristics of six or seven animals typically found in a zoo.

Materials needed

Medium-sized box
White paper
Crayons or colored pencils
Scissors
Pictures of zoo animals
Background scenes (grass, rocks, trees, shrubs, ponds)

What to do

1. Remove top and bottom of box and split it down one corner to open it up flat.
2. Fold it accordion-style along its four corners so that when opened it can stand alone.
3. Cover both sides with white paper.
4. Reproduce pictures, one for each child in the class.

5. For the Zoo's gate, write "Welcome to Our Zoo" in an arch and draw bars on either side. Under the arch make a signpost listing the names of the animals chosen and label each section of the box for one type of animal.

6. Tell the children they will study zoo animals with their very own zoo to keep in the classroom and visit anytime!

7. Present the box you've prepared, which will be the zoo. Tell the class you'll introduce one animal each day to add to their class zoo.

8. Pass out crayons and paper. Show the picture of the first animal you've chosen. Instruct the children to color it and describe its characteristics and habitat.

9. Choose some of the children's pictures to paste in the habitat.

More to do

Plan a field trip to a nearby zoo or call your local Parks and Recreation Department; often a mobile program featuring small domestic wild animals is available to visit your school.

Related books

If I Were a Penguin by Heidi Goennel
Joey Runs Away by Jack Kent
Roar and More by Karla Kuskin

Related songs

"We're Going to the Zoo" by Raffi in *More Singable Songs*
"Here Lies a Monkey" by Raffi in *The Corner Grocery Store*

—*Mary Ellen Baker, Mt. Airy, MD*

Olie Octopus   3+

The children will learn about the octopus as a form of sea life while practicing basic cutting skills and developing counting skills.

Materials needed

Purple and green construction paper, 1 sheet of each per child
Two milk creamers or egg carton cups (1 set per child)
Cereal "O's" or round noodle "O's"
Glue
Tape
Scissors
Crayons

What to do

1. Draw or photocopy patterns on the construction paper. Have the children cut out head and arms for Olie.
2. Glue eight arms along bottom of circle. You may wish to place numbers along base of circle so that children can cover up each number with an arm.
3. If using egg cartons for eyes, cut out to make two separate "eyes."
4. Color the center of the egg carton or creamer for eyes.
5. Glue on eyes (you may wish to use tape for this part).
6. Cover mouth outline with cereal or noodle "O's".

More to do

Visit an aquarium in your area. See if there are any octopuses. Collect pictures from nature magazines such as Ranger Rick, National Geographic, etc. Before sending octopuses home, make an octopus garden mural on the wall.

Related books

The Magic Fish by Freya Littledale
Six Foolish Fishermen by Benjamin Elkin

Related songs

"Row, Row, Row Your Boat"
"My Bonnie Lies Over the Ocean"
"Three Jolly Fishermen"
"The Owl and the Pussycat"
"Charlie Over the Ocean"

—Mark Crouse, New Minas, Nova Scotia, Canada

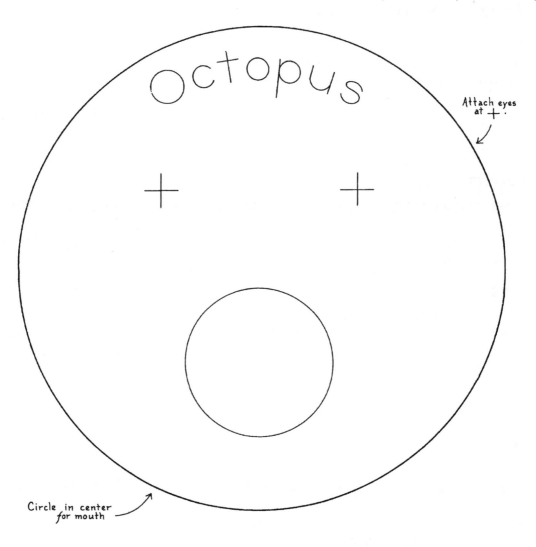

Head of Octopus

Octopus arms and legs

Snakes! 4+

This activity capitalizes on children's natural curiosity about snakes and provides them with the enjoyable challenge of making an unusual paper snake.

Materials needed

9" paper plate, one per child
Crayons
Scissors
String
Hole puncher

What to do

1. Have the children color the back of a paper plate and return it to you when they're done.
2. Turn the plate over. Starting from a single dot in the center, draw a spiral. The older children may want to try drawing the spiral themselves.
3. Allow the children to cut along the spiral from the outside edge of the plate (the tail) until they reach the dot in the center (the head).
4. Give the snake eyes using the crayons or a marker, and cut a small triangular snip for a mouth.
5. Punch a hole at the top of the head, pull a string through, and hang the snakes from the ceiling. The hanging snakes, gently turning as the air currents move them, make an interesting classroom display.

More to do

Have the children color the underside of the snakes to make them look really nice. After showing the children pictures of real snakes, you can talk about how the snakes have patterns on their skins. Show them what a pattern is (how it repeats itself) and practice making simple color patterns (for example, brown/green/brown/green, etc.) on strips of paper. Some children might like to make a snake with patterned skin.

Related books

Jump Frog Jump by Robert Kalan

—*Jyoti Joshi, Framingham, MA*

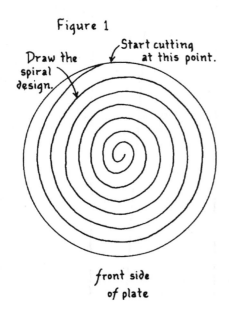

Figure 1

Draw the spiral design.

Start cutting at this point.

front side of plate

Figure 2

string

Lion: King of the Animals

A large heart turns into a lion in this interesting use of a paper plate! The children will practice fine motor skills as they cut and paste.

Materials needed

Small paper plate
Brown construction paper, one 3" x 6" sheet per child
Brown, orange and yellow yarn in 3" lengths
Scissors
Glue or glue sticks
Markers

What to do

1. Draw a big heart on the paper plate and have the children color it yellow. This is the lion's face (see illustration).
2. For the nose and eyes, fold the brown construction paper in half and cut three identical heart shapes along the fold. The older children will be able to do this themselves.
3. Glue two small hearts sideways for the eyes and one upside down for the nose and draw in the rest of the nose and the whiskers (see illustration). The children may need help with the drawing.
4. For a mane, glue the yarn around the edge of the plate. Point out to the older children that they can glue the colors in a repetitive sequence, for example, brown, orange, yellow, brown, orange, yellow, etc.

More to do

These may be made into lion masks by cutting eye flaps and holes on the sides for string to hold the mask in place. Small children are often frightened by masks so take care that you don't have lots of lions terrorizing your classroom. Give the lions a purpose, such as acting out a story or a play to end an animal, zoo or circus unit.

—Jyoti Joshi, Framingham, MA

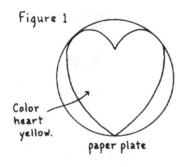

Figure 1

Color heart yellow.

paper plate

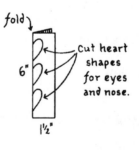

fold

6"

1½"

Cut heart shapes for eyes and nose.

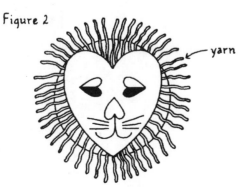

Figure 2

yarn

Tiger Bag Puppet

4+

Children make tiger puppets and learn about the appearance and mannerisms of tigers.

Materials needed

Brown bag (10 3/4" x 5 1/2")
Orange paper
Black crayon
18mm wiggle eyes
Scissors

What to do

1. Make a pattern for tiger head, tail and paws.
2. Cut orange paper to fit the front area of the bag and under the flap. Glue the paper to the bag and cut a V-shape at the base.
3. Have the children trace the head, tail, two paws and two feet on orange paper.
4. Ask the children to cut out all pieces.
5. Show the children how to draw stripes from outside of paper edge going in, then back out on head, body and both sides of tail.
6. After the children have drawn the stripes, ask them to color them in.
7. Show the children how to draw the tiger's triangle nose and color it.
8. Add mouth, whiskers, a line between legs and other features.
9. Glue the tiger's head on bag flap.
10. Glue the tiger's tail to back of bag.
11. Glue the paws and feet by inserting them into the bag side folds.
12. Glue on wiggle eyes.

More to do

Have a tiger puppet show. Visit the live tigers at the zoo.

Related song, to the tune of "Did You Ever See a Lassie?"

Did you ever see a tiger
Growl this way and that...
Stalk this way and that...
Pounce this way and that?

—Mary Brehm, Aurora, OH

Front

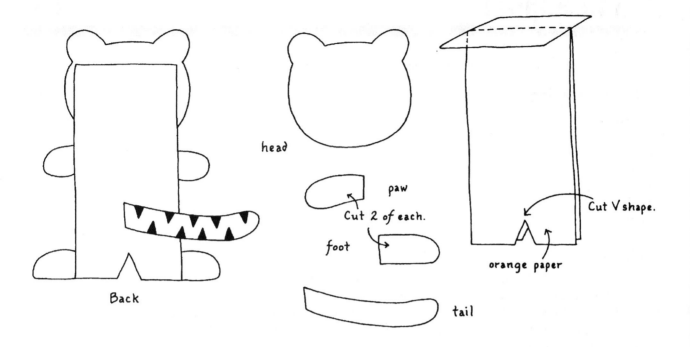

Back

head

paw

Cut 2 of each.

foot

tail

Cut V shape.

orange paper

Paper Zoo

4+

Children will learn about zoo animals and take part in a fun art activity.

Materials needed

Three different animal pictures (in color) per child
Crayons
Glue
Black construction paper

What to do

1. Give each child three animal pictures and three sheets of paper.
2. Have the children copy and color the pictures so there is one zoo animal on each sheet of paper.
3. Cut narrow strips of black construction paper (two 9" strips and many 2" strips per child) for fences.
Have the children glue the fence along the bottom of each picture (fence should cover only about one-fifth of the page)
4. Show the children how to tape the three pages together, side-by-side, to form a triangle. The "zoo" now stands up, and children can "walk around it" with their hands.

—*Cathy Chenoweth, Columbia, MO*

Panda Puppet

4+

Children learn about Panda Bears in the course of making Panda puppets.

Materials needed

White paper
Black paper
Black marker
15mm eyes
Glue
Scissors
Pencil

What to do

1. Roll 9" x 12" white paper into a cylinder and glue into shape.
2. Cut two ears, two arms, two legs and a face to be used as stencils.
3. Lightly trace a tail cutting line on the back of the cylinder where the ends are glued.
4. Lightly trace a half-moon-shaped area at the bottom front of the cylinder for children to cut. This will shorten the front slightly.
5. Using the black paper, have the children trace and cut out ears, arms and legs.
6. Help the children trace a face on cylinder using black marker.
7. Ask the children to color black circles for eyes and add a nose and a mouth.
8. Use black to color area under the Panda's chin in front and under its head in back.
9. Glue on ears, arms, legs and eyes.

More to do

Have children pretend to be Pandas eating, playing and walking. Using an atlas or globe, show the Panda's native habitats in China.

Suggested books

A Book About Pandas by Ruth Belov Gross
Giant Pandas by Jim Rothaus

—Mary Brehm, Aurora, OH

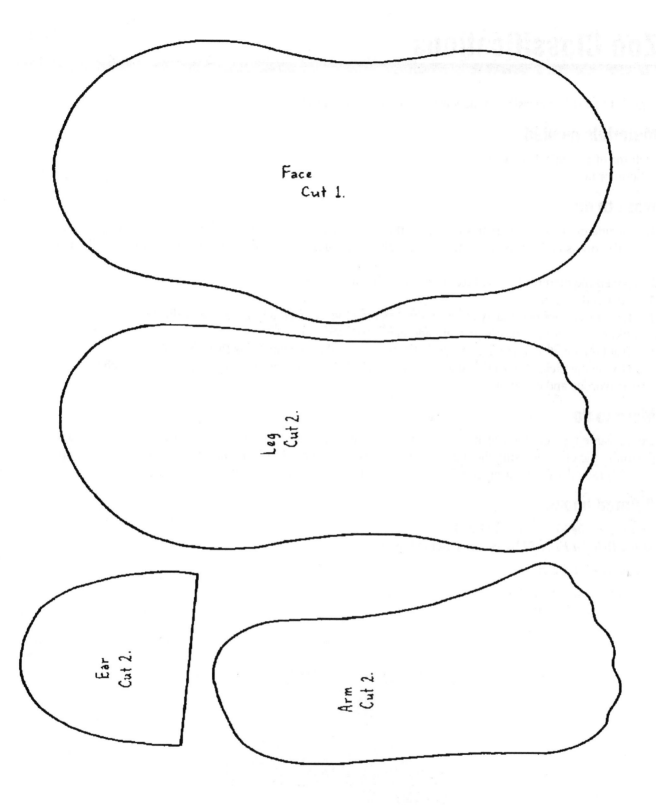

Face
Cut 1.

Leg
Cut 2.

Ear
Cut 2.

Arm
Cut 2.

Zoo Classifications

4+

The child learns to classify animals using specific characteristics.

Materials needed

Pictures of animals that live in a zoo
Ribbon or tape

What to do

1. Decide on the characteristics to use for the purposes of this exercise. (In this example, the characteristics are herbivorous and carnivorous, furry and feathered.) Divide a section of the floor in half with ribbon or yarn.

2. Assemble pictures that will exemplify the characteristics chosen.

3. Seat children in a circle.

4. If you have not previously done so, discuss the physical characteristics that indicate whether an animal is herbivorous or carnivorous (e.g., teeth and beak structures, etc.).

5. Hold up a picture and have children determine whether the animal is furry or feathered.

6. Divide the pictures into two stacks, placed on either side of the ribbon or tape, using the characteristics of herbivorous and carnivorous.

More to do

Do the same type of classifications using invented animals. Have children discover the identity of a specific person in the class by using the dichotomous key (blonde, not blonde; male, not male; tennis shoes, no tennis shoes), gradually eliminating groups until the identity of the selected child is determined.

Related books

Animals at the Zoo by Rose Greydanus
May I Bring a Friend? by Beatrice Schenk de Regniers

—*Elaine Root, Garland, TX*

Classifying   19, 23, 28, 30, 31, 102, 165, 171, 174, 206, 377, 382, 390, 468, 484, 506

Color Recognition   62, 73, 74, 78, 79, 80, 84, 85, 185, 221, 248, 254, 294, 337, 439

Comparing   20, 58, 106, 128, 284, 294, 300, 321,. 334, 372, 383, 388, 392, 482

Cooperating/Sharing/Taking Turns   18, 29, 78, 85, 100, 132, 133, 134, 164, 175, 178, 182, 188, 190, 200, 203, 228, 231, 295, 312, 313, 327, 337, 351, 423, 442, 446, 448, 452, 456, 459, 469, 472

Counting   95, 148, 190, 199, 213, 223, 233, 243, 330, 332, 333, 336, 339, 340

Creating   32, 33, 37, 38, 39, 42, 72, 99, 104, 108, 115, 116, 122, 127, 144, 152, 200, 202, 235, 257, 269, 288, 299, 318, 322, 325, 350, 354, 386, 402, 446, 453, 454, 463, 467, 479, 487, 490

Cutting/Pasting   24, 34, 40, 43, 44, 50, 67, 117, 130, 134, 149, 160, 162, 171, 172, 173, 195, 220, 224, 235, 244, 310, 311, 349, 424, 468, 497

Estimating   136, 267, 272, 276, 324, 374, 375, 380, 382, 383, 416, 462, 480

Exploring   34, 36, 38, 39, 70, 75, 81, 82, 83, 108, 129, 138, 193, 207, 211, 268, 292, 309, 315, 317, 356, 358, 361, 373, 374, 377, 378, 379, 382, 384, 399, 403, 405, 406, 410, 411, 412, 414, 415, 417, 419, 435, 436, 442, 458, 469, 475, 478, 480, 481, 485, 486, 492

Eye/Hand Coordination   26, 104, 105, 109, 112, 118, 120, 123, 135, 141, 159, 166, 170, 179, 181, 182, 184, 185, 206, 209, 219, 253, 256, 316, 330, 339, 344, 354, 434, 451, 455, 466, 488, 491, 494, 502

Fine Motor Skills   18, 27, 32, 35, 45, 47, 51, 52, 54, 57, 88, 90, 91, 93, 100, 108, 111, 113, 118, 119, 122, 138, 140, 144, 151, 152, 155, 164, 165, 201, 204, 209, 210, 213, 214, 215, 218, 222, 225, 226, 229, 230, 232, 233, 241, 242, 250, 252, 256, 259, 260, 262, 263, 278, 281, 290, 306, 308, 309, 312, 316, 319, 328, 344, 347, 349, 362, 368, 369, 370, 388, 410, 414, 417, 419, 422, 437, 443, 454, 459, 462, 464, 465, 467, 471, 476, 488, 493, 495, 500, 501, 503, 504

Following Directions   46, 53, 76, 84, 98, 102, 103, 106, 125, 179, 180, 182, 220, 242, 246, 254, 289, 301, 407, 494

Imagining   64, 68, 94, 102, 194, 255, 258, 269, 272, 287, 304, 305, 355, 356, 357, 367, 373, 440, 451, 452, 453, 455, 474, 484

Language Development   46, 49, 54, 59, 96, 108, 110, 126, 131, 133, 142, 146, 154, 155, 157, 158, 168, 186, 188, 194, 195, 199, 201, 208, 211, 212, 215, 217, 235, 238, 239, 240, 249, 264, 266, 267, 274, 279, 291, 293, 297, 320, 323, 326, 338, 342, 348, 366, 378, 380, 381, 384, 386, 390, 392, 397, 400, 408, 414, 418, 426, 437, 442, 457, 459, 477, 483, 486, 491, 496

Large Motor Skills   21, 57, 79, 84, 95, 107, 121, 141, 154, 159, 182, 183, 186, 193, 194, 196, 205, 216, 227, 231, 241, 246, 255, 277, 285, 286, 288, 289, 290, 291, 296, 298, 312, 316, 319, 409, 438, 440, 448, 466, 474, 478, 484, 496

Letter Recognition   13, 14, 16, 444, 447

Listening (Auditory Discrimination)   76, 79, 87, 121, 158, 183, 188, 221, 246, 273, 275, 276, 279, 292, 298, 300, 301, 305, 348, 376, 407, 413, 432, 433

Matching (see Visual Discrimination)

Measuring   98, 103, 294, 378, 395

Memory Skills   19, 26, 75, 157, 180, 189, 267, 334, 393, 400, 450

Number Recognition   219, 223, 243, 329, 332, 338, 340

Observing   20, 39, 58, 59, 81, 107, 131, 136, 189, 196, 197, 210, 254, 315, 320, 324, 326, 364, 366, 369, 372, 373, 376, 385, 401, 403, 470, 472, 478

Organizing   22, 166, 171, 173 178, 323, 457

Pre-reading skills   15, 17, 48, 80, 91, 92, 97, 146, 187, 266, 277, 304, 359, 428, 440

Problem Solving   124, 126, 131, 133, 136, 137, 203, 273, 289, 338, 469

Sequencing   14, 82, 114, 147, 168, 219, 245, 265, 275, 302, 304, 314, 329, 341, 346, 364, 366, 388, 390, 391, 405, 428, 432, 447

Shape Recognition   64, 65, 264, 349, 420, 421, 422, 423, 424, 426, 428, 429, 430

Social Skills (see also Cooperating, Sharing, Taking Turns)   88, 89, 149, 150, 192, 202, 214, 237, 271, 364, 394, 396, 441, 444, 445

Sorting   86, 93, 142, 143, 145, 163, 173, 175, 360, 404

Speaking   126, 274, 363, 398

Visual Discrimination (Matching)   55, 56, 60, 69, 70, 71, 78, 84, 139, 145, 148, 149, 155, 163, 180, 184, 187, 198, 223, 226, 247, 248, 280, 282, 307, 329, 331, 387, 430, 433, 441, 444, 489, 493

INDEX of SKILLS

Airplanes 338, 464
Alligators 117, 206, 495
Amphibians 31
Angels 424
Animal habitats 23, 28
Animal costumes 20, 21, 64
Animal footprints 19, 26, 120-121, 128
Ants 256
Apples 74, 105, 139, 142, 441
Applesauce 105, 287-288
Appliance box 356-357, 412-413
Aquarium 373-374
Archaeology 124
Baa Baa Black Sheep 342-346
Babies 149, 350
Balloons 54-55, 68, 113, 118, 123-124, 400, 480
Balls 286-287
Bananas 165
Banners 148
Bark rubbing 321
Barns 154
Beach 454, 455, 456-457, 458, 459-461
Beanbags 55, 179, 243, 292, 297, 301
Bears 26-27, 36, 98, 192, 267-268, 332, 405-406, 472
Beavers 130
Bees 258-259, 263, 326, 334-335
Big top 65, 68
Bingo 56, 79, 489
Bird terms 46
Bird feeders 46-47, 48
Bird nests 48-49
Birdwatching 52
Birthdays 214-215
Blankets 2932
Blindfolds 399, 433
Blocks 88-89, 93, 96, 203
Board games 282, 329-330, 337, 472
Boats 465, 466
Body parts 54, 55, 56
Bones 210-211
Bookmaking 126, 274, 388, 393, 491
Bookmarks 252
Braille 419
Bread dough recipe 98
Bridges 469-470
Bubbles 290, 481-482
Butter churning 107
Butterflies 253, 254, 255, 257-258, 260-261, 265

Calcium 210-211
Calendar 386, 388-389
Camera 11
Camping 451-452, 453, 457
Candy canes 333
Canoes 310
Carbon paper 382
Card games 85
Cars 463, 468, 469
Castles 204, 376-377
Casts 209, 210
Catch and look box 254
Caterpillars 255, 260, 265
Caves 205
Cellophane 268
Charade game 246
Charlie Brown 217
Cherry pie 106
Chinese New Year 239, 240
Christmas trees 231, 233-234, 235-236
Christmas 225-236
Cinnamon rolls 104-105
Circus animals 65
Clay 53, 109, 496
Cleaning up 136-137, 438
Clock 349-350
Clothespins 84, 152-153, 181, 198
Clouds 474
Clowns 62, 67
Coins 279-280, 281, 282, 284
Collages 18, 20, 39, 122-123, 144-145, 149-150, 195-196, 202, 208, 215, 358, 455-457, 467
Collections 93
Color blending 75, 81, 82, 83, 268, 288, 422
Composting 136
Constellations 354, 356, 358
Cookbook 274
Cookies 189, 274, 275
Corn shucks 38
Corn 170
Costumes 20, 21, 60-61, 64, 67, 70, 72 116, 272, 394
Coupon holder 250-251
Coupons 150, 190
Cows 155, 159-160
Crayon shavings 235, 257-258, 453-454
Crops 157
Crystals 39
Dancing 121, 288, 293, 298-299, 304
Days of the week 391-392

Dental hygiene   57, 206
Dinosaur dig   124
Dinosaur hunt   126-127
Dirt   320, 326-327, 417, 436
Dogs   340-341
Dolls   152-153
Dominos 78
Dragons   239
Dramatic play   266-267, 269-270, 272, 277, 351-353, 355, 356-357, 360-361, 367-368, 398-399, 440, 445, 451-453, 455, 457, 458, 471, 484
Ducks   53
Easter   247, 248
Egg cartons   73, 111, 231, 233-234, 260-261, 281, 372, 467
Eggs   30-31, 120, 123-124, 158-159, 247, 248, 258-259, 344-345, 361
Elephants   64
Epsom Salts   39, 249
Erasers   86
Faces   59-60, 401-402
Farm animals   154, 155-156, 157, 158, 159-160
Favorite things   400, 444
Fear   110
Feathers   49, 221, 222, 285
Feelings   397-398
Feet painting   299, 403
Finger painting   405-417
Fingerplays   272, 333, 347
Fingerprints   256
Fire safety   209
Fireworks   35
Fish   364
Fishing game   17, 180, 184
Flag   203
Flannelboard   15, 26, 62, 73, 147-148, 188,258-259, 264, 272, 274-275, 300, 304-305, 333, 340-341, 346, 359, 405-406, 420-421,426-427, 428, 432, 493
Flashcards   16, 273, 413
Floating objects   382
Flowers   73, 94, 145, 193, 249-250, 369, 370, 439, 440
Food groups   166-167, 171-172, 173-174 175-176, 178
Fossils   124, 129
Frames   119, 225, 232
Friendship   202, 238, 271
Frogs   361, 362, 364-365
Fruit   102-103, 163
Garage sale   136-137

Germination   193
Germs   211-212
Gifts to make   150, 230, 232, 249, 250-251, 386
Gingerbread man cookies   103-104
Goat   160-161
Goldilocks and the Three Bears   266-267, 289
Goose   162
Grapes   166
Graphing   22, 29, 30-31, 95, 199, 364-365, 374, 484-485
Grass   316
Gravity   379
Growing up   58, 395
Guessing game   276, 462
Halloween   216-220
Hammer   95, 200
Hamster   203
Hanukkah   222-225
Hats   70, 72, 116
Hickory Dickory Dock   349-350
Hives   258-259, 334-335
Home address   90, 91-92, 450
Honey   258-259
House sounds   432
Houses   88-89
Humpty Dumpty   344-345, 348
Ice castles   376-377
Ice   34-35, 373, 376-377, 486-487
Igloos   488-489
Impressionistic painting   38
Inclined plane   377
Interviews   445
Jack and Jill   349
Kangaroo   267, 273, 294-295, 448
Kick ball   312-313
Kites   260-261
Kwanzaa   236-237
Ladybugs   245, 264-265
Leaves   40, 84-85, 138-139, 140, 141, 144, 288, 388
Libraries   92
License plates   447-448
Lilacs   437
Lions   494, 501
Litter clean-up   133, 136-137
Little Red Riding Hood   80
Locks   182
Lotto game   433-434
Loud/soft   298
Luau play   459-461
Magnets   242, 253, 374-375, 383, 384, 423

INDEX of TERMS

INDEX of TERMS

Mail carrier 91-92
Mail 450
Mailing a letter 90
Martin Luther King 237-238
Masks 118, 160-161
Mass Production 471
Maze 203
Meadow 323-324
Medical supplies 207, 208
Megaphone 434
Memory games 180-181, 189, 400-401
Menorah 222-225
Milk jub 181
Milkweed Pod Cradles 350
Mirrors 268, 396, 402-402
Mittens 70
Mobiles 44, 47-48, 52, 132-133, 144-145, 318, 476
Moldy bread 385
Money 279-280, 281, 282, 284
Monkeys 286, 291, 329-339
Monsters 278
Months of the year 390, 393
Moonlight 325
Mother's Day 249, 250-251, 252, 253
Mouse 430
Murals 36, 134-135, 155, 157, 200-201
Musical instruments 298, 300, 301-302, 304, 306
Names of children 14, 441, 442-443, 444-445, 447-448
Names of Dinosaurs 127-128
Nature walk 23, 40, 140, 144-145, 318, 322, 361, 364-365
Necklaces 113-114, 118-119, 314, 437-438
Newspaper 97
Noah's Ark collage 18
Number lotto 329-330
Nursery rhyme play 351
Nursing home 88
Nutcracker 231
Nuts 142-143, 231
Obstacle course 205, 289, 291-292
Ocean 29-30, 132-133, 134-135, 453-454, 455-456, 456-457
Octopus 497-498
Oil slick 131
Old MacDonald Had a Farm 157
Olympics 296
Opposites 297
Organs of the body 60-61
Ornaments 223, 226-227

Overhead projector 59-60, 384-385
Owls 43, 45, 244
Panda 504
Papier-Mache 118
Pearls 113-114
Pears 403-404
Penguins 51
Pet store 87, 360-361
Pet care 360
Peter Peter Pumpkin Eater 344
Photographs 225, 232, 400-401, 433-434, 437-438, 442, 477
Picnic 267-268, 441
Piggy bank 280, 281
Pine cones 233
Pizza 102
Planting 193, 194-195, 196-197, 249-250
Playdough 27, 108, 339, 414, 422, 490
Pocahontas 309-310
Pockets 230, 273
Poetry 146, 277, 359
Poisons 206-207
Pollination 326
Pollution 131
Pond 316-317, 323
Post office 90, 91, 450
Potato prints 120-121, 151
Pots of gold 336
Puddles 474
Pumpkins 218, 344
Puppets 43, 87, 155-156, 210, 222, 269, 302, 339, 342, 346, 348, 462, 502, 504
Purse 117
Puzzle pins 112
Puzzles 124, 338
Quilts 37, 115-116, 443
Radishes 196-197
Rainbows 185, 476
Raindrops 475
Recycling 130, 131, 133-134, 135, 136-137, 204, 226-227, 328, 469-470
Red Rover 84
Reindeer 229
Robins 50
Robots 178
Rocket ships 354, 355, 356-357
Rocks 73
Roots 367
Rudolph the Red-Nosed Reindeer 229
Safety 209, 212
Sand painting 309
Santa 226, 227-228, 230

Scarf dancing 298-299
Seasons game 387, 390-391
Seeds 198, 366, 368, 372
Sewing 26-27, 115-116, 219, 250-251
Shadows 57-58, 292-293
Sharing 327-328
Sheep 342, 346
Shoes 69, 71
Show and tell 363
Sight 399, 419
Sign language 407, 408, 409, 418
Simon Says 76, 407
Smells 410-411, 412, 414-415
Snacks 99, 122, 125, 239, 403-404, 441
Snails 319-320, 324-325
Snakes 494, 496, 500
Sneezing 211-212
Snow fun 492
Snowflakes 488
Snowman 486, 490, 491, 493
Solar system 357
Soup recipes 100-101, 164, 386-387
Space station 357
Spiders 216, 219, 256-257, 259-260, 262, 341, 347
Spoons 184-185
Spring cleaning 438
Sprouts 367, 369-370
Squash 197
St. Patrick's Day 246-247
Stained glass effect 34, 42
Stars 354, 356, 358
Stickers 84, 85, 120, 187, 332
Stop signs 182-183
Stores 93, 94, 102
Storytelling 147-148, 152-153, 405-406
Streamers 484
Sunflowers 368
Sunshine 325
Syllables 273
Symmetry 254, 260-261, 264
Syringe painting 207
T-shirt art 322
Tag game 241, 295
Tape recorder 398-399, 432
Tape measure 395
Teddy bears 267-268, 441
Teeth 206
Telephone 213, 271
Telescope 83
Telling time 349-350

Tepees 311, 313
Textures 36, 405
Thanksgiving 221-222
Three Little Pigs 266, 381
Tic tac toe 192
Tiger 502
Timer 183
Tires 462-463, 469
Tissue paper 35, 39, 40, 42, 113, 253, 354, 457
Tool sounds 376
Toothbrush painting 33
Totem pole 308
Touch and feel objects 399, 406, 411, 412-413, 416, 417
Towns 93, 96, 459-460
Trains 340, 467
Treasure hunt 14, 214-215, 246-247
Trees 388
Tube art 201
Tugboats 465
Tulips 369
Tunnel 205
Turkeys 221-222, 285
Turtles 24
Valentines 241-246
Vegetables 415
Vehicle races 378
Voting process 89-90, 95, 364
Water lily 316-317, 370
Water table 378-379, 486-487
Water play 465, 466, 486-487
Waterfall 379
Watermelon 451
Weaving 119, 312
Wee Willie Winkie 347
Wild west 269-270, 272
Windsock 220, 478, 479
Witches 216-217
Wood sculpture 32
Wool dying 114-115
Worms 20, 32, 315, 317-318, 320
Wrapping presents 214, 226
Wreaths 225, 228, 322, 454
Xylophone 435
Yellow brick road 193

INDEX of TERMS